Of Singular Genius, Of Singular Grace

Horace Bushnell, 1847. Portrait by
Jared Bradley Flagg (1821–1899).
Courtesy of the Wadsworth
Atheneum, Hartford, Connecticut.
Endowed by C. N. Flagg and Com-
pany. © Wadsworth Atheneum

Robert L. Edwards

Of Singular Genius, Of Singular Grace

A BIOGRAPHY OF HORACE BUSHNELL

The Pilgrim Press
Cleveland, Ohio

The Pilgrim Press, Cleveland, Ohio 44115
© 1992 by Robert L. Edwards

Book design by Milenda Nan Ok Lee

Printed in the United States of America
The paper used in this publication is acid free and meets the minimum requirements of American National Standard for Information Sciences-Permanence of Paper for Printed Library Materials, ANSI Z39.48-1984

97 96 95 94 93 92   5 4 3 2 1

Library of Congress Cataloging-in-Publication Data

Edwards, Robert Lansing, 1915–
    Of singular genius, of singular grace : a biography of Horace
Bushnell / Robert L. Edwards.
        p.   cm.
    Includes bibliographical references and index.
    ISBN 0-8298-0937-6 (alk. paper)
    1. Bushnell, Horace, 1802–1876.   2. Congregational churches—
    United States—Clergy—Biography.   I. Title.
BX7260.B9E38   1992
285.'092—dc20
[B]
92-26773
   CIP

Dedicated to

one of America's oldest and historically most significant cities
the city of my seventeenth-century Edwards forebears
the city of Horace Bushnell
the city that, along with its environs
has given me my most rewarding years

"Biography" meant a book about someone's life. Only, for me, it was to become a kind of pursuit, a tracking of the . . . trail of someone's path through the past, a following of footsteps. You would never catch them; no, you would never quite catch them. But maybe . . . you might write about the pursuit of that fleeting figure in such a way as to bring it alive in the present.

—Richard Holmes
Footsteps, Adventures of a Romantic Biographer

Contents

PART 3   "MY BROKEN INDUSTRY"

Acknowledgments

MAKING ACKNOWLEDGMENTS is one of the delightful aspects of writing a book. Not only is it an opportunity to express appreciation, it stirs memories of rewarding associations with friends old and new who have taken a supportive interest in the project, from the beginning or along the way.

The idea of attempting a Bushnell biography first came to me during my tenure as the senior minister of Immanuel Congregational Church (United Church of Christ), Hartford, Connecticut. This church is the descendant of Bushnell's North Congregational Church, and its pulpit is dedicated to him. My first debt, therefore, is to this historic New England congregation for calling me to its leadership and sustaining me in it for nearly a quarter of a century.

In the absence of a regular corpus of Bushnell papers (see Bibliographical Note), I am also fundamentally indebted to the late Horace Bushnell Learned, one of Bushnell's great-grandsons, and Eileen, his wife, for opening to me their collection of Bushnell materials. With their confidence and their faithful interest in the book, they have treated me almost as though I were a member of the family, although without attempting in any way to influence the picture of Bushnell I have presented.

Over the years many libraries have provided skillful and cheerful help. I wonder constantly at the patience and willingness of these indispensable guardians of the past to serve friend or stranger without stint of time, usually without charge, and often with as much sympathetic interest as though the research were their own. The largest library collections of primary Bushnell materials are distributed among the various archives of Yale University. Other manuscript sources are widely and often sparsely scattered. The institutional holders are listed in the Bibliography. For aid in general research I must particularly thank the staffs of the Connecticut Historical Society, the Watkinson Library, and the Trinity College Library.

Several professional scholars have read all or parts of the manuscript and given valuable counsel. Here my primary debt is to Robert T. Handy, emeritus professor at Union Theological Seminary in New York, who encouraged me in this undertaking in its early stages and read critically the entire text. For their scholarly insights I am also grateful to John Dillenberger, Mabel C. Donnelly, Myra C. Glenn, Joan D. Hedrick, Robert G. Irving, Frank G. Kirkpatrick, Harry S. Stout, and David E. Swift. I need hardly say, however, that for all their expertise, final responsibility for these pages rests with me.

Since it has been my hope to provide a book general readers as well as professionals might enjoy, I have shared it in advance with family members and friends from various walks of life and have benefited from their wisdom. Some of them are colleagues of long standing in full-time church ministry. Particular appreciation is due to Richard and Josephine Aldridge, Heywood and Beatrice Alexander, James and Linda Cowdery, David L. Dickerman, William Gay, James and Helen Gettemy, Nathanael M. Guptill, Justin and Peggy Hartman, Ruth M. Knauft, Richard C. Norberg, Nancy C. Rion, George J. Ritter, and Jane W. Wielhouwer. For other valuable assistance I must also thank Jane Dillenberger, my sister Mary Parke Edwards Manning, Morris D. Pike, Avery D. Post, and many friends from the special community that is Hartford Seminary.

In an age of high technology a biographer, too, needs technicians. My warm appreciation goes to Roseann Lezak, who for years transferred my old-fashioned typing to a word processor, until at last I became a computer addict myself; and to Teri Vaughn, who not only led me deeper into the mysteries of computerizing but was there with her magic touch when problems arose that were quite beyond my amateur capability.

Finally, as for many other things, I am grateful to my wife, Sally, for her interest and support. Her own professional commitments as a teacher and preacher, in which I take pride, have prevented her from playing a major role with this writing. But she has kept a weather eye out for relevant sources, and she repeatedly has been ready with positive criticisms and suggestions. Best of all, she has endured with good grace my too-frequent preoccupation with Horace. The book is a better book because of her companionship and help.

"Did You Know Horace Bushnell?"

"DID YOU KNOW HORACE BUSHNELL?" With an air of excitement, Hartford, Connecticut, citizens who traveled in the United States or abroad in the late nineteenth century often were asked that question.[1] Almost certainly they could give a positive answer. If they had not enjoyed a personal acquaintance, they would at least have known enough about him to satisfy initial curiosity.

At his death in 1876 at the age of seventy-four, he was indisputably the first citizen of the Hartford community, a storied city that already could boast nearly 250 years of colonial and national history. Long before that his reputation had spread across the Atlantic, in minor ways on the Continent and conspicuously in England and Scotland. One eager Londoner, about to make his first visit to the United States, announced that in coming to these shores he had two main objectives. He wanted to see Niagara Falls, and he wanted to meet Horace Bushnell.[2]

The American personality this expectant British tourist had resolved to find was not the usual celebrity accomplished in politics or commerce, in war or the arts. Bushnell was an exceptional Congregational minister and Christian thinker at a time when Protestantism was still a determinative force in American culture, and the long arm of evangelical and benevolent Congregationalism reached far beyond the bounds of Calvinist New England. Moreover, Bushnell's practical versatility was such that in his generation he cut a considerably larger civic figure than is always associated with one of his calling.

Horace Bushnell (pronounced Bush'-nell) was born in 1802 in the invigorating atmosphere of western Connecticut's scenic Litchfield

Hills. As is occasionally pointed out, that rugged rural corner of the state, with its hard-scrabble fields and stone-walled pastures, probably produced more formative leaders for the burgeoning young republic than any region its size in the country. Among them were most of the irrepressible Beechers; John Brown of Harpers Ferry fame; Samuel J. Mills, the homely pioneer of the vastly influential overseas Protestant missions movement; and Collis P. Huntington, who helped spearhead the first transcontinental railroad.[3] Reared on his father's tidily kept acres in New Preston, Bushnell left home in 1823 for Yale College, where during his lifetime he received four degrees. Ten years later, unknown and untested, he was called to lead the prestigious North Congregational Church of Hartford, the only ministerial charge he would ever hold.

While serving this strenuous mercantile people, he emerged as an original man, in the sense that Jonathan Edwards had been an original. Increasingly Bushnell moved on the same astonishingly creative stage as Ralph Waldo Emerson, Theodore Parker, Leonard Bacon, Charles G. Finney, Henry Ward Beecher, Harriet Beecher Stowe, Henry James, Sr., and Frederick Law Olmsted, to cite but a few of his key contemporaries. He mingled familiarly with them all, sharply differed with some, and was their equal in importance.

Preaching was his first love. Less popular but more penetrating than his friendly rival, Henry Ward Beecher, Bushnell grew to be one of the great preachers in an age of pulpit princes. To an extent other leading ministers of the day did not, he also developed out of his discourses and pastoral experience a distinctive mode of Christian thought suited to new times. Without question he was the outstanding American theologian of the nineteenth century, and his fresh approaches, which challenged a magnificent but aging orthodox tradition, did much to reshape a large segment of U.S. Protestantism. For this spiritual pioneering, however, he paid the price nearly every genuine prophet pays. The legions of theological war were called out against him, and he was subjected to five years and more of punishing doctrinal controversy. It became so intense that he barely escaped being defrocked by a concert of high-minded but outraged New England conservatives.

[2]

Having survived these attacks, Bushnell not only pursued his innovative church leadership, but he energized an extraordinary range of civic and cultural undertakings. His abilities were so varied that he seems in retrospect to have been a flash of Renaissance genius on the midcentury American scene. He was at home in both political commentary and strategies for business. With a native talent for civil engineering, he held two U.S. patents (on home heating devices),[4] delighted in charting out routes for railroads and canals when these were all the rage, critiqued John Ericsson's famous "caloric" (hot air) engine for ship propulsion, and almost singlehandedly brought about the construction of Hartford's city park (now Bushnell Park), along with New York City's Central Park, one of the first two publicly financed urban preserves in the nation.

Concerned for quality education, Bushnell labored with Henry Barnard to improve the woefully inadequate Hartford public schools, and he also played an on-site role in the formation of the College—now the University—of California. He was a much-sought-after orator on public occasions, and with a wide range of writings he won for himself a place as a man of letters. It has been said of Bushnell's books that in "no other twelve volumes of American literature, unless it is Emerson's, is there such a wealth of thought on great themes."[5]

An avid mountaineer, fisherman, sailor, explorer, bowler, and equestrian, Bushnell would have been an ideal companion for Theodore Roosevelt in his legendary "strenuous life" a generation later. The claim has been made that many Protestant clergy in Bushnell's lifetime were becoming femininized.[6] If so, such a cultural change never affected him. He remained a thoroughly masculine personality. Yet he was beset half his days by an undiagnosed tuberculosis that wasted his frame and made him appear prematurely old and frail.

During his remarkable career, Bushnell touched the main currents of our midcentury experience at about as many points as any contemporary one can name. "Minister to a changing America," as one authority has described him,[7] Bushnell shared many of the period's romantically optimistic hopes. As a thoroughly human being, he also was involved in the limitations and tragic failures of the day, including the bitter dispute over slavery that shadowed his most active years. In it all, he believed he could see the finger of God at work, the God of the biblical message, whom he persuasively preached and convincingly trusted.

Over the years a few biographies of Horace Bushnell have been written. All but one, however, published more than eleven decades ago by his loyal and yet perceptive daughter, Mary Bushnell Cheney, are either technical or relatively brief. What has been missing is a readable, modern narrative of Horace Bushnell's life, dealing not only with the output of his inexhaustibly fertile mind, but with his colorful character and often adventurous encounters, and placing his story within the context of an eventful age. This book is an attempt to fill that gap.

It is not in the nature of this volume to offer an in-depth critique of Bushnell's theology. That fascinating task is the ongoing work of specialists. As the story unfolds, however, every effort has been made to capture the substance of his thought, and that of his opponents, and as often as possible in nontechnical language. These pages are intended for the general reader—in the pew or out—in academia or otherwise who is interested to rediscover a major contributor to our spiritual and, not too incidentally, our secular heritage.

It has been said of William Ellery Channing, the gifted Unitarian leader, with whom Bushnell, though never a Unitarian, has sometimes been compared, that he deserved "one of the front rooms in the house of history."[8] It is a fair claim to make for the great Boston liberal. It is also fair to claim that another of those "front rooms" rightfully belongs to Horace Bushnell.

PART 1

The Young Horace Bushnell

CHAPTER 1

A Birth in Bantam

THE CENTURY HAD JUST TURNED. The 1700s, at their peak so decisive for the original thirteen American colonies, finally had slipped away. The universally lamented death of George Washington only a few days before it closed, seemed to put a period to the age that was past. Now the 1800s stood out ahead, like the slenderest new moon, waiting to be filled in with events even more momentous.

To be exact, the year was 1802. Even the most active historical imagination has difficulty making the great leap backward from the modern era of space exploration, robotics, and genetic engineering to life as it was in a youthful United States in that long-ago year.

For one thing not many Americans were around. Including the remote territories of Ohio and Mississippi and a sprawling Indiana that also covered today's Illinois and Wisconsin, along with parts of Michigan and Minnesota, the population totaled just over five million, with its center only eighteen miles west of Baltimore.[1] Cleaveland (as it was originally spelled) was a cluster of cabins in a wilderness full of bears and wildcats. Even as a military outpost, Chicago did not exist.

The large majority of people lived on isolated farms, were seldom out of sight of the woods, and scarcely thought at all in city terms. These scattered citizens wrested a living from the soil with backbreaking labor, working fourteen-hour days in all weathers. Creature comforts were few. One former farmboy recalled the conditions of his childhood during this time as cheerful, but severely frugal:

> We had in winter only the fireplace, the brick oven, the foot-stove and once in a while an angelic form in the shape of a bed-pan [with

coals to warm cold bedclothes]. No matches, but flint and punk.
Tallow candles with their wicked light. Burn about 30 cords of
wood. No overcoats or underwear. No thermometers, so we didn't
know how cold we were. My great pleasure was to slide down hill
on a sled made by myself. There were no others. Never received a
penny for spending money. No Christmas. Yet we were full of fun,
dammed up for an occasional outbreak.[2]

With its constant exertion and plain living, society moved slowly.
People often kept time by the sun. Indoors grandfather clocks were
not uncommon, but barely one person in fifty had a watch.[3] The age
also knew a degree of quiet quite unimaginable now. At the opening
of the 1800s, no American ear had heard the shriek of a steam
whistle on a ship or train—though perhaps occasionally on a primitive factory—much less the wail of sirens in the streets or the roar of a
jet engine. Birdsong and the lowing of cattle were not yet drowned
out by the din of traffic, and the loudest peacetime noises were still
the sounds of nature—occasional claps of thunder splitting the un-
polluted air or the howl of a winter wind blasting its way across the
family farm.[4]

In this physical environment, one that varied little from father to
son and mother to daughter, thought frames, too, changed gradually.
Federalists, long used to power, angrily predicted that the election of
an agrarian, Deistic Thomas Jefferson, in 1800 would prove the
death-knell of the republic. When military or diplomatic problems
were on people's minds, it was not a Nazi Germany, a Soviet Union,
or some swaggering Middle Eastern dictator who was the arch-
enemy. It was the high-handed British—with Napoleonic France at
times a close second. Memories of the Revolution were still fresh,
and before long the insufferable Redcoats would invade the country
again, burning much of Washington in the process. Slavery was not
yet a sectional issue. Even Connecticut had few qualms about being,
at least *de jure,* a slave State.[5] Scientific ideas were few, and no college
in the country had a natural science course we today could recognize
as such.

Of all the contexts of thought, the most determinative was still religion; and for the most part religion meant Protestant Christianity. The churches had sunk to a new low during the Revolutionary period,[6] helped not at all by the influx of radical atheism that crossed the Atlantic in the wake of the French Revolution. But despite this decline in organized faith, Puritan views maintained their strong hold in many quarters, consciously or subconsciously, and the coming of the Second Great Awakening soon would give them a new vitality.

Among orthodox believers, the issues of existence were crystal clear. Creationism was beyond question. Personal life was a warfare in a fallen world, with the wrath of God never far away. As for the ultimate future, some were predestined by immutable decree to salvation, and the rest to a terrifying damnation. The only way for totally depraved human lives to get a clue as to which way they were headed was to undergo a radical conversion that would bring the favored sinner within the reach of saving grace. To make this salvation available, as every good churchgoer knew from the Apostle Paul, God in Christ had "done what the law, weakened by the flesh, could not do."[7] How one might come by such a saving change was God's own mystery. Sure it was, however, that no one, no matter how "good," could earn salvation, although living an upright life might be a sign that the gift had been given, or still might be. This severe brand of religion often made the strong stronger, with a force still felt in modern society. But to many others it brought an inner torment that is difficult by any standards to justify.

Rural, scattered, politically advanced but industrially primitive, and at least nominally attached to rigorous Christian doctrines—in broad brush this was the distant but excitingly seminal American world of 1802. That year, in an obscure corner of that world, Bantam, or Bantam Falls, Connecticut, close to patrician Litchfield Hill, but then part of the town of Washington, a boy was born on 14 April to Ensign and Dotha Bishop Bushnell.[8] He was their first child. His birthday fell on the Wednesday before Easter. The imminence of that high festival of faith, however, did not move the young couple to give their son a biblical name, such as had been carried by his paternal grandfather, Abraham, or his maternal great-grandfather, Jonathan Bishop. Instead his parents followed the classic trend then so pronounced: after the renowned Roman poet they scarcely could have read for themselves, they called him Horace.

Although his arrival attracted no special attention, even the humblest birth has somewhere ancestral roots. Bushnell's were anchored deep in four unpretentious but solid New England families: on his father's side the Bushnells and the Ensigns; on his mother's the Bishops and the Bradleys. All of them had made their exodus from the tense, high-handed England of Charles I in the second quarter of the seventeenth century. In many cases it is hard to verify exact times of landing in the New World, but it is likely that James Ensign was the first to arrive, very possibly reaching Boston in 1634.[9] The immigrant Bushnells probably came a year later, also entering at Boston.[10] John Bishop is listed as one of the covenant signers of Guilford, Connecticut, in 1639;[11] and the Bradleys, in a complex relay of travelers, landed in New Haven in the 1640s.[12]

Over the years these families generated the world's usual composite of saints and sinners. William Bushnell, who settled in Saybrook, Connecticut, in the mid-1600s, had a long and useful career in war and peace. For six generations the Saybrook area never lacked a William Bushnell.[13] By contrast, Bushnell's eighteenth-century maternal grandfather, Luman Bishop of Litchfield, was a scamp. Having married Horace's grandmother Lucretia Bradley in 1781, he abandoned her and their three children (including Bushnell's mother, Dotha) eight years later and absconded "beyond the seas" to Virginia. There he craftily announced that his wife was dead and cajoled an Anglican cleric into joining him in another marriage with a local woman of uncertain reputation.[14]

Occasionally Horace Bushnell gave passing thought to his family tree, jotting informal genealogical notes for himself.[15] When he did, one figure above all caught his eye and held it for life, his father's mother, Molly Ensign Bushnell. By the time Horace was born, she and his grandfather, Abraham, had left western Connecticut for the Green Mountain country of Starksboro, Vermont, starting their lives over again in a log house and hacking out a new farm from an ancient wilderness.

Twice as a boy, in 1808 and again in 1814 or 1815, Horace visited them there, lumbering along with his parents on a springless open wagon over roads that often were virtually nonroads. Once they reached their destination, however, the arduous trip seemed well worth all the hardships, especially as young Horace hung on the words and doings of his magnetic grandmother.

As he remembered her long afterward, she was a little body, less than five feet in height, but habitually erect, with a purposeful spring in her step and dark eyes that seemed to her grandson to "smite intelligence into people and almost into things."[16] For over twenty years she had a child every other year—thirteen in all—and when she and Abraham ended their days, they were well on the way to having 100 grandchildren.[17] A devout Methodist, Molly Bushnell was influential in leading into the ministry a teenaged Vermont giant with a booming voice named Elijah Hedding. Once launched on his career, Hedding became a tireless New England circuit-rider, and he later rose to be one of the most able of the pre–Civil War Methodist bishops.[18]

One Vermont letter of Molly's to her grandson Horace survives, written in reply to "a very agreeable letter" from him at the time he was thinking of entering Yale. Constant childbearing and the rigors of the northern frontier had taken their toll; over seventy, and suffering from a stroke and Parkinson's disease, she admitted that "old age has shaken me by the hand and left me a-tremble." After giving Bushnell spiritual advice from her own inner journey, she expressed hope that there might be one more visit between them. Whether or not that materialized, she pledged him to remember "your affectionate Grandmother . . . when she is no more to be sene in this vale of tears."[19]

There is no evidence that another visit ever took place. As for remembering her, that Bushnell gratefully did. "Though I knew her only in my childhood," he recalled in a brief memoir, "and then only on visits twice made of a few days each, she has been almost visibly with me . . . down to the present hour."[20] When he wrote those words, Bushnell himself had grown old, with the snows of more than seventy New England winters on his own head.

CHAPTER 2

By the Splash of Waterwheels

BUSHNELL'S FATHER, ENSIGN, was a farmer, but he was more than that. The first venturesome beginnings of an industrial revolution were stirring in America, and with some of his more enterprising contemporaries Ensign Bushnell thought he could see a commercial future for water power. Born in Canaan Falls, Connecticut, a month before the muskets of 1775 blazed at Lexington and Concord, he went as a youth with his parents to Vermont. But in his middle twenties some restless homing instinct brought him back to the Litchfield County scenes of his boyhood and eventually, somewhat southeast of his native place, to Bantam.

Here his instinct to return to western Connecticut was doubly confirmed. For one thing, there he fell in love with a comely young Dotha Bishop and persuaded her to marry him. For another, he was impressed by the wild white water of Bantam Falls. Flowing from Bantam Lake, then, as now, the largest natural body of water in Connecticut, the Bantam River dropped over 100 feet within a mile, a rocky, precipitous course that already had led to the "seating" of half a dozen mills with their dams and splashing water wheels. These included a forge and works that already had made Bantam an important name in iron.[1]

Under the shadow of sophisticated Litchfield center, Bantam still had its rough edges and was thoroughly small town. When the celebrated Methodist bishop Francis Asbury came to Bantam to preach in the 1790s, he decided he never had seen "any people who could talk so long, so correctly, and so seriously, about trifles."[2] Yet the combination of love and power was sufficient to persuade an enterprising Ensign that here was a promising place to settle. Accordingly, he scraped together enough to lease a "clothing shop" and a fulling mill (for cleansing homespun fabrics), exchanged vows with Dotha in 1801, and began raising a family.[3]

It was here in this rustic hamlet that Horace toddled around after his mother, formed his first words, and looked up with proper awe at his father. He was baptized in the local Episcopal church, the only congregation in town. A very Congregational Bushnell later enjoyed remarking that for all his supposed Calvinist antecedents, he had been "Episcopally regenerated."[4] Until he was three, Horace was an only child.

Then in 1805 all this abruptly changed. Another son was born to Dotha and Ensign, and for reasons not altogether clear the family pulled up stakes and moved only a few miles west to New Preston. It would appear that Ensign had done well in Bantam, as now instead of leasing, he was able to buy a house, barn, and another fulling mill.[5] Yet conditions on the East Aspetuck River, a fast-moving outlet from picturesque Lake Waramaug, were essentially the same as those he had left behind. Here, too, early settlers had been quick to capitalize on the powerful natural resource. As early as 1744, mills had begun to crowd the banks of the river, some of them with wheels as high as twenty feet. Primitive as this kind of manufacturing seems now, little "factories" like these formed part of America's earliest industrial empire, an "empire over the dam" that not only processed grains but produced textiles, iron, paper, twine, lumber, tools, and a wide range of related essentials during the early decades of national independence.[6]

In this New Preston environment of a demanding farm and a rudimentary factory Horace Bushnell spent the next eighteen years. Most of that time it seems to have hardly occurred to him that he would ever live anywhere else, or do anything other than work the land and manage minor manufacturing. As his father was a farmer and entrepreneur so, naturally, he would be. Nor would it necessarily mean a restricted career. The elder Bushnell was not only the undisputed head of his family, he also became a figure of consequence in the town, serving as a justice of the peace, and aggressively invested in land and marble quarries, in addition to carrying his routine responsibilities.[7]

A steady, practical man, he treated his children—eventually four sons and two daughters—firmly but fairly. Occasionally, when the household economy had yielded a surplus of marketable goods, "the wiry patriarch of homespun," as Horace once described his father, would swing his first-born up on the wagon, and take him along to what seemed to the boy the great cities of Bridgeport or Hartford. Except for the two trips to Vermont, these were his only early exposures to the wider world. As they plodded over the dusty or muddy miles, young Horace must have had questions for his father that prompted conversation, supplying some basis for a companionable relationship.[8]

Far more important to Horace's boyhood and youth was the influence of his mother. Most of what we know of her comes from a sketch Bushnell wrote late in life. Even allowing for the idealization of time and sentiment, however, she stands out as a woman of uncommon character. From her girlhood in a broken home to the day she died under the strain of a difficult move from Connecticut to western New York State in her late fifties, life seldom was easy for Dotha Bushnell. With no educational or social advantages, she managed to pick up a smattering of schooling. Whether from adversity, her own mother, or her religion, she also accumulated a wisdom of experience that Bushnell found a marvel. "She was," he wrote, "the only person I have known in the close intimacy of years who never did an inconsiderate, imprudent, or in any way excessive thing that required to be mended afterwards." He could not remember that she ever had given advice on any subject "that was not perfectly justified by the results."[9]

This poise and discernment seemed the more impressive in that Dotha maintained it under such heavy burdens of household management. Slender of build and of soft complexion, she gave no indication of special stamina. Yet her work was never done, and her energies were slow to flag. With her rested the care and feeding of a family of eight, plus taking in men from the mill and the dairy and serving her turn at boarding the local schoolmaster. It was up to her to haggle with peddlers, sometimes for a half hour or more, over a single needed article until she was sure the price was right—and that the limited family exchequer could stand the expense.[10]

With all this she did well, too, by her children. She kept careful track of the schoolwork and emerging talents of each child. Dotha was so supportive that her brood came to feel, as Bushnell put it, that "more than half our school life had its springs at home." As she observed Horace along with her other offspring, she plainly wanted to see him become a minister, and thought she could. It was a dream she had had from his earliest years, and she never let it go. When Bushnell turned to the study of law instead of theology in his late twenties, she was troubled but undeterred. "If he is not a minister," she remarked, "I shall not know what to think of it."[11]

Meanwhile Horace went through the usual minor misadventures and collisions of childhood. When he was still very young, he fell off a footbridge and narrowly escaped drowning. Intellectually, he got everything he could from the local schools, and socially he once increased his standing among his peers by thrashing the school bully in a tussle that was inescapably forced on him. In the largely self-contained business of a New England farm in this period, young people did not have to wait long before being pressed into service. "I did the full work of a man for at least five years before the manly age," the Doctor remembered, "holding fast the astronomic ordinance . . . of from thirteen to fourteen hours a day."[12]

Starting in 1817 he attended a high school of sorts in Warren, and then enrolled in the newly opened classical academy on New Preston Hill. Usually the next step would have been more deliberate preparation for college, and his parents offered to send him to Yale. But young Bushnell had no taste for any such notion. "Peremptorily," as he remembered his reaction, he declined and continued as an all-around farm hand.[13]

Yet more than he knew, decisive counterforces in his adolescent makeup were at work. The awakening of an inquiring and ingenious mind could not indefinitely be denied. He was not necessarily counted brilliant or always well focused. But once motivated, it was noticed that he could apply himself with an almost fierce intensity. At one stage, in an English class, he was so determined not to be out-done by some older girls that his mother heard him rehearsing parts of sentences in his sleep. Fascinated, she sat on his bed while he un-consciously finished the exercise, and in the morning she compli-mented him that he had made so few mistakes. Such concentration foreshadowed his adulthood, when he would come to lunch after a long session in his study with his mind still so absorbed in thought that he could not call the potato on his plate by the right name.[14]

He matured in the mechanical skills farming and milling required. Yet as he hurried about his chores, his eye increasingly took in land-scapes; he not only captivated by their beauty, but he sharply sur-veyed the outlines of hills and valleys, and as his daughter records it, imprinting them on his mind. These he would subsequently explore and study in greater depth.[15] It was the start of a lifelong delight in ob-jective visualization and would one day help to equip him to be a paraprofessional engineer.

Such mental expansion led him closer to second thoughts about further education, but the decisive push eventually came from reli-gion. New Preston was no more an unmixed community of model Christians than any other New England village, but in the words of one of Bushnell's brothers, faith "was no occasional and nominal thing" at the Bushnell homestead.[16] Mercifully, however, it was low key. Not all American young people of that time were so fortunate. In many early-nineteenth-century families, religion hung like a fright-ening dark cloud over the experience of childhood and adolescence. Catherine Beecher, who had lived in Litchfield close to Bushnell's first home, and was only slightly older than he, knew a good share of love and laughter as she grew up under the watchful spiritual tutelage of her parents, Lyman and Roxanna. Yet in any introspective reli-gious moment, it was not long before she was all but engulfed in ab-ject terror. "Up to the age of sixteen," she recalled, "my conceptions of religion were about these: That God made me and all things... that he knew all I thought and did... that I had such a wicked heart that I could not feel or act right in anything until I had a new one;

that God only could give me a new heart; that if I died without it, I should go to a lake of fire and brimstone and be burned alive in it forever."[17]

With a Methodist father and a sage Episcopal mother to temper the rigors of Calvinism, Bushnell was more fortunate. The religious impressions of his childhood, he recalled, were "not of fear, nor in a sense of wrong, but in a sense of the Divine beauty and majesty," a memory reminiscent of Jonathan Edwards's numinous youthful experience in his *Personal Narrative*.[18] The Bushnells habitually taught their children more by example than by precept. Neither parent was disposed to try to talk them into religion.[19] This did not mean, however, that the family failed to honor all basic orthodox disciplines. Sunday cessation of work, for example, began precisely at sundown, not just at any random moment between dusk and the next morning. Nor was even the worst weather an excuse for absence from weekly public worship. When Sunday dawned—hot or cold, stormy or fair— people hitched up the horses and prepared for a long day at the hilltop meetinghouse. Bushnell's often-quoted sketch of gathered New Preston Congregationalists has become familiar:

There is no affectation of seriousness in the assembly, no mannerisms of worship; some would say too little of the manner of worship. They think of nothing, in fact, save what meets their intelligence and enters into them by that method. They appear like men who have a digestion for strong meat.... Under their hard and ... stolid faces, great thoughts are brewing, and these keep them warm. Free will, fixed fate, foreknowledge absolute, Trinity, redemption, special grace, eternity—give them anything high enough, and the tough muscle of their inward man will be climbing sturdily into it; and if they go away having something to think of, they have had a good day.[20]

Surrounded by this atmosphere of earnest, but not overly forced faith, Bushnell struggled to find his own spiritual footing. Progress was slow and, as he remembered it, had "many turns of loss and recovery."[21] He may have been tempted at times by the heady Tom Paine–type of atheism that was going the rounds of the more rebellious young,[22] and there were the normal assaults of doubt. But in his better moments, more positive factors gradually prevailed. An important influence continued to be his feeling for nature. Horace could not be daily among the hills or in the fields without sensing at least dimly a mighty hand behind the mysterious wonder of Creation. Near his house there was—and still is—a big, gray boulder which became for him a kind of shrine. Drawn there every now and again to watch the sunrise, Bushnell would stay to lift a youthful prayer to the Maker of Light.[23]

Feeling after the God of nature, however, was not enough. Given the Calvinistic air he breathed, he had to come to terms with the God of Christian revelation. As he well knew from repeated exposure to biblical preaching and through the Westminster Catechism, which he had to commit to memory, becoming a genuine a Christian meant having a personal conversion experience of salvation in Christ. In search of this pearl of great price, Bushnell, in adolesence, began studying Scripture with new intent. Just how this slowly shed light on his search we cannot know. We do know that by March 1821, apparently without any notable crisis, he was persuaded that "the Lord, in his tender mercy, ᵘᵃˢ led me to Jesus." Eight months later, near Christmas, "in the presence of God and angels and men," Bushnell joined the local Congregational church, vowing "to be the Lord's, in an everlasting covenant never to be broken."[24]

It was not long after this that the idea of entering the ministry began to take serious hold. He needed no parent to tell him, however, that he never could achieve that goal without college training; thus he began reconsidering his hasty rejection of Yale.

But it was too late, or so at first it seemed. The local economic scene was changing rapidly. Trade disruptions from the War of 1812, the tariff of 1816 which greatly limited imports, and the spirited enterprise of a new generation of New England manufacturers had stimulated the growth of larger-scale textile manufacture. This cut drastically into the market for small-scale, individual production that had furnished much of the Bushnells' disposable income. Ensign Bushnell's little "shop" on the East Aspetuck presented a quaint figure beside the enormous, five-story Lowell mills rising on the banks of the Merrimac River in Massachusetts the very year that Horace finally was looking toward New Haven. What might have been managed with relative financial ease in 1818 when his family originally offered him the chance was next to impossible by 1823.[25] Yet thanks largely to the unswerving determination of his mother, a family council met and pooled ideas as to how to foot the bills. Whatever other students might wear to class or to social events, it was agreed Horace would wear only homespun. All books would have to be second-hand, and the cost of his last year he would somehow shoulder himself. Meantime, the most stringent economies would be practiced at home, where frugality already had gone about as far as it could go.

These arrangements made, a newly motivated Horace set about boning up on Latin, Greek, mathematics, and other required subjects. Then, two months before he was due to enroll, he impetuously rode to New Haven, took the examinations under a tutor only six years his senior, and passed. His examiner observed that he had a "rude, original and discriminating mind."[26]

In the fall of 1823, well into his twenty-second year, Horace Bushnell left New Preston, never again to return in the old way. College would be a totally new experience for him, intellectually and socially, and he could not be sure he would survive. But his course was set, and if ever he were to embark on this adventure, now was time.

CHAPTER 3

The Great World of Yale

WHEN BUSHNELL ENTERED "the great world of college," as he then thought of it, he faced a new Yale. In 1795, a generation before, Timothy Dwight had assumed the presidency of what he termed "a ruined college."[1] While it was an exaggeration, there was some truth in it. Despite the best efforts of his predecessor, the learned Ezra Stiles, enrollment had dropped, the number of faculty and administration was dwindling, and financing was meager. The only two dormitories were dismal and decaying, the chapel roof leaked so badly the building was virtually useless, and the refectory had not served a meal in four years.[2]

By 1823 Yale was anything but a ruin. Helped considerably by improved economic conditions, enrollment had more than tripled. At graduation the class of 1826, with approximately 100 graduates, was said to be the largest senior class in any academic institution in the United States.[3] Dwight had died six years earlier, but his successor, Jeremiah Day, whose family Bushnell had known from childhood in New Preston, presided over a faculty studded with stars: among them were Benjamin Silliman, pioneer teacher of chemistry; Nathaniel W. Taylor, brilliant theologian; and James L. Kingsley, professor of languages, "the [Joseph] Addison of America," as Dwight had called him.[4]

Although the college was enjoying high prestige, it still was almost unrecognizably different from the complex university of today. A tightly controlled Christian community, Yale had a limited curriculum and was small enough so that just about everybody knew everybody else. With uncanny ability to spot promising talent, however,

Dwight and Day had built quality into it, and the active, growing alumni began to exert a powerful influence on the rapid development of the country.

Of the members of Bushnell's class of 1827, more came from Connecticut than from any other state. But the roll included men from as far north as New Hampshire and from as deep in the slaveholding South as Alabama and Louisiana.[5] The majority hailed from small, rural communities, with only a scattering of city-bred students, whose sophisticated presence was nonetheless felt. In worldly finesse, Nathaniel P. Willis, the future poet and dramatist of Boston and Phillips Andover background, Adam Cox from Charleston, South Carolina, or Cortlandt Van Renssalaer, wealthy aristocrat from Albany, New York, could run circles around a rustic like Bushnell.

Whether or not this was a concern to him is unknown, but Bushnell may well have been uneasy about his age gap. Three-quarters of the class was younger than he. Son of a fellow of the Yale Corporation, Robert McEwen, who entered at fifteen, thought Bushnell "a full grown man" in comparison with his own tender age.[6] This may have led to a certain solidarity among those who were more nearly Bushnell's contemporaries. Some of them were to remain among his intimates long after college: Henry Durant, for example, with whom one day Bushnell would work on the founding of the University of California; or Theron Baldwin, a farmer from Goshen, Connecticut, with whom he later shared an active interest in the education and evangelization of the West.

Significant as his social ties came to be, Bushnell was chiefly bent on getting an education. That meant following prescribed courses that seldom changed and allowed no electives. At a time when everything from manners and morals to architecture and place names bore the mark of ancient Greek and Roman cultures, the curriculum at Yale also had a classical core. Instruction was in English; but depending on the ability of the student, Greek and Latin could become second languages. In their freshman year, Bushnell and his peers labored through five books of Livy's Roman history, followed in other years by solid doses of Cicero, Tacitus, Horace, and Homer's *Iliad*. Mathematics started out with arithmetic and algebra, quickly moving on to more demanding spheric geometry, trigonometry, and Euclidian geometry. For all the efforts of Silliman in chemistry, mineralogy, and geology, which appealed strongly to Bushnell, sciences were not much developed at Yale. In many respects, the senior year was like attending a theological seminary—Yale still was called a "seminary" about as often as a "college." At long last undergraduates had sustained contact with the college's president and senior faculty, who put them through their paces in logic, rhetoric, moral philosophy, and New Testament theology.[7]

In the pursuit of knowledge the Yale community adhered to a spartan schedule. Spring and fall students were routed out each morning at half past five—mercifully adjusted to half past six in the dead of winter (the early nineteenth century did more before breakfast than is the custom now). Chapel was held by flickering whale-oil lamps, and class sessions with tutors came before the meal at half past seven. Most days classes usually met twice more; there was Chapel again in the afternoon (not always wholly religious in tone), and on Sundays a student would be in church gatherings of some sort up to five times. Classrooms were heated by inefficient stoves that "reeked with oily odors," and fireplaces were the only source of warmth in dormitory rooms. On winter mornings water pitchers regularly froze over, and sustained exposure to frigid temperatures produced frequent chilblains. Bushnell may have been among those who on occasion resorted to standing barefoot in the snow outside his college hall to get a moment's relief from burning feet.[8]

Extracurricular activities were not highly organized, but Bushnell entered fully into those that were. Most students belonged to one or the other of two literary societies, Brothers in Unity or Linonia. He joined the Brothers, took part in debates, wrote a play in his junior year, and as a senior became president of the society.[9] In March 1824, he joined the Church of Christ at Yale, which in turn led to his taking a leading role in the formation of the Beethoven Society, a rejuvenation of a musical group dating back to 1812.[10]

At least twice he put his signature to student petitions asking for improvements in campus conditions. One protested bad food served in commons. "The present baker," so the petition read, is "a confessed *drunkard,* a dirty man, and a miserable baker." At a time when colleges put little emphasis on physical education, another student request in which Bushnell joined supported the construction of a gymnasium "to relax the mind and to promote health and bodily activity." The petitioners asked that it be so arranged as to be usable "in any weather and at all seasons."[11]

These efforts to influence the faculty seem to have been acceptable, but another such attempt landed Bushnell and most of his class in deep trouble. The celebrated "Conic Sections Rebellion," in which he took part in the summer of 1825, stemmed from an alleged promise by the faculty that certain corollaries in a mathematics course on conic sections would not be included on an examination. Yet when the test was given, there were such questions on it, as though no promise had been made, or even thought of. To a man, Bushnell's sophomore class felt cheated and betrayed. With an intoxicated sense of injured honor, they impetuously banded together and, without waiting to consult their tutors on the matter, adamantly refused to recite on those corollaries, pledging themselves "to share one common fate."[12]

The administration was in no mood to countenance insurrection, and it reacted swiftly. According to a faculty minute, signed by Tutor Edward Beecher, Lyman's eldest son, all sophomores refusing to perform the stated recitations were to be "indefinitely suspended." Soon the administration gave the screw another turn and threatened dismissal. President Day promptly followed up these actions with a stern letter to parents of the students involved, telling them that their sons had been found guilty of "direct disobedience to the order of the college government," and hence would be sent home.[13]

From then on the class of 1827 began to die by inches. Daily quotas of rebels were removed, until only a baker's dozen were left. As an active participant in the affair, Bushnell could not escape the penalty; on 22 July 1825, back to New Preston he went. Ostracized by their peers if they did not join the revolt, and disciplined at home if they did, students and their families agonized for weeks.[14] The affair eventually blew itself out, the faculty giving no ground. However the rebellion opened ways for undergraduates to capitulate without losing all face and to be readmitted on promises of good behavior. The class that had been in such serious straits reassembled, performed the required recitations, and continued on successfully to graduation.

Momentarily painful as it must have been for him at New Haven and at home, Bushnell never regretted his support of the resistance,[15] and it left no lasting mark on his record. As his four years passed, he increasingly won a conspicuous place for himself both as a Phi Beta Kappa student and as a well-coordinated athlete.

Many of the personality traits that were to mark Bushnell for life also emerged more distinctly during his campus career. Confident, intellectually bright, and "all energy," as one classmate described him, he was driven by a sense of duty and was known for inflexible integrity. He had a cheerful, outgoing nature, but at the same time an almost impenetrable private side, preoccupied with his own interior life. Bushnell was not especially religious, or even very philosophical, and was inclined to take a detached view of existence. He may have recognized this in himself, as he did in retrospect: "I loved a good deal the prudential, cold view of things." Lyman Coleman, the tutor who first admitted him, noted the same tendencies. Long afterward he still remembered Horace as "kindly to all" but as having "few confidential friends or intimates. He lived the life of a scholar, original, retired, peculiar, and independent." Coleman's was a perceptive memory. Although there always would be a certain aloofness to Bushnell, he combined with it a capacity for friendship that elicited more than simply respect. "Dear, dear chum!" one of his roommates exclaimed, looking back over their college relationship. "I loved him sincerely, and I believe he as sincerely loved me."[16]

This was the Bushnell who marched into Center Church with the graduating seniors on commencement day in September 1827. As with most colleges, commencement was Yale's oldest ceremonial tradition, and it regularly proved a city-wide, if not a state-wide, attraction.[17] Hours before the doors of Center Church opened, people stood jostling each other on the steps, having walked or ridden many miles in every imaginable type of vehicle in hopes of securing a seat, or at least access to a window.

They were in for a long day. Amid all kinds of solemn emotions and colorful excitement, the proceedings lasted the entire morning and afternoon. The Beethoven Society, of which Bushnell had been so much a part, supplied feature music, at one point filling the sanctuary with the triumphant sound of Handel's "Hallelujah Chorus." On the strength of his academic achievements, Bushnell won a place among the senior orators. He delivered what turned out to be a prescient discourse on "Some Prevailing Faults in the Eloquence of the Times." Customarily each speaker was applauded loudly, and occasionally a prettily dressed damsel would lean over the balcony and toss a bouquet.

Late in the day the exercises climaxed with the conferring of degrees. President Day intoned the time-honored Latin that went with the award, *"Admitto vos ad primum gradum in artibus."* He then gave his benediction, and the eighty graduates of 1827 went out into the world, arguably the ablest class to leave Yale since the days of Dwight.[18] Some of its members would rarely, if ever, see the college again. But it was not to be so with Bushnell. For him and Yale, this was only the beginning.

CHAPTER 4

Feeling after a Profession

FOR ONE WHO FINALLY IDENTIFIED his calling as clearly as he did, Bushnell immediately after college was extraordinarily adrift. Business had no appeal for him. He was too much in debt to pursue graduate study. And by his own admission, he was so "utterly gone down in religion" that any thought of the ministry was out of the question. "Unbelief, in fact," he once reminisced, "had come to be my element."[1]

Lacking any burning desire to do one thing over another, he first tried teaching school. Perhaps with a recommendation from his younger classmate, William Adams, who had taught there successfully as a precocious teen-ager prior to coming to New Haven, he took a job at the Chelsea Grammar School in Norwich, Connecticut,[2] a quality academy in an old aristocratic town. But it did not take Bushnell long to discover that he never was cut out to be a schoolmaster. His high-strung intellectual nature was ill-suited to handling squirming boys with provoking pranks. As early as October he was cautioning a friend that pedagogy was enough to "freeze the heart and dissipate the mind of the best man living."[3]

Dutifully Bushnell was making the best of his situation when a new door unexpectedly opened. Unbeknownst to him, the audience at his commencement a few months before had included a Norfolk, Virginia, lawyer, William Maxwell, who had returned for his twenty-fifth Yale reunion. Maxwell had just taken on the editorship of a recently launched New York newspaper, *The Journal of Commerce,* and something about Bushnell's graduation speech made him think the young speaker might be useful to him in this enterprise. As a consequence, Maxwell offered him the post of associate editor, an opportunity Bushnell gratefully welcomed. Immediately submitting his resignation and bidding Norwich a willing farewell, Bushnell made his way to Poughkeepsie, boarded a Hudson River night boat, and on the last day of February 1828 had his first view of New York City, half hidden in a morning fog.[4]

New York in 1828 boasted a population of over 200,000, and, thanks largely to traffic from the newly opened Erie Canal, the city was growing rapidly. It enjoyed social prestige and wealth, but was no utopia. Periodically it was devastated by uncontrollable fires and raging epidemics; the city was noisy and, on a hot day, noxiously odorous. Young Gideon Welles, later Abraham Lincoln's secretary of the navy and a Connecticut politician Bushnell came to know well, had occasion to sail into New York harbor in the spring of 1823. He fancied he could hear the "bustle of business" from six miles out, and once in the city itself, he confided to his diary, the stench was "almost insupportable."[5]

Among other accomplishments, the city had become the nation's newspaper capital, having outstripped even Washington's prolific political press. In this competitive setting, the *Journal of Commerce* was a newcomer. Started in 1827 by the reform-minded silk merchant Arthur Tappan, it maintained a lofty tone. It turned away theater or lottery advertisements and stood out boldly for religion and against slavery, Sabbath-breaking, and strong drink. When one editor was asked whether such straightlaced policies might not limit circulation, he answered testily, "I do not consult my subscription list to ascertain my principles."[6]

Soon after Bushnell began working at this virtuous establishment, Maxwell fell ill and moved away, leaving Bushnell to carry the main journalistic load. Even for a young man it was a rugged routine. Without typewriters or telegraph keys, writing was done by hand, and he often sat up half the night preparing stories for the morning edition. News constantly poured in. Abroad the Greek revolution was in full swing, polarizing the big powers of Europe and the Middle East. At home the raucous presidential race of 1828 was pitting John Q. Adams—"who can write," as the saying went—against Andrew Jackson, "who can fight."[7] Frequently, after covering the latest developments and snatching two or three hours' sleep, Bushnell would be back on the job again, digesting the latest dispatches and readying editorials for the next day.

He was not unsuited to the work, and at 100 dollars a month, he was able to repay his college debt and even lay aside some savings. Yet despite enticing offers of promotion, he found pressured journalism "a terrible life."[8] But what else should he do? At twenty-six he could not postpone a permanent vocational decision much longer. Horace was painfully aware of family hopes that he eventually he would choose the ministry. One in four of his Yale classmates already had done so, and over a third eventually would.[9]

The thought of entering the Congregational ministry, however, still left Bushnell unmoved. He was too tangled in doubts to commit himself to theology, and too engrossed in secular ambitions to set them aside. After months of indecisive floundering, he finally decided the way out was through the law. Nothing in his fragmentary written recollections gives us a clue as to why he thought this would be his answer. Nonetheless, in January 1829 he left the *Journal of Commerce* and enrolled in the Yale Law School, his third wandering attempt to arrive at a life work.

Going to a structured law school in the late 1820s was something of an oddity. The Yale Law School itself was small and only recently started.[10] Just as for generations men aiming at the ministry had done their training in the studies of local pastors, most aspiring lawyers learned their trade as apprentices in the offices of successful attorneys. Bushnell expected to leave Yale for a private lawyer's office after a semester. By the summer of 1829 he had made plans to join a legal practice in Ohio, where he could complete his training and begin to work his way into Western politics.[11] He was on the verge of going when matters suddenly took a different turn. While he was in New Preston bidding farewell to his family, a letter reached him from Yale's president, Jeremiah Day, offering him a tutorship at Yale beginning that autumn. Tutorships were coveted appointments for hand-picked, unmarried recent graduates. The position carried with it the rank of junior officer on the faculty and afforded occupants the opportunity to pursue graduate studies on the side if they wished.

Bushnell must have been pleased. So sure was he, however, of the attractive plans he had already laid, that he scarcely gave a thought to accepting this flattering preferment. Without hesitation he wrote back and respectfully declined the honor. What happened next is best told in his own words:

> As I was going out the door, putting the wafer in my letter, I encountered my mother and told her what I was doing. Remonstrating now very gently, but seriously, she told me that she could not think I was doing my duty. "You have settled this question without any consideration at all that I have seen. Now, let me ask it of you to suspend your decision till you have at least put your mind to it. This you certainly ought to do, and my opinion still further is"—she was not apt to make her decision heavy in this manner—"that you had best accept the place." I saw at a glance where her heart was, and I could not refuse the postponement suggested. The result was, that going on a wedding excursion the next day with friends, I was so long occupied by it that I felt a little delicacy now in declining the appointment. And then it followed, as a still further result, that I was taken back to New Haven.[12]

Unforeseen at the time, this chance parental encounter set in motion a chain of events that was to alter the whole course of Bushnell's life.

His tutorship was a sunny interlude. Tutors were more drill-masters than instructors and were not expected to help students in any substantial way with preparation of their standard-form lessons. Bumptious Norwich boys Bushnell could not gladly teach; Yale undergraduates he could relate to with verve. He quickly won their confidence in the classroom, and his athletic prowess was an asset. In the opinion of some he eventually became the most popular officer of the college next to President Day.[13] On top of all this, he still was excited by the law, and by the winter of 1831, he had finished his coursework, passed his examinations, and eagerly anticipated admission to the bar.

Then once again the unexpected crossed his path. That same winter a religious revival swept New Haven. Of the various Second Great Awakening revivals the town experienced before the Civil War, none was quite like this one. Although not marked by excessive emotionalism, as some were, an impressed Professor Eleazar T. Fitch of the Yale theological faculty could hardly restrain his excitement over what seemed to him an outburst of fervor "unexemplified since the primitive age" of the apostles.[14]

In our pluralistic, highly populated, secular day, it can be difficult to get the feel of these events in the simpler setting of small, homogeneous communities shot through with earnest Christian assumptions. Wherever a major revival struck, it transformed the whole atmosphere of daily living. At Yale, in this instance, the usual din of conversation at meals in the student dining hall "was hushed into very whispers" for days at a time, as one undergraduate recalled.[15] Churches filled up, prayer meetings were constant, and saving faith became the urgent first order of the hour.

For anyone with any Christian background at all, trying to ignore or resist such a powerful stirring was like trying to stand alone against a seventy-mile-an-hour wind. Bushnell did try to withstand it—not because he scorned it, but because he could not decide how in all honesty he could respond to it. He still was uncomfortable with traditional forms of belief, and only with considerable difficulty had he been able to take his required turns at leading daily chapel. Still spiritually at sea, he scarcely knew whether he could any longer consider himself a Christian at all.

In a sermon on "The Dissolving of Doubts," Bushnell described to a later Yale generation an undergraduate not forgetful of faith, yet determined to rethink it in his own manner; all independence, he had "resolved to have a free mind." Thus he went on year by year, as the Doctor portrayed him,

reading, questioning, hearing all the while the gospel in which he has been educated, sometimes impressed by it, but relapsing shortly into greater doubt than before. . . . He has not meant to be an atheist, but he is astonished to find that he has nearly lost his conviction of God, and cannot, if he would, say with any emphasis of conviction that God exists. The world looks blank, and he feels that existence is getting blank also to itself.[16]

Plainly the passage was autobiographical. At age twenty-nine, Horace Bushnell was that man.

With revival all around him the strain was even heavier, as his tutorial following was looking to him for a lead. One by one the other five tutors entered into the event, and gradually Bushnell realized that he alone among his young faculty colleagues had not responded.[17] When he could endure the pressure no longer, he burst out to his confidante, Henry Durant, "I must get out of this woe." The solution he found was to loosen the hold of his overworked, analytical head and give more of a hearing to his heart. Like a Saul turned Paul, he suddenly appeared in a meeting of tutors, flung himself into a chair, and, half smiling at his predicament and half dead serious, opened his soul and shared his confession, both hands running nervously through his black, bushy hair:

O men! What shall I do with these arrant doubts I have been nursing for years? When the preacher touches the Trinity, and when logic shatters it all to pieces, I am all at the four winds. But I am glad I have a heart as well as a head. My heart wants the Father; my heart wants the Son; my heart wants the Holy Ghost—and one just as much as the other. My heart says the Bible has a Trinity for me, and I mean to hold by my heart.[18]

Horace supplemented this leap of faith with a fresh moral conviction. Pacing up and down in his room, he reached the conclusion that there is a fundamental, unchangeable distinction between right and wrong. This, at least, he never had questioned. He then reasoned that if there is a God, "as I rather hope there is, and very dimly believe, he is a right God. If I have lost him in the wrong, perhaps I shall find him in the right." This approach proved reassuring, and he did indeed begin to "find him" with greater certainty. He went out from his wrestlings and prayers as though on wings, the most troublesome doubts about God finally "gone." A being "so profoundly felt," he joyfully decided, "must inevitably be."[19] With this radically altered outlook, Bushnell might reasonably have continued on his way as a reborn Christian lawyer. Yet for one of his temperament this never was a serious possibility. Once he glimpsed what to him was a new dimension of truth, he had to give it his all. Hence he was not long in plotting still another course for himself—the fourth in his long search for a calling. He finished off the year of his tutorship, said farewell to the undergraduates in his division in a labored but caring speech,[20] and headed for Yale Divinity School.

At Yale Divinity School Bushnell once again faced a different set of teachers, and in particular Nathaniel W. Taylor, the leading light on the divinity faculty. Taylor had been the faculty's original member and had become widely known as an urbane, astute, controversial theologian. The son of a well-to-do New Milford, Connecticut farmer-apothecary, he had graduated from Yale in 1807. He had been a favorite of Timothy Dwight, in whose home he lived as a theological student. He also served as Dwight's amanuensis. In 1812, while still a young man, he had been called as minister of New Haven's influential Center Congregational Church, and ten years later, when Yale instituted a separate theological department, he was appointed Dwight Professor of Didactic Theology.[21]

Taylor hardly fitted the usual stereotype of a seminary teacher. With the incongruous exception of his addiction to chewing tobacco—the only Yale faculty member to indulge this habit—everything about him had "class" and style. Always meticulously dressed, he was uncommonly handsome. He had a well-proportioned frame, a finely shaped head with flowing locks, and as one of his students remembered, "lustrous eyes betokening descent from beautiful women."[22] Fortunately, he was also robust. His Center Church parishioners liked to tell of a day when a roughneck met up with Taylor on the New Haven green. Offended by Taylor's good looks and flawless attire, which he took as signs of weakness, the tough young man taunted him, "If it were not for your coat, I would give you a whipping." Unruffled, Taylor looked him in the eye and replied, "I could take it off." At this retort the startled would-be assailant decided he had miscalculated and with no further word beat a sullen retreat.

From his position at the Divinity School, this refined achiever not only influenced generations of students, but he severely rocked the New England theological boat. He had not intended to do so, and it is not always easy to understand why he had the effect he did. Many of the minute doctrinal distinctions that gravely exercised different Calvinistic schools of yesteryear hardly seem now to have warranted all the uproar.

Below the surface, however, crucial issues sometimes lurked, and often they engaged genuinely gifted minds. Always, for example, there was the problem of God's sovereign power as opposed to our human ability. How radical is the imbalance? When it comes to ultimate salvation, can we contribute anything? Or does all depend on the the decisive coming of the Spirit? For years New England orthodoxy had held that the imbalance was total. We human beings are helplessly caught from birth, so they contended, in the toils of sin, in defiance of a holy God. The majestic, all-righteous deity, on the other hand, is omnipotent; and no saving relationship with him is possible until by an act of unmerited grace he touches us with forgiveness and, through the sacrifice of Christ's Cross, receives us home to himself. All a sinner can do is wait, live the best life possible, and hope.

Nathaniel Taylor's theological crime in the eyes of New England orthodoxy was that he ever so slightly modified this imbalance in favor of human initiative. For Taylor, human sinfulness was not an inherited state of being. Sin required a deliberate deed on our part. As he argued in his much-disputed 1828 *Concio ad Clerum* ("Address to the Clergy"), a distinguished annual Connecticut lectureship, "the sin is in the sinning." In our unredeemed, natural condition he believed we almost certainly *would* sin and so incur guilt. But with skilled logic he contended that we do not *have* to err. We have power to do otherwise if we will. On the positive side, he insisted we also have the ability to reach out and use such means of grace as Scripture, worship, sacrament, and prayer—practices many clergy maintained were blasphemous for the unredeemed. Contrary to the dogma of more conservative Calvinists, Taylor held that these resources were appropriate and always available, even to persons as yet unsaved, and that we can choose to respond, thus playing a small but significant role in winning our own redemption.[23]

Church history amply shows that Christian understanding of the tension between divine grace and human capacity is forever in a process of reinterpretation. There is good Scripture to go with both sides of the issue. "Work out your own salvation with fear and trembling," Paul counseled the Philippians in one breath, only to add in the next, "for God is at work in you, both to will and to work for his good pleasure."[24]

Not every New England Congregationalist in the early nineteenth century, however, could apply both halves of that counsel with any degree of evenhandedness. Convinced that God's absolute sovereignty, and our own total dependency, were unquestionable givens, orthodoxy saw in Taylor a dire threat. If allowed to go unchallenged, his teaching would cut the nerve of revivals, conversion, and the whole process of salvation as the establishment had understood it. Deeply disturbed, traditionalists set out with vigor to fend off this subtle attack. In 1834, under the leadership of Taylor's highly conservative Yale contemporary Bennet Tyler, a stocky, ruddy-faced Maine pastor, once president of Dartmouth College, they established in East Windsor the Theological Institute of Connecticut (now the very different Hartford Seminary). They then proceeded to engage in intensive pulpit, tract, and ecclesiastical warfare.[25] The resulting Taylor-Tyler rivalry sharply split Congregational opinion and developed into a bitter controversy, of which Bushnell's more radical pronouncements a generation later became the stormy second phase.

One might have thought that two such progressive minds as Taylor and Bushnell, each destined to divide the churches, would have been kindred spirits as teacher and pupil. To a degree they were. Taylor was no ordinary lecturer, and an audacious Bushnell could appreciate the stimulating climate of his classroom. Taylor had a first-rate intellect, and as he expatiated on the key Calvinist themes of freedom and necessity, sin and redemption, reward and punishment, he was alternately dynamic with logic and tearful with emotion. After his own presentation, he would take a pinch of tobacco and invite an hour or more of open discussion. "Now, young gentlemen, I will hear you," he would say in a manner unique to his classroom. He urged them never to shrink from investigation or argument, often citing the dictum of the eighteenth-century Connecticut theologian Joseph Bellamy, that "there is no poker in the truth."[26] Bushnell could relate to that. After the major role moral right and wrong had played in his 1831 conversion, he could identify, too, with Taylor's contention that conscience was part of the Living Creator in every person. Above all, he was grateful to his mentor for daring to teach in a dogmatic day "that it doesn't hurt a man to think for himself."[27]

So far the two ran well together. But in ways other than age and experience, they were different men. Taylor was no mystic. To him religious truth was made to be captured completely in definitions and propositions. When thus reasonably framed, he believed the Gospel message to be irresistible. He had little use for intuitive feeling, or for those wide margins of ultimate mystery already starting to be important to Bushnell. It followed that Taylor had unbounded confidence in the capacity of human language to contain and express adequately even "the deep things of God."[28]

From the beginning of his ventures into theology, Bushnell was unable to share that viewpoint. With the zeal of a convert, augmented by the impatience of many a young theolog with the traditional, he must often have been what his daughter says he was, "an inconvenient member of so small a school." No matter what position was being explained or defended by his professor, young Bushnell always seemed to be "on t'other side."[29] Taylor never quite knew what to make of Bushnell, either as one of his students or later when he had become a controversial theologian. In later years Taylor would complain in a pique of puzzled frustration, "Bushnell don't know anything."[30]

While Taylor was confronting his inquiring mind, Bushnell also drew on other teachers. One was Josiah W. Gibbs, regarded as America's finest Hebrew scholar. With his expert knowledge of biblical tongues, Gibbs helped open Bushnell's eyes to the symbolic meaning of language—words always having more significance than appears on the surface.[31] Another guide of utmost importance was a thinker who never walked under Yale's stately elms. As Emerson and other ground-breaking young intellects of the period had done, Bushnell gradually came under the sway of Samuel Taylor Coleridge, the opium-addicted, romantic genius of early-nineteenth-century English letters.

Among Coleridge's prose writings was the thoughtful but difficult volume *Aids to Reflection*. Written in 1825, it circulated in America in an 1829 edition with a courageous introduction by James Marsh, president of the University of Vermont. Coleridge was no friend of rigid Calvinism, whether in Old England or New. His central thesis was that this theological school had perpetrated "outrages on the common sense and moral feelings of mankind" and had made satisfying belief all but "inaccessible" to the majority of Christians. He objected to the attempt to contain the mysteries of religion in neatly boxed formulas, arguing that theological language was intended to be taken suggestively, not literally, and in such a way as to point to experiences that went too deep for words. Christianity, he asserted, was not a theory "but a life." As for those who were righteously preoccupied with the wrath of God and frightful punishments, Coleridge pointedly reminded them "that the purpose of Scripture was to teach us our duty, not to enable us to sit in judgment upon the souls of our fellow creatures."[32]

There was virtually nothing in Bushnell's traditional church background to condition him for such committed yet such broad and flexible faith. If Nathaniel Taylor opened the door a few inches for him on new theological horizons, Coleridge flung it wide, knocking over a good deal of familiar spiritual furniture in the process. The change, however, did not come easily, despite Coleridge's avowed purpose to write for young people and especially for "students intended for the ministry."[33] At first reading, perhaps in an English edition while in college, Bushnell felt Coleridge was "foggy and unintelligible," and soon laid him aside. Some time later he tried him again, but even then was "buried" under the book for six months before he sensed he was starting to understand its message. However slowly comprehension came, his efforts proved permanently rewarding. All his life he thought of this volume as more important to him than any other book, save the Bible. Once Bushnell acknowleged to a friend that prior to Coleridge his outlook had been "only landscape." Afterward, if only dimly, he began to see stars. "I saw enough to convince me of a whole other world somewhere overhead," he recalled, "a range of realities in higher tier, that I must climb after, and, if possible, apprehend."[34]

The climb was not long delayed. With his vision clarified by his 1831 change of heart, he understood more of Coleridge and used him in his divinity school essays. In one, "There Is a Moral Governor," Bushnell challenged a hypothetical atheist to Coleridge's kind of "reflection."[35] In an untitled essay on natural science and moral philosophy, he dealt with many strands of thought, now leaning on Taylor and taking sharp issue with him. Through it all, however, ran a tone that was all Coleridge: protest against excessive intellectual speculation; impatience with systems that tangled Christians in perplexity about God; and a plea for spontaneity as well as discipline in discipleship.[36] Such views he never learned from Nathaniel Taylor; they were the yeast of the Anglican poet-critic, gradually leavening Bushnell's thought.

Meanwhile, in the more practical sphere, Bushnell stood at the threshold of his career. Where it would take him he could only guess. On 1 August 1832, he was licensed to preach by the New Haven West Association, using as his sermon his "Moral Governor" paper.[37] Licensure accomplished, he planned to say goodbye to New Haven and cast about for a church.

But he had not reckoned with a happy factor new to his experience: he was falling in love. He had been teaching a Bible class made up of younger women at New Haven's Third Congregational Church, when he met Mary Mehitabel (biblical name meaning "God is doing good") Apthorp, a bright, attractive, twenty-seven-year-old who lived in town with her mother and sisters. After a few sessions of the class, Bushnell was reluctant—on her account—to leave town a moment sooner than necessary.

Also in August he kept an important commitment to preach his first sermon in his boyhood New Preston Church.[38] Quickly, however, he hurried back to New Haven to see Mary and spend the fall and winter pursuing his courtship. He worked up a supply of sermons and filled pulpit engagements here and there in the hope that one of them might result in a call. He was impatient to get started, and needed a salary before he could marry.

But his personal desires neither impressed nor spurred on the churches. Twenty years later his memory was that one or two committees had looked him over but passed him by "as not being sufficiently promising."[39] Finally, in February 1833, conceivably through the good offices of Jeremiah Day, whose brother Thomas was a member of the search committee,[40] a letter reached him from an unknown quarter, the North Congregational Church of Hartford. It invited him to fill its vacant pulpit for a six-week trial period, indicating that if he proved satisfactory he might expect to be called permanently. He was unfamiliar with the church, and he worried that his "very small mustard seed of Christian experience" might not be sufficient for him in trying to handle a city congregation.[41] He was in no position, however, to turn his back on such an opening. Private misgivings notwithstanding, he agreed to come, and did. As it turned out, this invitation, with the call that eventually followed, was the only pastoral position he was ever to accept. So theologically dangerous did he become, it may have been the only such overture he ever received.

CHAPTER 5

New Minister in a Port City

SOARING ABOVE AN UNPAVED Main Street, at what seemed a dizzy height, the spire of the North Church looked down on a Hartford still primarily a port. Strung along an easy, fertile bend in the Connecticut River, the city was on the brink of a major economic transition from ocean-going commerce to nationally recognized banking, insurance, publishing, manufacturing, and merchandising enterprises, a new chapter in what has been called Hartford's "century of marvels."[1] But at the time Bushnell arrived in town, many of the old ways still held, and merchants continued to go down to the sea in ships.

Eyes on fortunes to be made, successful firms operated busy packet lines to East Coast harbors from Boston as far south as Norfolk. In their search for rich cargoes, more adventurous shipowners sometimes sailed on their own topsail schooners to the West Indies, Europe, or even the Far East. Small steamboats carried goods upriver, and despite formidable obstacles, investors dreamed of navigating as far north as the Canadian border.[2] Charles Bullfinch's tasteful statehouse faced the water, not the main streets, for river traffic was so active that by the 1840s it was estimated 2,500 vessels a year berthed at Hartford, servicing some 24,000 passengers, not to mention handling a substantial tonnage of freight.[3]

This bustling trade not only kept the city from being wholly provincial. It had its effect on growth. For decades Hartford's homogeneous, Anglo-American population had idled between 5,000 and 6,000 souls. By 1820 this figure had begun to grow, and by 1830 was edging close to 10,000. This, in turn, would increase by 30 percent by 1840.[4]

Not only were there more residents, but inspired by Second Great Awakening revivals, more people were attending worship, and the churches faced the happy problem of overcrowding. A new Congregational Church had not been established in the city for over 150 years. There had been no need for one. The pews of Thomas Hooker's original Center Church, dating from 1636, and its dissident offshoot, the South Church, gathered in 1670, always had been sufficient for the dominant Congregational membership of the community. But no more. Under pressure from growth that already had occurred and optimistic about the future, certain leaders of Center Church decided in 1823 that it was time to form a third Congregational Society.

In typical Yankee fashion, movers of the plan set about raising funds for land and a new building by selling stock at fifty dollars per share and by soliciting advance rentals for pews. Their appeal was so successful that, by September 1824, a commodious new structure had been erected, and just over 100 founding communicants, many of them, it was noted, "in the morning of life," had constituted themselves as the North, or Third, Congregational Church.

Their first pastor, Carlos Wilcox, was a frail poet-preacher who resigned and then died soon after North Church's establishment. The second pastor was Samuel Spring, Jr., one of an old-line family of Congregational and Presbyterian preachers. A very different type, Spring had been a sea captain before entering Andover Seminary (while a blockade runner during the War of 1812 he had been captured by the British). In Hartford, Spring ran afoul of doctrinal disputes and left after a brief pastorate. Once approved, Bushnell was to be his successor.[5]

As Bushnell had partially discovered at Yale, theological New England in the early 1830s was no peaceful place. And it was about to get worse. Trinitarian Congregationalists, Unitarians, and adherents of the liberal New Haven School were everywhere at swords' points. Soon the Transcendalists would join the fray. All of these contentious persuasions were beginning to feel added pressure from the rise of the new sciences and the influx of liberal ideas from abroad, especially from Germany. In Hartford, revival-centered Congregationalists from the First Church differed sharply from ecclesiastically and socially more genteel Epicopalians. Still more locally, the North Church already was split between devotees of Taylor and disciples of Tyler.[6]

From the moment of his arrival Bushnell encountered conflict. He reached the city the first weekend in March, having ridden the Litchfield stage through a furious snowstorm,[7] and went immediately to the home of the chairperson of the search committee and settled down to a warm fire and the prospect of a relaxing dinner. In a matter of minutes, however, he discovered the delicacy of his new situation. His host suddenly announced he must bundle up again and make his way through the drifts to the house of another church member. Mystified at first, Bushnell learned later the reason for this was the Tyler-Taylor dispute: the balance of power dictated that he stay with a family of a different faction.

Thus "put in hospital," as he felt, he was nonetheless well entertained and went on to make his pulpit debut on a bitterly cold Sunday when the meeting may well have been "thin." He preached from Hebrews, "How shall we escape if we neglect so great salvation?" His feeling was that the morning had gone tolerably well, and in any case he concluded the experience had been personally rewarding for him. In a letter, probably to his fiancée, he mused that to have worked with so searching a text "was certainly a good thing for myself."[8]

The trial period was no casual passage. He had to produce sermons more rapidly than ever before. Moreover, he was among a strange and strenuous people, and some of his constituents were awesome. When Joel Hawes, the ranking Congregational minister in town, began his work at Center Church as a young man in 1818, he was all but unnerved as he looked down from his high pulpit on a congregation that looked to him much like a gathering of Roman senators and their families, so grave and eminent did many of the men appear.[9] As the North Church had been organized by prominent Center Church members, a nervous Bushnell looked down on some of the self-same imposing "senators" that had made Hawes so uneasy.

His trial weeks were also made difficult by the chronic theological tension. It began at the top; the two deacons, customarily appointed for life, were at odds on almost every religious issue. Seth Terry, a no-nonsense attorney, was devout but meticulously unbending in his Calvinist orthodoxy—a typical disciple of conservative Bennet Tyler. His junior colleague, Amos M. Collins, was a highly successful, self-made merchant, a future two-term Democratic mayor of the city, and, like Terry, a transfer from Center Church. By temperament Collins was more flexible—firm but progressive—in his views, almost certainly sympathetic to the position of Nathaniel Taylor. The two deacons managed some sort of Christian accommodation and served together for a number of years. But the disharmony they symbolized made life precarious for an untried Bushnell. In an often-quoted description, he said he felt "daintily inserted between an acid and an alkali, having it for his task to keep them both apart, and to save himself from being bitten of one, or devoured by the other."[10]

As time passed it became clear that he was succeeding. He had a way about him that parishioners soon liked and respected, regardless of doctrinal feelings. At a Good Friday church meeting the membership unanimously extended him a formal call, and arrangements were made for his ordination and installation on 22 May.

Many young Protestant ministers still experience an *annus mirabilis* when they secure their first charge, get ordained, and are married all in the same year. It was so in 1833 with Bushnell. The job was in hand; ordination was next, and it did not come easily. Part of the procedure was a theological grilling before the ecclesiastical council of the Hartford North Consociation, consisting of clergy and laity. Given the conservative bias of his questioners—including that of the moderator, Princeton-educated Nathan Perkins, the stern and ageing pastor of the church in West Hartford—and Bushnell's independent, half-formed convictions, there was no way the council could have gone smoothly. When Perkins solemnly asked the central question, "What reason do you have to consider yourself a Christian?" Bushnell did well. But when the body could not drag from him the answer it wanted to hear about infant baptism, approval hung perilously in the balance. Finally the delegates agreed to do what such councils often have done: sustain the examination on the ground that what then was amiss in the candidate's thinking would come right with time and maturity.

The vote duly recorded, ordination took place the same day. The sermon was preached by Thomas H. Skinner, an uncle, by marriage, of Bushnell's fiancée, Mary. He was an eloquent Presbyterian preacher, born in North Carolina, and was said to resemble "a moth-eaten angel." There followed the consecrating prayer and the laying on of hands, and the ordinand stood officially before the world as the Reverend Horace Bushnell.[11]

Less than four months later, in New Haven, he was married.[12] His marriage to Boston-born Mary Apthorp was a love match, and remained so for over forty-two years. For Bushnell socially it also meant moving several steps up. His own heritage had been in every way solid, but unsung; Mary's bordered on the dazzling. Her ancestry included Charles Apthorp, a wealthy official of the British Crown in colonial Boston; Apthorp's son William, who moved in the same circles as John Adams and the Otises; and John Davenport, co-founder, with Theophilus Eaton, of the New Haven colony. She also had collateral ties to such greats as Governor William Bradford, Solomon Stoddard, and Jonathan Edwards.[13]

Only one shadow lingered over all this blue blood. Mary's father, another Charles Apthorp of Boston, proved to be a ne'er-do-well. Unaccountably, he abandoned her mother with five young daughters and disappeared, perhaps into the Deep South. This left a void in the family circle that was hard to forget or forgive. Bushnell's daughter Mary used to refer to him coldly as "the grandfather I never knew and never loved."[14]

Bushnell took his bride on a honeymoon to the Litchfield Hills, introducing her to the life of fishing and climbing that always had refreshed him. In midautumn they returned to Hartford, and his ministry began in earnest.[15]

Bushnell's first priority had to be preaching. Whatever else he might attempt, he knew he had to deliver on Sundays, and often midweek. He put no trust in *ex tempore* performance or sketchy notes. His habit was to write out his discourses in full and, in the pulpit, read from his manuscript word for word. It is no mean accomplishment to be able to preach effectively in this fashion, but Bushnell was a preacher who could do it. Young and old alike, many of them long used to sitting restlessly through sermons while their minds wandered, began listening with unaccustomed attention. Here was a new voice with fresh and relevant teachings. Charles L. Brace, the widely known pioneer social worker among deprived children of New York City, was a mere boy at the time, but he never forgot the impact of Bushnell's early appearances. "Those were the eager and powerful days of the great preacher," he recalled, "when his language had a pure and Saxon ring...[and] when emotions from the depths of a passionate nature bore him sometimes to the highest flights of eloquence, and wit and sarcasm [against the false and the pompous] flashed from his talk."[16]

The manner of his preaching had to measure up. So did the theological content. New England Congregationalists of the period often took their Christian opinions as seriously as their politics. The laity generally was biblically literate, frequently could dispute fine points of doctrine, and usually knew what it wanted to hear from the lips of a preacher. In the North Church that meant a fair fraction of the pewholders had their ears cocked for the accents of Tyler orthodoxy, while another equally influential group was watching for signs of Taylor liberalism.

Bushnell felt his way along diplomatically and yet also boldly, recognizing the merits of both parties but not hiding his lack of full agreement with either. "I took my stand openly on all the vexed questions," as he put it, determined "never to act on a policy of concealment or suppression for peace's sake." Although he may not have been quite as confident at that time as he was when he wrote those words years later, it would seem that he was not uncomfortable with this approach. Already he was moving into that "vein of comprehensiveness," which for all the trouble it brought on him proved to be "in no small degree the happiness of my ministry."[17] To Bushnell "comprehensiveness" meant that, contrary to entrenched New England opinion, no one Christian system could contain all the truth. To progress toward ultimate reality it was necessary, he argued, to allow different, even contradictory, opinions free play, letting them correct and nourish each other until new levels of insight emerged and greater Christian unity was possible.[18] In this he was much influenced by the contemporary French philosopher Victor Cousin, whose writing was available in New England in the early 1830s. But Bushnell adapted Cousin's thought to his own uses.[19]

One of his earliest sermons helps illustrate his method. He called it "Duty Not Measured By Our Own Ability," a title that characteristically suggested a fresh idea. Using Luke's account of Jesus feeding the 5,000, he developed the point that each of us is responsible not simply for the ability we think we have but for the ability which, by God's grace in Christ, we *can* have. Thus, Jesus would not accept the puzzled protest of the disciples that they could not possibly stretch a mere five loaves and two fish among 5,000 people. He told them what to do; believing in him, they went about doing it and, beyond every natural expectation, found they could feed everyone and still have abundant food left over. Bushnell was saying here that all human ability is a gift. Just as the disciples were powerless to feed the multitude on their own, so we are powerless to do anything of significance, least of all regenerate ourselves "without drinking out of God's fulness." Conservative Tylerites, sceptical of any reliance on individual ability, were glad to hear that. At the same time he used the story to demonstrate that human ability can, to a degree, act on its own. Those who search for the answer of salvation must use such strength as they have to take hold of God's promises in good hope, as the disciples set about the work of feeding, not leaving everything to their Lord. Followers of the New Haven school felt at home hearing that, convinced as they were that human souls could contribute something to their own redemption.

Not stopping there, however, he wove these two insights together, telling his flock it was their privilege and duty to "co-work" with their Creator, trusting him to "give you all supply, just as fast as you need it, gaining abilities by using abilities, where necessary "learn[ing] to swim by swimming" and so serving and achieving beyond every merely human possibility.[20] Thus everyone in the congregation, conservative or liberal, was left with something to ponder.

The pulpit was Bushnell's first love. Especially at first he acknowledged that pastoral care lagged somewhat behind his preaching and writing.[21] Nonetheless, he was an affectionate man at heart and faithfully made his rounds, with Mary giving him good support. Together they would go on foot or by carriage to visit each North Church home at least once a year, apart from emergencies.

Pleasant as this was, there were pastoral difficulties, too. Some of them called for sustained help from the deacons and other church leaders and, in the end, discipline. Bushnell was hardly settled in before he and the church had to deal with Mrs. Clarissa Dodge ("Sister Dodge"), allegedly the keeper of a house of dubious reputation. In spite of two years of attempting to bring her around "tenderly and affectionately," as the church record states, in June 1836 she was excommunicated for subjecting the church to "reproach and scandal."[22] Congregationalists at the time were not squeamish about ecclesiastical rigor, and at least two other members suffered the same fate within a few years. Bushnell, however, found the procedure distasteful, and viewed excommunication as "a very cruel discipline." In another early sermon he laid it on his people to be watchful with a sense of family concern for "the first gentle declinings," so as to forestall the need for such severe penalties.[23]

His ministry bore fruit in slow but steady parish growth, handicapped by frequent member moves to larger cities in the East and to new ones in the West, losses over which neither he nor the congregation had any control. In 1832 the membership stood at 264. By 1836 it was 303, and by 1839 the number was 414.[24] It was not the kind of rapid revival expansion the churches dreamed of, and it left Bushnell with a nagging sense of vocational insecurity. Yet it was enough foundation to stand him in good stead when the winds of controversy began to blow.

Although the severest storms would not gather until much later, even his beginning years were buffeted. A recurring source of unpleasantness was Bennet Tyler's new Theological Institute of Connecticut. This highly conservative school was set up a few months after Bushnell was ordained, and "before a brick was laid," he once complained, it began to "meddle" with him.[25] Three prominent members of the North Church, James R. Woodbridge, Deacon Seth Terry, and Terry's brother, Eliphalet, an enterprising insurance pioneer, were early trustees of the Institute.[26] Very possibly it was one of these men who persistently pained Bushnell by peddling unfriendly complaints against him "in the east and in the west, in stages and in steamboats, at public tables and anniversaries." It dawned on such minds that here in their new pastor was a prime illustration of the dire consequences of the New Haven theology: a falling away from the doctrine of total human depravity, an exaggeration of human ability, and a deemphasizing of revivalism, election, and saving grace. Adding to Bushnell's troubles, one or two unfriendly pastors in eastern Connecticut made a point of spreading tales about him, stirring up the churches, and using his alleged heresies as leverage for fund-raising on behalf of the rock-ribbed East Windsor seminary.[27]

Bushnell managed to remain on viable terms with one or two of the Institute leaders,[28] but it hurt him that members of his own congregation, to say nothing of ministerial colleagues in the state, would stoop to attack him behind his back, especially when he barely had had time to establish himself with his people. The time came when he could no longer refrain from public outburst against this "brute conservatism." But for a decade he seems to have held his peace, keeping in some touch with many of his opponents and making all the allowances he could for their hostility."[29]

He could not be so patient when it came to the looming storm over African American slavery. Like Harriet Beecher Stowe, Bushnell had his first encounter with this problem at the time of the fierce Missouri Compromise debates in 1820–21. He was then an impressionable New Preston farm lad of seventeen, but his memory was that the whole town was stirred by the crisis, including children in the schools. The thought of slave territory being extended into the new state of Missouri, as provided by part of the compromise, outraged these rural New Englanders, whose minds were "full of liberty." The experience stayed with Horace, and he wrote on the subject while an undergraduate at Yale.[30]

In the interval, slavery had become an even more sensitive issue, but he was not long in addressing it from his Hartford pulpit. In practice Connecticut was largely free, yet there were qualified judges who held "that the State of Connecticut, from time immemorial, has been, and to a certain extent now [1837] is, a slaveholding State."[31] The census of 1840 showed there still were seventeen legally held slaves in Connecticut, albeit these were vastly outnumbered by 8,000 free African Americans.[32]

Territorially, the Nutmeg State was no part of the Cotton Kingdom, yet a city like Hartford had important economic, political, and social ties with the South. The Whigs were still a national party. In business, one of Bushnell's leading laymen, Normand Smith, Sr., to cite but one example, had been doing a flourishing saddle and livery trade with New Orleans since 1818.[33] Various members of the North Church had come to the Hartford community from such Southern centers as Lexington, Kentucky, Huntsville, Alabama, and Augusta, Georgia. Southerners and their Hartford friends often visited back and forth, and more than once during the 1830s Bushnell was called upon to perform intersectional marriages.[34]

Northerners with such interests and connections could have misgivings about the Southern attachment to slavery, but they were hardly disposed to be radical reformers. In Connecticut attempts in the 1830s by whites or African Americans to enlarge the civil liberties even of free African Americans usually met with strong opposition, if not outright violence. Prudence Crandall, a socially sophisticated, if not always tactful, white teacher in Canterbury, dared to enroll African American girls in her classes beginning in 1832. Infuriated local citizens savaged her house, clapped her in jail, and forced her to close down her little academy.[35] In 1831 an effort was made by a small group of African Americans and whites to establish a African American college in New Haven. The reaction in the city was one of unabashed horror. "A negro college by the side of Yale College!" "The City of Elms disgraced forever!" "It must not and shall not be," ran the excited protests. A meeting of some 700 aroused citizens almost unanimously voted the project down.

There were abolitionists in the state, and many who wanted to see the institution of African American bondage in the South more gradually removed. But for the personal future of African Americans, whether already free or some day to be liberated, whether in the South or in their own midst, Connecticut whites during Bushnell's initial years in Hartford showed little concern. What was attempted by a brave handful of progressive African Americans and whites in what one historian has called the most anti-abolitionist, anti-African American state in New England was routinely rejected.[36]

In this setting of caution and disdain, Bushnell followed developments closely, looking for a position he could commend to his people. Only two years into his ministry he risked tackling the issue as part of his first published sermon, "Crisis of the Church." He gave slavery top priority among pressing emergencies, already fearful that it might at almost any time "explode the foundations of the republic." In this, as in other aspects of the "crisis," he argued, all depended on respect for "the majesty of law" and reverence before God. On these firm foundations, he insisted, the country had been established. On them alone it could endure.[37]

This preachment was too general to stir much dissent. Four years later, however, in January 1839, it was different. In a full-length, weekday evening sermon, "Discourse on the Slavery Question," he focused entirely on the "hideous" institution. A full North Church, crowded with men and women, Whigs, "Loco's," colonizationists, and "abolitionists of every degree of temperature, from 55° to 210°," as one listener described the scene, waited to hear Bushnell.[38]

Read today, the speech has its puzzling contradictions and is tainted with racism. It also has eloquence and courage. Even to raise the subject was to invite serious discord. Bushnell knew well enough that nearly all his own people were opposed to the radical abolitionists, some were moderately antislavery and others "mad" against any mention of the thorny question.[39]

With half his discourse he gave comfort to nonabolitionists by attacking organized antislavery. In his opinion it tactlessly alienated the South, exercised overheated judgment, occasioned lawless riots, entertained too optimistic an opinion of the African American race, and fruitlessly tried to force the hand of God, who would bring in his mighty justice whether the American Anti-Slavery Society fulminated or not. Having said this, however, he did some fulminating himself. Passionately he advocated most the of things the antislavery leaders favored, only insisting, with many leading New Englanders of the day, that they be accomplished by individual means rather than in concert. In a slashing polemic against slavery itself, Bushnell was all but indistinguishable from an ardent abolitionist. If the lawyer in him kept him from saying slaveholding was under any and all circumstances a *malum in se,* a sin in itself—a matter much debated among the churches[40]—he did denounce it as an insupportable evil incurring "great personal guilt." It broke up families, subjected slaves to bodily cruelty, and deprived African Americans of moral and intellectual identity. No one with any human feeling could think of it without "pity, disgust and shame." "Away with it," he implored, "nothing can be worse—anything beside must be better."[41]

Moreover, the time for silently standing by was past. True Christians and true New Englanders must act, he contended, and "you cannot do it too soon." According to Bushnell, the pulpit, the press, and Northern politicians must speak out; Southerners must be prodded to lobby their legislatures. Let all free citizens "vote, debate, converse, write," he urged in a forthright—and provocative—sentence. Then, in a peroration not unworthy of abolitionist William Lloyd Garrison, Bushnell cited slavery as not a secondary cause but as the very "hinge" on which the integrity and future of the Union must depend, not to mention "the griefs of afflicted millions. Who of us shall be the truest friends of these immeasureable interests?—this shall be our strife!"[42]

"Strife" over any political or social issue was hardly what Bushnell's cautious, practical constituency wanted most. As people spilled out of the North Church, tightening their greatcoats and bonnets against a winter rain, reactions were predictably strong. A favorable letter soon appeared in the *Courant* hailing the address as a "master effort" and claiming what was said was received with "unqualified approbation."[43] That was a considerable overstatement. In a preface to the published "Discourse," Bushnell himself expressed his "sorrow" that he could not make his case more acceptable to those "who

differ with me." Francis Gillette, an abolitionist and later a Free Soil
U.S. Senator from Connecticut, wrote in a long review that neither
the antislavery people nor their opponents were pleased with Bushnell. In the eyes of abolitionists he had demeaned the Christian pulpit
as a voice of liberty. Among the conservatives, according to Gillette,
"many men" were deeply upset with his unexpected brand of activism.[44]

On top of this uproar the North Church Society soon met in a
stormy, inconclusive session to debate opening the church more
widely to abolitionist use. Both sides became so aroused that Bushnell feared his pastorate might meet "disaster."[45] Although he refused
to compromise his slavery stance, however, the worst did not happen, and before long he was pushing his brand of antislavery again,
this time from a different angle. In June 1840 he proposed calling a
special convention of Connecticut Congregational clergy to meet in
Hartford and prepare an antislavery address to the churches.[46] As before, Bushnell wanted to undercut the organized societies and offer
church members more religiously acceptable paths to abolition. He
tried to enlist the aid of his close friend Leonard Bacon, influential
pastor of New Haven's Center Church for his plan. Although recently disillusioned with colonization, Bacon was hesitant. Other
clergy leaders turned a deaf ear to so "needless and injudicious" a
meeting, and Bushnell's brainchild died a-borning.[47]

In the main these encounters fixed the outlines of Bushnell's
pre–Civil War approach to African Americans and bondage.
Whether or not his parishioners were likely to approve, he was fearless in speaking out against slavery and equally opposed to tightly organized efforts to abolish it. Although he knew there were exceptional African Americans—"I am far from thinking that the African
is incapable of elevation"—he shared the prevailing white opinion
that African Americans as a race, even if set free, had no significant
future.[48] And while he wanted to see the slavery conflict resolved by
gentlemanly, peaceful means, he was afraid from the beginning that a
violent solution might be unavoidable.[49]

In light of this, was Bushnell a racist? On that difficult question it
is only fair to move carefully, and with an eye to definitions. If the

meaning of racism is destructive hatred of minorities, Bushnell was no racist. If in his day racism meant condoning slavery, Bushnell was not a racist; he deplored Southern slavery. If racism is a prejudiced unwillingness to associate with racial elements other than one's own, or to respect or assist them, Bushnell does not qualify. He esteemed the few African Americans he knew at all well. He listened attentively to "Old Law," an untutored fugitive slave living in Hartford who called on Bushnell occasionally to talk religion.[50] He had at least a few professional ties with James W. C. Pennington, an African American minister in town, and once tried to get Jeremiah Day to admit Amos G. Beman, another rising African American leader, to lectures at Yale—a bold gesture for the year 1838.[51]

If, however, racism means the objective conviction, held without malice, that biological, cultural, religious, and moral achievements identify and separate the races of humankind, a highly complex Bushnell, prior to the Civil War, was a racist. He believed God had brought Anglo-Saxons to a unique degree of perfection in the United States, while other races, notably African Americans, lagged behind. During the nativist, racist age when he was most active in his ministry, it was a rare American—especially among intellectuals—who did not agree.[52]

Bushnell has to be counted among those able, dedicated, white Christians whose ambiguous racial stance (apart from their opposition to slavery) made them considerably more of a hindrance than help to the prewar African American struggle. Given his moral vision in other progressive causes, it is regrettable that Bushnell could not see further on this matter, especially since in the same period liberated Northern African Americans, with the help of a few determined whites, were making hard-won progress in education, business, voting rights, and church life. Ironically, the kinds of advances he and so many others thought impossible were already happening in plain sight.[53]

Throughout early controversy and his daily ministry, Bushnell drew strength from his family. When he and Mary first returned to the city as newlyweds, they made a temporary home with hospitable parishioners before settling into their own modest house on Ann

Street. Mary soon became pregnant, and their first child, Frances Louisa, was born in 1834. Another daughter, Elizabeth Davenport, was born two years later, bringing joy and then, abruptly, grief; she died before her first birthday in 1837. Bushnell helped to nurse her until she slipped away.

To ease their pain, the couple made an autumn excursion that year to Niagara Falls, stopping en route home to visit Bushnell's parents in Brockport, New York, where they had moved in 1836—a strenuous change for a man of sixty. The hardship of breaking ties of a lifetime and starting over again as pioneers on new land was proving too much for Bushnell's mother, Dotha. By 1838 she was dead. Bushnell never saw her again after this one trip, and he found it hard to forgive his father for making a change so difficult for her.[54] Shortly after their return, however, the Hartford household was brightened again, this time by the birth of their only son, Horace Apthorp. Bushnell was quite beside himself with delight over "the little gentleman," proudly reporting to his mother-in-law in New Haven the appearance of "a very gracious and meditative smile."[55]

Home was always an important center for Horace. Modern downtown Hartford makes it hard to imagine the green space he had there for a garden, shaded by a venerable oak. Natively a farmer, he enjoyed donning overalls and working the soil, grading his front yard, or laying a course of bricks.[56] On a salary of $100 a month, he was frugally comfortable. Like most ministers, he looked forward to holidays, when he could lay down the perpetual parish load and find refreshment. Some of his early vacations he necessarily spent alone, while Mrs. Bushnell stayed in Hartford or New Haven with the children. At times he "drifted off to sea," sailing and fishing with friends along the shores of Long Island Sound. At such times he could let go of formality; talk was not of theology or parish difficulties, but of persons and places, nature, current news, or the day's catch of bluefish. A smoker in college, Bushnell had given up the habit when he married. But away from home on such holidays, if a cigar were offered he could not always resist. With a mischievous twinkle in his eye, he would remark, "Let's sin a little!" Then along with his companions, he would light up and enjoy the usually forbidden luxury.[57]

In the late summer of 1835, he made the first of a number of treks to the popular White Mountains of New Hampshire. On a cloudless September day, with snow already on the summit, he and a friend climbed Mt. Washington from Crawford Notch. From the highest vantage point in New England he reveled in the magnificent panorama, gazing over the southern peaks with Chocorua's jagged tooth in the hazy distance. Looking east he may have caught a gleam from the Atlantic off the coast of Maine.

As he lingered there in the splendor, he took a fragment of birch bark, probably a souvenir from his ascent, and with fingers stiff with cold penciled a note to Mary in Hartford. "My heart longs for my dear wife," he wrote. "If my feet could travel as fast as my eye, how soon I would be by her side!" He added a note to his little daughter, tucked the bark back in his pocket for mailing, breathed a prayer of thanks to "the God of the mountains," and picked his way carefully down the steep, rocky cone toward the valley.[58]

The messages and moments are revealing of Bushnell as he was in his midthirties: vigorous, adventurous, having heart as well as head, and, for the most part, a happy man.

CHAPTER 6

First Steps toward Center Stage

FOR ALL ITS GROWTH AND POTENTIAL, Hartford could not long monopolize a figure with Bushnell's talent and drive. Once his ministry had fairly begun, out-of-town invitations began to come with flattering frequency. Academic centers were especially attentive. During his first dozen years at the North Church, he was twice called to Yale for major presentations and once to Andover Seminary. In 1836 he was asked to take a professorship in theology at the Western Reserve College in Hudson, Ohio, and in 1840 Middlebury College wanted him as its president. Two years later Wesleyan University, then a struggling institution, gave him an honorary Doctor of Divinity degree.[1] From that day on, he was always and everywhere known as "Dr. Bushnell."

He does not seem to have coveted the title too much, yet the lure of academia continued to disturb his peace. Although things were generally going well in Hartford, feelings about his career would not quite settle down. Often he asked himself how long he intended to remain in the ministry. There were moments when he felt he would do "better as teacher than...as a preacher." Hence, when the offer came from a "thriving" Western Reserve, he hastily sought advice from Jeremiah Day at Yale, half hoping he would encourage him to accept. Whether or not Day did so, Bushnell soon declined the place and decided to stay where he was.[2]

Then, in the winter of 1840, there came the tempting approach from Middlebury College. Founded in 1800 with the blessing of Timothy Dwight, Middlebury dreamed of becoming a northern New England Yale. At one point it had boasted over 150 students and, with the exception of the University of Vermont, was the only collegiate institution of any consequence in the state. Starting with the academic year 1836–37, however, "the town's college" had fallen on hard times. It came under the influence of radical, "anxious seat" revivalism, lost the support of many Vermont clergy, and was faced with a dwindling, rebellious student body.[3]

Unsettled as the scene still was in early 1840, there were faculty members who saw a great future for the school. Alexander C. Twining, a professor who alternately taught mathematics and natural philosophy and laid out railroads and experimented with astronomy, was a newcomer to the college and full of enthusiasm for it. He had known Bushnell at Yale and pressed him so hard to consider the presidency that the Doctor undertook a wretched March journey through Vermont rain and mud to get a first-hand look. He was well received and made a better impression than even his supporters had expected. But they could sense he was holding back in deference to his wife.[4] If he felt it his duty to accept, she was willing to go. But she was reluctant to leave Connecticut and had strong convictions about seeing her husband continue in the pastoral ministry. To her the ministry was "the noblest work ever committed to man."[5] Despite her misgivings, Bushnell had his own leanings and ambitions. Back in Hartford he agonized for days over the question, going so far as to inquire of his colleague William W. Andrews, Congregational pastor in Kent, Connecticut, whether he would consider becoming his successor.[6] Finally, however, as he had with Ohio, he decided to say no.

Before long he must have realized that these decisions were leaving him with the best of both worlds. He could stay with his parish and still retain outside scholarly connections. Andover Seminary offered an important example. Originally Andover had been set up as a bulwark against Unitarian Harvard, and standing on its commanding hilltop twenty miles north of Boston, it was known as the "West Point of orthodoxy." Each year the Porter Rhetorical Society at the seminary elected honorary members, one of whom was chosen to deliver an address the day before the September commencement. In 1839 this honor came to Bushnell. Without his knowledge, however, the ceremonies that year were advanced a week, and he suddenly heard he had hardly more than a day to prepare and travel before he was due to appear. He met the alarming deadline by shutting himself in his study, and with intense concentration he produced by sundown an eighty-page manuscript on revelation. Immediately he hopped a coach, bumped along sleeplessly through the night, changed stages at Worcester, and rode on to the Andover campus in the nick of time.[7]

His "Revelation" had to do with the mysterious ways in which God chooses to communicate with us. At the time Bushnell spoke, it was a question much disputed. As noted in connection with Nathaniel Taylor, prevailing theology was in love with the God of precise doctrine. It held that the Eternal reaches human beings through logically refined statements of faith, the same for all and adequate for every type of soul. Most New England Trinitarian leaders were convinced they had caught in human language the saving messages of God in a form so nearly exact as unlikely ever to need change.

Long as this view had predominated, the early years of the century were producing a slowly rising tide of opinion against it. Unitarians, Transcendentalists, natural scientists, and devotees of reason, not to mention many bewildered pewholders in traditional Congregational churches, began protesting that such tight creeds no longer addressed life as they knew it. There must be other ways of relating to the Gospel. This polarizing climate almost demanded that an emerging leader such as Bushnell declare where he stood on the issue. Did the revelation of God's love and will occur exclusively through precise creeds? Or might it beam its way to us also through more varied and imaginative channels?

As was his way, Bushnell's answer at Andover was comprehensive. Yes, God does speak to us through human language, as orthodoxy held, but through language that instead of being forever precise, was primarily suggestive, symbolic, and aesthetic. It was the insight Coleridge and Gibbs had given him, and it was to run like a bright identifying thread through the texture of his thought.

To his Andover audience Bushnell proposed that all language is two stories high: on the ground floor are words for *things;* On the second floor are words for *thought*. What the divine-human process of language does is take words from the first floor, and use them to

[59]

convey ultimate spiritual truths on the second floor. Thus the sky, which we can see (first floor language), communicates something of the glory of God, which we cannot see (second floor language), as in the Psalm: "The heavens are telling the glory of God; and the firmament proclaims his handiwork. Day to day pours forth speech, and night to night declares knowledge."[8]

For Bushnell, as for Emerson in his *Nature*,[9] all of Creation was "one grand dictionary of speech," language from the mind of God plainly revealing something of the Eternal Being and purpose. This kind of revelatory vocabulary comes to a clear focus in the Scriptures, which are crammed with physical images from the Old Testament—images of altar and law, of nature and history—which ultimately bear messages of highest truth in the New.

Such language, Bushnell went on to say, was not so much revelation by logic as by poetry. It was figurative and incomplete; but since it allowed room for imagination, beauty, and mystery, it was more powerful. Rightly used it would set preachers free from the "cold terms" of mere speculation to experience and share more of a living grace. It would open the way for science and religion to make new joint discoveries, and, best of all, it would help make God more immediately apparent to every believer. Speaking of such immediacy, Bushnell gave his own testimony: "I behold God by no deduction of logic . . . I see him with a direct gaze of simple inspection as I see any man through his bodily types of look and action. Here, then, in language, we have a revelation of God which shows, as in a mirror, one vast and varied image of his intelligence."[10]

Here were the makings of the most personal and artistic view of revelation New England had heard from its Trinitarian theologians since Jonathan Edwards's luminous "sense of the heart." But it was not what the traditional Andover community was used to hearing from its faculty. Bushnell felt he had tried to be cautious, but knew he had stirred "a little breeze" and would be criticized. As he thought about it, grandiose visions crept into his thinking. Could it be that this different approach was to be something akin to a new Reformation? If so, did he have the moral courage of a Martin Luther and his successors to take a lead in it?

Bushnell was not destined to be another Luther. His Andover address, however, began to link him to the wider unorthodox "flowering of New England"—and to the price to be paid for it. Already a young Emerson had delivered his "Divinity School" address at Harvard, and would not be invited back for nearly thirty years. His offense was having said of symbol, feeling, and spiritual imagination from the periphery of the church what Bushnell was saying from its center. Soon Theodore Parker's independent opinions would drive him from his West Roxbury parish; Margaret Fuller would bear the brunt of criticism for her role in *The Dial;* and a dissatisfied Herman Melville would embark on his literary "voyage chartless."[11] Bushnell included, these and others were revolutionary minds still in their thirties, looking, in Emerson's words, for "an original relation to the universe" and determined to do a new thing.[12]

With many of them the Hartford pastor had no close personal ties, although he knew Parker and George Ripley well and Emerson at least slightly.[13] He had radical disagreements with their views. Yet in his quest for greater, more relevant truth, Bushnell was their spiritual kinsman and would carry his full share of the rejection all of them had to endure. Andover was his earliest heresy and his first step toward a long, unwanted battle.

Other outside appearances were less pivotal, but they served to broaden his public. Before and after Andover he spoke at Yale. In 1837 he delivered the Phi Beta Kappa oration, which included a call for a truly indigenous American literature, expressing more briefly what Emerson said in his "American Scholar" address at Harvard two weeks later.[14] At the 1843 Yale commencement, he addressed alumni on moral trends in history.[15] In this presentation he made so many excursions into Greek art and Roman law that an irate "Catholicus" accused him in print of forsaking his Christian vocation. How could a Christian pastor, and a doctor of divinity at that, his critic inquired, hand out such teaching? "Are you one thing as Dr. Bushnell preaching in Hartford, and another thing as Dr. Bushnell addressing the Alumni of Yale College?" he wanted to know.[16]

No such challenge greeted a visit to Western Reserve College for graduation ceremonies in 1842. As a law student, Bushnell had dreamed of Ohio. When he actually saw it, it lived up to his every expectation. It was "a kind of garden at the West," he reported, New England recreated. Western Reserve was trying to make itself the Yale of the West, even to the point of duplicating its architecture.[17] Apparently these efforts were succeeding, as Bushnell claimed he saw more Connecticut people he knew than he would have met had he attended a commencement in New Haven. Ohio liked Bushnell, too. He was looked upon as a prophet from the East, and his discourses on "The Stability of Change" and "The Vital Principle" were so enthusiastically received that his listeners were loath to let him go home.[18]

But the glow of Western hospitality was followed abruptly by tragedy in Hartford. He came back to find that four-year-old Horace Apthorp was dying. The victim of a brain disorder, the child weakened as his parents stood helplessly by. He died in October. His death meant that Horace and Mary had been deprived of two of their four children—Mary, the fourth child, had been born in 1840. The distraught Doctor and his wife were comforted by the birth of their youngest daughter, Dotha, in 1843, but Bushnell never wholly forgot the loss of his one son. In time he did his best to learn from the experience, and did so with some success. There was evidence that the blow had deepened his preaching. In any event, he remarked wistfully that he had "learned more of experimental religion since my little boy died than in all my life before."[19]

Meanwhile Bushnell was an engine of activity in Hartford's church and civic life. With his younger friend, Henry Barnard, he labored to improve what he described as the "dirty shops of education" that too long had passed for local public schools.[20] One eventual fruit of their partnership was the establishment of the Hartford Public High School, created in part from the time-honored Hopkins Grammar School and, in 1847, equipped with a new building. He was active in the affairs of the General Association of Connecticut, still the only statewide Congregational body.[21] At the local ecclesiastical level, some felt by 1843 that the Hartford North Association of Ministers had grown too large and should be divided. This was done, and Bushnell was elected an early moderator of the newly formed Hartford Central Association. The same year he helped found *The New Englander,* a New Haven–based quarterly, the forerunner of today's *Yale Review.*[22]

With these demands it was a constant struggle to do justice to his parish. There, too, the pace was unrelenting, but he managed. Thomas Robbins, librarian of the embryonic Connecticut Historical Association, was new to town in 1844 and spent time acquainting himself with the churches. On an October Sunday he went to hear Bushnell preach and noted in his *Diary* that "the North Church congregation is a large and good one."[23] "Good" as his constituency and his own basic situation may have been, problems still could arise. During the presidential election year 1844, Bushnell deliberately plunged into another political controversy and again found his pulpit at risk. This time, in a sermon on "Politics Under the Law of God,"[24] he dealt even more directly with political specifics than in his slavery discourse.

Henry Clay of Kentucky was doing his usual utmost to win the White House as the Whig candidate and seemed certain to be opposed by a proslavery Democrat. Bushnell could stomach neither possibility. He saw the noisy race as further evidence of rank party politics that had departed from every religious and moral principle. He had said much the same in a sermon on "American Politics" during the raucous "Tippicanoe and Tyler too" campaign of 1840.[25] Now, however, matters seemed even worse. Not only was secular party rivalry more advanced in its hold on the electorate, but there was the strong likelihood that the national canvass would further the annexation of Texas, thus vastly enlarging both proslavery territory and the political power of the South.

Not despairing of democracy, but concerned for its spiritual grounding, the Doctor deplored all this as godless political manoever. It seemed of a piece with the disastrous Missouri Compromise, the more recent unjust expulsion of Georgia and Florida Indians from their ancestral lands, and with Thomas Dorr's disruptive "rebellion" in Rhode Island. "With a boldness for which some of you may not thank me," he accused the American people of "the most glaring wrongs," breaches that could only bring down Divine judgment, since "God cannot endure a nation which cannot endure him." Consequently he advised his people to reject both major candidates on election day and to ballot with "*a piece of clean white paper*" as an act of national repentance. This would also serve as a signal to politicians that spiritually insensitive, ethically unjust candidates from whatever party were no longer acceptable. He made no reference to Clay by name. Too transparently to be missed, however, he castigated him as the architect of the proslavery Missouri Compromise, "who therein took upon his soul the sorrows of millions of bondmen, and the moral desolation of the fairest portion of the globe."[26]

It was part of Bushnell's Puritan bent that he continually stressed the dependence of a healthy democracy on healthy religion, hence on a strong national as well as personal reverence. A merely human social contract was not enough. His congregation had heard him on that before. But here he was moving beyond generalities to immediate particulars, and his thinly veiled attack on an allegedly immoral Clay left the Whigs in the North Church stunned and angry. By dint of enormous effort, their party had managed to elect William Henry Harrison in 1840 only to have his sudden death rob them of their triumph. Clay's promising candidacy seemed to offer a way to redeem that misfortune and at long last bring into office a president to their liking. To have their pastor blacken the reputation of their cherished hope and link this with yet another blistering censure of slavery was too much to be borne. In greeting Bushnell's assault on Clay with respectful glee, the Democratic Hartford *Times* reported that the sermon had caused "a great commotion-motion-otion" in North Church circles, which were "enraged beyond bounds."[27] It was no exaggeration.

For whatever reason, Bushnell, at forty-two, had been going through one of his confident, almost cocksure periods. Earlier in the year he had all but lampooned Connecticut Episcopal bishop Thomas C. Brownell, first president of Trinity College and Bushnell's senior in age and status, in an ecclesiastical critique in the *New Englander*, a piece he later lamented.[28] In part his attack on Clay stemmed from the same self-assured, combative mood. Shaken, but still defiant, Bushnell acknowledged that his parish situation was perilous; but he told friends in unvarnished terms that if he must go, "I won't be kicked out."

He thereupon called for a good attendance at a Sunday evening service and openly faced his people. He told them with feeling that he regretted having caused them distress, but that he believed he had spoken God's truth. In effect he repeated what he had said in the sermon, that as a Christian minister he could not let politics alone until he should be convinced that political life was not as much under the government of God as any other sphere of human existence. If his critics expected their pastor to say solely those things they wanted to hear, with never an unwelcome word, they must have mistaken the vocation of a minister. So pliable an envoy of the Gospel would scarcely be worth supporting under any circumstances, and such an envoy Bushnell did not propose to be.[29] This blend of tact and conviction gradually stilled the storm. So effectively did he handle the crisis that his right to speak freely from his pulpit was never again challenged.

At times historians have said that Bushnell, like his future fellow-townsman Mark Twain, often was victimized by the Victorian prejudices of his constituents and found it necessary to adjust his principles to retain his public. In this respect he even has been portrayed as a prototype of supposedly malleable twentieth-century suburban ministers, blandly catering to the prosperous preferences of their conservative, commuter congregations.[30] It is difficult to find hard evidence for such a theory. The well-known New Haven author and landscape gardener, Donald G. Mitchell, who had opportunities to observe Bushnell over many years, was closer to the mark. Describing the Doctor in a volume of memoirs, he maintained that "he was never in any straits of politics, or of theologies, another man's man."[31] Bushnell may have been overconfident, but the Clay episode was also an example of the independence that marked the Doctor's style. At his best he was ready to adjust if he felt he had come upon a new element of God's truth. But seldom would he yield to merely human pressure.

Clay carried Hartford by a margin of nearly 3 to 2, but, of course, lost the election to James K. Polk, a defeat over which strong men wept.[32] The harassed Hartford pastor, however, may have been a prophet without honor in his own country. Although a minor factor in the election, his sermon allegedly had its effect. In New York State, where the Free Soil vote ultimately sealed Clay's fate, Bushnell's published discourse circulated widely as a campaign document. At least one onlooker estimated it had cost Clay "tens of thousands of votes."[33]

During these demanding years Bushnell's powers and reputation were on the rise. But so was an ominous personal problem. More and more he knew himself to be stalked by an enemy he could neither identify nor shake loose. Recognizable now as having been tuberculosis, one of the killer diseases of the period, it intermittently afflicted him with hacking coughs, low fevers, and sieges of what seemed to be flu or common colds, voice problems, and onsets of depression.[34]

As early as 1835, Bushnell began to have throat trouble, and by 1839 his condition was serious enough to justify a month at a spa at Saratoga Springs, New York. Treatment there may have provided some temporary relief, but after his "Revelation" address at Andover he admitted to his wife that "this disease hangs about me, and I am afraid is getting a deeper hold of me." Five years later he acknowledged that he composed his "Politics Under the Law of God" under the pressure of great bodily prostration."[35]

He was able to fend off the worst until the winter of 1844–45, when he fell seriously ill. Thomas Robbins took his pulpit one Sunday in January and afterward called on Bushnell, whom he found "quite unwell." When the Doctor failed to recover by spring, he took further leave from the church and traveled to North Carolina.[36] This trip south brought some improvement, but once home again, he suffered new setbacks. By then all concerned could see that a more radical solution must be found.

As many substantial churches did in such a situation, the North Church urged him to take a year abroad, his expenses paid and his salary continued. "My people say go to Europe," he told Leonard Bacon in New Haven. Since Bacon, too, had been laid up from overwork, Bushnell tried to persuade him to come along. The same age as

Bushnell, Bacon was well launched on his outstanding ministerial career while Bushnell was still in college. The Doctor soon caught up, however, and they became fast friends, Bacon often playing church statesman to Bushnell's theologian. "Be as sick as you can," Bushnell coaxed him, "and let your disorder have an eastward look."[37]

He was so eager to have Bacon accompany him that he even risked putting direct pressure on some of his Center Church parishioners to send him, arguing that Bacon's presence was essential to the success of a coming international meeting of the Evangelical Alliance in London that August. This embryonic anti-Papal (and partially anti-Anglican) confederation had significant American roots, and Bushnell considered it of critical importance.[38]

As it turned out, however, Bacon decided he could not go and left an ailing Bushnell to pursue travel plans on his own. While Mary braced herself for the long separation, with three young children to care for, Horace booked passage to England from New York. The *Courant* announced that he was set for his voyage, "worn down with arduous labors and duties of his station," and he made a few rounds himself to say personal farewells. Then on 1 July 1845, he boarded the fashionable 860—ton packet *Victoria,* and sailed out that evening among the tall ships of New York harbor, bound for the high seas, for England and the Continent, and hopefully for renewed health.[39]

CHAPTER 7

Europe

EVEN AS A SICK MAN, Bushnell took to the sea with zest. After his years among the hills and small lakes of New England, a far horizon that went full circle with an unbroken sky like "a great bowl" overhead was new and exhilarating.[1]

It was not long before seascapes stirred the preacher in him. Two Sundays out, he gave his fellow passengers a discourse, written in the cramped quarters of his cabin, on "The Moral Uses of the Sea." Anticipating something of Winston Churchill's metaphor of the Thames as "liquid history," he saw the ocean as "liquid acres of the deep," not only a key symbol of the depth and power of the Creator, but productive of challenge to human courage and of a civilizing commerce among the nations of the earth.[2]

With all his physical handicaps on land, he had one valuable strength afloat. He was almost immune to seasickness. As a consequence he was free to wonder at the magnificence of wind and wave and to make the most of shipboard life. Bushnell found *Victoria*'s master, Captain Morgan, highly congenial, and he felt surrounded by "a very pleasant company of passengers." But all this was not enough to offset loneliness. As the voyage wore on, he took to dangling his legs boyishly from the stern of the ship, gazing toward home and feeling "alone, alone."[3]

An unusual maritime encounter occurred shortly before England came into view. Bushnell was napping in his berth when shouts called him on deck to see an imposing armada of naval vessels flying the Union Jack. It bore down with "mountains of canvas," eight of the largest dreadnoughts in the British fleet, with two tenders, collectively mounting nearly 800 guns. Four days before at Portsmouth, Queen Victoria, Prince Albert, and the entire Board of Admiralty had dispatched this experimental squadron on secret maneuvers with full pomp and circumstance.

As *Victoria* sailed through the line of *Vanguard, Trafalgar, Rodney, Queen,* and others, an awe-struck Bushnell was not close enough to spot squadron commander Rear Admiral Hyde Parker, who had served against Boston in the War of 1812, on the quarter-deck of his flagship *St. Vincent.* Nor was he close enough to see three hapless crewmen on *Superb,* who that morning had suffered a brutal thirty-six lashes each for drunkenness. What did come clear was the "volume of thunder and power" represented in this sudden spectacle, the kind of naval muscle that had helped make Britain undisputed mistress of the seven seas. Even Captain Morgan watched in wonder; he thought it the finest sight he had seen in 121 crossings of the Atlantic.[4]

Twenty days out of Sandy Hook, the craggy cliffs of Lizard Point and Cornwall loomed up, and at Falmouth Bushnell went ashore. He lost no time getting started on his tour. The next day, 22 July, he rode the Royal Mail coach 100 miles to Exeter, getting initial impressions of English landscapes and local people. The peasant children (he often noticed the condition of children) "looked healthy and happy," and the womenfolk "fairly clean." But his orderly Connecticut farm background made him look askance at thatched-roof "hovels" with rude clay walls and "pigs at the door."[5]

From Exeter he made his way to London and then up through the midlands to Liverpool and Scotland, returning to London via Newcastle and York. En route he heard his first English sermon from a London preacher who denounced American slavery. Bushnell thought the discourse a "capitally good one," so effective that he hesitated to think of preaching in England himself. He found that American tourists still were something of a novelty. English reactions to the United States ranged from critical to uninformed (as yet "no railroads in America") to enthusiastic—citizens were both knowledgeable and eager to see the new land for themselves. One irrepressible coachman near Birmingham startled him by displaying enough familiarity with American customs "to herald me into town by playing Yankeedoodle on his bugle."[6]

London at first left him feeling lost and small as "a speck." With a population of over two million, Greater London in 1845 was six times the size of New York, and he thought it "bewildering." He visited the city's famous landmarks, not all of which suited his fancy. St. Paul's Cathedral seemed "too much cut up" with architectural detail, and its cavernous interior cold—"it wants a soul." He had entree to a few meetings of church judicatories, including a session of the London Missionary Society while its board listened to an account of work in Tahiti. But he was left to sit there uncomfortably, feeling ignored, and with a deflated sense that American churches were of little consequence in the eyes of the Society.[7]

Engagements with a few good friends eased the burden of strangeness. He spent a day roaming the city with Captain Morgan of *Victoria,* looking in at prominent places of business such as Lloyds, Baring Brothers, and the Exchange. At the National Gallery he acquainted himself with the works of Hogarth, Sir Joshua Reynolds, and Raphael. Later he developed other satisfying contacts, but by August he realized the summer was passing and he wanted to see Switzerland before bad weather set in. On 20 August he set out, apprehensive that he soon would be in countries where he was not only an alien but was unable to speak a word of the language. For all his anticipation of seeing the Alps, he "never felt more solitary."[8]

Providentially he ran across a New Yorker on the Channel steamer who spoke French and who also was bound for Switzerland. They struck it off well from the start and agreed to go on together. Politically the Continent was experiencing a lull before the outbreak of the major 1848 revolutions in France, Prussia, Italy, Austria, and elsewhere. New to Europe and linguistically limited, Bushnell was in no position to assess the trend of events. But as he made his way across Belgium and up the Rhine to Basel, he was historically awake. At Waterloo he walked the battlefields, apparently well posted on the disposition and movements of forces on both sides. In many respects he admired Napoleon extravagantly, and as he recollected this Armageddon—which happened while he was still baling hay in New

Preston—he asked himself with feeling, "What spot [is there] in the globe to match this?"[9]

On the Rhine the steamer passed Rudesheim, where he noted the palace of Metternich, then in the waning years of his repressive control of European politics. The sight seemed "nothing remarkable." At Frankfort Goethe came to mind, and at Worms he pictured Luther, projecting himself back to the 16th century and the struggles Luther faced. In Zurich it was Zwingli, and by Lake Lucerne the legendary William Tell, shooting the apple from the head of his son to mollify the tyrant Gessler.[10]

Swiss weather was kind to him, opening resplendent vistas of mountains and lakes. "I shall never forget this day," he wrote in a typical journal entry, after gazing on the most dramatic scenery he had ever seen. From there he rode over the Simplon Pass into Italy, thence north to France; by February he was back in London. In Florence he mingled with the colony of American artists; sculptor Chauncey Ives, also from Connecticut, chiseled a marble bust of him, now in the Wadsworth Atheneum in Hartford.[11] In Paris he heard a foreign policy debate between Premier Francois P. G. Guizot and his chief political rival, Louis Thiers. He dearly wished he could have understood the speakers, which without a command of French he could not. Even if he had, however, he would not have learned what surely would have astonished him mightily, that only six years later both he and the lean, animated Guizot would receive honorary degrees at Harvard University's 1852 commencement.[12]

For the most part Bushnell's *Wanderjahr* took him where other travelers routinely went. All the same, his journey had marks of its own. The experience was not all joy. He had come to Europe to regain his health, but there were times when fitness must have seemed as elusive as at home. One morning in Heidelberg he awoke to discover his eyes were so watery he could not see, added to which he was coughing up discharge from his lungs which made him suspect for the first time that he might be a terminal consumptive. Soon after he reached Florence he came down with a strain of Roman fever. Chills stiffened his muscles so badly he scarcely managed to reach his bed. Still sick, he had to move to other lodgings, where he was so wretched he prayerfully noted in his diary, "God grant that I may not see many such nights in the flesh."[13]

Except for these low moments, however, he continued to relish physical challenge. Always a climber, Switzerland gave him unprecedented chances to tramp and clamber. Not yet in the best of condition for an ascent, he nonetheless scaled the 6,000–foot Rigi-Kulm, finding himself "dreadfully sore" afterward. But he soon hardened up. Less than a week later, he and two companions negotiated Furka Pass (elevation 8,000 feet) "through snows up to our middle," only regretting there was not time to go up 2,000 or 3,000 feet higher. Instead they descended to the Rhone glacier and then trudged back up Grimsel Pass by a desolate trail, spending the night in a remote hospice. The next day they walked twenty-five miles back to the little town of Meiringen.

With some difficulty Bushnell had persuaded his friends to take along a horse to help with baggage and any emergency. They finally agreed on the ground that the Doctor, as an older man, might want a lift before the expedition was over. It is not clear whether Bushnell ever rode it, but it gave him secret satisfaction to report that before they reached their destination, "my two friends began to give out, and at last took their turns on the horse that was to carry me!"[14]

Adventure was in his blood, and for Bushnell the church involved adventure. As he toured country after country, it was a rare day when he was not observing some church building or visiting a congregation. Some of these were close in tradition and liturgy to his New England heritage; more of them were far removed. From a little Free Church in Scotland, attended by shepherds, to massive Anglican and Roman Catholic cathedrals; from modest gatherings of Swiss Protestants, to St. Peter's in Rome and St. Peter's in Geneva ("Calvin! Where art thou?" he exclaimed as he stood in its stony emptiness)— he surveyed them all with a practiced Puritan eye.

What he saw sometimes disturbed, or even angered, him. He was jarred to see white-robed English choirboys in Bristol cathedral joking their way through the Lord's Prayer from behind the chancel screen. In various places, too, he reacted sharply against the apparent insensitivity of Roman priests, lording it over their docile people. In

Antwerp he was sickened to notice confessions of trusting Catholic folk being heard by "a red-faced, sensual son of Eli, in his dirty habiliments." Likewise, in Fribourg it offended him to observe unappealing Swiss Jesuits, "who swarmed the streets like the lice of Egypt." Confronted by such scenes he burst out in dismay, "Merciful Heaven, what a Christianity is this! You need to see it and smell it before you can know it."[15]

Neither these adverse impressions nor his Protestant bias, however, kept him from appreciating evidences of genuine faith, even in forms alien to his own. This was particularly true of continental Catholicism. Once in Zurich he happened on a procession going from Mass to a churchyard to perform tender offices beside a recent grave. He learned it was part of a year-long series of attentions to a departed believer and was moved by it. "Can it be less than a merit of the Catholic religion," he asked himself, "with all the attendant superstitions of invocation, purgatory, etc., that it keeps up so close and intimate a relation between the living and the dead?" He felt so frozen out by the coldness and poor preaching in the English churches he visited in Europe, that he whimsically announced to his family, "I have now become a Catholic." The worship of one Jesuit church in Rome so impressed him that he wished he could equal it with his own congregation.[16]

Such appreciation notwithstanding, he remained at odds with the dictatorial ways of Rome and felt called upon to work against it where he could. Nearly everywhere he went he privately pressed the cause of the Evangelical Alliance. Its original aim had been to spread Reformation freedoms in Italy, but Bushnell wanted to expand it into a pan-Protestant league "to floor the Papacy."[17] The London meeting, for all its warmth of fellowship, fell apart over creeds, the American slavery issue, English establishment, and lack of agreement on a practical object. But Bushnell still was hopeful for some ecumenical effort. Meantime, Pope Gregory XVI gave the Alliance a certain unintended visibility by citing it in an encyclical and ordering "most lively vigilance" against "its plots and designs."[18]

While Bushnell was abroad, the papacy was widely viewed as weak and burdensome, and despite the repressive prowling of papal agents, anti-Catholic feeling was on the rise.[19] It was on the increase also in the United States, not because the Roman Church was weak, but because in a hitherto Protestant nation Catholicism was becoming strong and threatening. Beginning in the 1820s, anti-Roman riots and burnings had broken out in major American cities, and as immigrant Irish and German Catholics began pouring across the Appalachians it was easy to spread the insidious myth that they were all actors in a devilish Vatican scheme to take over the new West. In 1843 Bushnell wrote Leonard Bacon that he thought the papacy stronger in Cincinnati than at Rome.[20]

If that assessment expressed some alarm at Catholic growth at home, it also reflected the Doctor's confidence that in Italy the papacy was vulnerable and could be challenged. While he was on Italian soil he merely observed conditions under Vatican rule, keeping his contrary opinions to himself. But once he reached London again in the spring of 1846, he could no longer be silent. On his own responsibility he took pen in hand and wrote His Holiness an open letter. It was a communication from an obscure but aggressive Protestant minister approaching the height of his powers to an arch-conservative pontiff who was old and tired and at eighty would soon be dead of a painful cancer. Both in the Sistine Chapel and in the nave of St. Peter's, Bushnell had seen him at close range during the 1845 Christmas masses and noted how drowsy and frail he looked.[21]

In the opening of his letter, Bushnell paid his respects to the aging bishop, "not wishing to trouble an old man's end" and hoping the pope would not find him an "ungenerous adversary." As the long "Letter" (over twenty printed pages) unfolded, he did indeed write as an unapologetic adversary, drawing on the experience of his travels and pointing to grievous civil and spiritual abuses in the papal states. These, as he saw it, were the fruits of a mistaken ecclesiastical absolutism. But his main purpose was larger than this. He wanted His Holiness to let his church engage in an "open trial of truth,"lead where it might. Ignoring for the moment the vast difference in their respective stations, Bushnell appealed to Gregory, as though from one apostle of Christ to another, "to withdraw your bayonets, close up the grim doors of your prisons, and bare your bosoms to truth." If in this engagement "Protestantism is dissolved by Romanism, and this again by Protestantism, and so on, let it happen." Truth can be trusted, and it will liberate, he asserted, "whatever it turns out to be." "Emancipate the truth of God, and it will be wonderful if truth does not emancipate us." Moreover, Bushnell claimed, in the process a new ecumenism would occur: "We shall melt together into the love of a conscious brotherhood."

At its best the "Letter" was a further application of his theory of comprehensiveness, the conviction that no one creed owns all truth, and that many views, operating in good faith on each other, will at last yield more Christian light than any single tradition by itself. Appropriately, he closed his missive, "Yours in the truth."

It was a characteristically bold stroke, and although the author was little known, the "Letter" attracted attention. The Vatican placed it on its Index as a seditious document; it circulated in Italy as *Littera al Romano Pontifice, di Orazio Bushnell;*[22] and "Orazio" reported to Mary that he was hearing favorable reactions in London. At home the text appeared in Hartford, soon after being noted in New York, where the Protestant *Evangelist* praised its plea for religious liberty as "an appeal to the best feelings of all Christendom." The Hartford *Courant* made it available for two cents in its biweekly *Supplement.* Meanwhile, Catholic opinion at home was predictably hostile. In Boston, where Romanists already made up over a quarter of the city's population, the *Pilot* lashed out scathingly at Bushnell. It denounced him as a near-infidel and deprecated his work as "a trashy and inflammatory composition, intended for the edification of a red hot mob."[23]

His final three months abroad were spent in London. It was the proud capital of Prime Minister Robert Peel, doing his best to deal with Corn Law repeal, problems in Ireland, and Sikh wars in India. It was the London that idolized the old "Iron Duke" of Wellington, the London of the grim workhouses of Charles Dickens's *Oliver Twist;* and the London of a young Queen Victoria and her Albert and their brood of royal children. One day Horace set out to "waylay" the queen as she passed "in a chariot of gold and two cream-colored horses." He pressed close enough to see that she was "really a very pretty woman, looks better than her portraits."[24]

Never very comfortable with conventional amusements, Bushnell in the outer circles of London society was something of a Puritan in Babylon. On two successive days he was a special guest at dinners of ministers and other intellectuals. At one where he was the only one not drinking he created an awkward moment by protesting the amount of wine being served. One evening at a party he admired "some beautiful waltzing." But when at another soirée he watched a polka for the first time, he walked shyly away and wrote in his diary, "Did not try it myself!" Although he had this much access to the ranks of privilege, he did not entirely ignore the seamy side of London life. On occasion he would drift down back streets among the slums and gin mills, where he was overwhelmed by the "misery and degradation" of people "dirty beyond comparison."[25]

During this return visit to the English metropolis he also ventured another public letter. Washington and London were angrily arguing over Oregon; the British were holding out for a boundary much farther south than expansionist Americans were willing to accept. While "Oregon fever" and extravagantly hawkish cries of "54–40 or fight!" were in the air, Bushnell wrote the London *Universe,* citing the importance of Anglo-American solidarity and urging a peaceful settlement of the issue. His letter speedily crossed the sea and was read over Hartford breakfast tables.[26]

Secular issues caught his attention, but even in London Bushnell was at heart a minister. He ached for a chance to preach. English pastors, he complained in his journal, do not realize "what it is to be a minister recognized for so long a time in no ministerial way."[27] After a painful two months' wait, opportunity finally knocked when he met Caleb Morris, minister of the Congregational Fetter Lane Chapel. Unmarried, brilliant, and neurotic, he was as emotionally unstable as he was homiletically talented. When he felt up to preaching, few, if any, in London could surpass him. But if he were depressed, a Sunday morning might well find him hurrying distraught through the city streets desperately looking for a last-minute substitute for his pulpit.[28] On one such occasion he felt forced to appeal to Bushnell, despite an apparent hesitation as to whether the Doctor was up to the assignment.

As Bushnell began to deliver his sermon on "Unconscious Influence," hastily retrieved from his Hartford "barrel," Bushnell was not so sure either. In that unaccustomed setting, in a congregation of British strangers, his self-assurance for once deserted him. He was so afraid of failure that he left off his glasses, "because I did not wish to *see* the indifferent looks of the audience." When he sensed an unaccountable stillness among the people, he decided they must be falling asleep.[29]

He could not have been more mistaken. His listeners were captivated by the preacher's portrait of humanity as so sensitively interrelated that the influence we exert on one another on the most ordinary day, without being aware of it, is far greater than any deliberate effect we may set out to achieve. It was so, he explained, with the ministry of Christ. For Bushnell's own thought, and in its widespread impact at home and abroad, the discourse was one of his important utterances.[30] If his hearers were not comfortable expressing their feelings to Bushnell after service that morning, they said plenty to Morris later. Morris was so impressed by their enthusiastic reactions that he insisted the sermon be published and eagerly invited Bushnell back. The next time he came, parishioners felt more at ease with him and thanked him "with tears in their eyes."[31]

From then on things were different. He began to have almost as many preaching appointments as he could handle. There even was talk that he would "make a sensation" in the fashionable West End, where notables and their families would flock to hear him. His leave, however, was up too soon for that enticing possibility to materialize. By the end of April he was once more pacing the decks of *Victoria*, homeward bound from Portsmouth to New York.[32] Among those on board was young Bayard Taylor, somewhat the worse for wear after a walking tour of Europe, where he served as a correspondent for Horace Greeley's New York *Tribune* and the *Saturday Evening Post*. Taylor was grateful to the Doctor for literary advice that kept him from publishing some doggerel verse, and Bushnell later followed with interest Taylor's meteoric rise to fame as a traveler and writer.[33]

The return voyage had its rough passages. A week or so out a fierce gale blew up, and for the better part of three days and nights huge waves pounded the vessel unmercifully, driving it far off course toward the North Pole. At one point it swept past a forlorn wreck, its masts stripped bare except for a single rope, savage seas dashing over the hapless hulk and water gushing from stern windows whenever the stricken craft lifted. Somberly Bushnell wondered about the fate of the crewmen. Had they escaped before the storm, or had they gone down?

As for himself, in foul weather as in fair, he found the sea invigorating. "I felt scarcely willing to leave the deck night or day, whether in the rain, or the sun, or the moonlight," he wrote euphorically, claiming that he "never enjoyed any scene more in my life." When the tempest eventually ended, as quickly "as if cut off with an axe," he was left to ponder cosmic thoughts. What was the mere "straw" of a human being up against such a raging, titanic ocean? He answered as philosophically minded seafarers so often have: human hands devise the ships that defy the dread elements and make survival possible.[34]

As he drew near the East Coast such reflections were mingled with impatience to be home. It had been a long absence, and he needed now to be back with his family and back to his work. In time, hundreds, if not thousands, of copies of his books, as yet unwritten, would be published across the Atlantic and gain a considerable foreign readership. But he himself would never visit Europe again. His tasks were to be on American soil. When his ship docked in lower Manhattan on 2 June, he not only completed a perilous leg of his travels in safety. He was returning not healed, but improved in health, to the major scenes of his career.[35]

PART 2
The Crowded Middle Years

CHAPTER 8

Champion of Children

HOMECOMING WAS HAPPY, but not all happy. Telegraphy was still in its infancy, and no immediate news of *Victoria*'s arrival reached Hartford. As a result Bushnell arrived in town unannounced. For days his family had been watching expectantly, but when his wiry figure finally made its way along Winthrop Street on a bright June day, Mary and children were out for a walk. On their return, there he suddenly was, sitting alone in the house.[1]

For all the rejoicing, his being there so abruptly was almost too much surprise. He had been away the better part of a year, and his young children could not escape the impression he was a semi-stranger. Even Mary's relief at having her husband back was followed by a difficult adjustment. Prone to psychosomatic breakdowns, she was immobilized for weeks during the autumn, requiring special medical care in New Haven and New York.[2]

The North Church gave Bushnell a royal welcome, and it was not long before he was immersed in a schedule that as usual meant overload. He began a series of sermons, later the core of his *Moral Uses of Dark Things*, addressing the age-old problem of evil. Why does a supposedly good God permit such "dark things" as disease, pain, bad government, the venom of the snake, or acute hunger? The mere mention of these unwelcome realities was a challenge to Transcendentalists, Unitarians, and other romantic idealists who too easily found God in nature. "In the teeth of those who would prove the beauty of God from the harmonious beauty of the world," as Conrad Cherry has put it, "Bushnell hurls the dark things of nature and history." The Doctor exercised his positive theological imagination and one by one found believable "uses" for these apparent evils.[3]

In great haste he put together a very different address to the Hartford Agricultural Society, "Agriculture at the East," pointing out the potential of continuing to farm in the New England states as opposed to moving to the West. He did not wholly differ with Horace Greeley's "Go West, young man, go West!" but he was concerned over the heavy losses of the northeast's farm population and thought it not entirely warranted.[4] He also shuttled back and forth to Boston to speak for the Christian Alliance, which was still much on his mind. Of all that he accomplished during the year after his return, however, nothing came close in importance to the publication of his *Discourses on Christian Nurture* early in 1847. It was his first and smallest book, so wafer-thin there was scarcely room on the spine for a title. Yet it turned out to be the kernel of an American classic.[5]

The little volume had to do with the education, or "nurture," of children, spiritually and in general, a topic addressed by an array of authors during the mid-nineteenth century. Patterns of childrearing in this country had varied widely, and some were more severe than others.[6] In New England, among Calvinist evangelicals, methods could be, and often were, rigorously authoritarian. In what passed for public schools, physical surroundings were usually wretched, and teachers often abused their charges, sometimes cruelly. Even in allegedly caring homes children were dominated.

In religion, the childhood experiences of figures such as Horace Mann, Elizabeth Cady Stanton, and many of the young Beechers, read now like emotional horror stories. Jared B. Flagg, portrait painter, Episcopal priest, and a good friend of Bushnell during his years in Hartford, recalled the well-meant but terrifying teaching of his devout mother. When he was six, she took him aside and solemnly told him that the Creator not only had made this world but also had made "a great lake of fire, where the flames were constantly blazing, and the coals red hot; and into that lake he put little boys who were bad, boys who told lies and disobeyed their parents; and . . . he kept them there to suffer and burn forever and ever."[7]

Behind such dire threats lay faith in an inscrutable, sovereign God, whose justice would not tolerate disobedience. Arbitrarily he chose whom he pleased for his elect, and damned the rest. Even baptized children were looked upon as unelected rebels against this supreme deity, who might or might not give them a saving experience of Christ in their teens or early twenties. Lyman Beecher had no qualms about telling his nine-year-old son, Henry Ward, "Henry, do you know that every breath you breathe *is sin?* Well, it is,—every breath."[8]

Elements of this Calvinistic rigor had not been entirely absent from Bushnell's own childhood. But fortunately they were so tempered by the Methodist-Episcopal origins of his parents that his religious memories consisted "not of fear, nor in a sense of wrong, but in a sense of the divine beauty and majesty."[9] Undoubtedly these recollections were a leavening influence when he contemplated the spiritual situation of his parish children. More directly, however, Bushnell was driven to rethink religious education as a result of the difficulties he experienced over the doctrine of infant baptism at his ordination examination. In the judgment of his elders, his convictions on this sacrament had not been sufficiently "positive."[10]

For the first two years of his ministry, Bushnell pondered his near-rejection over that disputed point of orthodox dogma. Slowly he realized what had happened. He had been uncertain over infant baptism because he had been mistaken about Christian education. In the spiritual economy of Christians, baptism was not meant to stand alone. It needed the fulfillment of ongoing Christian nurture. If it was losing its appeal, it was for lack of attention to that all-important sequel.[11]

Along with the clergy of other denominations, Congregational ministers generally considered infant baptism desireable, even though they could not always agree on its meaning. When a sharp decline in the practice set in, as it did in the 1840s and 1850s, they deplored it.[12] But infant baptism was not what concerned them most. Their chief aim was to bring about saving conversions, whether of young people or adults. So solid an orthodox teacher as Leonard Woods at Andover Seminary cautioned pastors, and presumably his students, "not to magnify the subject [of baptism] beyond its real importance. After all," he argued, "it is an outward rite, and does not belong to the essential articles of the Christian religion." The real work of the Gospel was "the conversion and salvation of sinners."[13]

The conversions Woods had in mind, changes from a state of nature to a state of Christian grace, still were regarded as highly individual transactions between the suppliant, of whatever age, and God. With or without baptism, no influence of home or church was believed to make much difference as to whether or not the requisite "new heart" was granted the hopeful soul. Hence there was little purpose in anything like Christian education, and little interest in it. In the eyes of many, infant baptism, too, became incidental.

Bushnell's new understanding led him to a radical reappraisal of this whole matter. He would not disparage all revival conversions.[14] The fact was that he himself had been decisively affected by a revival at Yale. Later, moreover, when he came to discuss religion on the American frontier, he credited revivals there, crude as they often were, with breaking up an "age of frost" and giving a promising "new spring" to Western character.[15] But the extremism of most New England revivals he knew of had left him with serious reservations.

Likewise, when it came to baptism, he admitted that baptism was "in some sense and degree" a vehicle of grace.[16] But he no longer saw it as having the traditional sacramental power to transform infant souls and insure their the eternal life. To a considerable degree he sympathized with parents who doubted it could be of much benefit in that way. What, then, was the use of a ceremony that seemed to lead nowhere? It still left the child a rebellious sinner, barely recognized by the church. Children and adolescents still had to struggle through lonely spiritual lives, anxiously awaiting the explosive conversion moment that would make them real Christians.

As he weighed his discontent with this view, Bushnell came to find new meaning in baptism not "in what it operates" as regards the child. He discovered it in "what it signifies" to the parents, and also to the church. What it signified was the public sealing of the child into the Christian faith and character of the home and into the support of the congregation. In those basic organic relationships the child was to be intentionally nurtured from his or her youngest years until the emerging new life was able "to take the helm" of his or her own spirit.

To Bushnell, Christian baptism then became not so much immediate in its effect as "presumptive." It pointed to the future, with full confidence that God by his grace would assist parents in the rearing of their children, until they could make their own Christian decisions. Seen in this light, it became for Bushnell "the most beautiful and appropriate of all the ordinances of God."[17]

But it was only so when Christian nurture was understood to be its faithful handmaid, the means of achieving all that baptism anticipated. No one "ever objected to infant baptism," Bushnell concluded, "who had not at the bottom of his objections, false views of Christian education."[18] Out of this persuasion came the statement that became the hallmark of everything the Doctor wrote or said on the subject. In the Gospel according to Bushnell,

> the child is to grow up a Christian. In other words, the aim, effort, and expectation should be, not, as is commonly assumed, that the child is to grow up in sin, to be converted after he [or she] comes to a mature age; but that he [or she] is to open on the world as one that is spiritually renewed, not remembering the time when he [or she] went through a technical [revival conversion] experience, but seeming rather to have loved what is good from . . . earliest years.[19]

Beginning with two discourses in March 1835,[20] Bushnell spent a decade shaping, reshaping, and fostering this conviction in sermons and published articles. Occasionally a parishioner would take him to task for his opinions. As earnest as he was conservative, Deacon Terry respectfully wrote his pastor in 1839 that "his spirit sank within him" at the sound of such preachments.[21] For the most part, however, Bushnell's plainly unorthodox claims appeared to cause scarcely a ripple.

Then in the fall of 1844 he published an article in the *New Englander,* "The Kingdom of Heaven As A Grain of Mustard Seed." In it he expanded his convictions on the importance of steady, spiritual growth, as opposed to the lightning "conquest" of revival conversions.[22] Certain paragraphs in the article raised eyebrows in the Hartford Central Association of Ministers, and when Bushnell returned from Europe in 1846, he was asked to share his insights with the Association in greater detail.[23]

In preparation for this he refurbished his 1835 discourses using the same Ephesians 6:4 text he had used then: "Bring them up in the nurture and admonition of the Lord" (KJV). He developed his thesis still further, stressing especially that "Christian nurture" could only happen in a "Christian atmosphere," within supportive social ties, especially those of the family. He rebutted those of his parishioners who said of their children, "Their character . . . is their own, let them believe for themselves and be baptized when they will." Such "dry individualism," as he put it later, Bushnell could not abide.[24] The child's individual nature was to be carefully respected. Nonetheless, spiritual growth needed constant support. From the moment of birth, he argued, a child should be "bathed" in the atmosphere of a believing family, "the church of childhood," as he described it in Edwardsian idiom, where faith radiates out from parental commitment, and teaches trustful feeling long before intellectual doctrine starts to have meaning.[25]

These new discourses he delivered in the North Church and then read in abbreviated form to his colleagues. When his reverend brethren had heard their friend out at the church in Farmington on a steamy August day, there appeared to be no serious disagreement with him. Before the meeting casually turned to other business, Noah Porter, the long-respected minister of the Farmington Church, made a fateful motion. He moved that the discourses be published. His motion was adopted unanimously. Subsequently, at the urging of Bushnell's Yale classmate, The Reverend Joseph H. Towne, a board member of the Massachusetts Sabbath School Society in Boston, the Doctor sent the manuscript to the Society (in the first instance anonymously) for its consideration. Originally Bushnell had formed other plans for handling publication and had reservations as to whether the Society would be comfortable with the project. After many editorial changes and various delays, however, *Discourses on Christian Nur-*

ture appeared with the Society's endorsement early in 1847.[26] Proudly the author took a copy and inscribed it to his eldest daughter: "Louisa Bushnell from her Father. The first copy of his first book."[27]

For a while after publication all remained calm. Moderates in the churches assumed that since the publication bore the *imprimatur* of the Sabbath School Society it was acceptable teaching. Scattered favorable reviews appeared as far afield as Maine, Vermont, and Pennsylvania.[28] Presbyterian Charles Hodge, of conservative Princeton Seminary, responded in the *Biblical Repository and Princeton Review,* then probably the strongest theological journal in the country. While not entirely approving the book, he welcomed Bushnell's new emphasis on Christian education and applauded his organic view of society.[29]

The notice Bushnell liked best came from the pen of John W. Nevin, a leading voice of the German Reformed Church centered in Mercersburg, Pennsylvania.[30] Referring to Bushnell in the German Reformed periodical, *The Weekly Messenger,* as "one of the most distinguished preachers of New England," he faulted him for understating human depravity and making too little of sacraments and grace. But he was delighted with other aspects of the book, and Bushnell found him so thoughtful and discriminating that he wished he had opportunity to know him better.[31] Given the overall tone of such responses, there seemed no reason to doubt that the book would make its way peaceably.

But as the Doctor later remarked ominously, "the day was coming."[32] No sooner had the more conservative elements in Congregational orthodoxy awakened to the contents of the tiny tome than they reacted as though Bushnell were a new Copernicus upsetting the Ptolemaic universe.

Given their premises, they had good cause. To be sure, Bushnell thought of himself as more "orthodox" than his critics. He felt there was altogether convincing evidence from the church fathers, as well as in New England covenant theory prior to the Great Awakening, that children were meant to grow up inside, not outside, the community of faith. Like these forebears, he left room in his views for occasional revivals, for the individual, and for operative grace.[33]

But his basic assumptions were nothing that standard New England theology could allow. In the orthodox universe the religious revival still was critical. Bushnell's theory of steady, daily Christian nurture clearly diminished its importance. Among the orthodox, datable spiritual rebirth was a highly individualistic matter. Bushnell made it largely the fruit of organic, social development. As for infant baptism, conservative minds were unprepared for the Hartford minister's insistence on the importance of the rite and for his unusual interpretation of its meaning. Such teachings filled the high-minded but unbending guardians of the theological establishment with grave forebodings. In an open "Letter to Dr. Bushnell" Bennet Tyler paternally warned him, "You have been led...into very dangerous errors."[34]

This communication, dated 7 June 1847, was the opening gun in a vigorous campaign to discredit Bushnell's heterodoxy. As president of the East Windsor Theological Institute of Connecticut, Tyler long since had proved himself a conscientious and able man. His opinions were heard with respect. Both in Hanover and East Windsor he had been a pastoral president who cared about his students. Besides all this, he was an affectionate father to twelve children, one of whom, Eliza, preceded Harriet Beecher as Calvin Stowe's first wife.

But Tyler was also an unyielding and sometimes contentious theological conservative. While still young in the ministry he had bound himself with Shakespearian "hoops of steel" to rigid New Light Calvinism as it had developed since Edwards. At his retirement from his seminary in 1857, he told alumni with unconcealed satisfaction that during fifty years in the ministry his opinions had undergone "no change."[35]

Such a man could not take Bushnell lightly. In his twenty-two-page "Letter," he attacked his younger colleague for falsifying the true approach to Christian pedagogy and jeopardizing the immortal souls of parents as well as children. Given his influential status, Tyler's broadside set off an alarm for many others in the churches. Ministers who barely had noticed the volume began reading it and stirring each other up against it. Joel Hawes, Bushnell's Main Street neighbor at Center Church, busily marked up his copy, telling Tyler he had found "more places in it that were wrong than there were pages in the book." At least one interested customer who attempted to buy *Discourses* at the Massachusetts Sabbath School Society's depository was all but bodily ejected for his insolence. The New York *Evangelist* was swamped with negative letters.[36]

One of the most cutting press barbs came from the *Christian Observatory* in Boston. The right-wing monthly came close to insult in saying the Hartford author liked to indulge "a vicious thirst for originality and "can scarce drink from a chalice without seeking to kiss the brim on some part which human lips had [*sic*] never touched before."[37]

Money, too, began to talk. Lyman H. Atwater, minister of the affluent Congregational Church in Fairfield, Connecticut, reported with anxious concern that Lockwood DeForest, a wealthy New Yorker, was witholding his customary support for Christian publications for fear his donations would be used for literature of the Bushnell type. By September the Hartford *Religious Herald* was saying that debate over the *Discourses* had "gone over the whole country . . . and has penetrated every sect."[38]

Inevitably this hue and cry reached the ears of the Massachusetts Society's publishing committee. With a notable lack of spine, considering the care it had taken in screening the manuscript in the first place, its members "turned pale and recanted," to quote Bushnell's description. A mere three weeks after the appearance of Tyler's letter, the Society suspended all distribution to libraries and other institutions, limiting sales to individual buyers.[39]

The Doctor picked up the news on the streets of Hartford. Stung, but still hopeful that he could reassure the Bostonians, he went public with a spirited, and occasionally caustic, "Argument" defending his position with historical precedents and prophetic vision.[40] "Brethren, whether you will believe it or not," he confidently declared, "a new day has come. If we will, we can make it a better day, but it demands a furniture of thought and feeling such as we must stretch ourselves in a degree to realize." With a combination of conviction and openness that increasingly marked his approach, he added, "We must be firm for the truth, and, for that very reason, ready to detect our own errors." Although at one point he disingenuously claimed he did not care whether the Society resumed publication or not, his real intent was clear enough. He wanted the Massachusetts gentlemen to recognize the signs of the times, reconsider their hasty action, and help lead the way into the "new day" by allowing the *Discourses* to circulate freely.[41]

He could not have been altogether surprised that his plea fell on deaf ears. Shortly the Society backed away still further and ended all distribution of the disputed work. Lamely protesting that it had "no wish" to keep Bushnell from publishing the material himself if he so desired, it returned him his copyright.[42] Thereupon 1,200 unbound copies of the volume began gathering dust on the Society's shelves, and Bushnell had on his hands a commodity with interesting potential: a book banned in Boston.[43]

Quickly he decided that if the establishment would not make his work available to a puzzled public, he would. He put together the two sermons plus the "Argument" and several other related articles, and before the year was out he issued them as *Views of Christian Nurture, and of Subjects Adjacent Thereto.*[44]

Instead of easing the tension, the book added to the general furor. Tyler had replied to the *Discourses* with a single letter. In answer to Bushnell's *Views* he wrote seven.[45] As the debate escalated between conservatives and those in sympathy with the Doctor, restraints of courtesy and respect often were forgotten in "contemptuous" and "gross" violations of "generous and gentlemanly warfare." Bushnell's friend Noah Porter, Jr., a recent appointee to the Yale faculty who penned that troubled assessment, ruefully concluded that "the theological world of New England is again threatened with storm."[46]

The storm broke, causing more stir than any American theological book in a century, one modern student has suggested.[47] But unlike the far greater conflict about to overtake Bushnell, the tempest over the *Views* died down surprisingly soon, and the book survived. On his retirement from the North Church in 1859, the first task he undertook was to revise and expand it, issuing it simply as *Christian Nurture.*[48] By the time it came out in 1860, irreconcilable Bennet Tyler had been laid to rest, and the *Congregationalist* in Boston could smile at the original upheaval over the publication as having been "ridiculous."[49] This edition, with its radical supplementary proposals—such as qualified church membership for children and, under supervision, their admission to the Lord's Table—is the version we now have. Although it was half a century before the churches took it seriously,[50] it has been republished at least once a generation since it first appeared.

At heart what Bushnell had written was a manifesto, reasserting the Gospel right of children to a childhood that in many evangelical New England circles had been all but stolen away. Despite a certain wordiness, and its inevitably dated frames of reference, his text remains generally readable and relevant. Its appeal for good family communication; the sense of outrage against child abuse in the name of parental authority ("you are not to be a savage to them, but a father, and a Christian"); the stress on "the art of growth in the long run," coupled with insights into the psychology of infancy; and the need for early encouragement of a child's spirit—all this represents Bushnell's farsighted understanding of childhood as not merely preparation *for* life, but as an integral part *of* life.[51]

The book gains added credibility from his own relationships with children. Engaging closeness to his own family, and to many outside his own domestic circle, was one of the Doctor's attractive traits. "Remember me most affectionately to your husband and the children" was a closure to an 1849 letter. To another correspondent ten years later he wrote warmly, "Give . . . to the young friends of the house my best hopes of their future." In his theology, too, young lives continued to be of major interest. His 1869 address "God's Thoughts Fit Bread for Children" bespeaks as urgent a concern for them as the first version of his *Discourses* in 1835.[52]

His ability to relate to children included a sense of ease in talking directly with them about religion, something he later regretted he had not done more often during his pastorate.[53] In 1851 his daughter Mary, aged ten, joined the North Church. Some time afterward spiritual questions began to bother her mind, and she looked about for more light on the meaning of the momentous step she had taken. It was all but forbidden to interrupt her father in his study, but in her need she screwed up her courage and, with a schoolmate to support her resolve, knocked on his door. He was startled and could not help showing it. Yet he was swift to sense the situation, and laying other work aside he took time to listen "very kindly" to their inquiries. Soon he was conversing with them unhurriedly "with no thought of intellectual problems, and with little effort to instruct,... except by showing us how near God is to his children." Mary and her comrade went from the interview "extraordinarily happy" and as though in "a transformed world." "For the first time," Mary recalled, "I felt we knew what Jesus Christ meant."[54]

Bushnell family homestead, New
Preston, Connecticut. The maples
could well be trees Bushnell planted
in his youth or trees descended from
them. Courtesy of the late Dorothy
Averill, New Preston, Connecticut

Hartford in 1841, still the Connecticut River port it essentially was when Bushnell arrived in 1833. Spire of the North Church at far right. Painting by Robert Havell, 1841. Used by permission of the Connecticut Historical Society, Hartford

North Congregational Church, Hartford, built in 1824. It was Bushnell's only parish. Engraving by unknown artist, ca. 1853. Used by permission of the Connecticut Historical Society, Hartford

Amos M. Collins (1788–1858), merchant, twice Hartford's mayor, and one of Bushnell's senior deacons for most of his ministry. Reprinted from J. Hammond Trumbull, ed., *The Memorial History of Hartford County, Connecticut, 1633–1884*, 2 vols. (Boston: Edward L. Osgood, 1886), 1:660

Bushnell's Hartford home at 10 Winthrop Street. Built in 1840 and designed by Bushnell himself. The other side looked eastward across open fields to the Connecticut River. Reprinted from Mary Bushnell Cheney, *Life and Letters of Horace Bushnell* (New York: Scribner's, 1903), 514

Octagonal rotary desk at which Bushnell did most of his writing for nearly thirty years. Courtesy of David H. Cheney, Harwinton, Connecticut

Mary Apthorp Bushnell (Mrs. Horace Bushnell) in 1904 at age one hundred. She died in 1905. The only photograph of her that has come to light. Reprinted from Antoinette Cheney Crocker, *Great Oaks: Memoirs of the Cheney Family* (Concord, Mass.: Privately published, 1977), 3. Courtesy Mrs. Byard Williams, Kennett Square, Pennsylvania

The three surviving Bushnell children about the time of the Civil War. *From left to right:* Frances Louisa (1834–1899); Mary (1840–1917), later Mrs. Frank W. Cheney; and Dotha (1843–1932), later Mrs. Appleton R. Hillyer. Courtesy of the late Horace Bushnell Learned and Mrs. Learned, West Hartford, Connecticut

Leonard Bacon (1802–1881), minister of Center Congregational Church, New Haven, and another gifted Bushnell sympathizer and advisor. Engraving by L. S. Punderson after a daguerreotype by Moulthrop and Litch. Used by permission of the Connecticut Historical Society, Hartford

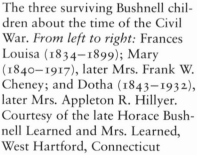

Noah Porter (1781–1866), for sixty years pastor of the Farmington Congregational Church. Bushnell's ablest supporter during the 1849–1854 doctrinal controversy. Portrait by Jared Bradley Flagg, 1847. Courtesy of Miss Porter's School, Farmington, Connecticut

Amos S. Chesebrough (1813–1897), Congregational minister in Chester, Connecticut. Author of the celebrated 1849 "Criticus Criticorum" articles defending Bushnell's theology. Courtesy of William Gay, Dayton, Ohio

Bennet Tyler (1783–1858), presi-
dent of the Connecticut Theological
Institute (now Hartford Seminary),
East Windsor, Connecticut, and an
aggressive Bushnell opponent.
Courtesy of the Hartford Seminary,
Hartford, Connecticut

Lyman H. Atwater (1813–1883),
minister of the Congregational
Church, Fairfield, Connecticut, and
a leader of the Fairfield West Association campaign to defrock Bushnell.
Courtesy of First Church (Congregational), Fairfield, Connecticut

Henry Ward Beecher (1813–1887),
famous preacher at Plymouth
Church (Congregational), Brooklyn,
New York. Bushnell's friendly rival
as a midcentury pulpit prince.
Courtesy of the Stowe-Day Foundation, Hartford, Connecticut

Cyrus A. Bartol (1813–1900), Boston Unitarian pastor, and beginning in 1847, Bushnell's closest ministerial friend. Used by permission of the Massachusetts Historical Society, Boston

Disheveled but central site Bushnell chose in 1854 for Hartford's city park. Worst areas not visible in photo. Lithograph by E. C. Kellogg from drawing by J. Ropes, ca. 1851–1854. Used by permission of the Connecticut Historical Society, Hartford

Bushnell Park today. *Left,* John Corning Fountain; *center,* Civil War Soldiers and Sailors Memorial Arch (1886). Courtesy Hunter Neal, Simsbury, Connecticut

Looking northeast from First and
Harrison streets, San Francisco approximately as Bushnell would have
seen it ca. 1856. Courtesy San Francisco Maritime Historical Park

Bushnell about 1861 as he entered
the years of his "broken industry."
Reprinted from Mary Bushnell
Cheney, *Life and Letters of Horace
Bushnell* (New York: Scribner's,
1903), 444

Main Street, Hartford, ca. 1868, looking south from the approximate location of the North Church. Used by permission of the Connecticut Historical Society, Hartford

Major Henry W. Camp (1839–1864), Bushnell parishioner and Yale scholar-athlete, a "knightly soldier" killed in action near Richmond, 13 October 1864. Reprinted from Henry C. Trumbull, *The Knightly Soldier: A Biography of Henry Ward Camp, Tenth Connecticut Volunteers* (Boston: Nichols and Noyes, and New York: Oliver S. Felt, 1865)

Lake Waramaug, New Preston, Connecticut, a favorite Bushnell fishing ground. Also location of Mount Bushnell and Mount Bushnell State Park (*right background*). Courtesy of the late Dorothy Averill, New Preston, Connecticut

Bushnell looks out from the east
wall of the Connecticut State Capitol in company with Jonathan Edwards, Noah Webster, and other
historic Connecticut leaders. Photo
by Arthur J. Kiely, Jr., West Hartford, Connecticut

CHAPTER 9

Pivotal 1848

IN WESTERN HISTORY, 1848 was so eventful as to be less a year than an epoch. It was the year that the Communist Manifesto of Karl Marx and Friedrich Engels, published late in 1847, was translated into nearly every European tongue, marking the effective birth of international communism and helping to topple thrones—at least temporarily—from Paris to Vienna. In the United States it was the year a New Jersey carpenter found gold in California, a discovery that touched off the first global gold rush and made Americans newly restless and materialistic.[1] In 1848 the Mexican War officially ended, and for the first time the United States found itself a continental nation. The vast expansion of new territory dangerously intensified the already smoldering slavery question. North and South heatedly debated whether the new lands should be slave or free, making eventual civil war all but inevitable. These and other crucial developments meant that much in the West was different once 1848 had come and gone.

For Bushnell in Hartford, 1848 was the same kind of watershed year. In the course of it he underwent an experience of spiritual enlightenment that heightened the urgency of all his preaching and writing. He poured out a wealth of theological statements from prominent platforms, considerably extending his public exposure. And beyond anything he sought, expected, or could have foreseen, he laid the groundwork for a bitter doctrinal conflict that far exceeded the hostile reaction to *Christian Nurture*. The clash of viewpoints came perilously close to costing him his professional career.

In the sense of momentous change, his year opened not so much in

January as in February. One dark morning during an unusually snowy month, he awoke and told his wife that the light he had long waited for in his inner seeking had dawned. "What have you seen?" she asked. His brief but joyful reply was simply, "The Gospel."[2]

What more he may have shared with her at that hour we cannot tell. By his own subsequent account, however, there was in that moment an important element of intellectual illumination. Much as Martin Luther had groped and agonized before he came upon his answer of justification by faith, or as Albert Schweitzer, laboring upstream on an errand of medical mercy in Africa, suddenly was given "reverence for life," a concept "unforeseen and unsought,"[3] so Bushnell had been probing for a key to unlock a truer Christianity than prevailing New England orthodoxy seemed to offer. His flash of enlightenment climaxed a period of "protracted suspense, or mental conflict" during which he had been trying strenuously to bring "into one theologic view" the complexities of the Cross. Working and waiting for what "could only be cleared by light," he received his reward at daybreak that bleak morning.[4]

With it came a powerfully moving mystical encounter. This, too, affected the rest of Bushnell's life, and he often referred to it in conversations with his family and close friends. "I was set upon by the personal discovery of Christ, and of God represented in him," he stated once in a letter. As late as 1871, when he and Mary were alone together one evening, conversation led back to the same subject. "I seemed to pass a boundary," he mused. "I had never been very legal in my Christian life, but now I passed from those partial seeings, glimpses and doubts, into a clearer knowledge of God, and into his inspirations, which I have never wholly lost. The change was into faith—a sense of the freeness of God and the ease of approach to him."[5]

Any such gift of grace is a mystery, but there were ways in which Bushnell had prepared for it. The previous five years had brought unsettling emotional setbacks. The loss of his one son, the adverse reception accorded his discourses on Christian nurture, and recurring spells of bad health—all these had moved him to reach for deeper foundations. "I swung, for a time, towards quietism," he confessed, and, more than was his wont, he took to reading pietistic literature. In particular he turned to the writings of the seventeenth-century French archbishop François Fénelon and to the life of Fénelon's quietist contemporary Madame Guyon as portrayed in a biography by Bowdoin College professor Thomas C. Upham.[6]

Across nearly two centuries, Bushnell found Jeanne Marie Bouvières de la Mothe Guyon an especially congenial spirit. Delicate of feature and socially charming, she had been born into the glitter of young Louis XIV's France in 1648. At fifteen, and much against her will, she was married to a wealthy but ailing aristocrat more than twice her age. She fitted easily into the life of a fashionable young Parisienne, and like Bushnell, had many practical abilities, including legal and financial talent. Yet increasingly she felt drawn away from her privileged connections to a career of religious seeking and serving. In time her devotion to biblically oriented faith displayed so many Protestant tendencies that the Roman Catholic king had her confined behind the twelve-foot-thick walls of the Bastille. Through this confinement and other hardships she lived out of an immediate, God-centered trust, calmly but impressively sustained by the presence of Christ and daily doing what she could to remain at God's disposal.

Quietism was not Bushnell's basic bent. But he was attuned to so much in Madame Guyon's quest that he recommended Upham's biography in a sermon. This caused a flurry of sales in Hartford and enough interest among the impressionable young misses of the city that Bushnell's conservative neighbor, Joel Hawes, felt obliged to mount his Center Church pulpit and issue a grave counterwarning against so un-Calvinistic a book.[7] As for Bushnell himself, his Gallic heroine helped him see that "there is another, fuller life that can be lived" and made him resolve to find it.[8] Then, on that February morning, his own vision came.

It had to find expression in a sermon. Without delay he prepared a discourse for the North Church on "Christ the Form of the Soul." The title came from Paul's yearning for his Christian friends in Galatia: "My little children, for whom I am again in the pain of childbirth until Christ is formed in you, I wish I were present with you now."[9] It is very possible that Bushnell also had in mind a paraphrase from Madame Guyon herself: "When Jesus Christ...is formed in the soul...it finds in him all good things communicated to it."[10]

Reminiscent of the late medieval Thomas à Kempis, Bushnell's discourse was an unflinching appeal for the "imitation of Christ," a phrase he used without acknowledgment. This, he was sure, was the key to all spiritual attainment. Not only in this sermon but later in his ministry when he repeatedly spoke of the ultimate importance of character, he had in mind more than developing a natural integrity. He meant progress in specifically Christly character, in becoming "charactered to Christ," with all that implied of faith and self-giving love. "Whether we speak now of growth, of sanctification, of complete renovation, or redemption, everything is included in this, the having Christ formed within us." He did not water down the difficulties of such discipleship, but he did lend encouragement. "The work is not yours only. God is in it," he proclaimed, and with "higher designs for you probably than you have ever conceived." That such an assertion might seem "a kind of daring" he frankly admitted. But "faith is a daring exercise."[11]

The encounter and the sharing of it were significant beginnings of a remarkable harvest of theological and literary activity. During this singular year, Bushnell delivered his "Discourse on the Atonement" at Harvard; his *Concio ad Clerum* at Yale; and his "Discourse on Dogma and Spirit" at Andover Seminary. He published his often-overlooked article "Christian Comprehensiveness" for *The New Englander* and prepared his focal "Dissertation on the Nature of Language." On a return visit to Harvard he gave his famous lecture "Work and Play." These were in addition to his regular Hartford preaching. As one perceptive critic has observed, all this was enough to fix Bushnell's own sense of vocation as a spokesperson for a new brand of theological thinking and to give him a place as "a representative American Victorian man of letters."[12]

In his series of doctrinal addresses, the discourse at Harvard came first. When he appeared there, the oldest institution of higher learning in the country had little of its modern size or prestige. It was a small college, struggling not too successfully to compete with such younger institutions as Princeton, Brown, Union, Dartmouth, and Yale. Nobody seemed to want the presidency of the place for long. Between 1846 and 1862, four "minor prophets," as they have been called, filled the office, none with much satisfaction or distinction. When the Harvard bicentennial was held in 1836, the presidents of academic communities all over New England were invited to take part. Only one bothered to accept.[13]

Harvard's problem was an only partially deserved reputation as a citadel of Unitarianism. None-too-popular president Josiah Quincy, "Old Quin'" to his students, boldly tried to insist in 1845 that the school was nonsectarian.[14] But the liberal label still stuck. Mainstream Unitarians at the time were unapologetically Christian and ardently biblical. Although they insisted that human beings were basically good, they had a doctrine of sin and revered Christ as more than a human savior, even if they stopped short of acknowledging him as God. At least for a time, some were even Trinitarians of a sort. So prominent a Unitarian as William E. Channing could refer to "Father, Son, and Holy Spirit" and add, "We all believe in these."[15]

Nonetheless, orthodox Congregationalists in Bushnell's day considered Unitarianism a virulent disease, eating away at the vitals of gospel faith. They charged it with being far too weak on sin and grace and too strong on the possibilities of human progress. Such Trinitarian gestures as Unitarians might make were regarded as vague and half-hearted. Worst of all, their concept of the work of Christ on the cross rejected the penal judgments of God exhibited there and denied that the propitiatory sacrifice of Christ paid for the sins of humankind.[16]

Unitarianism failed to gain much of a foothold in Connecticut. Even outside the state it had passed the peak of its power before Bushnell was fully settled in Hartford. As late as 1847 it was estimated that only one-eighth of the churches in Massachusetts were Unitarian, and Trinitarian Congregationalists in the Bay State were believed to outnumber Unitarians three to one.[17] The Doctor never had reason to feel threatened by the movement, nor, as is sometimes supposed, was he a significant factor in limiting its Connecticut growth. But if he disagreed with its main teachings, there still was something about its openness and magnanimity that attracted him. To the Boston Unitarian pastor James Freeman Clarke, Bushnell confessed that if he had been born sooner, when this dissenting faith was emerging, "I should have been found among its zealous adherents."[18]

As it was, he remained in his Trinitarian pulpit and dared (the only adequate term for it, and one he used himself) to fraternize freely with the dread Unitarians.[19] He was a welcome guest in the home of ultra-liberal Theodore Parker, and was on friendly terms with the Unitarian minister and editor Edmund H. Sears, now best remembered as the writer of the Christmas hymn "It Came Upon the Midnight Clear."[20] Occasionally he preached from Unitarian pulpits and found in the staunch Unitarian pastor Cyrus A. Bartol, of Boston's West Church, probably his most intimate ministerial friend.

Bushnell also frequented Harvard. In four years he gave three addresses there, and in 1852, as already indicated, he received from the university an honorary doctorate. In 1848 he was mentioned prominently for the coveted Hollis Professorship, and when Edward Everett resigned as president that year, the *New England Religious Herald* in Hartford suggested Bushnell would make a better Harvard president than such rumored nominees as Charles Sumner or Jared Sparks. He was not only a scholar and orator, but had close connections with both the orthodox and the Unitarian constituency.[21]

Gratifying as such attention was, it came at a price. The more he befriended Unitarians, the more the anger of the orthodox was kindled against him. In his effusive 1848 "Letters," Bennet Tyler could not forgive Bushnell for speaking well of Massachusetts Unitarians while chastising his Congregational colleagues.[22]

To hear Bushnell, the First Church in Cambridge on the evening of 9 July was crowded from galleries to doors.[23] His theme was the Atonement, or the work of Christ on the Cross. From apostolic days the ringing message of the New Testament has been that on Calvary's grim hill God did a profoundly sacrifical deed, uniquely restoring the loving relationship with himself that a wayward humanity had broken.

Magnificent as the claim is, however, Christians never have agreed as to how this was accomplished. Orthodox minds in Bushnell's Harvard audience would stoutly have held what was known as the objective view. It taught that on the Cross, Jesus, though wholly innocent, paid a one-time penalty for all the sins of humankind. This satisfied the absolute justice of an injured God and made it possible for him to forgive us and offer us eternal life. Such traditional doctrine was well expressed in lines of Cecil Alexander's popular hymn "There Is a Green Hill Far Away," written, as it happened, in this same year:

> There was no other good enough,
> To pay the price of sin;
> He only could unlock the gate
> Of heaven and let us in.

Consistent Calvinists regarded this view as "the very heart, soul, and life of Christianity."[24]

Schismatic Unitarians, as is well known, strongly protested. They could not conceive of a God so heartless as to look on his children as hateful sinners, or a God so unjust as to punish a sinless Christ for a guilty humanity. To Channing the whole penal scheme was "a fallacy." "Such a God," he protested, "we can not love if we would...and ought not to love if we could." To Unitarians the purpose of the Cross was not to reconcile an offended God, but to turn us back to God's grace through a moving, searching sacrifice they deeply revered without undertaking to explain.[25] This type of approach was generally known as the subjective theory.

Firmly but courteously, Bushnell announced at the outset that on this "hinge question" he intended to "speak [his] own sentiments" without fear or favor toward either side.[26] He undertook to show that each side was too narrow in its teaching and that Scripture called for a blending of both views. He did not delay long in expressing sympathy for the subjective, Unitarian persuasion. All talk of a blameless Jesus suffering at the hands of a vengeful God seeking to placate his justice filled him with "a sensation of horror." To him this was not biblical; it was simply "cool, speculative language."[27] The essential message of the New Testament was Paul's pronouncement to the early Christians in Corinth, "every word of which is power": "God was in Christ, reconciling the world to himself."[28] Here, Bushnell insisted, was not a hint of a stern Almighty exacting the pain of Golgotha to reconcile himself to the world. Quite the opposite. Here was a God of suffering love reconciling *the world* to himself. He was seeking "to re-engage the world's love and reunite the world, as free, to the Eternal Life."[29] Thus far truth lay with the subjectivists.

But not the whole truth. All high religions, Bushnell pointed out, instinctively have gone beyond subjective feelings, craving objective ritual forms to lift worshipers out of themselves and into the presence of the Holy. Thus Christian piety has pictured Christ as making, or being, "a sacrifice," as "the Lamb of God," as "bearing the sins of the world," as "offering" himself, and as achieving a new "righteousness." These "altar forms," as the Doctor was fond of calling them, God had consciously provided through the long years of Old Testament experience.[30] They were meant to prepare his people to grasp the full significance of the Cross when at last it should come. His subjectivism notwithstanding, Bushnell was convinced that over the ages of faith too many believers had been sustained by these forms for them to be cast aside.[31] That Unitarianism had done so was, to Bushnell, its great loss.

At the same time it was of utmost importance that this vocabulary not be taken literally. This in turn was the orthodox error. With its confidence in exact definitions, the New England theology, Bushnell thought, had worked these terms almost to death. They were not meant to be used in so literal, definitive a way. By their very nature they were inexact expressions, terms not of logic but of imagination, not of precision but of poetry and art. As such they helped preserve the unsearchable mystery of God and, in a way rational dogma could not do, impress on believers the unfathomable import of what he had done on Calvary.[32]

Bushnell's hope was that orthodoxy would see this and become more imaginative. Correspondingly, he longed to have Unitarianism recover these time-honored terms, in this aesthetic sense (as opposed to dogmatic), and draw once more on their true richness. For the Christian community to reunite on this subjective-objective basis, he

pleaded, would be to move out from the cold "starlight" of orthodoxy's dying dogma, as from the chill of a deprived Unitarianism,
and "to bask in the sun of righteousness and live."[33]

For all his eloquence, it is doubtful that he changed many minds.
An unfriendly *New England Puritan* in Boston acknowledged that
this sermon had been "one of the events of the times." But it only
showed that the preacher had emerged into "the glorious sunlight of
a Unitarian atonement"—hardly much of a discovery. Unitarians
found his objective "altar forms" a thinly veiled "fetch" to save face
with Congregationalists. If so, it was not enough to mollify all the
Congregationalists present. One whispered to his Unitarian pewmate
at the close of Bushnell's address, "We must turn that sermon over to
you." The Unitarian murmured in reply, "If I understand him,
though he was somewhat obscure, I do not know that we should object to it."[34]

Bushnell felt once again the sting of rejection. Disappointed, but
still in good spirits, he confided in his Unitarian friend, Bartol, "I
don't know but I am to be burnt out or smoked out of orthodoxy on
account of my heresies."[35]

Heretic or no, the Doctor had a commencement engagement the
next month at Yale. Here would be no concentration of Unitarians,
but a formidable gathering of doctrinally minded Congregational
clergy. To be invited to deliver the Connecticut *Concio ad Clerum*
was a signal honor. Given Bushnell's increasingly uncertain theological reputation, some wondered jealously how he ever came to be
asked.[36] That aside, however, his much-publicized appearance at Harvard had aroused an excited curiosity as to what this rising radical
from Hartford would say on the foundational theme assigned him:
"The Divinity of Christ."

For faith, the nature of Christ is never an idle question. Unless he
was divine, the one in whom "all the fulness of God was pleased to
dwell,"[37] he has no ultimate power to transform our lives and hopes,
which is to say, to save us. But divinity is not enough. If Jesus was not
also a genuine human being, "bone of our bone and flesh of our
flesh,"[38] we cannot make effective contact with him. Yet how could
one person have been both? And assuming his divinity, how are we

think of him in relation to God, and the promised Holy Spirit, without ending up with three Gods instead of one? This is ever the problem of the Christian Trinity. Such mysteries will always remain insoluble for finite minds. Yet finite minds cannot escape dealing with them. Bushnell's generation wrestled mightily with these questions—and usually with unshaken confidence. As he spoke to this issue from the pulpit of the North (now United) Church in New Haven, Bushnell had two goals. Both represented hard-won truths to him, and both, he knew, were likely to be unacceptable to many of his listeners.

At the risk of seeming to underemphasize his humanity, he wanted to reaffirm Christ's full divinity. Dogmatically minded theologians of the day had been unable to explain logically how Christ could have had two natures at once, nor could they admit that the majestic, sovereign Deity could suffer human emotions, least of all the pain and disgrace of an ignominious crucifixion. In this impasse they devised an out, an answer not entirely new to Christian history. They took the position that during Jesus' earthly ministry the divinity in him was suspended. He grew and and learned and taught. He experienced hunger, fatigue, and rejection and finally endured the Cross. All of this, however, he experienced solely with the human side of his nature. His divinity was not directly involved.[39]

To Bushnell this underplayed Christ's divinity, and, in any case, it was a fruitless, un-Scriptural speculation. It presumed the ability of limited human minds to define in detail the mysteries of Christ's inner being. This possibility Bushnell flatly denied. All such efforts, he insisted, were at best "raw guesses."[40] Moreover, this view obscured "the summit or highest glory of the incarnation," the fullness of God's life in Christ Jesus, which was the central purpose of his coming to bring us. Urging that we already have quite enough of the human as human, Bushnell maintained that "God, God is what we want, not a man; God revealed through man." Meanwhile, leave the structure of Christ's inward person to mystery, where it belongs. It is enough to accept him for what he conveys externally. To receive him in "simple unity" as the outward expression of God made flesh, "one person, the divine-human" who knows our joys and griefs and in them stands victoriously with us—this is sufficient. This is what he came to be and do.[41]

The Doctor's second aim was to revitalize the doctrine of the Trinity. Here, too, Bushnell accused New England divines of too much effort at impossible interior analysis. In attempts to combat Unitarianism, prevailing orthodox thought had gone to extremes in conceiving a "social Trinity," a kind of select society within the unity of the Godhead, a "celestial tritheocracy," as Bushnell derisively called it. Within that company, the three separate and equal members covenanted and conversed with each other, planned with each other, even dispatched one another on cosmic errands, all the while allegedly remaining one eternal God.[42]

Such conjecture had the endorsement of many first-rate minds, but to Bushnell this, too, was far-fetched and unbiblical. Not only did it make the real richness of the Christian Trinity a mockery to Unitarians, more and more it was becoming a source of "mental confusion" to thinking Congregationalists.[43] Again Bushnell pleaded, "Let God be God." Receive the Trinity in simple faith as God's outward self-communication, expressed in familiar, concrete terms we can understand, one God, reaching out to us as Father, as Son, and as Holy Spirit. Bushnell called this an "instrumental" Trinity, a concept for which he was heavily indebted to an essay by the great liberal German theologian Friedrich E. D. Schleiermacher, made available in English translation by Moses Stuart of Andover Seminary.[44] Bushnell, who has himself been called "the American Schleiermacher,"[45] offered it as a practical and "positive" alternative to a forbidding abstraction, "a vitalizing element offered to our souls, as air to the life of our bodies."[46]

Typically he closed on a pastoral note. He knew that his thought "differs in some respects from what is commonly held." He could only say he had known no other doctrine since he began to be a preacher of Christ. If it had delivered him from "agonies of mental darkness," it could not be wrong to hope that God would make the same truth "a deliverance equally comfortable and joyful to some of you."[47]

Again reactions were mixed. Some Boston conservatives, who

were beginning to find Bushnell's theology "revolting," likened him to Channing and pronounced his *Concio* "a fatal departure from the truth." Mirroring the Doctor's considerable popularity at Yale, the New Haven *Palladium* was impressed by his "richness of language" and ranked him "among the first orators of the age." Contrasting reviews in the press were matched by spontaneous reactions at the church door. One distraught woman was heard to lament, "They have taken away my Lord, and I do not know where they have laid him." Yet a young Yale student was beside himself with relief and gratitude. As he left the assemblage, he exclaimed unashamedly, "I could kiss the soul of Dr. Bushnell."[48]

Two such demanding appointments as these in Cambridge and New Haven would seem quite sufficient for one summer. But the pace continued. In a matter of days he was back at Harvard, this time to deliver the prestigious Phi Beta Kappa oration which he called "Work and Play."[49] Behind that deceptively elementary title lay one of Bushnell's most original utterances, and certainly one of his most charming.

Taking his cue from watching his children playing with a kitten on the parlor floor, he developed the thought that play is the highest fulfillment we can achieve, no matter what our field of endeavor. Work (also essential) was an activity *for* an end. Play was activity *as* an end. Play, though often built on work, rose far above mere exertion into experiences of freedom, spontaneity, and joy. Thus Christian faith at its highest level was not a hell-fearing struggle after God or a slaving over moral obligations one was forever breaking. It was the freedom of a Christ-liberated spirit, serious but sublime play. Bushnell asserted,

> Exactly this we mean when we say that Christianity brings an offer of liberty to humankind, for the Christian liberty is only pure spiritual play. Delivered of self-love, fear, contrivance, legal constraints, termagant passions, in a word, of all ulterior ends not found in goodness itself, a person ascends into power, and reveals, for the first time the real greatness of his or her nature.[50]

The poet Henry Wadsworth Longfellow was in the audience and noted in his journal that Bushnell had been "fresh, original, poetic."[51] Others apparently agreed. The Doctor's sparkling literary touch on this occasion so delighted his hearers, that they repeatedly interrupted him with applause.[52] The day was one of his high moments; and along with *Christian Nurture* and his views on language, this unusual address remains one of the keys to his spirituality. It offered Christians something better to hope for than the drudgery of a work ethic, or an endless effort of will. Without doubt it also reflected his recent liberating Christ-centered experience. A reporter present suggested as much in saying that Bushnell had given his audience "a daguerreotype of himself."[53]

In September it was on again to Andover Seminary's high hill to address the evangelical school's fortieth anniversary commencement. He spoke on "Dogma and Spirit," or, as his subtitle expressed it more accurately, "The True Revival of Religion." This time he was a man on crusade, dreaming of a fresh extension of the sixteenth-century Protestant Reformation, advancing further "the work Luther left incomplete." His target was not Rome, but the aging revival system of New England theology—"marvellously unspiritual," he was convinced, "having no real intimacy with God."[54]

Genuine Christian dogma—as he understood it—he did not oppose, and never did. Bushnell was no easygoing liberal sceptical of all traditional theological statements. It was not dogma, but what he regarded as a dying dogma*tism* that troubled him, a rigidity of thought that he was convinced had been allowed to overshadow lively faith and block the creative power of the Spirit among the churches. He stressed to his Andover listeners that his aim was "not to uproot opinions, not to stop the intellectual and scientific activity of the church, but simply to invert the relations of dogma and spirit, so as to subordinate everything in the nature of science and opinion to the spirit."[55]

He was sure he was not just speaking his own mind. As he had claimed from the same platform in 1839, and again in his *Views of Christian Nurture,* he sensed an awareness "among the most thoughtful Christians of our time" that "a new religious era" was about to dawn. In the new age he saw approaching, there would be a much-needed reunion of the separated New England churches, orthodox and Unitarian. But more. There would emerge "a grand catholic reviving, a universal movement, penetrating gradually and quickening into power the whole church of Christ on earth."[56]

The festive importance of the anniversary and Bushnell's own widening fame had attracted a strong attendance, representative of many theological opinions. Aging conservatives rubbed elbows with young seminarians. Harvard professors and Andover faculty shared the same pews, as did Unitarian divines and laypersons of differing sympathies. When Bushnell finished, many in this mixed audience were well impressed and glad he had spoken out so freely.[57] There were conservatives, however, who went away pained and puzzled. Judging by what he had said, it might be true that Bushnell was not really a Unitarian. But what was he? He occupied a traditionally orthodox pulpit, yet nearly everything he said seemed to challenge prevailing New England doctrine.

Hard as it was to classify him, it was not hard for loyal Calvinists to see that for them this man was going to spell trouble. They had trouble enough as it was. Congregational ministers were gradually losing the authority they long had enjoyed in New England and elsewhere. The industrial revolution was draining more and more people away from the country to the cities, and many clergy were feeling a financial pinch. Disestablishment in Connecticut and Massachusetts reduced their political power, and the spread of education and the rise of new professions meant they no longer could exercise the unchallenged intellectual prerogatives that once had been theirs. Denominationally they had been shaken by the Unitarian departure, and with every passing year, both in Eastern urban centers and on the frontier, they were facing increased competition from Baptists, Methodists, and Roman Catholics.[58]

The main asset they still had was their theological system. Doomed though it was, it had been a remarkable structure, and was still seen as such. One knowledgeable historian has called it "the single most brilliant and most continuous indigenous theological tradition that

America has produced,"[59] and here was this maverick minister from Hartford threatening to break that down also.

A coterie of Boston clergy began to perceive Bushnell as a traitor working from within to undermine the household of faith. "When orthodoxy is assailed from without, however furiously," they boasted, "its friends sit calmly in their impregnable defenses, without anxiety as to the result. But when we see one of the garrison with a lighted torch in his hand, arranging the magazine, it naturally excites some commotion till the danger is removed."[60] Something had to be done—and done soon—to deal with this treacherous insider. It would help if he were to publish his offending 1848 discourses in a book; his errors could then be shown up in detail, and there would be a firm basis in print for action against him. Bushnell knew full well that his adversaries were poised to strike with new force, and he was uneasy over the furore that publication might cause. Nonetheless, the dangerous Hartford pastor sent his copy to the printer and provided the public with a volume which friend and foe alike eagerly awaited.

CHAPTER 10

A Book New England Was Waiting For

"WHEN IS THE BOOK COMING OUT?" Bushnell was beseiged by impatient inquiries. Some pressed him because they wanted to see he was not in fact "mortally dangerous." Others could hardly wait for written proof that he was. There were unforeseen delays. The Doctor kept making extensive revisions, and at one point a heedless typesetter let a bundle of copy slip into his lamp and burn. Finally, early in 1849, *God in Christ* made its long-awaited appearance, published in Hartford and paid for out of Bushnell's own pocket.[1]

As expected, it contained the three controversial discourses. Unexpectedly, to most, they were preceded by an impressive "Preliminary Dissertation on the Nature of Language, as Related to Thought and Spirit."[2] Some early readers were irked by this insertion. Why should they have to wade through an irrelevant disquisition on language, before getting to the discourses? "Something queer is here," one Boston reviewer scornfully commented. For Bushnell to intrude an essay on language before he dealt with his theology was as though a concert violinist were to salute his audience by saying "I am about to play three popular airs with variations. But first I must give you a preliminary dissertation on fiddle strings."[3]

Bushnell's theological "airs," however, were so unusual for his time, that attention to "fiddle strings" was not dallying. Nor was it enough for his essay to be a mere appendix. Bushnell placed it first for a good reason. He saw in language the key to all that followed, and he felt it a "duty" to make it available to his readers. He was wiser than he knew. More than he could then realize, language became not only the clue to one book, but it became the key to the man himself and to much of his life's work.[4]

To a point, the "Dissertation" only published what he had said to a limited audience in his 1839 "Revelation." The theory of double-level language; the mysterious correlation between inward mind and outward matter; the power of physical objects to become signs of spiritual truth; and the expressive activity of the divine Logos in bringing all this to pass—anyone acquainted with his Andover address ten years before would have found these concepts familiar. Yet in other ways the "Dissertation" was different. Since 1839, for one thing, Bushnell had been reading extensively. The origins and capability of human language were among the scientific preoccupations of the age, both in Europe and in the United States, and literature was plentiful. Although, like Emerson, Bushnell was not usually a systematic reader,[5] he would now and again focus on an area that particularly interested him and study it in greater depth. It was so here. His preface is peppered with references to Continental, English, and American philologists. He had acquainted himself with the findings of such European scholars as Friedrich Schlegel, William von Humboldt, and Heinrich J. Klaproth. He had restudied Coleridge, Goethe, Bunyan, Milton, and other literary authorities. Among American writers, he had come to know, for example, the work of the New York banker and amateur student of language Alexander B. Johnson, including his *Treatise on Language*. Acquaintance with these authors enlarged his knowledge and gave him a surer touch.[6]

Then, too, in 1849, the Doctor was writing out of a different professional milieu. A decade before, he had been an obscure pastor. Now he was a spokesman for a disputed new theology and, for good or ill, was a household name in many quarters. This meant that he was more specific in taking issue with his opponents and more thorough in the defense of his own position.

Mainly, his quarrel was with the precise verbal premises of the eighteenth-century "common sense" philosophy, chiefly represented by the Scottish writers Thomas Reid and Dugald Stewart. The books of these influential thinkers were everywhere on American shelves, inside the churches and out. Thomas Jefferson came to know Stewart in Paris on the eve of the French Revolution and admired him for the rest of his days. John Adams considered him a profound genius.[7]

Reacting against the difficult idealism of the celebrated Bishop George Berkeley and the equally renowned scepticism of David Hume, the "common sense" thesis stated that our ordinary human senses can be trusted to put us in touch with reality. The corollary to this view was that words, while not perfect vehicles of expression and communication, are adequate to convey with precision the major truths of thought, including the teachings of the Christian religion. Thus, an ardent "common sense" disciple such as Nathaniel Taylor, at Yale, was certain that once the right words had been found and arranged in the right logical order, he could capture for everyone what it had pleased God to reveal through the Old and New Testaments. Consider his explanation of the mystery of the Trinity, which he emphasized with italics:

> *God is one being, in such modified sense of the terms as to include three persons in such a modified sense of the terms, that, by his tripersonality, or by the three persons of his Godhead, he is qualified, in a corresponding modified sense, for three distinct, personal, divine forms of phenomenal action.*[8]

With such meticulously chosen words, and marvellously labyrinthine logic, Taylor felt he had said it all.

In his "Dissertation," Bushnell resumed his long campaign against this rigid linguistic method of New England theologians. "This whole tribe of sophisters," these "unfructifying logicker[s]," as he mercilessly nicknamed his opponents, placed altogether too much reliance on exact terminology. Even words for everyday objects—a tree, a leg, or a stone—he found full of imponderables and nuances of meaning. The same was true of words strung together in logical sequence. If such ordinary, everyday terms were inherently imprecise, how should the weighty words of Christian thought—God, sin, incarnation, redemption, and all the vast range of the faith vocabulary—be unambiguous?[9]

Bushnell renewed his claim that language was "an instrument of suggestion" only.[10] Words were not made to contain major truths entirely, and major truths of faith were not made to fit the narrow spaces of finite words. Poetry and art, not science, set the standard for the proper use of language.[11] Thus the Scriptures should be read "not as a magazine of propositions, . . . but as inspirations and poetic forms of life, requiring also divine inbreathings and exaltations in us, that we may ascend into their divine meaning."[12] In a statement bound to scandalize the establishment, he actually cast doubt on the value of exact clarity in spiritual matters. "Of all the 'clear' writers and speakers I have ever met with," he protested, ". . . I have never yet found one that was able to send me forward an inch."[13] Like his mentor Coleridge, he felt undefinable mystery, beyond the power of words to express, was a part of truth. "Make any truth too definite," Coleridge once said, "and you make it too small."[14]

Bushnell's other linguistic complaint against most contemporary theologians was their blindness to the power of symbols. When applied to moral subjects, symbolism, to the Doctor, was "the real and legitimate use of words."[15] One need not have a sophisticated knowledge of language to know that symbols command perennial popular interest. The Statue of Liberty is above all a symbol. As such it says more about freedom to more people around the world than a thousand definitive treatises ever could do. Symbols, moreover, do more than convey information. They stir emotions. Those who see them become active participants in the area of experience they represent. Symbols, it has been said, "are places to live, breathing spaces that help us discover the possibilities that life offers."[16]

The chief end of all Bushnell's theological effort was to help people rediscover and reenter such "places to live" within the Christian faith. The way into that, he maintained, lay in an imaginative, responsive approach to language as symbol. Words in general, and biblical words in particular, were not nearly so much literal as symbolic. Turning the pages of Scripture was like walking through an art gallery. The poetic beauty and power of its symbols—God as Father or refuge, Christ as the Good Shepherd, the Spirit as a dove, not to mention a host of other Scriptural images—invited the reader to enter into a spiritual experience, and there to live. In explaining his "instrumental Trinity" at Yale, Bushnell hoped his listeners would receive it not as a puzzling abstraction to be gazed at, but as a symbol "to be lived in as a power."[17]

Bushnell's imaginative approach to language was a major contribution to American thought.[18] It helped people find a faith closer to their experience and freed them to consider Christian truth not just from one formalized perspective, as previously, but from many sides. It released them to ponder different creeds—each necessarily imprecise and incomplete, yet each helping to correct the errors and affirm the truth of the others. In easing feelings of guilt and perplexity, his method opened new avenues of faith for a growing number of seekers in both pulpit and pew. Some came publicly to his support. Bushnell was especially pleased that a young man from his North Church congregation, Henry M. Goodwin, then a student at Andover seminary, published an article of his own endorsing his pastor's stand, and in some ways putting the Doctor's case even more clearly. Bushnell read him "with greatest delight."[19]

As usual, however, the weight of reaction to the "Dissertation" was anything but friendly. The lengthy preface was labeled "baseless and delusive" and "bound to be of disastrous influence."[20] One of his former teachers at Yale, Chauncey A. Goodrich, deplored Bushnell's attempt "to destroy all confidence in language as a vehicle of moral and religious truth." If a tenth of what the "Dissertation" had said were true, Goodrich lamented, "society would long since have been thrown into inextricable confusion."[21]

The generally negative reception accorded Bushnell's efforts on language was gentle compared with the onslaughts against the main body of the book. One seminary after another sent out champions against it, booted and spurred with traditional arguments and determined to unhorse the troublesome black knight from Hartford.

From Maine came Enoch Pond of Bangor Seminary with a critique a third as long as the book itself. Pond acknowledged a few good passages in Bushnell's volume, but went on to assail it at every major point. Patronizingly, he cautioned the Doctor against raising "any *new theories*" regarding the person and work of Christ. The field had been thoroughly covered, he announced loftily, and he doubted that "anything essentially new is ever to come up." He was saddened that the author's "brilliant powers" had been so "prostituted," and his dour prediction was that most readers would look on Bushnell's pages with "grief and abhorrence."[22]

Among other Congregational voices Goodrich continued to speak disparagingly for Yale.[23] From as far west as the Illinois prairies, Julian M. Sturtevant, president of Congregationally founded Illinois College, anxiously asked his friends back East, "What are you going to do with the heresies of Dr. Bushnell?"[24] A front-page editorial in the *Congregationalist* called Bushnell "*guilty*" of "heresy in the first degree."[25] The far-Right *Christian Observatory* in Boston wondered whether the Doctor were "wholly sane," and in a mood scarcely short of rage it accused him of poisoning theology and arrogantly spreading "moral death through the community."[26]

Nor were most reactions outside the Congregational fold any less devastating. Charles Hodge, the so-called "Oracle" of Presbyterian Princeton Seminary, managed to pay Bushnell his respects, but then pronounced his work "a failure." He devoutly hoped, "for the honor of the race," that such a book as this is not about to turn the world upside down."[27] Unitarians reacted in their *Christian Examiner* courteously but firmly registering objections.[28] Orestes Brownson, once a Unitarian, but by this time a zealous Roman Catholic, depicted Bushnell as "a very ignorant man" who was "mentally and morally in a chaotic state"—"a bad theologian, but unhappily a worse philosopher."[29]

As he had vowed in his introduction, Bushnell remained publicly silent in the face of criticism. Privately, however, he shared his pain. In particular it hurt him to be shunned by ministerial colleagues. On a trip to Boston, he had amazingly pleasant talks with nearly all his most articulate enemies, but still met stares of "half horror." "I am looked at here by the mass as a kind of horned animal," he reported to his wife.[30] When Professor Eleazar Fitch of Yale awkwardly canceled a pulpit exchange with Bushnell, an arrangement Fitch himself had requested, Bushnell sadly wrote Leonard Bacon, "I hope you are not all going to cast me out as a reprobate."[31]

Not everybody did. "I have some friends who stick to me," he reassured Bartol.[32] Astute Noah Porter of Farmington always was there for him. Leonard Bacon stood by, though his review of the book in *The New Englander* was guarded.[33] The *Methodist Quarterly* gave a mixed, but generally friendly critique.[34] And a literary Baptist minister in Hartford, Robert Turnbull, was a comfort to him. Turnbull was in the process of publishing a book of his own and added a sympathetic supplement to take Bushnell's theories into account.[35]

His most effective support came from a source that was unexpected, and for a time anonymous. During the summer of 1849, articles began appearing in the Hartford *Religious Herald* mysteriously signed "C. C." It developed that the initials stood for "Criticus Criticorum" (critic of the critics) and that the author was Amos S. Chesebrough, the Yale-educated minister of the Congregational Church in Chester, Connecticut.[36] He undertook to defend Bushnell by showing that his attackers did not constitute a solid phalanx of agreement, as had been claimed. On the contrary, he maintained, they spoke in "a perfect Babel of tongues" and were as divided among themselves as they were vociferous against the Doctor. He imagined them giving contradictory testimony at a mock trial; by laying out their charges in parallel columns, he displayed Hodge opposing fundamentalist editor David N. Lord, Goodrich at odds with Pond, and the *Christian Observatory* poles apart from more moderate opponents.

Prominent North Church laymen, including former U.S. Congressman James Dixon and Lyman Beecher's son-in-law, Thomas C. Perkins, took pleasure in seeing to it that Chesebrough's pieces (not excluding some the *Herald* had refused to print) were collected in a pamphlet and given wide circulation. This exposed Chesebrough and the *Herald* to heavy fire. "Take care, Brother Chesebrough, or we will have you tried for heresy," one grim Middlesex Association minister warned him after hearing a preliminary reading of his views.[37] The booklet nonetheless made its mark. Unitarian Henry W. Bellows in New York thought it "perfectly annihilated" the reactionaries, and Bushnell came to feel the surprising tract had "saved his head."[38]

The furore over *God in Christ* not only brought down on Bushnell an avalanche of censure, inevitably it caused his name to be still more widely known overseas as well as at home. He began to be taken with a new seriousness in Britain, where already he had begun to be noticed. Frederick W. Robertson, the short-lived preaching genius among the workingmen of Brighton, had been aware of the Doctor for some time. Apparently he had been sufficiently impressed by his "Unconscious Influence" that he laid out a sermon of his own along the same lines, inviting suspicions of plagiarism, which Bushnell thought groundless.[39] Within a year of *God in Christ*, young Frederick Law Olmsted was on a walking tour of England with his brother John and an adventurous Charles L. Brace. In the home of a Ludlow (Shropshire) Congregational minister, they were amazed to discover a portrait of their pastor on the mantelpiece, sharing honors with the legendary Dr. Thomas Arnold of Rugby "and other worthies."[40]

At higher ecclesiastical levels, Henry H. Millman, recently appointed dean of St. Paul's Cathedral in London, felt obliged to inquire of Edward Everett at Harvard about Bushnell, of whom he was beginning to hear so much. Everett identified the Doctor as "a man of middle age, come of late rather suddenly into great repute, as an original thinker and teacher." On occasion Everett had spoken highly of Bushnell, and at least once during his Harvard presidency he had said he would be happy to have him on the Harvard faculty as Hollis Professor.[41] In correspondence with Millman, however, he blandly agreed with the London cleric's sceptical assessment that the Hartford preacher probably would experience only passing fame. Still, Everett predicted Bushnell would not lose caste with "his orthodox friends, with whom he evidently desires to remain in good fellowship."[42]

In his last observation the Harvard leader was right. No matter how towering his troubles among the Calvinists were, and for all his cordial ties with liberals, it never seriously entered Bushnell's head to take refuge with the Unitarians. "Bushnell, why submit to be buffeted by those Connecticut ministers?" prominent Boston Unitarians kept asking him. "You belong with us. Why not say so and join us?" Categorically he disagreed. "Gentlemen, I am much mistaken by many," he would reply with a trace of irritation, "but by none so much as by you. I don't belong with you, but the farthest possible otherwise, if only you knew it."[43]

He was indeed determined to keep his Trinitarian standing, and he did. But not before he had been battered and almost struck down by a long theological storm of epic proportions. In the midst of it he told his own people he felt at times as if "winds from the four quarters of heaven" had blasted him all at once for his "deadly" doctrine and his "appalling" heresy.[44] He was not exaggerating the fury of the gale.

CHAPTER 11

The Bushnell Battle Royal

MACHINERY FOR DISCIPLINING wayward Congregational ministers in Connecticut had been evolving ever since 1708, when the famous Saybrook Platform, in quaint but forthright terms, had laid down the basic principles.[1] As matters stood in 1849, a heresy trial for a minister could only take place in a district consociation made up of both clergy and laity. There was no higher court of appeal. An accused could be brought before such a consociation if the ministerial association to which he belonged voted to present him. Or, he could be required to appear if three members of his congregation testified against him, supported by one minister from another church.[2]

Although these procedures had seldom, if ever, been used,[3] Bushnell's opponents took hold of them and launched a warlike campaign to bring him to the bar of ecclesiastical justice. Three disgruntled members of the North Church could not be found. So there was no future to that method. From some source, however, an overture was delivered to the Hartford Central Association of Ministers complaining of Bushnell's theology as set forth in *God in Christ*.[4] Under the Saybrook rules, it then became the duty of the Association to meet as a kind of grand jury to determine for itself whether there was sufficient truth to the charges to justify presenting the author for trial before the Hartford North Consociation.

"In a rather delicate way," as the Doctor described it, the Association took up the issue when it assembled for its annual meeting in June 1849 in the rural setting of the East Avon Church, a few miles west of Hartford.[5] In what now would appear as a direct conflict of interest, Bushnell immediately took an active part in the examination of his own book, almost as though the fate of quite another minister were at stake. His colleagues did not seem to see anything inappropriate in this and accepted his suggestion that a special review committee be appointed. They even consulted him on the makeup of the panel, drawing the line, however, when Bushnell objected to including his old theological antagonist, Joel Hawes.

In the end, five men were selected: Noah Porter of Farmington as chair; Hawes of Center Church, Hartford; Charles B. McLean of Collinsville, the youngest of the five (age 34), whose ordination sermon the Doctor had preached in 1844; Merrill Richardson of Terryville, a forceful personality whom Bushnell later remarked "had always been for me;"[6] and Walter S. Clarke, the abrasively conservative pastor of Hartford's South Church.

Bushnell sized up the committee with a political eye and was uneasy. The choice of Hawes seemed to him a "dark sign," and he was so upset by it that for a while he was tempted to refuse all cooperation. Without doubt Clarke would side with Hawes against him. McLean and Richardson he considered "safe." That would leave Porter with the swing vote. He could not believe that Porter would desert him, but neither could he feel entirely sure. "Is it possible," he asked anxiously of Leonard Bacon, "that such a man as Dr. Porter, in this age of the world, can be so wrought upon by Omicron [Chauncey Goodrich, of Yale], Hawes, [Nathaniel] Taylor and others, as to think it best to cut off me [*sic*] from the church?" He tried to console himself with the thought that if Porter would only remain steadfast, he would be "quite willing to have Dr. Hawes as deep in the matter as he can be." Meanwhile, he set about taking the "cars" to New Haven to confer with Bacon in person, hoping his valued but busy friend would somehow make time for him even on short notice. "When you are a heretic," he not altogether jokingly promised, "I will try and do as much for you."[7]

Porter fell ill during the summer, delaying the scheduled July meeting of the Association for two months. Bushnell used the time to write a long defense—later his *Christ in Theology*—and met with members of the committee and with friends, picking up advice and encouragement wherever he could to sustain him in the "long, sore job."[8]

Amid his anxieties, it pleased him that Lyman Beecher, on a visit to Hartford from Lane Seminary in Cincinnati, came to his door late in August to hear Bushnell's side of the story firsthand. The two had "a full talk"; and as Bushnell reported to Chesebrough of the "C.C." papers, the aging, great preacher and crusader "rejoiced with tears" to discover his essential "soundness" on most points. Afterward Beecher unhitched his horse and drove directly to see Porter in Farmington. There, using some pointers from Bushnell, he took a hand in framing what it was hoped would be the majority committee report exonerating the Doctor entirely.[9]

At length, on 18 September, Hartford Central reconvened. Every member who could possibly be expected to be there was there, eager to hear what the committee reviewing Bushnell's book would say. As it turned out, the best that the Doctor could hope for happened. The committee had split three to two in Bushnell's favor and was unable to offer a single, united report. Instead it made three. The first report was limited to procedure and was recommended unanimously. The second was the report of the majority. This argued that although the language of the book was "apt to be peculiar" and Bushnell's thought patterns "not those which are common to the theologians of this country," there were "no views set forth in the book in question which are fundamentally erroneous." The third report was from the Hawes-Clarke minority. The longest of the three, it dissected *God in Christ* in minute detail. Its conclusion was that this "most studious and sorrowful inquisition" could only decide that "the book before us holds views which deny and subvert the essential facts of our common faith."[10]

Once the reports were accepted there was lively debate. Bushnell then took the floor and began his personal defense. He continued until late afternoon, when it became necessary to adjourn—as it turned out, for more than a month. The Association reassembled on a rainy 22 October in Hartford, and Bushnell resumed his defense, taking up the rest of the day. The next morning the long-suffering pastors met yet again and plodded through several more hours of deliberation.

It was a fatiguing business. At one point during the two-day session, Bushnell entertained a few of the ministers at his house for dinner. The atmosphere was heavy with talk of the debates and with uncertainty as to the eventual outcome. His children noted their father was tense with apprehension, more strained and anxious than they had ever seen him.[11]

Finally it came time for a vote on the key question as to whether the report of the majority should be adopted. If the motion to adopt failed, Bushnell would face trial by the consociation. If it passed, it would mean that in the all-important eyes of his Association, he was innocent of basic error and would escape the ordeal of further judicial process. Although none of the participants could foresee it, much future American religious history would be riding on the result.

The momentous polling took place in a hushed room of the Fourth Congregational Church. Seventeen members, led by Noah Porter, stood by Bushnell and voted "Aye." Three voted "Nay." Two of the three negatives certainly were those of Hawes and Clarke. It would appear that the third may have been cast by Thomas Robbins of the Connecticut Historical Society. The bachelor historian confided unhappily to his *Diary* that "the majority did not do as they ought," Bushnell having been only "moderately censured for his errors." Had Samuel Spring, Jr., of East Hartford not been sick and absent, there likely would have been a fourth "Nay."[12]

The Association had spoken. No other Congregational agency had authority to override its verdict. It was not a clear victory, for even though they supported him, few, if any, of his colleagues fully endorsed Bushnell's theology, and some remained distinctly opposed. But finding no *fundamental* error, as Mrs. Cheney expressed it in her biography, "they kept room for him."[13] It was enough. This vote became the rock against which all future waves of opposition to Bushnell eventually dashed in vain.

Immediate outside reactions to the Association's decision had no consistent pattern. In New Hampshire the *Congregational Journal* was glad Hartford Central had dealt kindly with its controversial member, optimistically hoping such treatment might lure Bushnell back to "old fashioned orthodoxy." This view was copied by the *Christian Mirror* in Maine. Bacon's New York *Independent* also applauded the decision, reminding its readers it had maintained a pro-

Bushnell stand all along despite retaliation from readers. Former Connecticut governor William W. Ellsworth already had written Bacon and canceled his subscription on this account.[14] Less friendly responses came from the "Old School" *Presbyterian,* which viewed the decision as "treason" to ignore Bushnell's heresy; the Hartford Baptist *Christian Secretary,* which claimed that the vote would satisfy nobody; and the Hartford Episcopal *Calendar,* which felt "disappointed and mortified."[15]

As for Bushnell himself, the vote momentarily lifted a heavy load from his shoulders. But that was all it did. Before long serious new troubles appeared and multiplied over five additional years of relentless attack, a bitter contest that wore him down and gave him no peace. The prime mover in the fresh assault was the Fairfield West Association, which had within its jurisdiction such prosperous towns as Fairfield, Stamford, Norwalk, and Bridgeport. For generations there had been a certain off-horse independence about Fairfield County churches.[16] In 1849 this independent stance was being maintained by a group of dominant leaders of traditional mind-set, patrician figures who were strong, devout, and profoundly sure of themselves.

If any was chief, it was Lyman H. Atwater of Fairfield, closely followed by Nathaniel Hewit of the Second Congregational Church of Bridgeport. Prominently affiliated with them were Theophilus Smith of New Canaan and Edwin Hall of Norwalk. Atwater, eleven years Bushnell's junior, had been a Yale undergraduate when Bushnell was a tutor. He lived comfortably in what one traveler described as "the best parsonage...in New England." This, however, did not prevent him from being a disciplined spirit, fair in controversy though capable of powerful invective. In every department of life, from education to women's rights ("a mad enterprise") to religion, he was certain that stability, not inquiry and change, was the only answer. Atwater liked and respected Bushnell as a man and as a Christian preacher; he had no confidence in him whatever as a theologian.[17] Among his colleagues, Hewit was so conservative a Calvinist that he once was part of a movement to put even Bennet Tyler on trial for heretical leanings.[18] Smith was a milder personality, of good practical judgment and exemplary Christian character. Atwater regarded him as the finest of Bushnell's opponents, as he considered Porter of Farmington the best of his defenders. Hall, among other interests, was a temperance man and had served his Norwalk congregation with unflagging conservative zeal for nearly twenty years.

These men constituted the "big four" of Fairfield West, but they were joined by supporters from other associations around the state. They were so sure of their particular Gospel and so convinced any other was wrong, that they all but turned their crusade against Bushnell into a second career. What they sought to do was convict the members of the Hartford Central Association of harboring a church law-breaker, which in turn would make that association an accomplice in theological crime.

They were impatient to get started. Even before Hartford Central had opened its investigation, Fairfield West prepared a special resolution for the 1849 annual meeting of the Connecticut General Association in Salisbury. It warned that body that fundamental Christian doctrines were being "impugned" under its very nose and exhorted all associations and consociations to "apply discipline mildly but firmly" to prevent further spread of error.[19] Bushnell was not named, but the aim of the resolution was clear. As by this time, however, Hartford Central had barely begun its inquiry, the General Association committee could truthfully report that it knew of no "culpable negligence" in this regard on the part of any association. Any action would therefore be "unseasonable."[20]

Thwarted at the state level, Fairfield West and its allies trained their guns directly on Hartford Central. With great care they documented their case in a "Remonstrance and Complaint." This paper summarized Bushnell's heresies in detail, strenuously objected to Hartford Central's refusal to prosecute him, and pressed it to repair damage already done to the churches and the cause of truth by rethinking its conclusions. Hartford Central gave a soft answer, arguing it could not reopen the case until new evidence was produced.[21] Without further consulting Hartford Central, the Fairfielders thereupon went public with their "Remonstrance" and Hartford's reply, printing both statements in a pamphlet and dispatching a copy to every member of every ministerial association in Connecticut.[22] They went further. In a highly questionable move, considering Congregational practice in Connecticut, they took it upon themselves to send a letter to each association in the state requesting it to meet and consider Bushnell's volume and report back to Fairfield West its reactions.[23]

The associations did not disappoint their Fairfield friends. Except for Hartford Central, which did not receive the mailing, all thirteen associations replied. Unanimously they expressed doctrinal sympathy with Fairfield's protest; none said anything supportive of Bushnell. Nine associations felt he should be brought to trial.[24] The New Haven West Association took the matter so seriously that Theodore D. Woolsey, president of Yale, and thirty others spent the better part of two days in the theological lecture room of the college carefully framing a position paper. Their final version informed Fairfield West that New Haven West could have "no fellowship" with the errors alleged to be Bushnell's, but they refused to say whether or not they were fundamental heresies.[25]

In some quarters the Fairfield request became an apple of discord. In the Tolland Association in eastern Connecticut, long a nest of anti-Bushnell intrigue, a minority objected to an over-hasty agreement with Fairfield West. There were words, and a relentless majority accused the dissenters of wasting valuable association time over an unworthy work full of "cold, damp and foggy reasonings."[26] In the New Haven East Association a few members vigorously contended that Fairfield's overbearing tactics verged on "ecclesiastical lynch law." If generally practiced, these dissidents argued, such behavior would deprive every minister in the state of legitimate protection.[27]

Such acrimony was typical of a growing tide of hostility toward Bushnell and his book. In midwinter, Henry Bellows, who did not hestitate at times to express disapproval of his unorthodox friend, visited Bushnell in Hartford. He found him in difficult straits. "His brethren hate him with a Christian hatred," he wrote Bartol in Boston. Yet he could not remember having seen the Doctor "so calm and self-possessed. I never felt so much drawn to him," he confessed.[28]

In this atmosphere the next annual meeting of the General Association took place in Litchfield in mid-June 1850. These yearly gatherings were of great importance to the life of Congregational Connecticut and were of considerable significance to Calvinistic churches nationally. Customarily they brought together some fifty ministerial delegates from Connecticut, often accompanied by wives, who came along in horse and buggy for the pleasure of the excursion and the opportunities for social contact. Representatives of "foreign bodies" (other General Associations) came from elsewhere in New England and from as far afield as Michigan, Wisconsin, and the prairies of Iowa. So did messengers from both General Assemblies (Old and New Schools) of the Presbyterian church. The church press usually was there in force, as were spectators from the neighborhood of the host congregation. The agenda allowed time for relaxed conviviality as relief from the strenuous pressure of business, which might begin with 5:00 A.M. prayer meetings and run with considerable intensity over two or three days.[29]

For such a gathering, the state had no more delightful village than Litchfield. Though its roads were still unpaved, and farmers could be seen leading cattle through the streets, the neatly fenced town was full of cultivated charm. Imposing homes and cool greenery were everywhere; towering elms offered graceful shade. The hilltop meetinghouse (which still stands with its stately Greek revival pillars and commanding spire) in itself lent dignity to the occasion.

Everyone knew that *the* business of this meeting would be Bushnell. He and his friends had armed themselves as best they could for a fight, and Fairfield West came prepared to do all it could to get the General Association to acknowledge the Doctor's "poisoning of multitudes" and do something to stop it. Ultra-conservative Nathaniel Hewit was chosen as moderator. It was hardly a hopeful omen that as he took the rostrum and called the meeting to opening worship he earnestly interceded "for apostates and heretics."[30]

Fairfield, with its allies at Yale, East Windsor, and elsewhere, took the initiative with a long "Memorial." It forcefully set forth the immediate theological situation as an acute emergency demanding decisive action. A special Committee of Thirteen was appointed to consider it, including five of Bushnell's most outspoken opponents.

Ostensibly this was an independent panel. It came out, however, that the substance of the report Fairfield hoped it would make had been prefabricated behind the scenes in New Haven in consultation with various Yale professors—this in the hope that their names would have weight with Connecticut preachers. Oddly, the maneuver seems not to have been called in question, and for the Bushnell cause it was, to say the least, threatening.[31]

Yet despite these elaborate, if not devious, schemes, the Litchfield meeting tamed the Fairfield lion, and Bushnell emerged unscathed. Partly this was due to feelings about Congregational polity. Fairfield's hard-line tactics seemed to many delegates to menace the independence of the local associations and, at least by inference, to grant too much power to the General Association. In Noah Porter's words, their high-handedness in dealing with the Bushnell question came too close to an "attempt to rule over us."

The outcome was also very much a result of Bushnell's personal participation. In his own defense, he was at times the lawyer Yale once trained him to be, addressing the assemblage as though it were a "jury." Vigorously pleading his own case, he drew on analogies from civil law and historical precedent, and for all he had said against "logickers" in religion, he fortified his arguments with powerful logic. Given his precarious situation, there were moments when Bushnell was astonishingly direct. Reminding the meeting that it could indeed bring him to trial if three of his own church members would speak against him, he challenged the meeting to find them. He even threw down the gauntlet personally to Hewit. "Go yourself, Mr. Moderator," he half coaxed and half taunted him, "and get your papers prepared." But in the absence of such accusers, he insisted that the decision of Hartford Central be allowed to stand. "You have no right," he lectured his colleagues," to repeat to an unlimited extent the agitation of such matters."

At other times he behaved very differently, counseling, cajoling, almost preaching as a fellow-minister and Christian brother.

> I wish very much that instead of spending your strength on so poor a subject as myself, you would set yourselves to work to change this

body from one of mere debate into one which should be promotive of a high spirituality.... It is easy to learn the art of theological war, and to find heresies to contend with, but it is a greater thing to be filled with the Spirit, and to grow into fellowship with God.[32]

Some were impressed. Others were not. As the debate continued, there were heated exchanges. "Do not drive us to revolution," an aggrieved Chauncey Goodrich warned Bushnell sympathizers at one critical juncture, and an exercised Edwin Hall came close to charging Bushnell with outright dishonesty. Yet just when patience was about to snap and deadlock seemed inescapable, the session underwent startling change. Whether from fatigue, the influence of the prayer meetings, or the pressure of time, the delegates suddenly began pulling together. The kind of basic faith statement Fairfield had sought was substantially achieved. In an undreamed-of combination, Atwater and Bushnell cooperated on a key procedural compromise, whereby if one association was troubled by the doctrine of another, it could complain, and the offending association was under obligation to reconsider its position. If in good conscience it could not reverse itself, it still was obligated to do all in its power "to satisfy" the plaintiffs. As adjournment came there were thanks to God for a harmonious conclusion of affairs, and the delegates, so recently sharply divided, emerged from the classic church as though leaving a love feast.

A number of sagacious leaders had played roles in the Litchfield drama, none more notable than Bushnell. Probably he never appeared to better advantage in a public forum. While to the end there were those who wanted to accomplish his "execution," and this depressed him (from a distance, Bellows suspected he had been "rather arrogant" toward his brethren),[33] in the estimation of many he gained new respect. Beyond what they had previously known of him, Bushnell had shown himself to be resourceful, courageous, large minded, and spiritually convincing. One participant felt the delegates had moved with great care for one reason. They were convinced that in judging Bushnell they were dealing with a man of God, even if he should be a man of God in error. Reflecting on these momentous events nearly fifty years later, Edwin Pond Parker of Hartford's

South Congregational Church struck the same note, summing up the Doctor's conduct at Litchfield as that of a man "not only of singular genius, but of singular grace."[34]

Once he had returned home, even Lyman Atwater decided he must take another look at his baffling brother. He wrote Bushnell asking for an interview, and Bushnell welcomed him fraternally to his Winthrop Street home. For most of two days they talked, toured Hartford, and prayed together. The Doctor thought his visitor left "greatly quieted." And as tensions seemed to ease, Noah Porter breathed a sigh of relief that at last "the whole earth was at rest . . . on this subject."[35]

So it was—but not for long. Atwater decided he had let himself be led astray by Bushnell's charm, and after a few peaceful months a belligerent Fairfield West returned to the battle. Having left Litchfield in peace, the association's leadership suddenly began using the faith statement made there as a weapon against Bushnell. Had not the General Association at Litchfield laid down the creedal basics of Christianity? Very well, Bushnell did not accept them. Had not the Litchfield meeting made it obligatory for one association to "satisfy" the doctrinal complaints of another? Quite so, and Fairfield had received no satisfaction.[36]

A disillusioned Noah Porter reported to Bushnell that another troublesome letter was forthcoming from Fairfield to Hartford Central insisting that Bushnell be brought to judgment. Other ominous rumors of anti-Bushnell activity floated about. The consequence of this *volte face* on the part of the Doctor's enemies was four more wearing years of theological altercation. The turmoil kept ministers, laity, Associations, seminaries, and even denominations in a state of unrest that refused to die down. Looking back over this period years later, Atwater called it a time of conflict "eclipsing all that preceded or followed it in Connecticut, if not in New England and the entire Congregational communion—the Unitarian defection excluded."[37]

Each year, indeed each month, brought its new crisis. Successive annual meetings of the General Association became scenes of battle. Associations likewise were disturbed, or worse. Into this stew of maneuvering and innuendo came a controversial address in 1850 by Edwards A. Park of Andover Seminary on "Theology of the Intellect and That of the Feelings." Although usually considered safely orthodox, Park seemed to side closely enough with Bushnell's emphasis on feelings to send new chills into the hearts of such orthodox leaders as Charles Hodge.[38]

The following year Bushnell's next book, *Christ in Theology*, reached the bookstores. It offered the public the substance of his defense of *God in Christ* before the Hartford Central Association two years previously, although with subsequent changes and additions, as the Doctor acknowledged in his preface that his brethren actually had heard only "about half" of what was in its pages.[39] Essentially it was a better-documented version of his former volume. In preparation for it, he again had laid out for himself an intensive course of reading, this time including the church fathers, Reformation thought (during this period he closely studied John Calvin for the first time),[40] and German and British theologians up to his own day. Investigation of the opinions of others was not a strong point with him, and he told Bartol that work on this book had cost him "five times the labor" of *God in Christ*. Leonard Bacon could hardly believe "the new thoroughness and insight" with which he had extended his researches.[41]

The more Bushnell read, the more he became convinced that he was more orthodox his detractors. Increasingly he felt that he was far from undermining historic Christianity; he was simply engaged in giving "fresh life to the faded and distorted truths of a genuine church antiquity."[42] This led him to urge with renewed conviction the same teachings he had advanced before: release from a lifeless "professorial Christianity" and a return to a Spirit-led Gospel, "the glory, joy, [and] sublimity of a true discipleship." He intended the volume as a contribution to peace and was relieved that it did not draw "the whole bushel of attacks" that had descended on its predecessor. Nonetheless, the new publication did little to pacify the insurgents.[43]

By this time the North Church was starting to feel itself a city besieged and had had its fill of harrassment. Hartford Central had been unmovable in its defense of the Doctor, but who could tell when circumstances might change? In that event Bushnell still could be in danger of trial before the Hartford North Consociation. To escape that Damoclean sword, the North Church, in June 1852, decided to withdraw its Consociation membership.[44] Quite apart from his precarious position, Bushnell considered the Consociation an out-dated vestige of Presbyterianism and did not oppose the move. The initiative, however, was not his, and for some time the break left him and his people newly on the defensive. It stirred all manner of ill will and was denounced by the Consociation as "irregular, uncourteous, and eminently unhappy."[45] Nonetheless, the departure did mean that whatever else might be done against him, there was no judicatory left before whom Bushnell could properly be tried.

As though in retaliation, the anti-Bushnell minority of Hartford Central declared it could bear its "impotent" frustration no longer and left to form its own Hartford Fourth Association. The split left a bad taste with Hartford Central, which saw it as unnecessary and largely the result of Fairfield West's incessant meddling. It grieved Bushnell, not so much because for the first time it institutionalized hostility against him, but because it still further divided the churches and marred the image of religion in the community.[46]

Meanwhile annual meetings of the General Association grew increasingly shrill. At Danbury in 1852, pro-Bushnell Samuel Dutton of New Haven told Edwin Hall to his face that he was guilty of "oppression and cruelty."[47] Before the gathering in Waterbury the next year, Hartford Central was incensed by a crafty, last-minute effort on the part of Fairfield West to deceive it. In a new set of charges, it accused Bushnell of propounding "another Gospel" and declared in blind outrage that it would not accept it "even if it were preached by Apostles or angels from heaven."[48] A serious division of Connecticut Congregationalists seemed imminent. The words of one emotional conservative sounded much like a Southern firebrand threatening secession from the Union:

> We have come to a crisis in the history of the churches of Connecticut. Obscure it as you will, the foundations are touched. The question is whether a man charged with treason against the truth of

Christ and the throne of God can be tried. Pass those resolutions [re-
fusing to condemn Hartford Central], and the answer goes forth to
the world, No! Division is the consequence.[49]

For all the violent feelings, time was running out for Fairfield
West. A reporter for the Hartford *Religious Herald* estimated opinion at Waterbury was running two to one for Bushnell—if not in support of his books, then in support of the man. The Fairfielders fell to
quarreling among themselves, and at the 1854 meeting of the General Association they were given a stinging rebuke. Moreover, their
leaders were growing tired, had died, or had left. Theophilus Smith
died suddenly during a steamer crossing of Lake George; Atwater
joined the faculty at Princeton College; Hall moved to Auburn Theological Seminary; and Hewit left his Congregational parish to serve a
Presbyterian church. Even without "the big four," Fairfield led a few
last desperate efforts. Late in 1854 they were joined by the Pastoral
Union of East Windsor in a final despairing "Protest" to Connecticut
pastors and churches.[50] But all these bids failed; and with more of a
whimper than a bang, organized opposition largely ended. Bushnell
was never brought to trial.

His survival was due to a variety of factors. First among them,
however, has to be the unwavering loyalty of the Hartford Central
majority and the membership of the North Church. Through five
punishing years they both stood by the Doctor. Among his ministerial friends some, notably Goodwin and Chesebrough, were relatively young. Others, especially Noah Porter and Leonard Bacon,
were seasoned churchmen. These respected leaders went as far as
they conscientiously could to preserve the bonds of Christian unity,
announcing repeatedly that they opposed as earnestly as the disaf-
fected members of the Fairfield West coalition the heresies *alleged*
against Bushnell. But that he was guilty of them they adamantly refused to admit. Thus adroitly and patiently they won their long war
mostly by not letting it be lost.

Even they, however, were not wholly successful. Fairfielders and
their associates were denied the official trial they had so aggressively
pursued, yet in devastating measure they achieved what they had set

out to accomplish. By giving national publicity to the supposed horror of Bushnell's errors, they isolated him almost completely from contemporary mainstream Congregationalism. There was truth to what the unfriendly *Puritan Recorder* in Boston told its readers after the General Association meeting at Waterbury: "At the bar of the common sense of the ministry and churches, as a body, he [Bushnell] has been tried, and...the verdict is unanimous. He is now essentially out of the fellowship of the orthodox ministry and churches. And no trial is needful to declare that fact."[51]

CHAPTER 12

Meanwhile, a Christian Pastor

BUSHNELL WAS SENSITIVE AND SOCIABLE, and the isolation hurt. But some of his woe he had to expect, given the boldness of his views. Moreover, as a reformer he, too, was quite capable of fighting—"magnificent fighting," as his disciple and chronicler Theodore Munger once referred to it.[1] A Bushnell who could speak of current New England theology as "decadent and dilapidated"—a foreshadowing of Oliver Wendell Holmes's satire on aging Calvinism in "The Wonderful 'One-Hoss Shay!'"—and disparage Congregational polity as an "ecclesiastical brewing of scandals and heresies, . . . wirepulling, [and] . . . schemes to get power or keep it" could hardly expect to be treated gently by the establishment.[2] As was pointed out now and again by his sympathizers, had he lived in the Middle Ages Bushnell might well have lost his head or been burned at the stake for his supposedly flagrant heterodoxy and his forthright words.[3]

Outbursts on his part, however, were less characteristic than a generally good-tempered restraint. He was sure enough of his ground that he did not need to respond to every sling and arrow that came his way. He was also mightily sustained by his faith and his people. "God is left," he could write believably to a younger friend, "and he is the best public to me." As for his people, he could say with confidence to the same correspondent, "These know me and love me, and I pray that God will enable me to lead them into his green pastures."[4]

Without question the bond between pastor and people was exceptional. The makeup of the congregation, however, was not. Bushnell's parishioners were no spiritual elite somehow drawn out of the nineteenth-century mainstream to appreciate and enable a rare ministry. Along with other Hartford congregations, they *were* the mainstream. In the variety of their backgrounds, and in their responses to *ante bellum* American life, they were typically urbanized, largely middle-class New Englanders. Economically the strongest of them were optimistic and determined. Politically they were involved, but conservative. Many were self-conscious social climbers, at their best paternally kind to the disadvantaged but often unapologetically racist. In religion they groped in the midst of change, but they remained consistently earnest.

Imagine yourself a member of Bushnell's North Church.[5] Each Sunday you find yourself in a well-appointed sanctuary with some 400 other communicants. Scattered among the pews are some seventy-five additional souls who find the requirements of formal membership too demanding but attend with considerable regularity. Young or old, you probably are native to Hartford, or at least to the greater Hartford area. There is about one chance in four that you came to the city from elsewhere in Connecticut or from afar—from Mississippi, Georgia, Maine, Kentucky, or Canada. The chances are about the same that after a certain time with the church you will find it necessary to move to New York or Ohio or possibly as far west as California.

You may be one of the local captains of commerce, ranking *ex officio* among the city fathers. If not a Normand Smith or a Deacon Collins, a Charles Boswell, president of the Farmers and Mechanics Bank; an Austin Dunham, head of a prosperous cotton commission house; or a Christopher Columbus Lyman, an officer of the Hartford Fire Insurance Company who loved music and occasionally wrote a hymn.

If a man, you could as well be an intellectual John P. Brace, who succeeded Catherine Beecher as head of the Hartford Female Seminary and, later, out of a dingy, book-lined little sanctum, edited the Hartford *Courant;* William N. Matson, a lawyer; Asa Newton, a dentist; Ira Ford, an auctioneer. Or you could be bookseller Lucius Hunt, machinist Jason Howe, or jeweler Thomas Steele.

If you are a woman, you live obediently under the shadow of the men, and it hardly occurs to you to expect much visiblity for yourself. But you are still important to the church as part of its majority. If not the very proper Mrs. William Ely, widow of a successful Dutch East Indies merchant, or equally respectable Mary Beecher Perkins, wife of lawyer Thomas C., you might be Margaret K. Jordan, whose husband, Octavius, English-born and Hartford's first fully trained resident architect, designed an elaborate Italian-style mansion for Hartford's renowned arms manufacturer, Samuel Colt.[6] You could be a very different sort, an East Hartford widow, entirely alone, "with no company but Christ," as Mrs. Bushnell found her one afternoon; or a comparably semi-destitute woman, long separated from a merciless husband yet still bearing the marks of his abuse.

You could be a child in that congregation—one of the Doctor's own children, perhaps, scampering home in the middle of a morning service to retrieve her absentminded father's sermon manuscript before the second hymn ended! You could be subdued, mentally handicapped Sophia Root, in need of special support. Or you could be frisky Charles "Charley" H. Clark, in need of no special support at all. Bushnell once rescued young Clark from drowning and so saved him to become another editor of the *Courant,* a director of the Associated Press, and a member of the Yale Corporation. Whether he wanted to or not, Charley always went to church. In his own words:

> Sundays I went regularly, because I was taken, to the Old North Church, where I counted the tassles on the pulpit cushion, thirty-nine of them there were—the thirty-nine articles of the Church as far as I knew any—studied the forms and the faces of the deacons, who presented some very interesting contrasts in American citizenship, wondered at the attire of certain old-school gentlemen among them who persisted in wearing swallow-tail coats, furtively calculated the different angles at which several mouths in the choir gave forth their sweetest notes, and went home as no doubt children do today, with impressions of various things that were not all in the sermon.[7]

In the face of this congregation, Bushnell did at least two things unusually well. For one, people appreciated his prayers. He knew of prayer firsthand in his personal life and took spontaneous praying, as distinct from saying set prayers, so seriously that he even objected to the use of the Lord's Prayer in public worship.[8] Though doubtless longer than we would find comfortable, his pastoral prayers had an authenticity that lifted the faith of his congregation. "Dr. B. is the only minister I know who prays," a worshiper once was heard to say. "Others tell God their creeds and what they know. He pleads with God for what he wants and needs."[9] In 1861, after he had been banished for fifteen years from the pulpit of the South Congregational Church of Hartford, Edwin Pond Parker, newly arrived as minister, invited him back. Parker was then young and progressive, but he was also impressed by the older man. "The praying was as wonderful as the preaching," he recalled.[10]

The other outstanding feature of any service Bushnell led was the "wonderful" preaching. It is difficult, and usually fruitless, to compare the greatness of Christian preachers. But, as in other professions, a few are distinguished by an edge of excellence that sets them apart. In the Victorian age Henry Ward Beecher and Phillips Brooks had that edge among American ministers, as did Frederick W. Robertson, Charles Spurgeon, and Frederick D. Maurice in England. And Bushnell had it. There is no need to claim he excelled these other pulpiteers. What is clear is that his contemporaries did not hesitate to speak of him as their equal.[11] To the Scottish biblical scholar George Adam Smith, Bushnell was a preacher's preacher in the same way Edmund Spenser had been a poet's poet.[12] In Hartford it was said that Bushnell had made the pulpit of the North Church "one of the thrones of the world,"[13] and a *New York Tribune* critic surveying the century's preaching scene ranked Bushnell's discourse "Every Man's Life a Plan of God" as one of the three most notable sermons of the age.[14]

In the 1930s Bushnell enthusiast Dean Charles R. Brown of Yale still found the Doctor's sermons "alive to their finger tips." Today it is not always possible to say so much. Yet even now attentive minds can recapture some of the power they had when first preached, and selections from his discourses continue to be published.[15]

Their appeal frequently starts with the title. Bushnell had a way with these designations, keeping them arresting and yet tasteful and using them to summarize the entire content of what followed: "Living to God in Small Things," "Spiritual Things the Only Solid," "Christ Waiting to Find Room," or "A Great Life Begins Early." He liked to choose subjects that teased the imagination of his biblically literate listeners and at first blush seemed implausible. What could he possibly do with a sermon on "Christ Asleep," for instance, or "The Dignity of Human Nature Shown from Its Ruins" or "Loving God Is But Letting God Love Us" or "The Small Saints That Are No Saints"? A visitor to Hartford met Bushnell on the sidewalk of a Monday morning: "Doctor," he asked him quizzically, "what did you preach about yesterday?" The confident reply came, "I preached a sermon to show that we know more of the future than we do of the past," almost certainly referring to his "Unconscious Prophecy," even now a mind-stretching discourse with a moving climax."[16]

He was equally effective with texts. "Dr. Bushnell could preach more of a sermon in the selection of a text," a businessman once remarked, "than any ordinary minister could in half a day's discourse."[17] He preached the main biblical themes, but he also lighted on passages few others would think of using. When he was looking for a text for his pre-Freudian sermon on "Unconscious Influence," which he had delivered with such good effect in London and at home, he turned to a plain half-sentence in John's resurrection account of the empty tomb, "Then went in also that other disciple."[18] The point was that both Peter and John ran pell-mell to the sepulcher, John arriving first. Yet before a hesitant John would enter the tomb, he needed the bolder, unwitting example of Peter, who passed by him and dashed in ahead. Neither one, as Bushnell pointed out, was aware that he was exerting influence or being affected by it. Not many would think of drawing on so uncommon and, on the surface, unpromising a text for such a purpose.[19]

He was imaginative, too, in matching texts with current public issues. More than once before the Civil War, Hartford went through financial depressions that alarmed and discouraged the business community. In the mid-1840s, when one of these ebb tides was dragging down the economy, certain leaders thought of obtaining new waterpower by tapping the Connecticut River north of the city and bringing it down by a canal along the west bank. The idea intrigued

Bushnell's engineering and biblical mind. Turning to Scripture, he discovered an episode in 2 Chronicles in which a threatened King Hezekiah of Judah "stopped the upper watercourse of Gihon, and brought it straight down to the west side of the city of David."[20] The plan never was adopted, but Bushnell applied the parallel in an encouraging Sunday evening discourse on "Prosperity Our Duty." He not only explored the scheme, but drawing on Hezekiah's experience he threw out practical and spiritual challenges to the city to create a new and different kind of economic future for itself.[21]

Since Bushnell hammered out much of his theology in the North Church pulpit, his week-in, week-out Sunday messages reflected the same basic viewpoints as his lectures and books. In a lyceum-like manner, more eloquent than the old Puritan plain style and less emotional than that of the revivalists,[22] he preached a majestic, omnipotent God who was also closer and kinder than the Deity of current New England orthodoxy. In a sermon on the "Gentleness of God," he portrayed a Creator who always has ultimate power but "lays gentle siege" to us, working by indirection and leaving us room to respond to his will freely according to our own gifts.[23]

He also preached of a humanity in critical need of a saving Christ. Bushnell's liberal image has at times obscured his depiction of our human lot as radically conditioned by sin. It was one of his major differences with the Unitarians. In his thinking, sinfulness was a kind of "wild" disorder, a "lost inspiration." We strangely, willfully cut ourselves off from God and turn away from reality. Not without sympathy he concluded that "we are down under evil," and without help, "we are in it forever."[24]

The only sufficient "help" was God's grace in Christ. But this did not rule out all human initiative. From behind those tassels on the pulpit cushion, the Doctor told his people they could and should "win the first inch" of their own salvation. The essential power, however, was still of God. A self-reliant Emerson, pointing to a neutral God, could claim that "nothing can bring you peace but yourself."[25] Unitarians could put their trust in evolving human goodness, and the spirit of the times could exult in automatic progress, religion or no. But in the Gospel according to Bushnell, this was largely illusion. The sailor must set his own sail and the farmer must sow his own seed, but the wind and the harvest are of God, as is the supreme gift of new life in Christ.[26]

That new life, he announced, was available to all regardless of age, talent, or condition. He could speak of the change from his own immediate knowledge. In Christ everything was different. "Life proceeds from a new center," he assured his flock. "The Bible is a new book" because now there is the light of God by which to read it. "Duties are new" because faith "has changed all the relations of time and the aims of life." The world itself appears "in new beauty and joy to the mind" because now it is seen as the very symbol of the living God. Here Bushnell in his century was speaking the same language that Jonathan Edwards, with his "new sense" of things, had spoken a century before.[27]

All this was personal gospel. Did anything socially prophetic come from the North Church desk? Bushnell warmly shared many of the commercial dreams of the merchant princes in his congregation. As he put it in one of his later sermons, it was possible to be "a Christian in trade."[28] All the same, he did not let his leading men forget where the priorities lay. Ultimately gold was a "toy." In the light of eternity, big bank accounts were "husks" and the security of "ledgers and stocks" a mirage. "O thou Prince of Life!" he prayed sermonically one Sunday, "come in Thy great salvation to these blinded and lostmen, and lay thy piercing question to their ear, 'What shall it profit a man to gain the whole world and lose his own soul?'"[29]

He similarly confronted fastidious moral complacency. In a forceful sermon on "Respectable Sin," he took his people to task for knowing little of the harsh world just outside the church doors, where raw, *un*respectable sin ran rife. What would happen, he urged his people to imagine, if a real cross-section of Hartford humanity came to church some Sunday? What would happen if not only the regular members, but pickpockets and gamblers should turn up in the pews; if the oaths of drunks were to be heard in the vestibule, "and their hungry, shivering children were crying at the door for bread"—"in a word, if actual life were here?" To Bushnell, as to many in his day, such derelicts were usually the victims of their own mistakes, and he did not stress the effects of social injustice. Still, it was strong medicine for a fashionable congregation to be told that the Christ of the New Testament found the virtuous pretensions of untroubled, respectable churchgoers as bad, if not worse, than the faults of the unrespectable rabble.[30]

Bushnell loved to preach. "I could go on to the world's end, or to mine," he exclaimed in the early 1860s, "for there is nothing I so much delight in as preaching."[31] No matter how zealously gifted, however, no minister can reach everyone, nor could he. There were those who found him too intellectual or too long or theologically irritating. Some Sundays his fountain flow of ideas would run away with him, and he would overplay his argument. A sermon on "The Employments of Heaven" so dramatized the ongoing activity of eternal life that one tired working woman commented, "Well, if heaven is such a place for work, I don't care to go there. I hoped I should rest."[32]

Nonetheless, the influence of his preaching was immense. Nowhere was it more striking than with young men. When he was a Yale undergraduate, Charles L. Brace reported to his father that because of Bushnell's "originality, his liberality and his independence," the students liked him "to distraction." Timothy Dwight the younger, president of Yale at the turn of the century, recalled from his days as a student, and later as a tutor, that Bushnell was the most popular of all visiting ministers, not excluding the most famous.[33]

In Hartford, too, he had a strong following of young people. Many of those who frequented the North Church came from favored backgrounds with doors of opportunity open to them to make a difference in American society. Such lives Bushnell's preaching and friendship helped shape permanently, with consequences that came to be felt nationwide. Frederick L. Olmsted took from the North Church and his companionship with the Doctor convictions about organic community, aesthetic values, and a lively interest in the emerging American city. They contributed materially to his achievements in landscape architecture, evidence of which is still to be seen from Central Park in New York City, to university campuses in California.[34] Charley Clark expressed his pastor's teachings on citizenship and literary integrity in a lifetime of journalism that had lasting importance. Charles Brace carried the message of the Doctor's "Unconscious Influence" and his teachings on children into the streets of New York City, where he pioneered work with juvenile delinquents and helped found the Children's Aid Society. Henry Clay Trumbull translated Bushnell's theology into service as a Christian educator, editor, and organizer, touching the lives of millions.[35] Bushnell's liberal preaching was also a major factor behind the unconventional, forty-year Elmira, New York, pastorate of Thomas K. Beecher, "Father Tom," as he was known, the most original of Lyman Beecher's many minister sons.[36]

So, too, people from everyday walks of the city's life were grateful for the stimulus and support of his words. One Sunday Bushnell took up Jesus' saying in Matthew that "He that is not with me is against me."[37] One hearer exclaimed that the sermon "went through us like grapeshot." Sometimes parishioners could hardly contain their enthusiasm. "You ought to have been at our church yesterday!" a merchant frequently burst out as he entered his place of business on Monday mornings. "You would have heard one of the greatest sermons ever preached." Whereupon he would rehearse the outline to his startled partners and clerks, adding his own utilitarian peroration. "Now, let's do a big week's work!"[38]

To their parents' delight, even children could find interest in what he had to say. Julia Chester, of New Haven, later the wife of Episcopal bishop Ozi W. Whitaker of Pennsylvania, recalled a childhood visit to Hartford during which she went to the North Church. She expected to be bored, as she usually was by adult sermons. Instead she carried away a positive memory of the minister and his message that she never forgot.[39]

In the public eye as much as he was, Bushnell was bound to be compared with his greatest pulpit rival, the hugely popular Henry Ward Beecher in Brooklyn. According to Leonard Bacon's droll saying, the United States at midcentury was composed largely of "saints, sinners, and Beechers,"[40] and for fifty years Lyman Beecher and his multitudinous children were involved with Bushnell and his family. As Beechers did on most subjects, they had pronounced opinions about their Hartford friend. A veteran of earlier theological wars, Lyman himself was marginally implicated in helping to strategize the Doctor's battles. When in Hartford, he would stop by to see Bushnell (at one sensitive point in "*profound*" secrecy) or to hear him preach.[41]

Catherine, the eldest of his offspring, once held up Bushnell as a model of effective ministry—ironically during the same early Hartford period when Bushnell still was plagued by self-doubt. Later she partially agreed with his theories of domesticity and the rearing of children and, like him, opposed suffrage for women. Although not during her administration, Bushnell served for many years as a trustee of the Hartford Female Seminary Catherine had founded. But in her 1857 *Common Sense Applied to Religion,* she turned her anti-clerical sharp stick on her father, as she did on some of her brothers.[42]

Edward Beecher, from the day he helped discipline Bushnell as a Yale undergraduate, was highly critical of him, especially as an orthodox Congregational preacher and editor in Boston.[43] Harriet was on generally friendly terms, and Bushnell was impressed by *Uncle Tom's Cabin.* Although she shared cautiously in his religious liberalism, she later was more than unhappy with his negative views on women and the vote.[44] More conventional Mary Beecher had been content to stay home many Sundays until she and her husband joined the North Church in 1849. Thereafter she counted it "a real loss" to miss a single sermon and remained Bushnell's loyal parishioner.[45] Erratic Isabella, married to John Hooker, apparently liked Bushnell's approach to Christian nurture (she let the Perkinses take the Hooker children to the North Church), but she could not abide his opposition to women's suffrage.[46] Off-beat Thomas was the Doctor's devoted disciple. As he wrote Harriet in 1848, he worried that the strains of doctrinal controversy would overwhelm the Doctor's essentially pastoral mission. All the same he was convinced that his Hartford friend "has got hold of the life of religion." In 1851 Bushnell preached Tom Beecher's ordination sermon in Williamsburg, just across the East River from New York, when an unreliable Henry let him down at the last minute and left him "in an abominable corner."[47]

Henry Ward Beecher was eleven years Bushnell's junior and seems to have drawn some help from *Christian Nurture* during the formative stages of his ministry, when he was still struggling to free himself from the severity of his father's type of Calvinism. His younger brother, Thomas, further quickened Henry's interest in the Doctor. He did not always share Thomas's devotion to Bushnell, nor was he entirely pleased to be compared with his senior colleague from Hartford;[48] but in 1847 Henry wanted Bushnell to be part of his installation service at Plymouth Church. Bushnell went to Brooklyn, heard his former Yale pedagogue, Edward Beecher, preach the installation sermon, and offered the prayer that concluded the solemnities.[49]

The two were similar, and yet at the same time vastly different, personalities. Both men were convinced of the supreme importance of Christian ministry, and once settled they were happy in the profession. Beecher exuded tact and charm and moved easily among strangers of both sexes. Especially with people he did not know, Bushnell was more reserved. Impatient with most theologizing, Beecher's chief interest was in applying Christian truth. Bushnell was primarily concerned with discovering and reformulating it. Both men gave the heart priority over the head in religion, but Beecher was more comfortable sharing his experience than was his Hartford colleague. Increasingly Beecher was accepting of personal wealth and loved the feel of uncut gems loose in his pocket. Although he was not indifferent to money, such a desire would scarcely have entered the mind of a frugal Horace Bushnell.[50]

As they were comparable, and yet different men, so also as preachers they were alike, yet different. Soon after Beecher's arrival in Brooklyn, a new admirer of his preaching wrote him that it made him "laugh" to "hear *you* likened to Bushnell! to whom I venture to intimate a suspicion that you are just the moral (and of course intellectual) *antipodes*—As thus: he is a man who thinks head-foremost—you are a man who think[s] heart-foremost."[51]

There was truth to the contrast. Beecher was emotional, even theatrical, as he rode his "chariot of fire." Bushnell was intellectual and steady. Beecher had success with revivals; Bushnell seldom—if ever—did. Yet "antipodes" was too strong a word. There was thought in Beecher's popular sermons, and in Bushnell's more solid discourses there was warmth and comfort. Both men preached a modified Calvinism, starting from the same traditional baseline of a sinful humanity in need of Christ, and both moved out from this into a new optimism toward individuals and society. Unlike their Puritan forebears who stood ten feet above criticism in their high pulpits, Beecher used no pulpit, and Bushnell would stoop down from his to identify more closely with the struggling pilgrimages and problems of his people. He was a good listener and knew his parishioners well. "My friends," he would say, while wrestling with some weighty theme, "let me come a degree nearer to you now, and lay the question side by side with your experience."[52]

Such affinities made it possible for each man to find strong points in the other. Although Beecher missed in Bushnell a certain "outward sympathy" to match his inward convictions, he was glad to acknowledge that he "lives toward God, toward truth, toward the good, the beautiful, the perfect."[53] Likewise, Bushnell faulted Beecher for lack of firm intellectual foundations, but willingly acknowledged that he was a master preacher. When visiting family in New York, the Doctor more than once boarded one of the crowded Brooklyn ferries of a Sunday morning and went to hear the golden-tongued orator of Plymouth Church. After one such visit he wrote Mary that he had heard one of Beecher's best. In his philosophy, Bushnell said, Beecher was "unspeakably crude and naturalistic;" but Bushnell was "greatly moved" nonetheless and felt the close "was eloquent enough to be a sermon by itself."[54]

In his ministry Bushnell did one thing Beecher explicitly told his people they could not expect: he made pastoral calls.[55] These calls symbolized the close, informal ties he developed over the years with his parishioners outside the pulpit. As demands on his time mounted, he had difficulty living up to his early intentions to make regular visits, but he kept at it. One day it would be a casual stopping by; he would "swing that hospitable, easy gate," as he told one parishioner he liked to do, "and drop in at almost any hour with your cheery and lively circle, and then be off."[56] Another day it would be to respond to an urgent crisis such as might interrupt him at any time. "I was called off suddenly from dinner," he wrote his brother George in 1851, explaining a delay in correspondence but without saying whether the contingency was a death or a lesser emergency.[57]

Along with routine contacts, Bushnell had a way of being present where and when need was greatest. A man who was poor and blind heard a knock on his door one afternoon, and when he opened it the Doctor was there. Autumn chill was coming on, and in a day well before sophisticated social workers the lonely man had waited a long time for someone to help him put together a stove that lay disassembled on his floor. In addition to visiting with him, Bushnell handily set up the stove, lighted a fire, and left the man warmed in body and cheered in spirit.[58]

What the Doctor could not always manage for every household, he made a point of doing for as many shut-ins as he could. Thomas Winship, a deaf shoemaker, had an invalid daughter, Mary. When he was not away, the Doctor came faithfully on Monday mornings to see her. "It did not seem to me possible," her father remembered, "for any man to manifest more tender sympathy and care for her spiritual interests than he did." With the same fidelity he was in the habit of calling on another invalid who was terminally ill. A day or two before she died, she was too weak to get herself out of bed. She insisted, nonetheless, on being carried to the chair in which she customarily received him. She "*knew* he would come," and he did.[59]

As resourceful pastors do, he devised myriad ways of his own to keep in touch. Often he was on the streets talking with people at random. About as often he was in and out of business offices, and there was always his haunting of bookstores. These last were like cracker-barrel gathering places where he encountered friends and strangers, "chatting...with all sorts of people," as one of his colleagues remembered, "upon all sorts of subjects—the news of the day, the doings of public men, the affairs of the city...politics, farming, mechanics, inventions, books, or whatever else might turn up."[60]

In a mode of ministry with a modern feel to it, he devoted an evening a week to personal counseling (though not called by that name), making himself available at the church to anyone who might wish to come in. Younger men in particular regularly availed themselves of these hours when they could converse privately with their pastor.

One would come troubled by an unruly temper; another had been reached by a sermon and wanted to explore its implications further. A number came with problems of Christian ethics in business, and Bushnell would help them think them through.[61]

On occasion he would ask someone to visit him at his house for further talk. It could happen, however, that he would absentmindedly forget he had issued the invitation. One young hopeful, after being introduced to the great man for the first time, was encouraged in all sincerity to come to his home at a later date to pursue the acquaintance. But when he arrived on the appointed day, already nervous about the interview, he found Bushnell so absorbed in work that when interrupted he simply stared at the trembling youth, his hair all a-bristle, and blurted out, "Who are you?" His visitor was so unnerved at this unaccountable reception that he scarcely could speak his own name. Yet once Bushnell had had a moment to recollect, his original cordiality returned, and soon he was conversing with the young man before a cheerful fire in so easy a way that a lasting friendship was born.[62]

When he was away from Hartford he did pastoral work by correspondence. A woman broke her arm and feared it was a penalty laid on her by God. Bushnell refused to let her wallow in that kind of guilt and wrote to reassure her that the care of the Eternal for her was as close and strong as ever.[63] Early in 1849, when controversy was boiling around him, he took time to send a letter of sympathy to a friend bereaved of her sister. He could not hope to take away the pain of her loss, he told her, "but I can at least signify my willingness to add some expression of sympathy or consolation that will assist you to bear it."[64]

In March 1855, his long-time friend Thomas Day, who had been instrumental in bringing him to Hartford, died while Bushnell was out of the country. Bushnell wrote his widow that there was "no privation so total as that which an aged love is compelled to mourn when its object is taken away." Then with a rigor and expectation modern faith cannot always summon, he suggested her own days must be numbered and urged her to press forward in trust, "looking for and hasting the day of your [own] release.... With much love," he signed himself, "I am yours in Jesus Christ."[65]

It was one sign of the affection in which the Doctor came to be held that letters like these were highly prized. An area resident once recalled that "a line from Dr. Bushnell...was so precious as to be passed from hand to hand until worn out; or if of too confidential a nature for that, was turned down and extracts read."[66] Very possibly his personal letters reached some persons at a deeper level than did his sermons and books. If so, it was another measure of his own "unconscious influence."

Such was the pastoral relationship that withstood the assaults of five years of bruising dogmatic encounter. While controversy still raged in May 1853, Bushnell completed twenty years with his North Church constituency. The occasion gave him an ideal opportunity to review his Hartford experience and to express gratitude to his people for their unflagging support.

His "Commemorative Discourse" was in part a sentimental journey, but not so nostalgic that he was not honest about his parishioners and about himself. "It would be too much to say that I have seen nothing in you to reprove or blame," he told them. Had such been the case, "there would have been nothing here for me to do." At the same time he acknowledged his own uncertain beginnings and the risky crises in which he had involved them, politically and theologically. Yet in sum he rejoiced in the special "cementing" of ties that had come out of their mutual travail, concluding that "no pastor was ever happier in his relations to his people or had ever greater reasons to thank God always upon every remembrance of their patience with him and their fellowship with him in his official burdens."[67]

It was important for Bushnell's own self-assurance to be able to make so positive a summing up. At that moment it was also important for his flock to hear him give it. In the spring of 1853 the battles were far from over, and there were gaping wounds all around. In voting to have the discourse circulated in print, the church meeting hoped it would not merely be of significance to posterity, but help more immediately to remove "the unfavorable impressions which have so extensively obtained respecting both him [Bushnell] and ourselves."[68]

That was as close as the inbred Puritan reserve of the North Church members could come to admitting they needed a renewed good feeling about themselves. As the encourager he nearly always was, Bushnell was able to rekindle that confidence, and with little distortion of the truth. In simple fact, the experience of the congregation in a stressful time, and Bushnell's pastoral connection with it, had by any standards been historic.

CHAPTER 13

Burning Issues, Hazardous Journeys

BUSHNELL'S DAYS AS A FULL-TIME journalist ended with his year in New York. Likewise, his interest in practicing law died with the revival of 1831. Yet he never lost interest in public affairs; he followed political developments closely, read the newspapers hungrily, and expressed his own opinions freely.

Increasingly, however, there was added to his secular concerns a vigorous spiritual emphasis. He was convinced that even in an America dedicated to the separation of church and state, society ultimately would be shaped by religion, as every other society had been.[1] No aspiring politician, such as he once dreamed of being, could have delivered a more ringing critique of the presidential campaigns of 1840 and 1844 than he did in his sermons on "American Politics" and "Politics Under the Law of God." When he spoke out in this way, however, he did so not merely as a political analyst. He was speaking without apology as a Christian prophet, trying to trace the purposes of God as well as the designs of human striving.

His two political sermons, and to an extent his letters from Europe on Oregon and those to the Pope, had stirred ripples of general interest. But the document that first brought him considerable national attention as a social critic was a discourse prepared for the American Home Missionary Society (Congregational) in the spring of 1847, to which he attached the striking title "Barbarism the First Danger."[2] It had to do with the rapidly accelerating settlement of the West and disturbing trends there that seemed to him to menace the degree of Christian civilization the country had thus far achieved.

When northern Protestants in this era thought of the opening of the West, they mingled pride with anxiety. For many there was the dream of a vast Christian commonwealth stretching from the Atlantic to the Pacific. It held out the promise of a powerful, free, benevolent realm the like of which the world had never seen. Yet it might not happen. The lack of binding traditions, the wild mobility of frontier populations, and the chaotic fragmentation of the churches into strange new denominations made many others wonder whether, after all, the Union experiment could succeed.[3] Aggravating these underlying fears was concern over the spread of slavery and, preeminently, over what seemed the threat of a rapidly growing Roman Catholicism.

At the moment Bushnell was preparing his discourse, foreign immigration was reaching the highest level in proportion to population in U.S. history.[4] This wave of newcomers included hundreds of thousands of Catholic believers. From these and other sources, the American Roman Catholic hierarchy had continued to gather such strength, in both the East and West, that by 1866 it could assemble in Baltimore the largest formal conciliary body summoned by Rome since the famous sixteenth-century Council of Trent.[5]

A Bushnell who once wanted to be an Ohio lawyer could not easily forget the West. In 1835, in his first published sermon, "Crisis of the Church," he joined the alarmists in citing the rapid Roman expansion across the Alleghenies. He did more than preach. That same year a group of Hartford merchants and religious leaders set up a secret organization cryptically called L.U.P.O. (Look Upward, Press Onward). The purpose of the Society was to offset Roman Catholic growth on the frontier, especially among German immigrants. It chose for its traveling agent Thomas H. Gallaudet, Hartford's pioneer educator of the deaf. Although perhaps not a prime mover, Bushnell was involved in this clandestine effort along with Deacon Seth Terry and likely other North Church members. Even select Hartford "ladies" were quietly clued in and made donations. Personally Bushnell had little or no money to offer. But he could give advice. When the Society brought over two young German missionaries from Basel, Switzerland, in the spring of 1836, he was among those who conferred with them during their visit of several months in Hart-

ford, helping to brief them (presumably with the aid of an interpreter) on American customs and New England theology before they
left for St. Louis.[6]

Soon the Doctor was taking part in another Protestant initiative to
evangelize and educate the frontier. He became a founding director
of the Society for the Promotion of Collegiate and Theological Education at the West, a determined Congregational agency opened in
1843 and headquartered in New York City. As an offset to the educational thrust of "the crafty Jesuit," it was dedicated to giving financial aid to such embryonic Protestant colleges as Beloit, Illinois,
Wabash, and Marietta, as well as Lane Seminary in Cincinnati. Later
it extended its outreach to schools in Iowa, Oregon, and California.

In part the idea of this influential Society had been hatched between Bushnell's Yale classmate Theron Baldwin, who initiated the
concept, and Edward Beecher while they bumped along on the dusty
stage from Farmington to Hartford during the summer of 1842.
Once in Hartford the two immediately conferred with Bushnell on
the scheme, "and he approved," as did Bacon and other ministers in
New Haven.[7] From then on Bushnell encouraged the cause, educating
his people from the pulpit as to its importance and taking up annual
collections for it. His deacon, Amos Collins, and many of his Yale
contemporaries were in the Society's leadership, and one would have
expected this connection to have been a cordial and productive relationship.

Yet it was not always so. Bushnell's theology became an irritant,
and he could be contrary in matters of policy. Opposing the Society
board's consensus, he favored aid for existing institutions, such as
Oberlin or Western Reserve, with only limited support for additional
new ones. He also felt that primary and secondary schools should
have priority over more colleges. Thus by 1853, Julian M.
Sturtevant, president of Illinois College, was saying Bushnell was "an
unsafe man," and Baldwin, the Society's able executive, later known
as "the father of western colleges," was admitting that the Doctor's
influence had been "against real progress." He thought of dropping
him from the board, but stayed his hand when he recalled the burden
of doctrinal controversy then weighing down his friend. Such a move

at that moment, he decided, would look "a little like persecution."[8]

Administratively Bushnell might have his difficult moments; nonetheless, he could still act as an eloquent spokesman. By 1847 his anxiety had gone deeper than conventional anti-papacy. Historically, he pointed out, wilderness frontiers were places where the restraints of home were easily discarded, and communal as well as personal disciplines of education, duty, and faith readily forgotten. Such laxity, he predicted, could foster a ruinous decline in the whole health of the country. Secondarily, such "social confusion" might create fertile soil for a superstitious Catholicism. But that was not the main threat. "Our first danger is barbarism," he warned. "Romanism next."[9]

True to that thesis, his discourse was not at heart an anti-Catholic diatribe. Housed under the ample roof of Rome, he generously stressed, "we know are gathered many great and accomplished men, and many nations farther advanced, in some respects, than we." For the work of laying solid Christian foundations in the untamed West, he would not shut out high-minded Catholics. Somewhat patronizingly, perhaps, he nonetheless he urged an inclusive ecumenical partnership, open "even to the Romanists themselves, when we clearly find the spirit of Jesus in their life."[10]

His approach thus defined, he attacked his chief target: a wild, religionless reversion to primitive behavior that ruthlessly squandered natural resources, kept company with slavery, and generated such unconscionable conflicts as the Mexican War. Negatively, he argued, slavery and its offspring, war, must be ended and the roughness of politics tempered. Positively, education needed to be furthered, and lines of communication, meaning railroads and telegraph wires, must be sent "spinning into the wilderness" to bring the West into closer touch with more stable and cultivated sections of the country.

Undergirding all these efforts, in his view, must be the dissemination of an intelligent, living faith. He knew of no society anywhere that had been able to sustain itself on human resources alone. "Religion," he urged with emphasis, "is the only prop on which we can lean with any confidence." Without overlooking the importance of overseas missions, he issued a call for home missionaries to spread themselves everywhere over the West and save the nation from becoming "a frustrated and broken experiment." Let this be done, Bushnell preached, and barbarism would fail. In its place the wilderness would "bud and blossom as the rose." The country would be filled with "a manly and happy race of people," united by "the bands of a complete Christian commonwealth" spanning the continent.[11]

It was a powerful speech. It was also significant. With its sweeping survey of history, its good sense and uncommon breadth of spirit, it illustrated the tension between millennial hope and acute anxiety that marked the period as it tried to foresee the American future.[12] Bushnell dealt vigorously with both views but characteristically tipped his balance toward optimism. In May and June he repeated the address to major audiences in Brooklyn, New York City, Worcester, Boston, and elsewhere. And as it circulated in print, it unquestionably gave added impetus to frontier evangelism and education.

When he delivered this address in Boston's Park Street Church on "Brimstone Corner," he not only made a strong impression, but he reaped an unanticipated personal reward. It was here that he first met Cyrus A. Bartol, who, as we have seen, became in many ways his most intimate ministerial friend.

An elfish little native of Maine, Bartol had graduated from Bowdoin in 1832 and three years later from the Harvard Divinity School. After a pastorate in Cincinnati, he came to the West Church in Boston to assist the venerable Charles Lowell, father of the poet James Russell Lowell. In time he succeeded him and for half a century was a leader of Unitarian and literary thought in the city. His Chestnut Street home was frequented by the Transcendentalist circle led by Emerson, Margaret Fuller, and George Ripley. As a preacher he was, like Bushnell, original and imaginative. His parishioners said his mind "was like a mint, continually striking off bright coins of thought and speech."[13]

From their first meeting, the two differing preachers constantly conversed and corresponded and delighted in the association. An expansive Bartol once wrote he had been "living on Bushnell" and found his company "like being in a vineyard or grapery with no possibility of eating the whole of the luscious crop." Since he, even more than Bushnell, also was close to Henry W. Bellows in New York, a triangular friendship emerged that kept Bushnell in touch with trends in Unitarian thinking.[14]

Bushnell found time to make a long sequence of public addresses of the "Barbarism" type. He was so productive that he won the reputation of having delivered more orations and occasional discourses than any clergyman in New England.[15]

Before Christmas 1849, he spoke to the New England Society of New York, which met annually to mark the comfortless landing of the Pilgrims in 1620 with a dinner and an address. At first he called his talk simply "The Fathers of New England," but he later changed the title to "The Founders Great in Their Unconsciousness."[16] As the revised heading indicates, he returned to his "unconscious influence" motif, this time projecting it on a national rather than merely personal scale. According to the Doctor, the "unconsciousness" of the founding fathers consisted of the unknowing way they laid the groundwork for future democratic institutions, even though they themselves were in no modern sense democrats. They did it by encouraging education, mutual trust, individual self-discipline, and loyalty to law above princes. They succeeded, Bushnell felt, not by consciously setting out to give the world new forms of statecraft, but by everywhere putting religion and these related disciplines first and, despite risks, letting forms of government follow from what God and "high constructive instinct" might direct.

The flow of speeches went on. With full official fanfare, including a special train from Hartford for Governor Thomas H. Seymour and members of the legislature, the State Normal School was opened in June 1851 in the neighboring village of New Britain. Henry Barnard was the first featured speaker. After a sumptuous dinner, Bushnell followed with a "Speech for Connecticut," an historical "estimate" of the state. He could size up its story in a single descriptive line: "independent, as not knowing how to be otherwise."[17] Two months later he returned to his native Litchfield County for its centennial celebration. Among the leading orators, Samuel Church, also a native son and at the time chief justice of the state, covered the usual type of historic highlights in an address so long it required an intermission.[18] By contrast, Bushnell went behind Church's scenes of prominence and focused on the common people as he remembered them from his boy-hood—a notable early example of social history. He called his address "The Age of Homespun," after the type of domestically woven clothing then in general use. To him the essential sources of a great society were not "the Doctors of Divinity, the Generals, the Judges, the Honorables, the Governors, or even...the village notables called Esquires." The true heroes were "the sturdy kings of Home-spun" and "the good housewives that made coats...for their children's bodies, and lined their memory with catechism." With these, and with the artisans, teachers, and unsung church leaders, lay the real secret of community achievement.[19]

Not only history, but current public issues proved quite irresistible to him. One sensitive matter was the increasing presence of Roman Catholic children in the nation's public schools, accompanied by a growing Catholic demand for a share of tax revenue for their own parochial schools. Protestant resistance to these efforts became so violent that in New York City in 1842 they had engaged Romanists in open street combat. The future poet, Walt Whitman, then a Manhattan editor, had attacked Catholic bishop John Hughes as "a hypocritical scoundrel" and his followers as "bands of filthy wretches."[20]

The Catholic population of Connecticut also had skyrocketed. From some 700 communicants in 1835, the diocese of Hartford (covering Rhode Island as well as Connecticut) had grown to tens of thousands by 1853. As Catholic pressure on the school issue mounted, the Protestant press in Hartford charged Romanists with "a systematic plan...to break down the Common School System of this country."[21]

Bushnell responded to this tension in a Fast Day sermon in March 1853 on "The Common Schools: A Discourse on the Modifications Demanded by the Roman Catholics."[22] It was an eleventh-hour attempt to help mediate the dispute, at least locally. He could not conceive of education without religion. But he was also a passionate defender of "our beautiful system of common schools" as basic to all that was good in republican America. For *either* Catholics or Protestants to break away from the practice of public education was not only un-American, but "a bitter cruelty to the children," distorting normal peer relationships and curtailing their training for citizenship.

Again his approach was more irenic than polemic. The solution he offered was for Protestants to recognize that anything like Puritan common schools, or even purely Protestant common schools, were things of the past in a pluralistic society, but to see that still "we can have common schools." He acknowledged Catholics had causes for complaint and recommended enough flexibility on the part of the Protestant majority to make room for children of all Christian bodies. He favored allowing use of the Douai as well as the King James version of the Bible; working out a selection of Scripture passages acceptable to all parties; preparing a booklet of Christian morality to be taught without doctrinal bias; and setting fixed hours during the schoolday for release-time religious instruction.

He conceded that it might be too late for compromise to have much of a chance, but he appealed to the Protestant community to make a last-ditch effort to meet Catholic objections and to find a way "to set them [the children] together under Christ, as his common flock."[23] His proposals failed, and though without public funding, parochial schools already started by the Sisters of Mercy continued to go forward.

From public education he returned to the most volatile problem of all, Southern slavery. No observer of events in the 1840s and 1850s could avoid this topic for long, and Bushnell has been faulted for seeming, at least, to try. After the heated repercussions in his parish over the Henry Clay sermon of 1844, so the theory goes, he sidelined himself for a decade.[24] To the extent that he did, allowances must be made for his year-long absence in Europe and for his exhausting involvement in controversy over *Christian Nurture* and, immediately afterward, *God in Christ*.

Even so, he was not altogether quiet. His "Barbarism" address, repeated many times, contained pages of merciless assault on the "peculiar institution" of the South. "A more withering attack upon slavery I think I never met with," one listener was moved to comment.[25] He also continued to express himself freely through private channels. His parishioner, James Dixon, a conservative Whig congressman from Hartford in the late 1840s, supplied the Doctor with a steady stream of government documents and speeches. When Dixon spoke out in favor of the ill-fated Wilmot Proviso that sought to exclude slavery from territory acquired from Mexico, Bushnell was delighted. He read Dixon's remarks aloud to Mrs. Bushnell at breakfast and wrote Dixon to applaud his resistance to Southern pressure on "this dismal fact of slavery."[26] He was beside himself with anger over the "abominable" Compromise of 1850 and declared he would never abide by the Fugitive Slave Law. He told Bartol that any compliance with that hateful provision would amount to "damning sin."[27]

Whatever excess public silence there may have been during these years, Bushnell broke with a vengeance in the spring of 1854. The occasion was the proposed Kansas-Nebraska Bill, which was making its tumultuous way through the Senate and the House. This explosive piece of legislation undertook to organize the 400–million-acre region of Nebraska as a new territory, leaving the question of slavery or no slavery to be decided by the people who settled there on the basis of "popular sovereignty." The chief advocate of the bill was the eloquent, pugnacious Democrat senator Stephen A. Douglas, the "Little Giant" of Illinois. The bill's reckless central feature was the explicit repeal of the Missouri Compromise of 1821. All of the prospective new territory, which reached to the Canadian border, was north of the 36'30", a vast region that under the terms of the Missouri settlement supposedly had been forever closed to chattel slavery.

Why Douglas suddenly made this politically risky and morally vulnerable move never has been entirely clear. Yet despite his own prediction that it would "raise a hell of a storm," he pushed it through the Senate with a final speech that even his enemies admitted was as splendid as any ever heard in that body.[28] Then he reaped the whirlwind. While the House debated the measure further, he was personally execrated as "Douglas Iscariot," or as "the Benedict Arnold of 1854." He confessed he could have ridden from Boston to Chicago guided solely by the light of his burning effigy by night and his hanging effigy by day. Even in the South reactions were mixed. In the North, usually placid figures such as Emerson and Edward Everett erupted in protest, and voices long familiar in the antislavery cause were heard from with almost uncontrollable indignation: Horace Greeley in New York, Henry Ward Beecher in Brooklyn, Wendell Phillips in Boston, and Abraham Lincoln in Illinois.[29] Bushnell joined the chorus of outrage with a Good Friday sermon entitled "The Northern Iron."[30]

His unusual "iron" metaphor came from words of Jeremiah: "Shall iron break the northern iron and steel?"[31] Modern scholars have scratched their heads over the original meaning of this query on the lips of the great Old Testament prophet, but Bushnell took it at its face value. Northern iron, manufactured near the Black Sea, was well known in biblical times as the hardest available. Mere iron, made farther to the south in Israel, was of softer, lesser quality. Jeremiah's question asked whether the softer southern iron could hope to break the harder northern product. The parallel to American sectional differences over slavery stirred Bushnell's imagination.

The heart of his address was that for too long the North had given in to Southern pressure. Beginning with the 1787 constitutional provision that allowed a slave to be counted as three-fifths of a human being and running through the Missouri Compromise, the Mexican War, the Compromise of 1850, and now this "perfidious" Kansas-Nebraska Bill, the North had yielded repeatedly and spinelessly to Southern slavery interests. This was enough, and more than enough. It was high time for "northern iron" to show its mettle, Bushnell preached, and force a halt to such shameful concessions. Even Southerners, he claimed, were losing respect for the North, convinced that Yankees had no real convictions about freedom and cared only for "the main chance of money and trade." He was persuaded, too, that Northerners were succumbing to a faint-heartedness, as though the South had won out so often that the weaker iron actually would finally break the Northern iron and steel.

"This is not my opinion," he confidently countered. For the moment, the South might still have the votes to work their will. But the spirit of the age was against it. One nation after another was abolishing slavery, until the United States, "the model republic of the world," was "left almost alone" in permitting it. Population trends were against it (one of his favorite arguments), as was the commercial enterprise of the North, the powerful influence of Northern literature—conspicuously *Uncle Tom's Cabin*—and the free spirit of Northern institutions, to say nothing of the dynamic of the Gospel. Let the North take courage in considering these silent, but irresistible forces constantly working to undermine the entrenched evil.

Fifteen years before, Bushnell had shown a certain patience, even a half-sympathy, with Southerners in their unique predicament. In "Northern Iron" he was closer to bluster. "The time of delicacy is now gone by," he proclaimed. He feared Congress might, after all, succeed in passing the Kansas-Nebraska Bill. If it did, "we will as certainly repeal it," he threatened, "waging the appeal as a holy crusade till it is carried." He did not wish to court a civil war. He could not believe the entire South would attempt secession. But if it made so drastic a move, the North would block it. "We will keep it [the Union] safe. This we have the power to say, and make the saying good."

He went so far as to toy with the opposite extreme: if matters continued to get worse, it might be better for the North to secede than to remain in a nation so corrupted by the slave system. Quickly, however, he thought better of this and ended with a do-or-die summons to his free compatriots to "take our ground firmly, and declare to the world, God helping us, that we will save both our principles and the Union."

This time the Doctor had pulled all his stops. In promising Bartol a copy of the discourse, he suspected he had been "fanatical." "Open your windows to make ready for the explosion," he warned him.[32] He need not have been so fearful. The mood had changed drastically since 1839 and 1844, when such antislavery pronouncements had landed him in deep trouble. Now he was running with a turned tide. There seemed no end to Southern successes in Washington, nor any appeasing of Southern appetites for slave territory. As though continental expansion were not enough, there was evidence that proslavery freebooters were conniving to annex Cuba, Haiti, Santo Domingo, and more of Mexico.[33] These rumors, plus the ominous events following the war with Mexico, had alarmed even conservative Northerners. Feeling against the Kansas-Nebraska Bill rose to fever pitch.

Instead of attacking their pastor for his blunt views, his congregation requested that his address be printed.

The bill finally passed both houses of Congress, though four of the six Connecticut delegates to Washington voted "Nay."[34] It was discouraging, but still there was hope for a nonviolent solution. Almost immediately, however, such hope was again shaken. Bushnell's sermon barely had time to circulate before "Bleeding Kansas " became a reality, and not long afterward John Brown let loose his savage raid on Osawatomie. It began to appear that the conflict over human bondage would prove irreconcilable and would finally be settled less by Congressional debate and pulpit suasion than by the deadly fire of Samuel Sharps's breechloading precision rifles. Grimly, when the time came, these lethal weapons would be manufactured in Hartford, within walking distance of Bushnell's church door.[35]

While all this tension was mounting in national affairs, other problems were building for Bushnell personally. His health still would not hold. Within months of his return from Europe he was telling Leonard Bacon that he was "in such a tremor of exhaustion that [he] could hardly sit in [his] chair."[36] He seems to have done passably well during the acute phases of his theological controversy, but by the summer of 1852 he was again in serious difficulty.

Along with other factors, illness made it quite out of the question for him to consider an invitation in August to head Antioch College, just then taking shape in Ohio.[37] A disturbing episode during an out-of-town preaching engagement, when he coughed blood,[38] sent him off again to the mineral springs at Saratoga, New York. He chafed there for several weeks without lasting benefit. By October he had to drop everything. He decided on a trip to Minnesota, where he could visit his brother and sister-in-law, the John Frazier Heads, at remote Fort Ripley on the upper Mississippi, where Dr. Head was serving a tour of army duty. The journey was meant to restore Bushnell's health, but at one it point nearly proved fatal.

Western travel in the 1850s was arduous. He rattled along in slow trains, subjected to "mortal poundings" as he sat up night and day, and then waited endlessly for delayed steamboats. His first major stopover was with the celebrated evangelist Charles G. Finney and his family in Oberlin, Ohio. Finney had just assumed the presidency of the college, and Bushnell had come to know him the previous winter while they participated in a series of revival meetings in Hartford. One notable fruit of his Oberlin visit was Bushnell's change of heart about coeducation. Observing this still unusual practice for the first time, he felt an unexpected "new chapter" opening in his opinions on the subject. Formerly he had been "shocked" at the very mention of combining the two sexes in the same school. Under Finney's weekend tutelage, however, he became persuaded it was "the only plan which is really according to nature," mutually beneficial to both men and women students.[39]

They were a strange pair, Finney and Bushnell. Both had come off Litchfield County farms and pursued the law before turning to the Gospel ministry. But there any close resemblance ended. Finney was older by ten years and had a booming voice and a powerful six-foot-two-inch frame that towered over the moderate height of his younger friend. With his fiercely intent gaze, he was everything in the way of an aggressive revivalist that Bushnell was not. This led to marked theological differences.

Yet there was a genuine attachment between them. They spent hours discussing doctrine as they visited in each other's homes and corresponded as long as they lived. While he was in Hartford during Bushnell's days of controversy, Finney preached in the North Church pulpit and did what he could to soften the hostility of the Doctor's unyielding opponents, appealing especially to Joel Hawes. Bushnell, too, was supportive. In a letter of introduction for Finney to use on his 1859–60 travels to England and Scotland, Bushnell assured British friends that Finney was "apostolic" and "no fanatic." Elsewhere he spoke of him as "pure gold." Yet the Doctor had to ask himself how he could feel that way toward so dominant a figure with whom he often disagreed and who sometimes wearied him with his stubborn arguments. "I do not know how it is," he once mused, "but I am drawn to this man, despite . . . the greatest dissimilarity of tastes, and a method of soul . . . wholly unlike." On further reflection, however, he did know: "It is because I find God with him."[40]

Via Chicago, Galena, and St. Paul, the Doctor covered the last 100 miles to Fort Ripley "by a hard-fought battle" with the wintry elements. He had a brief but satisfying family visit, but it was so cold he wanted to name the place "the North Pole, *alias* Fort Ripley."

All this, however, was nothing compared with his journey back to St. Paul. He was making his way down-river in a bark canoe, when "a tremendous snow-storm" blew in, forcing him to transfer to an open wagon. The driver had extreme difficulty finding his way across the trackless prairie, blindly struggling through the howling blizzard in total darkness. By some combination of human instinct and divine guidance, they reached a filthy hovel of a "hotel," where Bushnell spent a freezing night. The only fire in the ramshackle building went out, and he lay for hours on the floor, chattering with cold, in the company of a half-breed Frenchman, his Irish wife, and other stranded travelers. The next morning, while he was waiting for the storm to abate, an immigrant Englishwoman was brought in, miraculously still alive after having tramped all night, barefoot and alone, through the gale and the snow. Amid further hardships he eventually reached St. Paul safely, but shaken and exhausted. Had he stayed in his canoe he doubted he could have survived, and even on land it was a close call. Snow and ice assailed him all the way to St. Louis. He was not one to complain easily of physical hardships, so it was a good deal for him to admit that for the whole two weeks he had undergone "torturing anxiety" and "suffered prodigiously." No matter how long he might live, he wanted "no more of prairie in any shape."[41]

Strenuous as it had been, the break seems to have given him new strength, but only briefly. By the summer of 1853 he was back in Saratoga "among a great herd of eaters and sleepers." At one point in 1854, he could say he had been enjoying "magnificent health," but this turned out to be only a lull before the worst collapse he had suffered in years. In December he confided in Chesebrough that he had been "quite disabled" for nearly two months, reduced to "a wreck, a waif—one of the vestiges of creation."[42]

Deeply depressed, he entered the year 1855 in New York at the home of his other brother-in-law, Joseph Sampson, who was married to his wife's younger sister, Emily. Sampson was a successful merchant and auctioneer who lived well at Broadway and Bond Street in the same fifteenth-ward neighborhood with Daniel Drew, Cornelius Roosevelt (grandfather of Theodore), Bushnell's ministerial classmate William Adams, and a *nouveau riche* Cornelius Vanderbilt.[43] He was devout and philanthropic by nature, and he and Bushnell enjoyed a close relationship. He was the only person to whom the Doctor dedicated two of his books: the collection of sermons in *Christ and His Salvation* in 1864 and his important *Vicarious Sacrifice* two years later.

Seeing that his friend was ill and discouraged, Sampson offered to send Bushnell to California. The thought hardly could have been wholly new to to Bushnell. Four of the Doctor's Yale classmates already had preceded him there, or were about to, at least two of them hoping to find the warmer West Coast climate helpful to diseases similar to his own.[44] Yet he hesitated, pondered, and protested; he could not comfortably accept so much from his in-law friend. Finally Bushnell decided to try Cuba instead.

He was in no mood for more travel anywhere and left Hartford in a fret. He tried with only partial success to comfort himself with a visit to Bellows in New York before sailing. Bellows found him annoying; "Bushnell lives too much on himself and in himself," he complained to Bartol. The strain was somewhat relieved by a breakfast meeting set up by Charles L. Brace. In addition to Bushnell and Bellows, such New York literati as Henry James, Sr., George Ripley, and Olmsted were there. Conversation ranged over a variety of topics. At one point it turned at considerable length to a discussion of Henry Ward Beecher and his rise to fame. Half-disparagingly Bellows suggested that his secret was a combination of "high sentiment and a very low manner—the union of the moral philosopher and the comedian." Similarly, Bushnell remarked that much as he disliked Beecher's preaching method, he thought he had succeeded spectacularly because he had a heart "as big as that of an ox."[45]

It was a hard voyage to Cuba. At first the bitter weather was like a repeat of the Minnesota prairie. As the ship crossed the Gulf Stream there was a snowstorm, and the sea was so rough that "almost every soul on board was sick, even old seamen." But not Bushnell. Writing home from off the Bahama Banks he announced with evident satisfaction that he had "stood it out, as usual, went to every table, shaved every morning, and kept on my way."[46]

Cuba opened to him a luxuriant, tropical world entirely new to his experience. He never had been so far south before, and he marveled at the variety of colorful vegetation. In Havana contacts from Hartford helped him get settled just outside the city, and before long he was in touch with people who "want to do more for me than I am willing to have them."[47] Not all his encounters were this pleasant. Unexpectedly low temperatures were disappointing as the "snow skirt" of a severe northern winter was felt even in Cuba. The casual Catholicism he met everywhere distressed him, as it had in Europe. Cubans lived in constant dread of invasion by U.S.-backed adventurers seeking to annex the island. Even more upsetting were his brushes with slavery, in this case involving not so much African Americans as Chinese coolies. African American overseers whipped them so brutally in the sugar cane fields that suicide among the poor wretches was routine.[48] One of Bushnell's landladies, a fiery-tempered virago, flogged three of her servants until the Doctor could barely stand "their hideous screams."[49]

None of this helped his health. "My disease is very stubbornly fastened," he wrote home after a month, and two weeks later he was still "greatly discouraged."[50] The upshot was that he abandoned Cuba ahead of schedule, made stopovers in Savannah and Charleston, and was home by mid-May. Hartford doctors shook their heads over him, and he offered to step down from his pulpit if it would help the church. A meeting of a North Church committee at his house, however, quickly vetoed this idea. In the words of Deacon Amos Collins, it was decided instead to "sit at the window of Providence and look out," awaiting the lead of the Spirit.[51] In December Bushnell turned down a professorship at the University of Wisconsin,[52] writing Bartol the same day that he was "still an invalid."[53]

At this dismal juncture he decided there was but one course left to him. It was time to accept Joseph Sampson's standing offer and try California.[54] But in going he would leave unfinished a task that had been important to him since 1853: the creation of a public park at the heart of Hartford. Along with Central Park in New York City, it was to be one of the first two urban parks in the country.

CHAPTER 14

"An Outdoor Parlor"

AS LATE AS 1857, no American city of any size could boast an urban park. The average citizen who might want to while away a leisure hour on green grass, look up through the branches of a tree at a bird or a scudding cloud, or perhaps indulge unhurried long thoughts had few choices: a scenic cemetery, perhaps; an inconvenient trip to the country; or possibly a small town common, where profit from rentals or the sale of hay was of more consequence to city fathers than upkeep for the refreshment of men, women, and children.[1]

Then suddenly, as it had happened earlier in Europe, the need for parks began to be felt. The impulse came primarily from a just-in-time awakening to the urban consequences of the Industrial Revolution. The shift from an agricultural economy to large-scale factories had lured droves of workers to cities. Many of them were foreigners, and most of them lived in slums. Such minimal housing not only disfigured the cities, but it left laborers and their families trapped in dingy surroundings while a rising managerial class bought up much of the best real estate for commercial development or private residences.[2]

City leaders nationwide had been slow to think of setting aside natural acreage for the refreshment of future generations. Finally, however, they began to see that what was at stake was more than incidental aesthetics. Parks would mean more appealing municipalities, higher property values, less pollution, better public health, and outlets for sport and holiday festivities that could reduce the potential for social unrest. There also were those who believed that putting the simple beauty of nature within the daily reach of city dwellers would do much to preserve the desirable rural values of hard work, morality, and religion, even in an urban setting.[3]

As a result, parks appeared in a burst on the city scene, as they had earlier in Europe. By 1870 the park commissioners in New York could say that "few cities of considerable population on this continent are now without schemes more or less advanced for the establishment of extensive parks for the pleasure of their people."[4]

In Hartford the idea of a public park was not totally new. While Bushnell was still a Yale senior in 1827, his future deacon, Amos Collins, was among petitioners to the mayor and Common Council for the creation of "a Publick Square or Promenade" to "add beauty and interest to our city."[5] Nor was the thought new to Bushnell. Enamoured though he was of the New England countryside, and at first sceptical about cities, he could see that urban centers were growing fast. The task, then, was not to resist them but to shape them. In the 1830s he advised one young man to settle in Hartford, arguing that it was destined to grow in population and importance, and that among other improvements it would one day have the advantage of a public park.[6] In the 1840s, while in Europe, he took note of foreign parklands. Observing one in Frankfurt-on-Main on an August day in 1845, he noted that the benches were occupied by nurses, many of them with their arms full of children. It impressed him that that this kind of facility plainly did much for "the character and happiness of the common people."[7] With these incentives he began to mention the idea of a park for Hartford as he chanced to converse with various citizens. From many he seemed to get "a hearty response."[8] He concluded that support might be mustered for the project, and he decided to act.

Bushnell brought to his self-assigned endeavor a combination of foresight and practical engineering, along with a keen legal and political sense that was not often equaled, even among the New Yorkers who first promoted Central Park. "He was a man born to lead," Episcopal bishop Thomas Clark of Rhode Island once said of him. He could "plan a house, or lay out a park, or drain a city," the Bishop maintained, "better than many of our experts."[9] Wisely the Doctor started by thinking out his purpose. Behind his dream was his view of a Christian democracy as not simply a collection of isolated, self-reliant individuals, but as a dynamic, interrelated community. To him, the chief agencies of civilized society were the church, the home, and the school, places where people of all types lived and grew together as they exerted unconscious, as well as conscious, influence on each other. The park would be an urban extension of these organic instruments of civilization. His hope, which by no means every American of the time believed feasible, was for

> an opening in the heart of the city itself, to which citizens will naturally flow in their walks . . . a place where the children will play and the poor invalid go to breathe the freshness of nature; a place for holiday scenes and celebrations; a green carpet of ground, . . . where high and low, rich and poor, will exchange looks and make acquaintance through the eyes; an outdoor parlor opened for the cultivation of good manners, and a right social feeling. It must be a place of life and motion that will make us conscious of being one people.[10]

As to the location of such an ideal resort, he had not reached his conclusion lightly that it should be "in the heart of the city." Common sense at first seemed to suggest otherwise. A park on the edge of town where unspoiled open land was easily available, had strong appeal. Proponents of Central Park in New York initially took that approach. But Bushnell had two criteria that ruled out such a plan. The park must be constantly visible, he thought, because only then could it hope to ornament the city and be assured of good maintenance. Secondly, it must be easily accessible to everyone. Independently, in the same year, 1853, Bushnell and the New Yorkers came to be of the same mind—a city park must not be peripheral, but central.[11]

In both cities, however, the nature of central space presented a severe problem. Sizeable sections of the land finally chosen in New York were foul to every human sense. In Olmsted's words, they were "steeped in the overflow and mush of pigsties, slaughterhouses, and bone-boiling works" where "the stench was sickening."[12]

The center of Hartford was no better. Set in a geologic depression, it consisted of an uneven rectangle of about forty acres, partly used as a garbage dump, partly the scene of dilapidated Hartford and New Haven Railroad yards, and partly the site of outhouses, squatters' huts, and ramshackle, odiferous soap and tanning works. A heavily polluted river, once the beautiful Little River, but later known as the Mill or the Hog, wandered sluggishly along the edges of the property on its way to the majestic Connecticut. Alternately its mucky waters were used by horses for drinking and by determined Baptists for immersions. Bushnell was so appalled by this wasteland that he called it "a Gehenna [Hell] without fire."[13]

But with his customarily hopeful view of things, he was grateful that at least such unpromising real estate had been saved by its very degradation from being preempted for some other permanent purpose, and was still a possibility for the park of his dreams. How, though, was he to persuade the present owners—including several influential old-time residents who, despite change and decay, had hung on in the area—to part with their properties? If that were somehow done, how was he to convince cautious Yankee councilmen to put public funds into such forsaken land for a purpose as yet almost unheard of among American cities?

Carefully concealing his object, he probed the situation privately, quietly talking with various owners to see whether they would be open to reasonable offers. He gained the impression that the Hartford and New Haven Railroad would be willing to negotiate. In 1849 it had completed a new depot just north of the meandering river, and the management might be glad of the opportunity to relocate its yards in that vicinity. One grist mill operator seemed receptive. Other than that, as Bushnell remembered, "I could get no terms for anything."[14]

He decided that not much could be done until the city could exercise the right of eminent domain. As its charter stood, it had no such power, but a legally trained Bushnell was undaunted. With the help of one of his North Church parishioners, Nathaniel H. Morgan, an old hand at city hall, a park provision was added as a rider to a pending petition to the state legislature on an unrelated land issue. The petition was granted by the lawmakers, and with the aid of some deft politicking by Bushnell himself—"the first and last time" he allowed himself such activity—the charter change was ratified by Hartford voters. Thus, as of July 1853, the city was authorized to "lay out parks or public grounds,...taking the same measures as [it]...is now by law required to take in laying out highways in said city." With this seemingly modest victory, the first formidable obstacle to a park was cleared away.[15]

Then came the time of persuasion. It was by no means settled that there should be a park, nor was there any agreement on a site. Among those who favored a park somewhere, ideas for its location sprouted like weeds. One interesting proposal was that it be situated just west of the core city on what later became the celebrated "Nook Farm," literary paradise of Mark Twain, Harriet Beecher Stowe, Charles Dudley Warner, and others.[16] None of these proposals, however, bore fruit during the summer of 1853, and in September Bushnell sensed the moment had come for him to step forward with his novel plan for a central ground.

When it came to making "the worse appear the better cause," Bushnell was a master. In this instance he had prepared his case thoroughly, including a sizable map of the area on which he had sketched his idea of a park layout.[17] His petition for a hearing before the Common Council caused a ripple of amusement when it became known what he was about to present. Nevertheless he was granted time on the evening of 5 October before an informal, extra-legal session.[18]

Attendance was good. The twenty-nine aldermen and councilmen present were some of Hartford's acknowledged leaders, though none appear to have belonged to the North Church.[19] Presiding was Mayor William J. Hamersley, a progressive Jeffersonian Democrat who had won election largely by opposing an outworn puritanical ban on dramatic productions in Hartford and favoring licensed theaters.[20] He was an unusual character, bald and bespectacled, well-read and witty, but he lacked easy graces and had an explosive, often disagreeable laugh. When he was not serving as mayor—he was twice elected —or running the Hartford Post Office as an appointee of the Buchanan Administration, he was a stationer and book dealer. Although no churchman, he had published an edition of Bushnell's *God in Christ*. His children were intimates of Bushnell's daughters, and his wife, with a heart as ample as her enormously stout frame, had no rival, so her friends fondly quipped, as "Patroness of Disorganized Charity."[21]

Under the wondering gaze of the mayor and Council, Bushnell hung up his map and held forth for over an hour. He played freely on the imaginations of his hearers, convinced that "if the imagination was carried, the judgment would be."[22] Verbally he led them over the land he was proposing, making the most of the stark contrast between the disaster area it then was and the spacious lawns, drives, fountains, and vistas he was convinced could be developed. Hartford, he reminded them, was not known for its beauty. A park on this site would do much to end criticism of the city's appearance, help induce moneyed families to build new homes along its edges and furnish an easily available playground for the poor, who needed a park more than any other class. Prophetically, as it turned out, he imagined a day when there would be need of a new statehouse, and what more appropriate setting than overlooking the pleasant greens of such a park?

Practically speaking, he would not attempt to estimate the cost, but he was certain the city could afford it. The crucial factor, as he saw it, was not money but time. The moment was now, Bushnell stressed; let this chance go, and the railroad likely would dig in for a long stay and additional marginal factories, with their parasitic tenements, soon would dominate the scene. The neighborhood would then be lost forever to the possibility of a park. He urged the leadership before him to hesitate no longer and to seize the opportunity with prompt and positive action.[23]

The Council was impressed. Amused scepticism largely evaporated, and without delay the members appointed a blue-ribbon committee, chaired by another civic-minded publisher, David F. Robinson, to investigate the proposal in detail. A month later this panel submitted its report, plainly influenced, and in part probably even worded, by Bushnell himself. It endorsed the bold project, including a cost estimate of $105,000, most of which it recommended "should be a tax on the City Treasury." In all likelihood this was the first time in United States municipal annals that such a suggestion had been made for financing a wholly new park. With only two dissents the report was formally adopted, the Council going on record that "it is expedient to proceed . . . to lay out a new Park."[24]

Immediately there were other expressions of encouragement. Both major newspapers, the *Times* and the *Courant,* endorsed the basic idea and the unusual choice of location. Even Hartford's effusive, nationally celebrated "Sweet Singer," Lydia H. H. Sigourney, whose inevitable poems for every prominent local funeral were said to add a new terror to dying, chimed in with sentimental lines, hoping the new park would come true:

> I dream'd—and o'er my raptured eyes
> New scenes of beauty seemed to rise.
> Unsightly roofs, and rail-road track,
> And stagnant waters green and black,
> Had fled—and in their place were seen,
> A mirror'd flood, like diamond sheen,
> And smooth-shorn verdure, richly green . . .[25]

All this was heartening, but a rocky road still lay ahead. There could be no park without the approval of the citizenry, and all citizens were not disposed to vote for it. At a boisterous preliminary meeting to decide on the timing and method of balloting, an incensed Maj. N. Seymour Webb, quartermaster general of the state, whose property would be affected, fumed against the whole idea. If there must be a vote, he testily suggested, put it off until 1900! A letter in the *Courant* from "Stone Bridge" complained that the proposed taking of land for the park was "outrageous and morally wrong." Not mentioning Bushnell by name, he referred to the park plan as simply one minister's "new hobby," a "Quixotic," fiscally irresponsible notion that would drive businessmen and capital away from the city. When the votes were counted on 5 January 1854, however, the park won handily, 1,687 to 683.[26] The Doctor was delighted. "A very great thing for Hartford," he gloated, "much greater than most people know."[27]

Success at the polls was one thing; completing a usable park was quite another. Bushnell thought of the new ground as a benefit to the poor. But the park would also displace the poor. For all its dreary aspects, the area to be renewed was home to some 200 people, more than half of the them unskilled Irish laborers and African American servants and their households. Most of them owned no land and thus had no voice in the outcome.

Yet there were exceptions. Noble Jones, an African American waiter at the Exchange Hotel, had a small holding and summoned enough courage to object to being dispossessed. So did a handful of Irish workers. A struggling African Methodist Episcopal chapel that also housed a small elementary school for African American children was threatened. In an effort to defend themselves, the church leaders retained a young white lawyer, Joseph R. Hawley, later a popular Civil War hero, governor of Connecticut, and a U.S. senator.[28] Such voices were heard by the Council, but no private grievances were deemed sufficient to override what it regarded as the public good.[29]

Now and again there was an element of tragicomedy to the struggle. During the spring of 1854 two factories mysteriously burned down at opposite ends of the hoped-for park property. An anonymous letter writer accused the Doctor of having set the fires to further his project. The matter might have passed off as a humorous aberration, except that one of the companies involved insisted it would rebuild, park or no park, and actually obtained a license from the Common Council to do so. An alarmed Bushnell got wind of the vote, and realizing all the undoing to which it could lead, he rallied his friends and leaped into the breach to protest. A week later the Council rescinded the license.[30]

For Bushnell, this action was more overt than usual. Generally he limited himself to working "from behind committees," as he put it. All the same, he spent himself prodigally on the effort. "It became a tremendous load upon me—this park matter," he told Bartol. "If I had known beforehand how much thought and anxiety it would cost, I am afraid I should have played Jonah." His preoccupation was such that he worried about its effect on his parish ministry. "Why should I carry a park to bed with me," he asked his Boston friend in the same letter, "and yet be so little exercised in the magnificent work of the Gospel and the care of souls?"[31]

In New York it took three years to gain full title to the land needed for Central Park; Hartford took longer. There were times when progress was so slow that public interest sagged, and yet another time Bushnell had to help stiffen the spine of the Common Council. Finally, in April 1858, the Council's park committee could report with long-deferred satisfaction that at last it had assembled the pieces and secured title to "all the remaining lands to complete the entire park."[32] Still the task was not done. Now there was need of a design. Depending on the taste and skill of some landscaping expert, the *Courant* observed, "the Park will be a gem of beauty, or a stiff, mechanical abortion."[33] The Council's park committee followed New York's lead and advertised a competition, offered a first prize of $300 and a second of $200 for the best proposals, and set up a panel of seven judges, Bushnell being one. Upwards of a dozen designs were submitted.[34]

After this promising beginning, nearly everything went wrong. The judges played favorites, argued with each other, and endlessly changed their minds. On two ballots the city engineeer, Seth E. Marsh, seemed to have won the top prize, but the mayor, Timothy M. Allyn, a carpet manufacturer, could not endure the outcome. With arm-twisting and oratory he brought about a reversal of the decision in favor of a former British-born resident of Hartford, Gervase Wheeler, then living in New York. Whereupon Bushnell dug in his heels and refused to accept the Wheeler plan. To him it was "totally ruinous." An effort to combine the two winning designs failed, and after heated debates, and at least one shouting match, the Council accepted an offer from the Doctor to work with Marsh on a modification of his plan and to complete the park on a budget of no more than $30,000.[35]

Within a year even Bushnell knew he and Marsh had overextended themselves and that their plan could not succeed. Marsh was a competent surveyor and engineer, but he was no artist. Bushnell had been courageously instrumental in pioneering the park, but he had no talent for the detail of aesthetic design. Moreover, in 1859, the Doctor became so ill he had to resign his pulpit, and the same year Marsh, protesting bitterly, was dismissed along with the unsatisfactory Middletown contractor.[36]

Despite cessation of work, the park was being used more and more. The grounds had to wait for professional care until Swiss-born landscape architect Jacob Weidenmann took over as superintendent of parks in 1861.[37] Then, at long last, the park began to receive the enduring form neither Marsh nor Bushnell was qualified to give it. In later years Bushnell took full responsibility for the failure. "If there was any blame in the matter, it belonged to me," he acknowledged. But he remained convinced that his sidetracking of the elaborate Wheeler plan had saved Hartford from a monumental blunder.[38]

Among those originally invited to submit designs for the new ground was Frederick Law Olmsted, eventually the most eminent of American landscape architects. As a young man he was just then beginning to develop Central Park in New York. It has long been thought that he also played a leading role in creating Hartford's Central Park, as it was first called. This is readily understandable. After all, Olmsted was a Hartford native; he liked the community; and early on it was suggested he might be willing to take charge of the projected Hartford park without charge, just for love of the city.[39] He never entered the contest, however, and there is no shred of evidence that he had anything to do with initiating the Hartford enterprise. During the first four difficult planning years, from 1853 to 1857, Olmsted was a Staten Island farmer, a writer, and a correspondent in the deep South for the *New York Daily Times,* sending back letters which resulted in his celebrated book *The Cotton Kingdom.*

While Bushnell was pushing ahead, and contending with one obstacle after another, Olmsted was in no position to help with a park anywhere. He never had attempted such landscaping and had no idea he ever would. With mingled amusement and amazement, he used to say that until the Manhattan opportunity unexpectedly came his way in August 1857 he had "no more thought of becoming a landscape architect than a [Roman Catholic] cardinal."[40] After that, he was too absorbed in his New York responsibilities to think of helping elsewhere, even in his own town.

Yet this is not the whole Olmsted-Bushnell story. In his formative younger years, Olmsted knew Bushnell well. The Olmsteds bought the Bushnell's Ann Street house in 1840, and the North Church pastor was a thought-provoking revelation to Olmsted in his teens and twenties. Hitherto he had known only harsh, overbearing Calvinist ministers who damaged for life any feeling he might have had for organized religion. However, Bushnell's unconventional Christian views and his fearless activism fascinated him. Routinely he heard his sermons and studied them in print. With his friend and confidant Charles L. Brace, Olmsted sometimes listened to them read aloud and constantly discussed them with Brace and other companions. Like the essays of Emerson and Carlyle, he once wrote his father, they "are not worth much without real, hard study."[41] Bushnell's Harvard discourse on the Atonement he found especially helpful. "I think Dr. B. has set it all right," he wrote his brother John. "It's a glorious, reasonable view" which, he was glad to say, "has influenced me for good."[42]

Equally exciting to him was Bushnell on the public scene. He enjoyed seeing him take on the pope and was intrigued to watch him at crowded city meetings, joining in the crossfire of debate with Democratic governor Isaac Toucey in defense of a free public high school for Hartford. He also found him an exhilarating outdoor companion. "The Doctor and I had a *jolly time* in the 'Susan Nippers,'" he told Brace in 1847, referring to a brisk ten-mile sail from the New Haven lighthouse east to Sachem's Head. Bushnell, he concluded, seemed "born for a sailor."

The same summer on the Connecticut shore, he and Bushnell teamed up for a game of ninepins against George Geddes, son of one of the engineers on the Erie Canal, and Chief Justice Greene C. Bronson of the New York State Supreme Court—"a clever old fellow," according to Olmsted. In some quarters at that time a minister could lose his job for playing ninepins at all. But Bushnell and Olmsted won so handily that Geddes vowed in astonishment that he would never again roll with a Doctor of Divinity. While a tickled Doctor crowed a little over the victory, Geddes declared Bushnell had mistaken his calling and "was cut out for a gambler."[43]

These varied associations—personal, pastoral, and intellectual— left a permanent imprint on Olmsted. His genius as a landscape architect was affected by many "prophets," as he called them, but Bushnell remained one of his heroes.[44] Before Olmsted had any thought of entering the landscaping field, Bushnell had pondered the future of urban life and given far-sighted leadership to the cause of city parks. Olmsted learned much from his friend and minister of the power of natural beauty to lift the human spirit and about the mysterious, organic interdependence of all life. As to Olmsted and Bushnell Park, the real question is not so much whether Olmsted shaped the park; the deeper question is the extent to which Bushnell shaped Olmsted, and thus made a contribution to the array of famous Olmsted parks from New York to California. Without question, that influence was considerable.[45]

The park in Hartford gradually won acceptance, and other aspects of the city improved as a result of its increasing attractiveness. On a warm August evening in 1859, Mrs. Bushnell took a solitary stroll through the still-unfinished park grounds. As she walked about and traced some of the walks her husband had planned, she wondered whether others passing through thought to be at all grateful to him.[46] It may have been too early for that, but fuller appreciation was on the way. By the late 1860s, memories of controversy had faded for the most part. Bushnell judged that the park's enemies were gone and that the parkland was "universally popular." Even the "old economic gentlemen" who had been so set against the venture, he could report, had changed their minds. Many of them were joining its original backers in saying all over town, "the best investment our city ever made is the park."[47]

CHAPTER 15

California in the Wake of the Gold Rush

"THAT I MAY NOT SEEM TO HAVE ELOPED, I must let you know that I am off to California on the 5th of March. Oh, how I wish I could have your company!" So Bushnell notified Bartol of his impending departure in the late winter of 1856. He wished with all his soul that he could escape the necessity of setting out alone—again.[1] There was some hope that in the warmer, drier climate of the West Coast he could regain a measure of health. But he could not be at all sure. "It really looked, for a time," he admitted later, "as if it was about an even chance that I had come here to die."[2]

Given his condition, he could not have gone at all except for the completion in 1855 of the Panama Railroad across the isthmus. Prior to its construction, all three routes from the eastern seaboard to the newly opened Eldorado in the West were extremely risky—whether "the Plains across, the Horn around, or the Isthmus over," as the saying went among the Forty-niners. Compared with the 3,000–mile trek across the continent or the dangerous long voyage around Cape Horn, a mere forty miles through the jungles of Panama from Chagres to Panama City seemed the easiest way even before the rail line was built. But appearances were deceiving. Many of the brash, greedy prospectors who hastily tried that pathless crossing, battling searing heat and torrential rains, never reached the Pacific shore. Those who did, staggering into Panama City hollow-eyed and half dead, warned the folks back home not even to think of attempting it. "I say it in fear of God and love of man, to one and all," one veteran expressed it, "for no consideration come this route."[3]

These hardships ended with the opening of the new railroad. It was constructed at huge cost—money and lives—by a combination of bold investors led by William H. Aspinwall of New York, and Bushnell took advantage of it. Having reached Panama by ship, he paid out the required twenty-five dollars in gold for his rail ticket, and in a little more than three hours he could look out over the vast expanse of the Pacific Ocean. He laughed at the idea of carrying a firearm on this short, routine crossing, as some did. Later, however, he had second thoughts. A month after his ride an anti-American riot broke out in Panama City. Twenty passengers like himself were killed, and twenty more wounded by hostile Panamanians.[4]

Observant naturalist that Bushnell was, it is disappointing that we have no word from him on the brilliant life of the jungle through which he passed. Passengers were treated to astonishing glimpses through the windows of the gaudily painted train as it moved along at fifteen miles an hour, while the rattle of the cars and the high-pitched blasts from its steam whistle frightened monkeys to the tree-tops. They were awed by swarms of blue butterflies, multicolored birds, and the dazzling lush green of the hills, which in the eyes of one Vermont traveler put the Green Mountains of his native state to shame.

At Panama City Bushnell transferred to the vessel *Sonora*. Twenty-three days out of New York, he sailed through a bridgeless, breath-takingly beautiful Golden Gate into San Francisco Bay, a body of water large enough to shelter all the navies of the world at once.[5] As he set foot for the first time on California soil, it dawned on him with sobering finality that there was now "a continent between me and all I hold dear on earth."[6]

Lonely and unwell in a strange land, he reached out for touches of home. Despite his need, however, not every transplanted New Englander was eager to welcome him. Frederick Billings, a rising young San Francisco lawyer from Vermont, had heard from his parents back East that an infirm Bushnell was coming to the coast. In a sceptical response the future president of the Northern Pacific Railroad and active conservationist (he gave his name to Billings, Montana) tartly declared that Bushnell, along with Henry Ward Beecher, had drifted off dangerously into mysticism and was mixing politics and

religion in perilous ways. Hence, for a time Billings remained sceptical and distant.

As so often happened, however, with those who were at first un-
sure of the Doctor, Billings changed his mind once he came to know
him. Bushnell, who always was attracted to promising younger men,
was in turn quickly drawn to Billings. The two neo-Californians soon
discovered they had legal, religious, and educational interests in common, and the friendship became one of the warmest of Bushnell's life.
They worked closely together helping to lay foundations for a university for California. Billings eventually read most of Bushnell's books,
as did his wife, who had known of Bushnell's writings before her
marriage, and for years they enjoyed leisurely, talkative visits in each
other's homes in Hartford and Woodstock, Vermont.[7]

Other California welcomes were more immediately forthcoming.
Within days of his landing, the Doctor took a steamer up the Sacra-
mento River and beyond to Marysville, where he attended a joint
meeting of the Congregational Association of California and the
Presbytery of San Francisco. The faces were mostly new, but the
church setting and the procedures were familiar, and he found one
old friend. His Yale classmate, Henry Durant, who had come out
three years before, was heading a small academy in Oakland that
bravely called itself the College of California. At this meeting Durant
was chosen as moderator of the Association and helped introduce
Bushnell, who was elected a corresponding member. He was the only
D.D. to have sat in that company, but he was pleased with the caliber
of the pastors he met. "They have an excellent body of ministers,
here," he wrote Mary, "fine-spirited, talented, and generally accomplished men."[8]

Not a New Englander, but the next thing to it, was his eventual
California host, Elias L. Beard, an upstate New Yorker with whose
family the solitary Doctor soon settled in at Mission San José southeast of the Bay.[9] Beard was an experienced, if not always astute, businessman, energetic, hospitable, and optimistic. He had a way of projecting his financial undertakings on a larger scale than always was
prudent, and hence was subject to wild swings of fabulous prosperity
followed by seasons of near bankruptcy. When Bushnell first came to

his vine-covered, adobe hacienda, Beard was slipping into a down cycle, due chiefly to loss of income from his plundered 30,000 acres, far more land than he could effectively police. Nonetheless Beard could produce phenomenal crops. One of his four-pound potatoes was said to be enough to feed a dozen people,[10] and Bushnell at one point hoped he could carry home a pear from Beard's orchards that weighed more than three pounds.[11] The Doctor came to think highly of him and also of Mrs. Beard. Originally from Indiana, she was a far cry from the sheltered woman he later allegedly idealized. "Mrs. Beard is one of the finest and most interesting of women," he told his own Mary, "one of the outdoor characters who has seen all sides of the world, the rough and the elegant, and meets them all with a welcome."[12]

On horseback and by water, Bushnell made excursions from this pleasant place and took stock of the California scene. He found it a mixture of beauty and barbarism, the latter the very frontier condition he had considered "the first danger" to the country in his 1847 address. Left to itself, the California landscape was a paradise. On a ride from the mission to Oakland, he thought he was passing through "the richest garden of the creation." On another day he made his way up into Stockton Pass, where the views seemed "the nearest thing to the Garden of Eden" he ever had experienced.[13] The redwood forests left him nearly speechless. Writing for readers of the New York *Independent,* he was tempted to call the Calavaras "Big Trees" "the Park of the Lord Almighty."[14]

Since the beginning of the Gold Rush, however, the natural wonders God had wrought in the Golden State had hardly been left to themselves. The marks of human destruction seemed everywhere. Bushnell grimaced with anger when he saw the wanton slaughter of redwoods. Such ravaging of irreplaceable resources "surpasses all contempt," he burst out. He was similarly scandalized by the huge gashes left in the hillsides by rapacious gold miners, the ugly abandoned pits and tunnels, and the unsightly piles of tailings.[15] The influx of miners was only seven years old, yet already the human impact had left its fatal blight on the countryside. Gold and desolation seemed to go together, Bushnell concluded. Of one ruined region he could only say hopelessly, "If some camp of demons had been pitched here for a year, tearing the earth by their fury, . . . they could hardly make it look worse."[16]

Politically and socially the California scene was a comparable patchwork of the hopeful and the vicious. Daily Bushnell met dedicated men and women who had come out not only to gain a new living, but to help establish solid moral and religious standards in the new land.[17] He also found "great honesty and frankness" in many of the rough frontier emigrants he met. But these highly motivated pioneers often seemed to be fighting a losing battle. The Gold Rush had passed its peak, and the new state was in the throes of a prolonged economic depression. The number of murders and suicides was frightening. Under a headline that screamed, "Blood! Blood! Blood!" the *California Daily Chronicle* detailed a massacre of foreigners in which fanatical Americans simply had gone beserk.[18] San Francisco was the nation's toughest town, and corruption had wormed its way so deeply into the elective process that it seemed next to impossible for responsible officials to be chosen.[19]

Twice, when violence seemed out of hand, vigilante committees had taken control in the Bay area. About the time of Bushnell's arrival, a notorious San Francisco gambler, Charles Cora, shot and killed a drunken U.S. marshal, allegedly in self-defense. In another instance, as part of a newspaper war, one James P. Casey, a shady figure with a Sing Sing record, gunned down in the open street the editor of a rival paper for having insulted him in his columns. Convinced that justice would never be done through normal channels in these brutal cases, a vigilante committee forced the sheriff to surrender Casey and Cora, secretly tried and convicted them both of murder and publicly hanged them.[20]

Bushnell witnessed some of these grisly proceedings and was deeply disturbed by them. In a pseudonymous letter to the *California Chronicle,* signed "Mediator," he sided with the vigilantes to the extent that uncontrolled murder could not be countenanced. But he urged restraint in the future, on the ground that fraud at the polls was an even more heinous crime. Even more than murder, he argued, political corruption undermined the very foundations of democracy.[21]

No sooner had his letter been published than new violence erupted. The volatile chief justice of the state supreme court, David S. Terry, got into hand-to-hand combat with a vigilante constable, and nearly knifed him to death. The constable pulled through, but for days he hovered on the brink of death while a nerve-wracked city held its breath, and the vigilante committee stood poised to wreak instant vengance on Terry.[22] At such times Bushnell all but despaired of a California reduced to "a truly wretched state."[23]

In the midst of all this harrowing discord he was offered a public platform considerably more influential than a letter to the press. The First Congregational Church of San Francisco was about to install a new minister, Edward S. Lacey, and Bushnell was invited to deliver the sermon. It was a strong, prestigious congregation that included numerous vigilantes, and he knew he would be reaching influential ears. He knew, too, that to get a hearing he must do more than address the ordinand; in Christian context he must speak to the critical social and spiritual condition of the state. What he gave "a grand audience," in his words, was a discourse under the ambitious, if not presumptuous, title "Society and Religion: A Sermon for California."[24] It was based on God's commission to Jeremiah, setting him "over the nations and kingdoms" and, contrary to every feeling in the young prophet's soul, dispatching him "to root out, and to pull down, and to destroy, and to throw down, to build and to plant."[25] Improbable as it may have seemed to minds attuned to separation of church and state and confident of natural human progress, Bushnell drew from Jeremiah the moral that "religion is the arbiter of a state and nations." Or, as he put it even more emphatically, "true religion, including the pulpit and the church, is the only sufficient spring of order and social happiness."

He went on to argue that the character of a state stems from the character of its people. That character, in turn, has faith as its ultimate source. Focusing then on the particular condition of California, he noted the efforts of both vigilantes and elected authorities to restore order by force. But what a troubled California society needed was not physical force so much as religious conversion. "Every torment of your social state in this crisis of peril," he declared, "is but a sign that, as a people, you have broken loose from God." If there are riots in the street, what else can be expected when Sunday worship is ignored, and week-end dissipation "ruins more character than all the other six days together?" What better conditions could develop, he asked, as long as the main feature of California life was greed for gold and as long as those who find it immediately take it back East with no regard for the welfare of California itself? Rising to a more fervent evangelism than he always displayed, he told his listeners, "You will settle into order as you gravitate toward God and Christ, not otherwise." Let Californians get for themselves "a Christly heart," one that could effectively aid just law and clean politics."

The sermon reverberated widely. Ten laymen, including vigilante leader Ira P. Rankin of the Pacific Iron Works, were so pleased that they arranged for its publication. *The Pacific,* a Congregational weekly considered by many the leading newspaper in the state, secular or religious, spread the discourse over two issues.[26] The *Chronicle* in San Francisco summarized it for its readers and spoke of it in glowing terms.[27] By August copies had reached Hartford, where it was published in pamphlet form. Taking notice of it, the *Courant* observed that the Doctor clearly had lost none of his powers,[28] and the *Religious Herald* earnestly suggested that a copy should be placed in the hand of every citizen of the far-away state where it had been-preached.[29]

Among those in California who took special account of the sermon were the trustees of the fledgling College of California. They were on the lookout just then for a prominent figure to serve as president, someone who could give their "literary institution" heightened visibility and prestige. To that need Bushnell seemed a providential answer. Two days after he preached for Lacey, the board of the college invited him to consider the post and called him in personally to hear his response.[30]

At that time the "college" was no more than a small preparatory academy that had been in precarious existence for seven years. It was so inconspicuous that when Bushnell first came to Oakland to see it he would have walked right past it had not Durant called out to him, "Dr. Bushnell, don't you know what a college is? This is the place."[31]

Small as it was, the trustees, generally able men, both clerical and lay, many with New England backgrounds, had limitless hopes for it. In their minds it would one day be a strong, ecumenical Christian institution. Not only would it be a center of learning for the state, eventually it would be the counterpart of Harvard and Yale on the Pacific Coast and the equal of the best European universities—Oxford, Padua, Salamanca, or Heidelberg.[32]

As to the presidency, Bushnell gave the only answer he could. He was honored by the invitation, and he would interest himself "at once" in the institution. But his first responsibility still was to his congregation in Hartford. "I am a Christian pastor," he wrote the board after a day or two of reflection, "holding a very peculiar relation to my flock." He must remain with his people as long as health permitted. How long that would be, only time would tell. In the interval, however, he would do what he could privately and without charge to stir public interest, help raise funds, and search for a location more suitable than Oakland, a quest which the board was much concerned with pursuing.[33]

The press quickly picked up the story, and Bushnell had to reassure his family that he was "not yet settled in the office." With a light touch he wrote his parishioner Elijah H. Owen, then busy trying to make his way into national Republican politics, "You will not get rid of me, till it is proved that I am good for nothing to you." More earnestly he advised the North Church that he had neither accepted nor definitely declined the appointment and would await the will of the Almighty.[34]

In his commitment to assist the college, he was as good as his word, especially with regard to seeking out a permanent location. Within days he began exploring. In the terms of his Harvard Phi Beta Kappa address, this for the Doctor was "work" that was "play." It gave him a healthy, purposeful occupation that kept him out of doors, roughing it by land and riverboat, and largely in the saddle, where he was as much at home as on his own feet.

From then on, in all kinds of weather and over every sort of terrain, Bushnell roamed the entire Bay area. It has been said that his search was "the most thorough ever made for a college or university site."[35] He soon became convinced that the best possibilities lay on the eastern and northern circuit of the Bay, and he surveyed that region extensively. He began with an inspection of Martinez, north of the city. Representatives of the trustees checked it with him, and all agreed it lacked sufficient water. Subsequently he explored the Suñole Valley near Mission San José, the region around Oakland, especially Clinton (Brooklyn, as it also was then known)—a choice he much favored—and the shores of San Pablo Bay. He then prospected farther north in the Petaluma, Sonoma, and Napa valleys.

Little escaped his eagle eye. The quality and flow of water was always a primary consideration, as were wind velocity and weather. He checked for supplies of sand, wood, gravel, and stone and sampled the texture of soils. He took into account grade levels, distances, population, the proximity of other colleges, and general environment. He looked for views of mountains and bays that would be attractive. He also kept in mind larger considerations. If a certain location seemed appealing, he had to ask himself what effect a new railroad coming through would have on that site. There were as yet no certainties, but there was much talk of a line reaching San Francisco from some direction. He had the problem constantly in mind and examined possible routes with care.[36]

There was also the interesting question of whether proximity to the city life of San Francisco would be an asset or a hindrance. That problem he could see both ways. He leaned toward a sequestered locale because it would better suit a "literary" institution. It would also mean fewer city temptations for students and keep them from becoming involved in the ways of the world before they were ready—from getting "their ship launched before the keel is laid." But there were plusses the other way, too. A university close to a city would run less risk of being locked into provincialism. Daily life would probably be more convenient, interesting, and colorful, and the chances of developing a good library would be greater. Somewhat surprisingly, he also thought the moral tone of San Francisco better than that of the average California small town, the reverse, he noted, of the usual situation in the East.[37]

Frequently his searches led to exposure and adventure. Alone and unarmed in "a fearfully wild place" in the Suñole Valley, he was convinced that he narrowly escaped an encounter with a grizzly bear. In all likelihood he did. During a crossing of San Francisco Bay, his ship was beset by a howling gale that carried off one of the wheelhouses and nearly swamped the vessel. The terrified crew gave up hope and got drunk, leaving Bushnell and a few other level heads to pump out the hold and save the day.

He would set next-to-impossible schedules for himself. One September day in remote terrain, "[I] drove a pair of mules ten miles and walked twelve miles, working at engineer's tools all the while, and keeping my feet all day from morning to night, except what time I was in the wagon. I ate nothing until dusk." The next day he was at it again, this time on horseback. "You would have laughed," he wrote his wife, "to see me running with the rod from one station to another, sometimes half a mile."[38]

In the course of his survey he dealt with leading citizens. He also rubbed elbows with coarse frontiersmen. On one occasion, near San Pablo Bay, the only available lodging was in a "dirty little shell of a place." He ate a so-called dinner with hostlers, drivers, land speculators, and other rough characters and spent a restless night "between dirt, and cold, and fleas, and a very good-natured bed-fellow."[39] Under happier circumstances, in the Napa Valley, he met the celebrated trapper Capt. George C. Yount. A native North Carolinian, Yount had come to California in 1831 and knew as much about the state as any man alive. To a group sitting around a friendly fire, he told of his daring rescue of stranded emigrants desperately trying to making their way over the Sierra Nevada in winter. Bushnell was enthralled with the heroic tale and later used it in one of his books.[40]

Thorough as his search was, it was ultimately inconclusive. When he left California in January 1857, he had enthusiastically recommended to the trustees a site in the Napa Valley. Following his lead, the board voted unanimously to accept it as "the site for [the] college" subject to a number of important conditions of title, water, and assurance of local support. Unfortunately, these conditions were not met. Weeks after Bushnell had left the state, the trustees turned to the site that eventually became Berkeley, a name suggested in 1866 by

Billings in a moment of sudden inspiration when he thought of the eighteenth-century Irish bishop George Berkeley's celebrated words, "Westward the course of empire takes its way."[41]

Often it has been stated that Berkeley was Bushnell's preferred choice. Probably confusing nearby Clinton with the the location of what became Berkeley, Mrs. Cheney believed this, knowing that her father did indeed consider Clinton seriously. Bushnell students still go beyond her statement to say he actually chose the Berkeley locale.[42] Tempting as it is to want to add this important decision to the Doctor's achievements, there is no support for the claim. Either alone or with some of the trustees, he may well have visited the Berkeley location, once the grainfields of the aristocratic Spanish soldier Don Luis Maria Peralta.[43] Late in life, Samuel H. Willey, who had been secretary of the trustees in the earliest days, recalled that Bushnell inspected the property but rejected it "at once" for lack of adequate water.[44] The Doctor never made reference to the Berkeley site in any of his meticulous reports to the trustees, in his "Appeal" to the people of California, his numerous letters home, or in his writing about the West after he had returned to Hartford. Even if he had recommended it, the actual choice would have rested not with him but with the trustees.

This is not to say, however, that his labors were fruitless. With tireless care he had scoured the entire region, giving the board an overview of the options and thus a valuable basis for comparison when the final choice was made. With his personal prestige, his speaking and writing, and, to a degree, through his fund-raising efforts, he helped give the college visibility in a difficult stage of its infancy. One of his last efforts before leaving was a written "Appeal" to the public that was published along with a statement from the trustees. He again cited the crucial importance of the projected school and urged generous financial support for it—not in "mites and fractions." Boldly he suggested $300,000 to start with. Striking an earthy note as to the affordability of such a sum, he estimated that "if only we had [the cost of] every twentieth cigar consumed in the state," it would be money enough.[45]

His main purpose in coming to California was to recover his

health, not helping to found a university. In this, too, he fell short of success. Even when he could report progress, his accounts had a tentative note to them. In June 1856 he wrote James T. Hyde, the minister who was standing in for him at the North Church, that his condition had "greatly improved." But he added half playfully and half cautiously that "*if* things go on well...I am afraid you will have to clear out and make room for me."[46] After being away nearly nine months, he reported to Mrs. Bushnell, "I feel very well, able to work and stir, and do, and wear, and yet I have certain vestiges of bad sensation which shake a little my confidence of the future."[47]

Once home again in February, after a "comfortable voyage," he remained full of optimism for the college and worked hard to promote it. James Walker, president of Harvard, invited him to speak on California in the university chapel, after which he talked at length with Walker on the merits of an urban, as opposed to rural, site for a seat of higher learning. In a burst of hopeful enthusiasm he told a Boston millionaire that if he would endow the college, he himself would "go and spend my life in it."[48] In New York his Yale classmate William Adams put him in touch with the enormously affluent dry goods merchant Alexander T. Stewart. Once Stewart had been a student for the Christian ministry, and for all his penny-pinching in some respects, he was known to have made substantial charitable gifts. He seemed a likely prospect. Bushnell tried to lure him with visions of becoming the John Harvard or Elihu Yale of the West Coast; but as earnestly as he put his case, he never got his money, and he began to weary of "prospecting in the stingy heart of mankind."[49]

Unknowingly he was also losing sight of California realities. At the 1857 meeting of the Connecticut General Association in Lyme, he delivered a talk on California, which was generally positive. He did, however, include a few critical remarks about the California churches. The press avidly seized on these negative comments and, out of context, spread them all over San Francisco. The result was so injurious to the Doctor's reputation that Billings felt forced to tell him his credibility on the Coast had been irreparably damaged.[50] Shocked and pained as he was, Bushnell decided he had said nothing out of malice and would not retract. But he did attempt to smooth feathers with a long article in the *New Englander* giving an affirmative estimate of California's characteristics and prospects.[51]

He also found that his strenuous fund-raising efforts were not universally appreciated. Some who had worked most closely with him in the West began to fear that his abortive efforts to obtain big money were making it hard to raise any dollars at all. After years of discouraging efforts to get the college on a firm footing, Henry Durant had been ecstatic when the Berkeley site finally came within reach in 1857, so he wrote Theron Baldwin in New York.[52] But when finances continued to drag, his elation turned to anger, especially against Bushnell. He was convinced that the only monetary hope for the College of California was to aim for more modest gifts, and he lashed out at his old Yale friend whose inflated funding hopes seemed to be threatening the very future of the institution. "We sinned greatly in tolerating Dr. Bushnell's vagaries," he exploded to Presbyterian trustee Edward B. Walsworth, "and now we are justly visited for it by the infamy of his speeches."[53]

History might suggest that the Doctor had more vision than Durant. He was only anticipating the kind of educational endowments Matthew Vassar, Ezra Cornell, Leland Stanford, and others soon would be providing on the handsome scale Bushnell had in mind. At the moment, however, Durant undoubtedly was the more practical. A less ambitious canvass did succeed in keeping the college alive until more substantial support was at hand.[54]

Despite all the negative publicity, the college trustees did not waver in their determination to have Bushnell for president. His unexpected appearance in the new state still seemed to them a heaven-sent "omen of good," and they were reluctant to let him go. Much as they respected his sense of loyalty to his Hartford congregation, they clung to the possibility that they could persuade the North Church to free him for what they felt would be "the crowning act of his useful and honored life."[55] The board's salary offer still stood;[56] and more than a year after his departure, *The Pacific* reported that friends of the college were leaving "no effort untried" to secure his "invaluable services."[57]

Bushnell agonized over his decision much as he had over Middlebury. When his brother George inquired which way he was leaning, the Doctor did not "know what answer to make." Privately Jeremiah Day felt that "if Dr. Bushnell takes charge of the California College, I think he will make something go there." [58] Ultimately the recurrence of ill health settled the issue. He grew too weak to handle his well-organized church down the street, let alone consider heading a struggling new college a continent away. Claiming that he thought the trustees had understood long before that he must decline, he made it official in July 1861, expressing continued interest in the university enterprise, and invoking on it "God's perpetual favor and blessing."[59] In 1868 the state legislature chartered a new State University of California, of which the college became a part. Two years later Henry Durant appropriately was elected its first head.[60]

Nonetheless, California did not soon forget Bushnell. In 1865 Frederick Law Olmsted came to the state in part to advise on the laying out of the college grounds. He heard much talk of Bushnell's work there. Accordingly, when asked for ideas as to what to call the new college town, his list included calling it "Bushnell" or, somewhat more aesthetically, "Bushnellwood." (Aware of Billings's role, he also suggested "Billings" or "Billingsbrook.")[61] Well into the twentieth century, a street leading to the campus was called Bushnell Place,[62] and still today there are visitors to the university who expect to find his name on the face of Founders' Rock, where in fact no names at all are inscribed.

As memories lingered on the West Coast, his California experience also became an integral part of Bushnell himself. "I am more grateful to God than I can express for . . . this California visit," he acknowledged to his daughter Mary.[63] Repeatedly he referred to it in sermons and books. In 1867, when he paid a leisurely visit to Washington Gladden in western Massachusetts before preaching Gladden's ordination sermon, he was still full of the West and reminisced about it at length.[64] Among other impressions, his ten months in California furnished laboratory confirmation of what he had said about the ominous roughness of the American frontier in his "Barbarism" discourse a decade before. His stay also reinforced his Christian convictions about the human condition. California was beautiful enough and vast enough to stir awe in the most heartless traveler, but the terrible damage done to it by human greed only illustrated again the disruptive ways of a blundering humanity always in need of saving grace.[65] To the Doctor, California was an exciting new world, certain to exert decisive influence on the American, if not the global, future.

Yet for that capability to be realized, he was persuaded that the turbulent new state, along with the rest of the expanding West, needed to follow the lead of New England and New England values. A generation later other interpreters of the frontier, led by Frederick Jackson Turner and Woodrow Wilson, would dispute this parochial view and celebrate what left Bushnell largely—though by no means wholly—uneasy: an American West populated by a new breed of Americans, shaped by indigenous democratic influences drawn from many parts of the country.[66] To the Doctor in the 1850s his native region still represented the ideal for the country. There were those in the new California leadership, also Yankee in origin, who earnestly agreed with him. For success in emulating that model he and they exhorted California to take seriously the priorities Protestant New England had long esteemed: intelligent religion and enlightened education.

CHAPTER 16

"Fresh Married to My People"

THE NORTH CHURCH WAS RELIEVED and delighted to have Bushnell safely home. "I count it no vanity," he reported to Billings, "to say that my friends and people are glad to see me—giving me a universal welcome." On his first Sunday in the pulpit late in February 1857, the pews were so crowded that benches had to be placed in the aisles. Even then some regular members had difficulty squeezing in.[1]

He preached a "sermon of reunion" on "Spiritual Dislodgments," drawing again on Jeremiah and this time using the prophet's figure of wine that cannot be allowed to stand indefinitely in its original container without going stale. So, he pointed out, with a Christian life. Undisturbed prosperity and security can result in a flatness of spirit. From time to time we may well need to be "shaken out of our places and plans" and emptied from vessel to vessel until the sediment of self is filtered out and we are again "prepared to the will and work of God."[2] The application of such a teaching to his own interrupted experience, and that of his congregation, was evident enough.

Having been without him for the better part of two years, the church wanted to see him often and hear him regularly. That meant renewed contacts outside of Hartford would have to wait. "I am now fresh married to my people," he wrote Bartol in postponing a trip to Boston, "and cannot leave them until I get a little old. . . . [T]hey are as eager to keep me as I am to be kept."[3] However, his new start was clouded by a bad cold and by a severe fall when his horse stumbled on a loose stone. The accident left him with a sprained foot and a painfully bruised leg.[4] Such setbacks made his wife wonder whether California had done him any lasting good. None too hopefully, she unburdened herself in a family letter, fearful that her husband "never again" would be able to carry a full load and all but convinced that "his work here will be brief."[5]

Despite all, he made it through the winter, and by summer he began to enjoy altogether unexpectedly a spell of good health. "What a blessing it is to be well again!" he exulted. "It comes over me occasionally like the sound of a hymn, and I stop to listen." In July he took a trip with Sampson and others to Niagara Falls, Canada, and the White Mountains and then attended his 30th Yale reunion in August.[6]

More important, he was able to relish preaching again. His new physical vitality, linked with full maturity of thought and experience, gave added power to his sermons. Originality of conception and his characteristic blend of imagination and conviction were demonstrated afresh as he dealt with a wide range of basic themes. Some Sundays he was primarily doctrinal: "The Finite Demands of the Infinite" or simply "Power from On High." Other weeks he was more practical, holding forth on "Our Unthanking Way Accounted For" or "The Eternity of Love." In some of his discourses he drew freely on his travels, as when he described the roar of the Niagara Rapids in speaking of "Preparations for Eternity" or used the timeless, towering California redwoods as material for "The Power of An Endless Life."[7]

As usual there were addresses for special occasions. In October 1857 he gave the installation sermon for his future successor, Nathaniel J. Burton, then assuming the pulpit of Hartford's Fourth Congregational Church.[8] In April 1858 he spoke to the senior class of the Hartford High School.[9] Nationally he continued to be much concerned over events in bleeding Kansas. During the troubled summer of 1857, Federal troops were called in to restrain impatient free-soil citizens of Lawrence, who in the absence of a stable territorial regime had undertaken to organize their own local government. An aroused Bushnell joined forty-two other Connecticut leaders, led by Silliman of Yale, in dispatching a letter to the White House protesting this action as excessive. He and the other signers objected to efforts to force people to obey laws which "they never made, and rulers they never elected." His inept administration already on the defensive, James Buchanan quite relished the chance to cross swords with "the Forty Fools from Connecticut," as one Southern sympathizer labeled them. Even more, however, he made good use of the letter to defend his Kansas policy and curry sorely needed favor with the South.[10]

Despite the stir, the Lawrence affair soon passed off without incident. In the autumn, when Bushnell felt sure the proposed proslavery Lecompton Constitution would fail, positioning Kansas to become a free state, he delivered an exuberant Thanksgiving Day sermon on an otherwise glum holiday, predicting that "human slavery is now doomed in the United States."[11]

The reason for the seasonal gloom was the financial panic of 1857, which had hit Hartford hard. During the summer the pages of the *Hartford Courant* had dripped pessimism. In an attempt to lift morale, Bushnell gave his much-publicized "Week-Day Sermon to the Business Men of Hartford." Understandably he himself never had accumulated any wealth, though he managed well enough what he had and thought he might have been a success in the business world. At times he even imagined the excitement there must be in making money.[12] His strong Puritan work ethic always kept him from sympathizing with the nascent labor movement,[13] but when need arose he could identify with the troubles of the mercantile community.

On this occasion the Doctor took the story of Paul's shipwreck on the Mediterranean (the only body of water on which he himself ever came close to getting seasick!) to help keep hope alive. Steer the ship of commerce with as much tenacity driving downwind as you would beating upwind in better times, he sturdily advised the bankers and tradesmen; hold fast to integrity and to faith in God's ultimate control. In New York, Bushnell's old paper, *The Journal of Commerce,* complained that clergy were preaching too many "panic sermons." All the same, the Doctor's effort in Hartford was well received.[14]

As had happened before on the American scene, the economic crisis was followed by a sweeping religious revival. Along with New York and other cities, Hartford was swept up in an outburst of spiritual earnestness, laypersons and ministers alike pouring prodigious energies into supporting and guiding it. The Doctor joined them and experienced a surprising new dimension in his preaching. Lacking time to write out daily sermons, he took to preaching *ex tempore*. So effective was his spontaneous delivery that his deacon, Amos Collins, remarked to friends, "Dr. Bushnell must never preach any more written sermons. He may write to print, but not to preach."[15]

There were other parish concerns. In the fall of 1858 Deacon Collins suddenly died, depriving Bushnell of one of his closest Hartford friends and a mainstay of his ministry.[16] For some time the church had been considering a move to a more strategic location, which would involve the construction of a new building. Bushnell was sufficiently concerned about preserving good taste and liturgical fitness that he took time he hardly had to go to New York and confer with the architect on the proposed design.[17]

The year 1858 also brought the silver anniversary of his pastorate. Since the revival was in full swing, there was no repeat of his "Commemorative Discourse" of five years before. What did mark the occasion was a heartfelt exchange of letters. A communication from the deacons, signed by the entire membership of the North Church, assured him of their "united affection." Recognizing that he was again in frail health, they nonetheless wished to consider him their pastor, whether he could preach or not, or even if he could no longer attend services of worship. The Doctor replied in equally warm terms, deeply grateful for "the tender pledges" his flock had offered him. He invoked the Lord's benediction on each and every one, "by name, you and your children."[18]

A feature of Bushnell's post-California ministry was the publication of two important books. One was his first collection of discourses, *Sermons for the New Life*. Included in it was a representative selection of his pulpit work from his early Hartford days to the year of publication. "Every Man's Life a Plan of God" led the table of contents, and favorites such as "Unconscious Influence" and "Living to God in Small Things" were accompanied by twenty other sermons, some of them offered to the public for the first time.

With religious revival in the air, books of sermons were enjoying a new vogue. A collection of Henry Ward Beecher's discourses sold 30,000 copies in less than six months. Bushnell's volume went through five editions in a year, and for some time it was the most popular of all his books.[19] Previously severe critics gave him good reviews, "non-plussed," as the *New York Independent* reported, by "the solid orthodoxy" they unexpectedly discovered in its pages. "Even the *Puritan Recorder* is out for me!" a delighted Bushnell exclaimed, hardly able to believe it after the Boston paper's history of hostility toward him.[20]

In these pages many readers met a Bushnell they had not known before. Instead of the troubling controversialist whose very name had come to imply error, here was the faithful pastor standing before his congregation week by week and preaching a generally orthodox, yet unmistakably relevant, Gospel. A response that especially pleased him came from Edward N. Kirk, the conservative, Princeton-educated minister of the Mount Vernon Congregational Church in Boston. Writing from Cambridge, Kirk confessed he previously had opposed most of what the Doctor had written but found his *New Life* sermons undeniably different. "They occupy a ground of supreme importance," he told his friend, "which I have no recollection of traversing under the guidance of any other teacher." He much regretted not having realized sooner "the style of your ministrations at home."[21]

The other book was weightier. *Nature and the Supernatural* had been simmering in Bushnell's mind for many years. It had its origin in his Dudleian Lecture at Harvard in 1852,[22] an address he had hoped to expand to book length before he left for California. Failing in this, he worked on it while he was there; and having prayed earnestly that he might be allowed to live long enough to complete it, he finally finished it in Hartford in 1858.

His theme was nothing less than the survival of distinctive Christianity in a naturalistic, scientific age. As he looked out on the world from his Winthrop Street study, it seemed to him that the essential Gospel was losing ground to what in effect was a new gospel of nature. An intoxicating science was unlocking hitherto unknown secrets of the physical world. Some appeared to contradict the Bible and to make religious faith appear naive or even superfluous. Transcendentalism, under the high priesthood of Emerson, was teaching that God was contained in nature. Radical Unitarians, led by Theodore Parker, were reducing Christ to a good teacher who saved humankind by interpreting nature. Voluntary reform associations, which still were profliferating everywhere, assumed that they could produce utopias by reorganizing society along the lines of nature and that the politics of a discordant democracy rested on a theory of social compact rooted in nature and nature's God. "Nature is the god above God," Bushnell concluded, summing up what appeared to him the disturbing trend of the times.[23]

For all his concern, he was not altogether opposed to these celebrations of the natural. In his usual comprehensive way he saw these movements as "friendly powers," each one capable of contributing something to "the higher completeness of the Christian faith." Science, for example, he welcomed as "the certain handmaid of Christianity."[24] What worried him was the drift away from the unique supernatural dimensions of the New Testament, "the great problem of life, and sin, and supernatural redemption, and Christ, and a Christly Providence, and a divinely certified history, and of superhuman gifts entered into the world, and finally of God as related to all..."[25] Could it be that these convictions were all "a mistake" and that supernatural Christianity was about to follow the mythological religions of Greece and Rome into distant oblivion?[26]

The Doctor was sure this ought not—and need not—happen. His approach to the problem was to show that the exciting new world of science was not its own self-enclosed territory, nor was the sphere of the supernatural an alien, independent realm of mysterious improbability. The reality was, as Christian faith always had claimed, that nature and the supernatural together constituted "one system of God."

He took time to define his terms. Nature, he acknowledged, had many meanings. For his basic understanding, however, he sat again at the feet of his lifelong teacher, Coleridge. In his *Aids to Reflection*, the poet-philosopher had declared that "whatever is comprised in the chain and mechanism of cause and effect...is said to be *Natural*; and the aggregate and system of all such things is *Nature*."[27] Bushnell essentially agreed. Nature was that part of Creation which operates under fixed laws of cause and effect "determined from within the scheme itself." Thus, by law, severe cold causes water to freeze; fire causes dry wood to burn; gravity will cause a stone to fall. Nature by itself has no power to evade or modify these limitations; its God-given destiny is to live forever within them.[28]

When he came to clarifying the supernatural, he again stayed close to Coleridge, perhaps also influenced by certain "common sense" teachings from Taylor at Yale.[29] To Bushnell, the supernatural was any force "that is either not in the chain of natural cause and effect, or which acts on the chain . . . in nature, from without the chain."[30]

From these definitions Bushnell drew some intriguing conclusions. One was that in God's total universe, nature, locked into law and unable to act on its own, was far less powerful and determinative than the supernatural. In a metaphor very possibly overdrawn, Bushnell announced to a generation infatuated with the natural that in the divine system nature was but a single, subordinate element, "a mere pebble, chafing in the ocean-bed of its eternity." More imposing by far were the unseen powers of the supernatural, which God had erected into "another and higher system, that of spiritual being and government, for which nature exists."[31]

Another conclusion he drew was that the supernatural was no faraway "ghostly" realm dominated by apparitions and visionary marvels. Shocking as he imagined it might seem to say so, he claimed that the supernatural meets us first in what is most concrete and familiar, in ourselves. As creatures of free will, imagination, and choice, as nature is not, human beings have the power to act on nature's chain of cause and effect and to produce new combinations nature itself cannot achieve. This makes us supernatural beings, even workers of minor miracles.[32]

Nature, as Bushnell pointed out, "never made a pistol, or gunpowder, or pulled a trigger." Nature "never built a house, or modeled a ship, or fitted a coat, or invented a steam-engine, or wrote a book, or framed a constitution."[33] It takes supernatural human beings to do these things, and we can do them all without ever violating nature's laws. To elaborate further than Bushnell did, the woodsman who fells a tree to provide lumber for a house does not interfere with the law of gravity that held the tree firmly to the ground. He acts supernaturally on that law, applying it in a different way so that the same gravitational force causes the tree to fall when needed. A sailor hoisting a sail to the wind, does not violate the fixed natural laws of aerodynamics. But acting from outside the laws of wind and wave, he makes newly creative use of them by spreading his canvas so that they move his ship and bring it to a desired haven. To the extent that he thus acts on the laws of nature to accomplish what nature alone could not do, he proves himself to be an original power or, as Bushnell claimed, to be supernatural.

This brought Bushnell to his major conclusion. If without breaking the fixed laws of nature human beings can act on the them supernaturally, how much more can God do the same.[34] From this point on, the Doctor came as close as he ever did to writing a systematic theology.

Human life, to begin with, was created when God acted on nature from outside the chain in a supernatural initiative unconnected with prior terrestrial developments. This theological position inevitably left Bushnell totally at odds with the theory of evolution, which Charles Darwin would announce in his *Origin of Species* only a year later. But Bushnell was dogmatically sure of his ground, and hardly alone in his opinions. He took pains to point out that Louis Agassiz of Harvard, probably the foremost American scientist of the time and highly regarded in Europe, held the same view.[35] Harvard authorities continued to feel so strongly on the subject that shortly they threatened to keep future philosopher-historian John Fiske, a Hartford native, from graduating because he was an evolutionist.[36] James D. Dana, Benjamin Silliman's Yale successor, whom the Doctor knew well, took a similarly conservative position. Reviewing *Nature and the Supernatural* only months before Darwin's radical hypotheses burst on the world, Dana could write that "science is moving further and further away from any proof of the creation of species through nature's forces."[37]

Science always was important to Bushnell. "God is in the book of science," he asserted, "quite as certainly as in the book of religion." Convinced that science and religion should mutually inform each other, he was comfortable making adjustments in biblical interpretation to accommodate indisputable scientific findings. But with evolution, the greatest scientific discovery of the age, he never came to terms. Ironically it escaped him, as it did most of his generation, that the God he believed worked organically in human society could also work organically to produce the race. As late as 1868, when Darwinism had been visible for nearly a decade, he clung to his opinion that the theory "may be true, but it never can be proved." If it were one day shown to be a fact, he wrote darkly, "we may well enough agree to live without religion."[38]

As he believed humankind had been born through God's creative action from without the chain of nature, so sin was the supernatural work of disordered human beings. It was the "bad miracle" resulting from abuse of our originating powers.[39] Bushnell took the awesome doctrine of sin with great seriousness. More of a Puritan than the Unitarians, yet more liberal than New England orthodoxy, he was hopeful and even ambitious for humankind. This made him unwilling to attribute sin to total depravity, or to any kind of preordained necessity. God "did not care to rule over an empire of stones."[40] Nonetheless, he accepted the fall of Adam and Eve not literally, but as a powerful myth indicative of the dire human predicament. [41]

The sin of Eden left the race in a "condition privative" (a term similarly used by Jonathan Edwards),[42] a state in which it lacked the necessary experience, moral training, and saving grace not to err and to do the right.[43] The consequence of this "very great, world-transforming, world uncreating fact," was disastrous.[44] It was the source not only of personal difficulties, but of social injustice, serious physical and mental diseases, and assaults on nature that turned the physical order into a chaos of "unnature." Our lapse into the "condition privative" had broken the egg of life as God intended it to be. Bushnell was convinced that all the prevalent theories of individual self-improvement and automatic social progress, unassisted, were as helpless to put the egg together again as all the king's horses and all the king's men were in mending Humpty-Dumpty after his great fall —although the Doctor did not draw on the Mother Goose analogy.[45]

The only possible remedy was some divine supernatural act, again coming from outside the chain of nature and the laws of morality, a deliberate bestowal of divine grace. To Bushnell this was the meaning of the miracle of Christ. Without violating any cosmic laws, God had come among us in the person of the unexpected Galilean. Through Jesus' unique ministry, his excruciating death, and startling Resurrection, the Divine had acted to win us back and to restore not only us but eventually all Creation to harmony and eternal liberty.[46]

Bushnell's tenth chapter, "The Character of Jesus Forbidding His Possible Classification With Men," took on a life of its own. On one level it was a literary, Scriptural, and somewhat sentimental portrayal of Jesus as a human personality, a figure so exceptional in Bushnell's eyes that he had to be superhuman—that is, the unique God-man. On another level Bushnell was putting the spotlight in a fresh way on the centrality of Christ and the possibilities of studying him objectively, taking up the New Testament "as if it were a manuscript just brought to light in some ancient library."[47]

In probing Jesus' nature, the theological habit of the time had been to begin with his divinity and work down to his humanity. In a way that made him more approachable for the average intelligent believer of his day (and very possibly for modern Christians as well), Bushnell in this chapter began with his unique human character and worked up to his divinity, reasoning, in the common German expression, *von unten nach oben* (from below upward).[48] Legitimately enough, the question for New England orthodoxy generally had been, "How can we believe that the all-righteous, transcendent God became the flesh-and-blood man, Christ Jesus, living in first-century Palestine?" With equal legitimacy, Bushnell was posing it the other way: "How can we understand a very historical, human Jesus, walking the common streets of Nazareth and Jerusalem, also to have been the everlasting God?"

Somewhat the same courageous attempt at scientific inquiry had been made by David Friedrich Strauss in Germany and, as Bushnell noted, in Boston by Unitarian Theodore Parker. Soon it also would be adopted in France by Ernest Renan, though at great cost to his career. But whereas this method left these bold writers sceptical of Christ's divinity in the traditional sense of the term, Bushnell's study reinforced his belief in it. For him no other viable explanation was possible than to believe that the unparalleled graces of the Nazarene signified the very presence of God. For the appearance of such a character to be just another natural, merely human occurrence in the brutal world of Caesars and Herods was as far-fetched a possibility, the Doctor concluded, as "a Plato would be, rising up alone in some wild tribe in Oregon."[49]

The chapter quickly turned out to have popular appeal. It came out as a small separate volume, and for the rest of the century it was published and republished in the United States, England, and Scotland and even in a Spanish translation.[50] At Yale Noah Porter, Jr., ebulliently considered it the finest handling of the subject in English literature. Only to have written it, he thought, was "honor enough for a single life."[51]

Hoping that his book, on which he had labored so long, might be recognized his best achievement, the restless Doctor hardly could wait to learn what public reaction to it would be. Twice he dashed off impatient letters to Bartol eager to know what was being said in "Boston above all." In time responses came from all the leading theological capitals, and most of the news was good. Bartol himself reviewed it for the Unitarians. Bushnell had urged him not to "spare me because I am your friend," but the elfish liberal found that the book swept him along like a novel. Having read it in a day, he questioned Bushnell's stress on sin and wished he had shown more appreciation for the positive, beautiful aspects of nature. But he pronounced it in many respects "the chief theological work of the time."[52]

Most orthodox reviewers from Andover to New Haven to Princeton to Mercersburg adopted a similar tone, taking issue with Bushnell at various points but treating him with far more respect than had been the case with *God in Christ* and *Christ in Theology*.[53] When conservative readers had taken up the Doctor's previous works, they had perceived him as a maverick, dangerously threatening the faith. This time they saw him more nearly as a defender of the Gospel in a day fraught with cross-currents of new thought. Nevin of Mercersburg, who had thought so well of the Doctor's discourses on Christian nurture, characteristically faulted him for underestimating the role of the church in the operation of the supernatural. But he liked the way the book grappled with "the life-questions of the age," doing so with "poetical charm" and "words that glow and burn."[54]

A glaring exception to favorable reviews came from conservative David N. Lord, the New York fundamentalist merchant and lay theologian. In his *Theological and Literary Journal* he tore Bushnell to bits, attacking him for inconsistencies, alleged errors of fact, and all manner of false interpretations of Scripture. He compared the Hartford heretic to the theological wanderer Orestes Brownson, predicting that the "false faiths and unbeliefs" which led that misguided pilgrim, as Lord thought, into "the superstitions and idolatries" of Roman Catholicism would surely bring an erring Bushnell to the same "apostate" end.[55]

By now a scarred veteran of controversy, Bushnell had no fear of reviewers' barbs. What he did need to fear was the alarming decline in his physical condition. For much of 1858 he had been in poor health. That summer one of his young parishioners, George Dunham, had drowned in a Yale crew accident on the Connecticut River while practicing for the Yale-Harvard boat race. Bushnell took part in his funeral, and one of Dunham's classmates noticed that he seemed "utterly broken down in health," barely able to speak and looking as though he had not long to live.[56] "I am doing poorly just now," Bushnell confessed to his brother George at Christmas.[57] Early in 1859 matters grew much worse. His doctors were advising that he return to California, or try the cold, dry air of Minnesota.

By March he had to face the reality that he was not likely to recover sufficiently to be of use to his people, and Bushnell submitted his resignation. Even under these critical circumstances, the church was in no mood to let him go. Twice it suggested a five-year leave of absence, or longer if need be, and offered to give him an associate. The Doctor was grateful for their loyalty, admitting he would like to stay and end his days "as a Hartford man, and nothing else," yet he could not conscientiously agree to these proposals. On a third vote in June, the church yielded to the inevitable and, with great reluctance, acceded to his "urgent request" that he be released.[58]

The day before the Fourth of July, he pulled himself together for "parting words." As he had so often done of late, he turned to Jeremiah, "Weep . . . not for the dead, . . . but weep sore for him that goeth away." The prophet was speaking of a Judean king, not dead, but exiled to Egypt, whence he never returned. Bushnell felt his own coming exile worse than death, leaving him "alive without the chance to live." The pain of giving up his flock after twenty-six years of "the happiest of pastoral relations" was more than he could trust himself to describe. Perhaps he would be able one day to return to the city, and he might manage "a fractional ministry by the press." But the hand of the Lord was upon him, he told his shaken people, "and I must go." The man since known as the father of nineteenth-century liberal Christianity warned his congregation to beware of "vapid liberalism" and to hold fast "a supernatural Gospel, for there is, in fact, no other." Saying in nautical simile, "I look back on you now as a ship looks back on a receding shore," he bestowed his final benediction: "The grace of our Lord Jesus Christ be with you all—in this, Farewell."[59]

More personal goodbyes were difficult on both sides. The church gave him a generous retirement gift of $10,000, payable in five annual installments, to ease financial worries for him and his family.[60] He dreamed of returning to California, but the arduous journey was more than he could face. Minnesota would be as much "exile" for him as was Egypt for the biblical king, but any distant place likely to help him would be the same. So despite his hardships there in 1852, he decided to head back to the cold, drier air of Minnesota.[61] Arrangements were quickly made, and in a matter of days he packed his bags, wearily boarded the railroad cars for the Mississippi and St. Paul, and left.

PART 3

"My Broken Industry"

CHAPTER 17

Minnesota and the Eve of Conflict

THE SPANKING NEW, YEAR-OLD state of Minnesota was rapidly joining Cuba and California as a haven for Americans with lung diseases. Bushnell found himself surrounded by "invalids from the entire Mississippi Valley...from New Orleans upwards," as well as by numbers of people "flocking this way from the east to medicate their pulmonary troubles." On arrival he established himself in St. Anthony Falls, just across the Mississippi from Minneapolis, then a rising semi-frontier town of 5,000 inhabitants. To his relief he discovered the weather had none of the "dark, codfishy Newfoundland fogs" of home. He was encouraged, too, by the number of sufferers he met who had come out thinking they were about to die and then had regained robust health in the Minnesota climate. It was a fine place, he decided, to "cheat disease of its nervousness and gloom."[1]

Publicly he kept up a cheerful front; privately he was beset by severe bouts of depression. Lost without a church, finding it hard to sleep, and feeling weak, lonely, and useless, the thought of suicide nagged him. In part he was rescued from that grim shadow by regular letters from his wife, who sternly remonstrated with him and stiffened his resolve. A spouse, he decided, was "a kind of feminine Providence that never sleeps," and he was grateful for her "tender persecutions."[2]

His mood changed when Mrs. Bushnell joined him in midautumn. Typically, they settled in with "a good, hospitable New England family" at the Falls and began working out their new mode of living.[3] To his children back home, their being alone together suggested a blissful second honeymoon "without any children to molest you."[4] Actually their days were quiet—almost to the point of boredom—filled with resting, and nothing much more exciting than horseback and sleigh rides.

The cold was sharper—if drier—than any they had experienced. In a Spartan fashion they washed in the morning with ice water obtained by pounding a frozen pail with a stick. Bushnell got a frostbitten ear before he finally agreed to buy a cap. "You would laugh to see his outfit," his wife wrote one of their daughters during the winter. "Fur cap, drawn down over his ears and forehead, fur shoes and mittens. Leggins reaching to his hip, his blanket shawl, worn like a long scarf round his neck and body."[5]

Far from home though they were, Bushnell was still in demand. Henry Barnard, not well himself, had just become chancellor of the University of Wisconsin. When he learned that Bushnell also had come West, he urged him to come and work with him. It was one of several attempts on Barnard's part to lure friends to his faculty. But the Doctor did not want to interrupt his new Minnesota regimen and declined.[6]

Preaching in St. Paul was another matter. The House of Hope Presbyterian Church asked him to supply its pulpit during the winter, an assignment he felt physically strong enough to accept. It was a sizable and distinguished congregation, including the Minnesota governor, Alexander Ramsey, and his family, plus various members of the state legislature. With a touch of wifely pride, Mrs. Bushnell felt that from that platform he was in effect "preaching to the state."[7] The Ramseys and others in the church opened their homes to the Bushnells in hospitable ways, thus considerably enlarging their limited social circle.

There were those, too, who responded with little less than awe to the sermons of the visiting Hartford minister. One young physician, with a privileged Pennsylvania background, felt he never had heard such preaching anywhere. "To have such a man as that in this wild frontier town, as it then was," he recalled later, "—it seemed almost an Angel visitation." After one sermon, he wrote a friend, "it took me hours to cool down."[8]

While they enjoyed the warmth of this Christian fellowship, they sorely missed their own home, especially their children, who by the

winter of 1860 had matured into distinct personalities, "the very opposite elements of our own household," as Mrs. Bushnell once described them.[9] Frances Louisa was a brown-haired young woman of
twenty-five, rarely in good health. She was romantic and possessively
attached to her younger sister Mary, to whom she always felt inferior. Yet with her own share of gifts she later taught at the Hartford
Public High School, became a minor poet, and, with the friendship of
Charles Dudley Warner of the *Courant,* developed civic concerns. At
least once deeply in love, the breakdown of her romances was a lifelong disappointment and left her feeling something of an outsider.
Wistfully she wrote in one of her poems,

> Once upon a time I, too, had a lover,
> Gallant and full of grace. . . .

At nineteen, Mary, the Bushnells' middle daughter, was brimming
with vitality. She was bright and attractive, was a conscientious student, loved parties, and had a wide circle of friends. During her parents' absence in Minnesota, Mary taught at Sarah Porter's fashionable finishing academy in Farmington, though she was scarcely older
than the girls in her classroom. She was to marry relatively early and
exceptionally well, would mother twelve children, edit and re-edit
her father's writings, and manage a monumental South Manchester,
Connecticut, home.

Dotha, "Dottie" to the family, was sixteen—steady, affectionate,
and not unaware of being the youngest sibling. While her father and
mother were in the West she boarded with various relatives in Hartford and New Haven and picked up a good education. As were her
sisters, she was devoted to her parents. Marriage in her midthirties to
the already established Hartford banker, Appleton R. Hillyer, was to
bring her wealth that would enable her to establish a professorship at
Yale in her father's honor and to give Hartford its Bushnell Memorial Hall. She was destined to be the only Bushnell daughter to get a
college degree—an honorary M.A. from Trinity College in 1930.[10]

Unlike the Henry Ward Beechers, whose domestic life was difficult, the Bushnells were a happy family. They were seldom without

problems of health, and the pressures of a pastor's household were constant. Yet through it all they were notably congenial. "We have come to the conclusion that we like each other very much," Frances Louisa wrote in the early 1860s.[11] As a result of this closeness, the breakup of the family circle when Bushnell had to resign was acutely painful. They never had been so separated before. For two years they did their best to keep in touch with long, newsy letters, but always there was the nagging fear they might never again be together under the same roof.

Meanwhile, in Minnesota the Bushnells continued to have the North Church on their minds. Mrs. Bushnell had special difficulties handling her feelings as she looked back. From Farmington, daughter Mary tried to reassure her mother that the parish transition was going quite well and that the Doctor's successor, George N. Webber, was showing promise in the pulpit.[12] But this only seemed to inflame her discontent. Normally a balanced and intelligent woman, Mary struggled in vain not to resent the drastic change in her situation. When she thought of another minister in her husband's place, she was glad to be 1,500 miles away. Deprived of her prerogatives as the minister's wife, she even pictured herself as another Josephine, heartlessly cast aside by the congregation in favor of a younger minister's spouse, much as Napoleon had exchanged his empress for Marie Louise of Austria. For a time she dreaded any return to the city, "even for a visit." "It is my home no longer, and what else can it be?" she lamented with uncharacteristic petulance.[13]

Whether or not they should return, or what they would do if they did, became more and more of a puzzlement as the months slipped by. In a note to Bartol, Bushnell said he was of half a mind to "settle down in this paradise" and go back to farming.[14] Given all their ties with Connecticut, however, this could only be a fantasy. By May they knew they were going home.[15] Just where they would live was not clear, though it did seem that Bushnell himself could not appropriately settle either in Hartford or New Haven.[16]

Casting about for alternatives en route east, they stopped over at a spa in Clifton Springs, New York, to see what it might offer the Doctor for the summer. They were pleased with it, and there he passed the season "in the general slop of Water Cure," looking on everything "with disgust" but making use of the time to revise and expand his *Views of Christian Nurture* and prepare his *Character of Jesus* for publication.[17] He appeared to benefit from his stay, enough so that after a brief visit in Hartford he decided to return for the winter, taking Frances Louisa with him. When Thanksgiving came, he led a holiday service of worship for the convalescent community. After some revisions, he made use of a sermon he had preached a year before entitled "The Census and Slavery."[18]

Since his antislavery address on "Northern Iron" in 1854, the storm clouds of approaching conflict had grown steadily blacker. As crisis followed crisis, it seemed that armed encounter must erupt. Yet each time it held off. The presidential campaign of 1856 generated enough sectional anger to start a fight then and there. But war did not come. 1857 brought the carefully manipulated Dred Scott decision, which, among other things, brazenly declared the Missouri Compromise unconstitutional and denied Congress the power to permit or prohibit slavery in the territories. This, too, caused a firestorm, but no war. By 1858 radical Northerners, including Wendell Phillips and Theodore Parker, were calling for the North to secede from an unbearable South—a course Bushnell had publicly suggested four years earlier[19]—and the Lincoln-Douglas debates were giving the question of human bondage the sharpness of a razor's edge. Yet despite these events, and John Brown's warlike raid on Harpers Ferry in 1859, the Union managed to hold together.

But by late 1860, pent-up political and moral feelings were too powerful to be restrained much longer. With Lincoln's election they began flying out of control, and when South Carolina departed the Union in December, the irreversible breakdown of secession set in.

Following the Kansas-Nebraska years Bushnell had watched the darkening skies with deep concern, and within the limits of ill health and other pressing duties, he had spoken out. One June day in 1855 a bulky young Unitarian minister from Worcester, Massachusetts, named Edward Everett Hale presented himself at the Doctor's door.

Hale was going the rounds among Congregational clergy drumming up moral and financial support for the New England Emigrant Aid Company, a five-million-dollar Massachusetts corporation designed to help colonize a divided Kansas (Hale spelled it "Kanzas") with free-soil settlers. Apparently already acquainted with the future author of *A Man Without a Country,* Bushnell received him warmly, encouraged him, and passed him along to Leonard Bacon in New Haven. He endorsed Hale's position as "exactly mine" and wrote Bacon that his cause "is succeeding, ought, must, will, completely succeed, and cannot fail unless our steel loses temper and changes to iron."[20]

Later in California he would pick up a newspaper, read a few lines, and throw it down in despair at the proslavery trend of events. An unwary Nantucket Yankee at his hotel once sputtered a few words on bleeding Kansas that seemed supportive of slaveholders. Bushnell could not contain himself and "blew him out in such an explosion as I think he will remember. I never gave such a setting down to any mortal," the Doctor reported. The next morning he felt he had overreacted and wanted to make amends, but the offender had "absconded before breakfast."[21]

In his Thanksgiving sermon of 1857, Bushnell optimistically had thought the end of slavery was in sight and without conflict. Neither he nor anyone else could then foresee all the bitter tragedy that was about to overwhelm his sanguine prophecy. But it is hard to fathom how he could have spoken as auspiciously as he did at Thanksgiving three years later in his refurbished sermon.

Using the national statistics of 1850 (Theodore Parker also had studied them on the slavery issue),[22] he argued that if permitted to work themselves out population increases and sociological changes would of themselves put an end to slavery. The country had only to forgo radical activism and "manage, by much patience and forbearance, to get by fifty or sixty more years." The relentless growth and energy of the white population would thus prove "our principal reformer," and the extinction of slavery would come about "peaceably" with no "woes" of transition and "in a way so natural and beneficient as to carry the consent of everybody." With God thus marching on his "awful census tramp," there was no need for continued human agitation of the problem. Indeed, such efforts were essentially as futile as trying to enlarge the Mississippi River by feverishly adding to it a few extra drops of water.[23]

Combining faith and demographic logic, this was Bushnell's last public utterance on slavery before war came. What faith might have hoped for in the face of impending hostilities is not clear. Waiting on God for signs of his will in historical crises before rushing into activist "solutions" can be a tenable political stance for Christians.[24] The Doctor was trying doggedly to maintain it, yet events had come close to overwhelming his position. Desirable as it may have been, his plea for restraint seems to have been strangely out of touch with passions of the hour. Already radical Southern hate mail was piling up in Lincoln's Springfield, Illinois, office, calling for his immediate execution by dagger, gun, or hangman's noose. No other chief executive had endured such malignant correspondence.[25] South Carolina was about to leave the Union in a rage; Northern tempers were getting short; and the scent of war was in the air. It was a dubious moment to speak of "fifty or sixty more years" of nonviolent endurance.

Yet in fairness it needs also to be said that the Congregational clergy generally remained moderate and hopeful until the last minute,[26] as did Lincoln and many other elements in the North. On the very morning the Confederates attacked Fort Sumter, the *Hartford Courant* was saying feelings of outrage in the North seemed to be subsiding and the danger of war receding.[27] Bushnell's basic trust in the God of nations was not misplaced. It was only that he, along with many others, failed to read the signs of the times. The unsearchable Lord of history was not going to move any longer to the methodical tempo of "census tramp." He was about to "loose his fateful lightning, and his terrible swift sword." Beginning in 1861, justice was going to be bought not with population trends, but with blood and sacrifice.

A further weakness of the "Census" sermon was its renewed negativism towards African Americans. It was "a sorrowful thing," the

Doctor confessed, that the possibility of emancipation "brings no hopeful promise for the colored race." If ever Bushnell could fairly be labeled a racist, it was in this address. African Americans represented "a stock thousands of years behind, in the scale of culture." "Since we must all die," he coolly observed, why be so concerned if African Americans should slowly die out and superior whites survive? As before, he admitted there were "single examples" of character among African Americans and even cases of "brilliant endowment." But as a race, they were "too low" and could not rise, even though white Christians should do "what we can for their improvement."[28]

With the puzzling inconsistency he occasionally showed in large matters, the Doctor in his "Census" sermon could sweep aside Malthusian pessimism as applied to white population—"for I believe that other and better facts are possible, and that we are to be an example of them."[29] Yet when it came to the prevailing pessimism about African Americans, he could not imagine "other and better facts" or bring himself to advocate being "an example."

Generations later these views are not pleasant reading. Yet again, he was hardly alone in holding them. It would be hard to exaggerate the amount of *ante bellum* Northern energy that went into arguing that there was scientific proof of African American inferiority, devising means of colonizing or otherwise removing Africans from the country, or hopefully predicting that in time they would simply die out for lack of stamina to survive. Extremist rhetoric wrote them off as "parasitic," "barbarous," "disgraceful," "a blot" on a fair, white country, or a primitive race suited only to the tropics, as oranges and bananas were. Such judgments often made Bushnell's strictures seem mild by comparison. What he was saying was not noticeably different from what Lincoln was saying at this date, or Walt Whitman or William H. Seward or even so militant an abolitionist as Theodore Parker, who, not in public, but in private, could see no future for African Americans after emancipation. What was missing from all these voices was recognition of the intelligent leadership of "black prophets of justice," and the courageous pride of thousands of free African Americans in being Americans.[30] With notable exceptions, "the black image in the white mind," as one modern scholar has put it, was in these years dismal indeed.[31]

But a change was coming. It did not altogether clear the racial air, or even come close to doing so. But the searching ordeal of the Civil War was to cause many whites to reassess the abilities and potential of African Americans and to make the first serious national effort to integrate them into the American body politic.[32] Bushnell was among those whose minds underwent this kind of elemental transformation.

CHAPTER 18

"This Gigantic and Fearfully Bloody War"

NEWS THAT THE CONFEDERATES had attacked Fort Sumter staggered Hartford, as it did communities across the country. No one could know it at the time, but once Jefferson Davis and his cabinet had authorized Gen. Pierre G. T. Beauregard to open fire on the parapets of the Federal fort in Charleston Harbor at dawn on 12 April 1861, a war began that slaughtered as many Americans as all our subsequent wars combined, including Vietnam and World War II.[1] After it was all over, Bushnell rightly described it as "this gigantic and fearfully bloody war."[2]

Word of the attack reached the city on Saturday, 13 April. Never in living memory had any bulletin caused such excitement. The treasonable assault—as it seemed to most Connecticut people—was called "the greatest crime committed since the Crucifixion of our Saviour." Crowds pressing around the offices of Hartford newspapers were so dense it was all but impossible to distribute the latest editions anxious citizens had come to buy.[3] The next day churches were jammed, most congregations singing "My country, 'tis of thee" with "heavy hearts but exultant patriotism," according to one account. In the afternoon a huge assembly met in State House Square to raise the flag and sing the hymn again, many breaking down in tears before the ceremonies were over.[4] That morning the North Church congregation came to worship with feelings taught as bow-strings, stunned, and yet half caught up in a "thrill that ran through us all," as recalled by one of Bushnell's merchant parishioners.[5]

The Doctor himself was still trying to convalesce in dreary Clifton Springs. He was restive and hard for his daughter to handle. "I see very plainly," she wrote her sister Mary, "that he must never leave home again without Mother, for he won't mind anyone else."[6] Soon after the outbreak of the war, he could stand it no longer and made his way back to Connecticut. This time it was for good. He was tired of chasing will-o'-the-wisp remedies for his health. "This, I think, is going now to be our lot from this time forward," he wrote Mrs. Bushnell, "a stay in old Hartford, and no more experiments, letting the clock run down as it will."[7]

Once home he was glad to sense "I have still a call," and he did. The next decade was one of the most productive of his life. He more than doubled his literary output of books and articles, had opportunities to preach often, and followed public affairs closely. Early on he formed a hopeful opinion of Lincoln as a long-overdue improvement on a spineless Buchanan. He liked what he saw of him as an honest man of principle, yet at the same time he feared for him. "What a load poor Lincoln has upon him!" he commented when he read of the inauguration.[8]

After a spring wracked with terrible political and military problems, the war broke out in earnest at the First Battle of Bull Run in July. To most Northerners it was unthinkable that the Union forces could lose. With a naiveté that is hard to conceive, Washingtonians put together picnic baskets and flocked to the battlefield, expecting to see a display not unlike a sporting event. While they lunched and huzzahed, they jauntily assumed they would watch the "Grand Army of the Republic" make the upstart Confederates bite the dust.[9]

Then reality set in. General Irvin McDowell's largely volunteer army was routed by Southern troops under Beauregard and Joseph E. Johnston. Both armies were green, and not all the running away was done by Union soldiers. But along with much heroism, there were the horrible scenes of suffering and loss that would be repeated countless times in the next four years. High-spirited young men in fighting trim one minute were shot dead the next. Riderless horses gone beserk plunged around half blinded by their own blood. Hundreds of wounded lay scattered about, screaming in agony as they died untended. "Don't ride over me!" one maimed cavalryman pleaded, holding up two bleeding stumps. "Both hands are gone!" Beginning with this initial disorganized fighting, the Civil War was all of the hell General Sherman said it was. The day ended with a frightful chaos of Northern sightseers and panicky soldiers stampeding back to Washington, leaving a rainy, gloomy city frightened and defenseless.[10]

Much of the South was delirious over its success.[11] The North was dazed. At first it could not believe the defeat, but once it had recovered itself, it turned defiant. Admittedly the storybook war was over, and no one could say how long or how costly the mortal struggle would be. But if a battle had been lost, the war was not yet lost. The Democratic *Hartford Times* continued to say the whole bellicose involvement was mindless and never could bring the Union back again;[12] but the *Evening Press* spoke for greater numbers in predicting that "whoever thinks the grit is gone, will someday discover his mistake."[13]

In addition to the lurid details they read in the newspapers, members of the North Church had a personal tie to the Bull Run debacle. The Reverend George N. Webber, Bushnell's successor, had been at the front as chaplain of the First Connecticut Volunteers. On his return he gave his people a first-hand account of the experience.[14] But in his absence the Sunday after the calamity, his parishioners needed a familar voice, someone who could serve as a seasoned interpreter of the unprecedented disaster. For this they asked Bushnell to resume his old pulpit.

Seldom had he faced a greater challenge or preached in a setting where people were more likely to hang on his every word. His terse title, "Reverses Needed," reflected both the hard facts and the positive rigor he would apply to them.[15] Half the discourse was a look "down the track of our history" that had led to the Bull Run disaster. At an hour when feelings were fastened on love of country, he began by faulting the very leaders who had founded it—above all Thomas Jefferson. One could speculate that had Jefferson and Bushnell known each other they might have discovered congenial points of contact. Both had ingenious, inquiring minds. Both were as much at home in the practical as in the theoretical. They shared a concern for quality education, a strong sense of moral duty, and, from different perspectives, were sworn enemies of narrow religious dogmatism. Jefferson was not the total atheist Bushnell thought he was. He was a Deist, and there was more than a little religious "comprehensiveness" in Jefferson's thinking, as there was in Bushnell's.[16]

But rooted as he was in Puritan tradition, Bushnell could not forgive the Sage of Monticello and his colleagues for one "immense oversight."[17] In founding the Republic, they had assumed, at the expense of transcendent faith, that a merely human social contract, after the manner of Rousseau and the French Enlightenment, would be a sufficient foundation for a lasting government. As Bushnell viewed the case, Bull Run and all that went with it were proof that these otherwise brilliant fathers had been severely mistaken in this.[18] Here was the central meaning of the battle.

As he had in other situations, he paid his respects to the Declaration of Independence, the Constitution, and the laws developed under these historic charters. "Better and more beneficent never existed." But for him, providential American history did not commence in 1776; it started with the Pilgrims and Puritans and evolved under God from that point. At the time of the Revolution, Jefferson and his colleagues did the right things but in the wrong, faithless way. This left the newly independent nation without a conscious, binding sense of reverence toward the Ruler of all Creation, who was beforehand with all governments.[19]

In the absence of this sense of spiritual obligation, reaching "above the mere human level," there was nothing to keep different sections of the country from separating at will. The final consequence was secession and Fort Sumter. To Bushnell this denouement had been as predictable as gravity. "We began with a godless theorizing," he maintained, "and we end, just as we should, in discovering that we have not so much as made any nation at all."[20]

Given, then, this grave predicament, what to do? Armed with Christian faith, learn from difficulties. This was the other half of his message. It was one thing to confront the challenge of Fort Sumter with a wave of fervent patriotism. He felt grateful for this spontaneous upsurge of loyalty, but more than a momentary flush of feeling for the Union would be needed to restore it. The conflict almost certainly would be long and bloody. In order to sustain the sacrifices required to win it, the country and its laws needed to be reinvested with an aura of the sacred, a significance more than human, "And this requires adversity." He proceeded to offer his people a Churchillian prospect of blood, sweat, and tears:

> There must be reverses and losses, and times of deep concern. There
> must be tears in the houses, as well as blood in the fields; . . . Reli-
> gion must send up her cry out of houses, temples, closets, where
> faith groans heavily before God. In these and all such terrible throes,
> the true loyalty is born. Then the nation emerges, at last, a true na-
> tion, consecrated and made great in our eyes by the sacrifices it has
> cost![21]

Viewed in this light, Bull Run was only a temporary setback, and was "almost glorious."[22]

The sermon was one of the major expressions of determination among the Northern churches.[23] As for "adversity," the next few years brought more than enough to exercise the staying power of those in the North Church and throughout the free states. Creating the Union armies very nearly from scratch proved a monumental task. Finding leadership was next to impossible. Lincoln had numerous generals to choose from, but among the early ones nearly all were limited to experience in the Mexican War—and the Civil War was not the relatively minor Mexican conflict over again. One after the other of these supposed experts in military science—George B. McClelland, Ambrose E. Burnside, Joseph Hooker, Don Carlos Buell, and the rest—proved unequal to high command. Defeat followed discouraging defeat, and political pressure on the White House became all but insupportable. Late in 1862 one woman visitor to Washington noted that Lincoln was pale as a ghost and stooped like an old man. President Lincoln himself had about decided there was no hope and that "the Almighty is against us."[24]

With his interest in maps, engineering, and strategy, Bushnell kept close track of the field commanders and their campaigns. From the start he had looked for a "new Washington," and for a while thought he might have found him. "If I were a prophet, I would almost dare to whisper his name," he ventured in "Reverses Needed." Almost certainly he had in mind McClellan, whom he personally knew "slightly" and regarded highly.[25] With reservations, he approved of "Little Mac's" plan for the Peninsula campaign and was so heartened by Ulysses S. Grant's winter successes at Forts Henry and Donelson in Tennessee, and Burnside's capture of Roanoke Island in the Eastern Theater, that he wrote his brother George that he thought "the beginning of the end is heaving in sight."[26]

Yet adversity had barely begun. McClellan's highly touted campaign between the York and the James rivers was a horrible failure. After him, Burnside suffered such murderous losses at Fredericksburg that even as a leader supposedly steeled to the brutality of war he wept when he thought of them.[27] Two days after this hideous slaughter, Bushnell feared dangerous damage had been done to the Northern cause and wished mightily that "that grand army were only on this side of the [Rappahanock] River again, and, shall I say? McClellan at the head of it."[28] Then came Lee marching into southern Pennsylvania at the high point of Confederate fortunes. Mary Cheney remembered this as "the darkest hour of the war."[29] But Gettysburg rekindled Union morale, and if Lee was not destroyed, as Lincoln had so hoped, he was never to be such a threat again.

For Bushnell, all this was more than a tense drama he could observe from the safety of his study. Although he had no son to enlist, his relatives and friends did. In July 1861 he wrote Lincoln's Navy Secretary, Gideon Welles, asking him to find a place as a regular midshipman for James H. Bushnell, a cousin from New York State who already had enlisted before the mast.[30] His future son-in-law, Frank W. Cheney of Manchester, Connecticut, was almost killed at Antietam.[31] Henry W. Camp, *beau ideal* of a Yale scholar-athlete, and one of the finest of the younger members of the North Church, fell leading a charge outside Richmond in 1864.[32] Henry Clay Trumbull, chaplain to the Tenth Connecticut Regiment, was captured at Fort Wagner, South Carolina, in July 1863 and imprisoned as a suspected spy.[33]

Despite the best efforts of peace societies, war in the nineteenth-century raised few ethical problems. To Bushnell it was tragic, but when inevitable it could be touched with a certain splendor. Peace was for angels, he stoically told his people. War was for imperfect human beings, one of God's stern moral schools designed to strengthen human spirits, purge their souls, test them, and equip them for sacrifice. Without this, in a fallen world, some great ends could not be achieved. In his Civil War sermons he reminded people of the stern moral courage of the Roman soldier. He was something of a Roman himself toward Hartford men in Federal blue, encouraging in them an unflinching sense of duty, mingled with the Christian ideal of self-sacrifice.[34]

One of the active members of his former church was George Metcalf, serving in Virginia as an officer with the First Connecticut Volunteer Light Battery. One day while Metcalf was in Hartford on leave, Bushnell met him on the street. In his usual direct manner he greeted him. "Glad to see you, Metcalf. Killed anybody yet?" "I don't know as I can say that I have," came the reply. "Time you had. That's what you went out for," a rigorous Doctor countered. In May 1864, Metcalf was mortally wounded in a battle near Drewry's Bluff, almost within sight of Richmond church spires. A very different but equally forthright conversation then took place with a Union army surgeon bending over him. "Lieutenant, you've got to die. Are you ready?" "Oh, yes indeed, Doctor! If I hadn't been, I shouldn't have been here." Whereupon he opened his eyes one last time to look understandingly at the medical officer, and then closed them forever. When Bushnell heard the news he was moved with sympathetic pride. Grieved as he was, he also was gratified that another of his "children in the faith" had lived and died for a great purpose.[35]

For the most part Bushnell supported Lincoln's conduct of the war. There were times when Father Abraham seemed to have about him "a certain grotesqueness and over-simplicity" that left Bushnell wondering as to his competence. In the end, however, he came to praise him without stint as a leader "original and quite unmatched in history."[36]

As he was loyal without stint to the Union cause, so generally was Hartford. With its Colt and Sharps arms factories, the city was among other things a major Union arsenal. Yet throughout the war years there was also considerable pro-Southern, Copperhead, activity, aided and abetted by the dissident *Hartford Times*. This kind of stubborn dissent disturbed Bushnell and moved him to publish an article in the *New Englander* on "The Doctrine of Loyalty." In it he reminded his readers that the idea of national loyalty in America was still a relatively new concept. He defined it as less a legal than a moral and spiritual disposition, and as one much in need of further cultivation in the ongoing struggle.[37]

A year later he preached on the sensitive subject of "Popular Government by Divine Right," reiterating his belief that popular, democratic government cannot stand unless it be government under God, the "Founder before the founders" of the republic. Human rights, he boldly declared, are never merely human. They originate in God and their final validity comes from that source alone.[38] Bellows in New York and Orestes Brownson in New Jersey and a notable Philadelphia layman, Charles J. Stillé, later provost of the University of Pennsylvania, were delivering similar messages on the role of faith in national affairs, and all to listening ears. They were assisted by another revival of religion in 1863 and 1864. In the midst of it the federal government had issued the first coin with the motto "In God We Trust," and a movement arose to amend the Constitution to include fitting reference to God. Recovery of national reverence Bushnell took to be the ultimate goal and meaning of the war, and here, sooner than expected, it was actually happening.[39]

Bushnell has been criticized for these utterances as a reactionary undercutting the very democratic principles the war was trying to preserve, seeking to make people once more dependent on the churches, and urging on them blind submission to traditional "divine right" authority.[40] He himself sometimes felt he was in danger of leaning too far in this direction. Perhaps here and there he did,[41] yet for all his desire to see the nation brought more fully "under God," as did Lincoln, Bushnell was always assuming "popular government." The whole record of his thought is evidence that he opposed political absolutism and clerical domination. Primarily he was not a seeker of power; within his human limits, he was a seeker of truth. What he wanted of American citizenry was not that they should discredit the Declaration of Independence or the Constitution. What he sought was to have them baptized with renewed reverence and so empowered to solidify the Union and its liberties.

When the end finally came at Appomattox, Hartford went wild. Celebrations broke out everywhere. So many church bells suddenly rang that the fire department rushed out, thinking there must be a serious conflagration. Bonfires were built, and Chinese lanterns bloomed out of nowhere. People stood at windows waving flags and handkerchiefs, and students of Trinity College rushed out of their dormitories to join the downtown jubilation. In Bushnell's park a 200–gun salute was fired into the evening air.[42]

Five days later came Good Friday. It seemed a fitting time for thanksgiving and remembrance, and services were held throughout the community. Little did the thousands who attended these solemn rites realize what the awful climax of that already solemn day would be. The next morning the newspapers were heavily leaded in black as they carried news of Lincoln's assassination, and abruptly a jubilant Hartford was plunged into grief and anxiety. Reeling from this new blow, the whole city closed down the following Wednesday, and again people flocked to the churches. Bushnell was among those who paid tribute to the fallen president. His sense of history irrepressible, Bushnell compared Lincoln's murder to that of William the First, Prince of Orange, cut down in 1584 after trying to unite the Low Countries against the power of Roman Catholic Spain. But to Bushnell even that storied Protesant leader was not the equal of the victim from the White House. "There never was such a man," he eulogized, "as Abraham Lincoln."[43]

The weeks following the asassination brought an unsettling confusion of events—some stunning, some stirring. Lincoln's funeral train moved people to tears as it made its solemn way north and then west; John Wilkes Booth died in a burning barn; the Confederate armies surrendered one after another; Jefferson Davis escaped and then was captured; the Mississippi steamboat *Sultana,* loaded with hundreds of liberated Union prisoners bound for home, exploded.[44] Under the influence of this kaleidoscopic swirl of circumstance, the public mood twisted and turned. It was inclined after Appomattox to be lenient toward the South, but after the death of Lincoln, it was bitter toward the Confederacy. On Easter morning the rector of Trinity Church (Episcopal) in New York declared Lincoln had been by nature too gentle to deal with the South. The job of the presidency now called for a leader who could "hew the rebels in pieces before the Lord."[45]

Part of this aftermath was a series of elaborate public memorials to those who had bought the victory, including a major ceremony at Yale. At its 1865 commencement, the college spared no pains to honor more than 700 of its alumni who had served in uniform, particularly those who had sacrificed their lives. Ten Union generals were in attendance, among them Robert Anderson, the defender of Fort Sumter. A special band imported from New York led a long procession featuring scores of veterans, many of them with bronzed faces and wearing trim army blue.[46]

For such an occasion an orator was needed. The invitation went to Bushnell as a well-known public speaker and a Yale alumnus of high standing and popularity. Every inch of pew space in Center Church was taken up. The Hartford pastor was introduced by another son of Yale, William M. Evarts of New York, a long, lean attorney, twice a Lincoln emissary to London, twice a top candidate for Chief Justice of the U.S. Supreme Court, and ultimately secretary of state under Rutherford B. Hayes.[47] Looking drawn, but neat and alert, Bushnell took the platform, and for ninety minutes he spoke on "Our Obligations to the Dead."

In the main his message was a fulfillment of what he had anticipated in "Reverses Needed" and his other wartime utterances. He had predicted then that the agony of the ordeal would not only restore the Union, but do so in a profound new way, consciously binding the nation together under the providence of God and so making it once more a compelling beacon of liberty and hope. Now the conflict was successfully closed. At least nominally the Union was a reality again, and "a new age of history" lay ahead. It could be a time when government and faith drew closer, and "the sense of nationality becomes even a kind of religion." This priceless opportunity was what the dead had purchased with their blood.

For that Bushnell paid them full homage, citing some of the great commanders but celebrating even more the private soldiers, and the ancestors who had shaped them over the generations into men willing to make such a sacrifice—much as he had done in lifting up obscure citizens of Litchfield County in his "Age of Homespun." As he had prepared for this Yale occasion, he was putting the finishing touches on his study of the Christian doctrine of the Atonement. Clearly this sacrifice was much on his mind. He drew a close parallel between the saving work of the Cross and the new nationhood he believed had been achieved by the sufferings and losses of the war. If it took the bloodletting of the Crucifixion to create the redemptive Gospel, he maintained, how much more would "a selfish race" need to be sanctified by "fearfully bloody sacrifices" before becoming a great, reunited people? In the real world, he reflected, it is mysterious, but true, that "most noble benefits" have "a tragic origin."

He then turned to the obligations the dead had thus laid on the living. One was sustaining a newly elevated national consciousness born of the high deeds of the war. "We are not the same people that we were, and never can be again." Under the inspiration of the sacrifices and heroism of the war, he looked for a new national devotion in every area of occupational life, from business to teaching and preaching. To support this, there was the obligation to create a new American literature. Along with Emerson, Brownson, and numerous others, he had sounded this note long before, but here it was again, and with new motivation. The searching trauma of the war had so shaken and sifted the nation that he could see enough material "to feed five hundred years of fiction," not to mention poetry. This rich new supply of "historic matter" must be shaped and expressed in a style not English, but distinctively American.

To Bushnell's mind, no obligation was heavier than removing "every vestige of slavery." There was no surprise in that. What was unexpected was his outright appreciation and support of African Americans. In a radical reversal of his previous views, he no longer spoke of them as too idle, too damaged, and too inferior to be citizens, or even to survive. On this July day Bushnell saluted African Americans who had fought heroically and urged that out of a sense of obligation to these dead, all African Americans be "put upon the footing of men, and allowed to assert themselves somehow in the laws." "We are bound, if possible, to make the emancipation work well." He hoped that the old plantation habit of white dominion might yield to "gentleness and consideration" toward former slaves.

Nor did he stop there. At a time when few in the North were willing to go so far,[48] he declared African American suffrage "indispensable." In a foreshadowing of the Fifteenth Amendment five years later, he proposed a Constitutional change that would make representation in Congress proportionate to the number of free male voters, regardless of color, and apply to all states alike. Not anticipating that the right to vote would not necessarily guarantee the ability to cast a ballot, he thought the South would accept the plan in order to maintain its full representation in the councils of the nation.

Civil rights for African Americans, Bushnell maintained, were not forms of "soft sympathy" or "whimpering" over the wrongs done to them in the past. They were a matter of practical duty. One only needed to recall the "hundred thousand" freed African Americans who had fought "our common battle," those fallen at Fort Wagner in South Carolina, at Fort Pillow in Tennessee, or on the James, where "the ground itself was black with dead." God forbid that these noble casualties should be "robbed of the hope that inspired them!"

Standing there in a moment of rare opportunity to affect public opinion, the Doctor not only pleaded the cause of African Americans, but tried in a pastoral way to moderate sectional feelings. He had been no friend of the Confederacy, and the lawyer in him could not forbear favoring punishment for a "few." But mostly he took his cue from the Northern dead. If they should judge, "there is no revenge in them now. . . . [T]he thoughts which bear sway in the world where they are gathered are those of a merciful Christ, and Christ is the judge before whose bar they know full well that their redress is sure." Moreover, the Doctor was certain that even during hostilities there had been many in the South with suppressed feelings of loyalty to the Union. Let there be, then, no concern for sectional victory or sectional defeat. Let this long suppressed attachment to the federal government be accepted and encouraged as part of the foundation of the new Union.

It was a commanding address at a teachable hour. But not everyone rushed to congratulate him. The *New Haven Evening Register* intensely disliked his broad suffrage proposal and classed him as one of the "clerical politicians" giving out "Negro harangues."[49] The Democratic *Hartford Times,* still unreconciled to the war as a whole, remarked sourly that Bushnell and his friends should know by now that war experience was not the ennobling ordeal he had described. The war was debasing and left in its wake new elements of "roughs and toughs" to open the floodgates of "vice and violence."[50] Other observers were more impressed. Chaplain Trumbull, still on duty with his regiment, thought his hero "never grander," intellectually, spiritually, and physically (in the sense of combat with disease) scarred by more battles than the veterans sitting before him.[51] The supportive *Courant* felt no summary it might provide could hope to do justice to Bushnell's words.[52]

More significant than quick reactions to the discourse, however, was its conciliatory tone and the depth of its insight into the meaning of the epic encounter. Bushnell was not the only one to speak in forgiving accents. Nonetheless, as the most conspicuous theologian of the North, he inevitably was one of the more influential voices.

On both sides there was a plethora of very different oratory, loudly judgmental and vengeful. Among Northern ministers, Henry Ward Beecher was hard on the "mighty miscreants" of the South, and even Bushnell's mild-mannered protégé, Theodore T. Munger, spent years castigating the Rebels, glad that the war had lasted long enough to reduce a "diabolical" South to a hopeless wreck.[53] In the South, Presbyerian pastor Robert L. Dabney, once chaplain to "Stonewall" Jackson, whom he worshiped, was so incensed by the defeat of the Confederacy that he wanted to see the entire South migrate to Brazil, or even Australia.[54]

Some of the lofty hopes Bushnell had entertained were briefly realized by positive aspects of Reconstruction. Many more were undone not only by the violent determination of the South to remain "a white man's country," but by postwar materialism and corruption in the North, where people were feverishly starting to make more money than the world had ever seen.[55]

Yet it is impossible not to note similarities between his interpretation of the war and the simpler, more memorable words of Lincoln. Both men reflected on the tragic conflict as a national, not merely sectional, experience. Neither was vengeful or willing to boast absolute righteousness for the Northern triumph. Both wanted to see differences forgotten and a new consciousness of Union achieved. No great distance separates the resolve of the Gettysburg Address—"that this nation, under God, shall have a new birth of freedom"—or the charitable judgments of the Second Inaugural from Bushnell's Yale vision of a redeemed nation with a new future.[56] It is understandable that in singling out the most penetrating nineteenth-century interpreters of the war, modern scholars have at times turned to three spokesmen above others: Philip Schaff, a Swiss-born, German-educated immigrant who became a leading American theologian and church historian; Horace Bushnell; and Abraham Lincoln.[57]

When he could, Bushnell liked to see things for himself. The war over, he was eager to observe firsthand the scenes of battles and other important events he had followed with such concern. Consequently, in the spring of 1866 he made a swing through the mid-Atlantic states, visiting Gettysburg, Baltimore, and Fortress Monroe before riverboating up along the peninsula to Richmond. Whimsically echoing the old Northern war cry, he jubilantly wrote his wife on his sixty-fourth birthday, "You will see by this that I am 'on to Richmond,' and have taken possession."[58] He found a city that was functioning, but scarred with ruined buildings, crowded with refugees from the surrounding countryside, short on utilities, and battling crime.[59] Apparently wanting to observe some of the life of freed African Americans in the Old Dominion, he spent his only Sunday morning in the city at "the great African church."[60] After the weekend, he went on to Petersburg and possibly to Antietam.

Sites were still fresh enough that earthworks remained in place, and he could gain vivid impressions of key points in major campaigns. All the while, however, he was seeing more than gun emplacements and torn terrain. In keeping with what he had said in New Haven, the suffering sacrifice symbolized by these battlegrounds was what moved him most. As he exclaimed about Gettysburg in that birthday letter to Mary, "Oh, what a grandeur hangs over that sacred valley and town, where the fires of true devotion to the country's life burnt with a vigor so glorious!"

CHAPTER 19

The Cross "Wickedly" Perverted

DISRUPTIVE AS THE WAR HAD BEEN, people behind the lines had done the best they could to keep up with familiar daily routines. In the Confederacy, elite Mrs. James Chesnut, whose husband was an aide to Jefferson Davis, increasingly had her troubles. Yet her famous diary also records social seasons that buzzed with amateur theatricals, sumptuous dinners, fine wines, and late parties.[1] The voluminous correspondence of the Charles C. Jones family in coastal Georgia shows a household not only preoccupied with the conflict, but one full of politics and religion, the price of cotton and cattle, and the problems of managing slaves.[2] Up North, where normalcy was somewhat easier, Wall Street investors kept scurrying after wartime profits, and Broadway flourished with opera, plays, and circuses much as though there were no war.[3]

In Hartford, too, much went on as before. During the winter of 1861–62 the Bushnell family enjoyed being together for the first time in nearly three years—"a real home-time," as one of his daughters described it.[4] At the height of hostilities, in November 1863, came Mary's brilliant marriage to Frank W. Cheney. As they would have in more peaceful times, the newlyweds enjoyed a Niagara Falls honeymoon followed by a business trip to England and the Continent, with Mary already pregnant.[5]

For Bushnell, the 1860s marked a period when he could spend long, undisturbed hours in his study. Out of that carefully placed sanctum, with its bucolic view of the Connecticut River, came a stream of pulpit discourses, lectures, occasional addresses, articles for journals and popular magazines, letters, memoranda, and books. Joseph Sampson, his New York brother-in-law, encouraged him to think of his activities in forced retirement as a "ministry at large." With a typical flourish of his own, the bodily handicapped Doctor came to speak of these activities as "my broken industry."[6]

While the guns of Petersburg, Atlanta, and Winchester were dominating the news, booksellers in 1864 received some of the first fruits of this industry: copies of *Work and Play* and *Christ and His Salvation*. They were of Bushnell's authorship, but they were also the products of concerted family editing. Domestic "councils of war" were held over proofs of both volumes. As his four women critiqued his content or his choice of words, Bushnell would defend his versions vigorously. But "he would listen to the criticism of a child," so his daughter remarks, "if it were intelligent," and in the end he often yielded to the judgment of his wife and daughters.[7]

Bushnell gave his *Work and Play* the alternate title of *Literary Varieties,* having in mind that only two of the chapters were sermons. The rest consisted of addresses he had given, or prepared for delivery, over the previous quarter of a century. In addition to "Work and Play, "The Age of Homespun," and other stock items, it included an address on "Religious Music." Initially he preached this in his own church. He gave it again as part of the 1852 Yale commencement festivities at the dedication of the first organ the tradition-minded college ever had allowed within its walls.[8]

Although it is not known whether he played any instrument, Bushnell loved to sing. He had been fond of music ever since he first learned the rudiments of it from his mother in New Preston.[9] In a period when instrumental music was widely suspect in church and academic circles, he wanted to see it given more attention in both. To him music was a pervasive presence throughout the universe—"the soul of music is in the heart of all created being." He felt that the best religious music, however, must be more than naturally or technically competent; it needed a spontaneity born of the Spirit. The finest Christian music was "the voice of truth . . . a discoursing of heaven in the language of the heart, . . . a holy baptism of sound." As such it could have immense power to move and change lives.

Christ and His Salvation was all sermonic. The gratifying success of his *Sermons for the New Life* encouraged him to feel that there still was a wider audience for his preaching than he could reach in person, and that the public would welcome another set of his discourses.

For the most part the contents of the book were noncontroversial, and the public response did not disappoint him. By 1866 the volume was in its third edition. There were a few passages, however, especially those having to do with the Atonement, that raised the old orthodox hackles. "The blade is keen," wrote the *Boston Recorder* in summarizing the book, "and always opens an original vein." Nowhere is the writing "dull or common-place." But in central matters of theology the reviewer lamented that Bushnell was "the most superficial, positive, and irreverent of preachers." The author wrote with a certain pontifical overconfidence, so the paper implied, as though there were "nothing in God's plans and ways which are [*sic*] not easily comprehended by Bushnell."[10]

A major event occurred in his former parish in the winter of 1867. The North Church moved a short distance west to a site beside Bushnell's park and became the Park Church. At the first service in the new Gothic structure, he preached a history sermon on "Building Eras in Religion," later the title given to one of his posthumous books.[11]

Writing much and preaching when needed, he also continued to be Bushnell the citizen. When Henry Barnard became national commissioner of education in 1867, he suggested that Bushnell come to Washington, apparently to help him found a university in the District of Columbia. His health just then slightly improved, the Doctor was momentarily tempted and would not "absolutely shut the door" on the idea. But nothing came of it.[12]

In May 1866 he had received an unexpected invitation from Navy Secretary Gideon Welles to serve as a visitor to the Naval Academy at Annapolis.[13] Fond of things nautical, and perhaps remembering that his distant forebear, David Bushnell, helped father the American submarine,[14] he was pleased with the opportunity. He told Welles he would do his best to accept, yet in the end he had to decline. A double murder suddenly had come over his horizon, and being the pastor he was he felt obliged to devote his attention to the convicted felon.

In the small hours of 1 August 1865, while they were sleeping at home, Mrs. Benjamin Starkweather, a widow, and her daughter, Ella, were gruesomely killed with an axe and a butcher knife on the outskirts of Manchester, Connecticut, east of Hartford, and their beds set afire. Mrs. Starkweather's son, Albert, who had been sleeping downstairs, reported the crimes to a neighbor about four o'clock the same morning. He claimed that intruders looking for money had broken in; he displayed cuts and bruises on his own body, suffered, so he said, in a scuffle with the robbers.

After extensive questioning, Albert himself confessed to the crimes, was tried in Hartford's superior court, and convicted by a jury that took only twenty minutes to bring in a verdict.[15] The defendant stood impassively while Chief Judge Joel Hinman of Cheshire sternly told him, "Starkweather, you must die!" After his trial he made a more complete confession, owning up to an appalling array of other offenses ranging from forgery to arsenic poisoning to burning down a neighbor's barn.[16]

During Albert's boyhood the Starkweather family had been loosely associated with the North Church. Bushnell was deeply troubled by the felonies and the sentence and visited the condemned man in his cell a number of times, intending to help prepare him for death. In the course of his interviews he became convinced that Starkweather was seriously mentally ill, and that this was at least partly the consequence of an unfortunate upbringing, which Bushnell knew had been one of hardship and damaging neglect. Accordingly, he sent a lone petition to the judiciary committee of the state General Assembly, urging that the sentence be commuted to life imprisonment.

Bushnell had sometimes defended capital punishment as part of upholding the stern majesty of the law.[17] But here his strong pastoral sense took over, and he pleaded Starkweather's cause. It was hardly a popular move. The community had been outraged by the murders, and many were impatient to see justice done. At an emotional meeting in Manchester, one citizen argued that if the sentence were changed it would not be long "before Dr. Bushnell, or somebody equally wrong-headed, will petition for his release," only to have more tragedies follow.[18]

Nonetheless, the Doctor appeared before the committee and stated his case. In his judgment the prisoner might not be insane, but he was "in a morbid state," thus lessening his accountability. It was because of this hearing that Bushnell reluctantly had to forgo Annapolis. As he explained to Welles, "I see no way out of the case but to stand by my petition, for that is a matter of life."[19]

For a while it seemed that public opinion might change in Bushnell's direction. After allegedly having tried to bribe, or even kill, his jailer and escape, a deluded Starkweather was reported to have boasted that the noose never would go around his neck and that both he and Jefferson Davis eventually would be let off. The committee, however, let the verdict stand, and he was hanged in the Hartford jailyard in August 1866. Reporters flocked in from New York and New England, and a crowd of local citizens collected to watch the dread punishment. By this time a professor from Trinity College was attending him as chaplain. There is no evidence that Bushnell saw him die.[20]

In pronouncing sentence on Starkweather, the earnest judge had assured him that if he should repent of his awful deeds, the Cross of Christ could mean salvation, "even for you."[21] As he spoke the words, a new Bushnell volume was starting to circulate, dealing with that very question of redemption by the Crucified. He gave it the ponderous title *The Vicarious Sacrifice, Grounded in Principles Interpreted by Human Analogies.*[22]

Dealing with the Atonement, of course, was no new thing for Bushnell. Now, however, he wanted to go beyond his earlier interpretations and develop his theme more fully. On New Year's Day 1859, when he was on the verge of retirement, he wrote a friend, "I think the day is at hand when something can be done for a better conception of the work of Christ. Here is the great field left that I wait for grace and health to occupy."[23]

By the "work" of Christ, of course, Bushnell had in mind not the preaching, healings, and other miracles of Jesus' unique ministry. He was referring to the mighty saving change wrought on the Cross and confirmed by the Resurrection. The ground he proposed to occupy was a place where the average churchgoer could experience in a living, relevant way the tremendous power of this event and respond to it at a new level of discipleship.

As he had sized it up so often, current New England theology, with its remote legalisms, metaphysical bargains, and awesome penalties, was making firsthand experience of Calvary difficult. He was persuaded that such barriers to faith never were meant to be, and that when carefully considered, both Scripture and the best in theological history supported his simpler understanding.

He divided his argument four ways. In the first section he developed the provocative thought that the Cross of Christ has about it "no superlative, unexampled, and therefore unintelligible grace." It is "not something higher in principle than our human virtue knows . . . but it is to be understood by what we know already, and is to be more fully understood by what we are to know hereafter, when we are complete in Christ."[24] The Cross did not go beyond universal obligations of right and duty that are binding on all committed Christians, and Christ did "what any and all love will, according to its degree."[25]

For the most part prevailing New England thought was ill-prepared for such strange doctrine. It continued to picture the Cross as an event entirely apart, a once-and-for-all penalty paid to appease an angry God offended by human sin. Only an innocent, sinless Christ could make this cosmic restitution. It was quite unthinkable that anyone else could have any share in this unique sacrifice.[26]

Bushnell disagreed. To be sure, he cautioned, "we are not to set ourselves up as Redeemers of the world," and not every Christian will be called upon to surrender his life. The fact remains, however, as he arrestingly put it, that "I have the same kind of ethical nature as God." Scholars have pointed out that in citing such a principle of commonality between the Creator and human creatures Bushnell was not all radical. In a measure he continued a New England theological tradition stemming from Timothy Dwight, Nathaniel Taylor, and William E. Channing. The considerable difference was that for them the heart of this shared nature was duty or happiness or judgmental law. For the Doctor it was love—selfless, suffering love. To him the supreme purpose of the vicarious sacrifice, therefore, was not to pay an ultimate legal penalty. It was "to beget in human character the same kind of sacrifice that is found, or revealed in Christ."[27]

Bushnell felt his view of a shared sacrifice was firmly grounded in Scripture. What else did Christ mean when he commanded anyone coming after him to take up his Cross and follow him? What else could Paul have meant in bidding Roman Christians to "present your bodies as a living sacrifice?"[28] Unmistakeably, he was convinced, the New Testament spoke in closest terms of the relationship between Christ and his adherents, calling them "to be with him in all the sublime economy of sacrifice by which he is reconciling the world [to God]."[29]

He was pleased, too, to discover support among the theological giants of church history: Peter Abelard; John Wyckliffe; Martin Luther, in his experience, if not so clearly in his dogma; and, closer to Bushnell's time, Immanuel Kant and Friedrich Schleiermacher. Among these, his favorite early figure was Anselm, archbishop of Canterbury during the tumultuous reigns of England's William Rufus and Henry I. He perceived Anselm as having pioneered the understanding of the Cross not as the "revolting" outcome of God's sending his innocent son to die a painful death, but as the inevitable result of a Christ who unflinchingly obeyed God's law of right and love regardless of consequences. The Doctor worked directly from the Latin of Anselm's *Cur Deus Homo?* (Why Did God Become Man?) and found it "really wonderful." It was a joy to him that so authoritative a Christian teacher living so long before him had freed himself from the chilling account-book readings of the Atonement so dear to nineteenth-century New England conservatives.[30]

This was the main thesis of the book. The rest, even though it ran to great length, was mainly commentary. A second section dealt with the vicarious sacrifice as the focus of Christ's healing ministry, taken in the broadest sense to include sin, guilt, anxiety, doubt, and destructive anger. The moving spectacle of the Crucifixion, he taught, had power to draw people away from every slavish sickness into a healthy, restored relationship with the God of all life. Especially by prayer, all Christians may share also in this ministry.[31]

In an extensive third section he set about defending the rigor of the Divine law. In exhaustive detail he insisted that his more flexible "moral influence" approach to the Crucifixion in no way undermined this law, as critics had charged, but exalted its eternal honor and demand as never before. Likewise, by grace, all Christians in their moral lives will exalt this law of right and of love, "doing and suffering each for each," thus forming what Bushnell called the "Complete Society."[32]

The final section elaborated on what he had said in 1839 and 1848, that the Cross as changing the heart of humankind, rather than the heart of God, gave new meaning to the ancient sacrificial symbols of the Bible: the altar, the priestly function, costly offerings, the sprinkling of blood—everything that went with the art and drama of what he liked to call "religion for the eyes." Cleansed of penal misconceptions and put in right perspective, such symbols forever bring the worshiper close to Christ as no mere words can do, inspiring growth in Christ-filled character.[33]

Time and again Bushnell knowingly challenged establishment thinking. Evangelical teaching held that Christ came expressly to die on the Cross and thus to square accounts with Divine justice. Bushnell thought the reverse, following his interpretation of Anselm: Christ did not come to die. He died because he came, and he remained obedient to the law of right and love despite all a hostile world could throw at him.[34]

Dominant thought looked primarily at God's exacting justice when it considered Calvary. Bushnell set forth a God not only just, but merciful. The Deity is not obliged to be "a precisionist," he protested. The God of Jesus Christ has a "justice above justice," shaped by the higher law of righteousness and love. Thus what we see on Golgotha is not a frowning Providence, watching from a distance to see stern justice done. We are witnessing an intertwining of God's everlasting justice and God's everlasting mercy—"pearls that are alike, on the same string," neither outshining the other.[35]

Most significant of all, *Vicarious Sacrifice* made much of a suffering God, while the New England theology placed the majestic Divine Governor far above susceptibility to human pain. When Bushnell had dared to present this view in *God in Christ* in 1849, Chauncey Goodrich of the Yale faculty was so exasperated that he brusquely swept it aside as unworthy of serious comment.[36] Goodrich and other old champions of orthodoxy were gone by 1866, but their doctrine still held. "Christ brought nothing of the Godhead with him into the world," as another conservative of the 1860s had emphasized.[37]

An overall effect of the Doctor's theology was reducing the distance between God and human life. An important expression of that was his belief in an eternally passible—that is, feeling or suffering—Creator. The conviction runs through this book as one of its most appealing motifs. To Bushnell the Cross was "no new thought . . . taken up by Christ in the year One of the Christian era." The whole of God had been in it "from eternity." "Nay, there is a cross in God before the wood is seen upon Calvary," he maintained in one of his best-remembered statements. Or again, "There is a Gethsemane hid in all love. . . . By that sign it was that God's love broke into the world, and Christianity was born."[38]

Beginning with *Sermons for the New Life* and *Nature and the Supernatural,* Bushnell had produced six books that were widely accepted and often praised. As a consequence some readers had been lulled into thinking that the Hartford theological leopard had been gradually changing his spots. A mere glance at the opening pages of *The Vicarious Sacrifice* brought a rude awakening, and the floodgates of controversy again flew open. To tamper with the Crucifixion was to touch the heart of all that orthodoxy held essential. From Chicago to Princeton, from New York to Hartford and Boston, church critics fell avidly on this new evidence of the Doctor's heterodoxy. Theodore Munger, who felt Bushnell had produced here a work "of the first order of intellectual greatness," nevertheless thought the attacks on it were more severe than "on any previous book" Bushnell had written. Especially outside of New England, he recalled, "the condemnation was total."[39]

Even before it was published, the mother of Phillips Brooks, the future great Episcopal preacher and bishop, learned that *The Vicarious*

Sacrifice was soon to appear. She warned Brooks against having anything to do with it. Appalled by what she already read of Bushnell's thought, she told her promising son, then in Philadelphia, "I would rather never have you preach Christ's blessed gospel than wickedly pervert it as Bushnell does."[40]

In Chicago, young Charles H. Fowler, later a leading Methodist bishop, leveled biting criticisms at the Doctor through his denominational quarterly. He could not recognize Bushnell's Anselm; he faulted him for failing to define "vicarious" adequately; he found him unrealistic about love; and he could not accept the book's attempt to portray Christ and ordinary Christians as redemptive partners whose natures differed in degree only. Fowler had come to the book hopefully, as he had found other Bushnell writings helpful. To his disappointment, he had discovered "*more errors,* and *more false* doctrine, than we have ever met *in the same space.*"[41]

The twenty-eight-year-old Illinois pastor wrote with flare, articulating the feelings of a broad segment of church opinion. Free-lance philosopher and theologian Henry James, Sr., always ready with a sharp opinion, had been critical of the Doctor in the past.[42] He was no less so in a *North American Review* article on *The Vicarious Sacrifice,* complaining that his Hartford acquaintance excelled at putting new wine in old wineskins, with the results predicted in Jesus' parable.[43]

In Hartford itself Calvin Stowe presided over a meeting of the anti-Bushnell Hartford Fourth Association, whose member William W. Andrews read out an eighty-one-page critique of the book that took it apart piece by piece. He was the same Andrews Bushnell had approached to be his successor at the North Church many years before. No doubt mindful of this earlier tie, Andrews tipped his hat to certain "true and beautiful passages" in his friend's work. But he deplored as "unfair" the Doctor's un-Scriptural undermining of the accepted penal understanding of the Cross.[44]

As before, Bushnell had friends as well as opponents, though this time they tended to be more tolerant than enthusiastic. James Freeman Clarke, the Boston Unitarian leader, acknowledged that Bushnell's volume was not at all a Unitarian book, but that it came from "a living mind and heart, and from a free spirit."[45] In the *New Englander* Noah Porter, Jr., was generous, though he could see relatively little in what he read that did not derive from such suspect European liberals as Schleiermacher, Coleridge, and the English theologian and preacher John Frederic D. Maurice.[46]

As Bushnell himself freely admitted, no teaching on the Atonement ever has been definitive.[47] The New Testament is clear that on the Cross Jesus did something *for* us, as orthodoxy held, opening the grace of God to us more fully than ever before. But it is equally clear in the Gospels that on Calvary he did something *to* us, as Bushnell claimed, in a uniquely deep and powerful way moving human hearts into a fresh relationship with the Eternal. Christian history has lived in the tension between these two poles, the focus of faith moving now toward one pole, now toward the other. The Doctor's book renewed the ancient tension. Quite apart from the disputes of major theologians, it was no easy thing for people rooted and grounded in the Cross as a penal sacrifice to contemplate his very different treatment, even when they highly esteemed him personally.

Henry Clay Trumbull, then a rising Christian education executive, and briefly Bushnell's Boswell, encountered such difficulties. Although a war veteran with hard experience as a prisoner, and not readily carried away, he exclaimed to Bushnell once, "O Doctor, you are simply grand! How good it is to be with you! There's no one in the world like *you*." "Oh, no! Trumbull," Bushnell protested, "I just look at truth from another corner of the room, that's all." Yet even for so enthusiastic a follower, Bushnell's Atonement views from "another corner" were not automatically acceptable. During their frequent walks Bushnell would prod his reluctant friend to study his understanding of the Cross, including an article he had written for the magazine *Hours at Home*.

> "Have you read my article yet, Trumbull?" he asked him one day.
> "No, I haven't," Trumbull confessed.
> "Well, I want you to," the Doctor insisted.[48]

Two weeks later he still had not done his assignment. Bushnell thereupon seized both his hands and, looking him kindly in the eye, said, "Trumbull, I *want* you to read that [article]. I ask you to read it for *my* sake. Now promise me you will." Eventually his young protégé did as he had been told. Still unconvinced, he pleaded for more time to think it over. Bushnell's eyes brightened, and poking his thumb gently into Trumbull's side, he exclaimed in a tone of good-natured triumph, "Ah! The pizen's workin'."[49]

In Trumbull's case "the pizen" did slowly work. In the end he felt his mentor's teaching had "rent the veil from before my mind," and that he never again could be "a blind child" in the face of what "the noonday sun brought to light." Yet when they discussed the never-ending issue sometime later, it appeared that if Trumbull had become more liberal under Bushnell's influence, Bushnell himself had become more conservative. Without abandoning his position, he told Trumbull he could "see now the truth there is in many forms I once vigorously opposed" and thought he could pass "a pretty good examination in the Westminster Catechism,...or almost any other catechism."[50]

Trumbull was but one of the many younger ministers Bushnell influenced during these years. It has been said of Emerson that he was "a great encourager and inspirer" for emerging writers just entering the literary profession.[51] "The Emerson of Hartford," as Bushnell has been called,[52] was the same to a new generation of church leaders.

This amiable trait was the outgrowth of a long-standing interest in men just starting out, or still finding their way. Such "saplings," as Mary Cheney referred to them,[53] often occupied his pulpit, and the Doctor listened supportively to them all, looking hopefully for good things even in mediocre sermons. When a new preacher did well, he was especially delighted. "Wasn't that fine?" he beamed to a friend after hearing a man fresh from seminary.

> When he announced his text I busied myself thinking how he would treat it. I was greatly pleased with his opening. Then I tried to keep ahead of him in my thoughts. At every point he was up to the best I

could think of, or better. And when the sermon was finished I felt like throwing my arms around him and kissing him.[54]

During the end-of-the-century's "Gilded Age," three preachers dominated the religious life of Hartford: Bushnell's eventual successor, Nathaniel J. Burton, at the Park Church; Edwin Pond Parker of Hartford's South Church; and Mark Twain's great friend, Joseph H. Twichell, at Asylum Hill. All of them exercised ministries that extended beyond Hartford. All of them became members of the Yale Corporation. All of them, though not always in full agreement with Bushnell, were his ardent followers and gladly acknowledged that they owed more to him in theology and personal faith than to any other figure in their long careers.[55] Farther afield in Philadelphia, Phillips Brooks disregarded his mother's warnings to burn Bushnell's books. Instead he bought them. Avidly he devoured *Christian Nurture, The Vicarious Sacrifice,* and other Bushnell writings. *Sermons for the New Life* made such an impression on him that he wrote a sonnet to it.[56]

In 1858 Bushnell noted a seminarian at Yale, Moses Coit Tyler, subsequently an Episcopal priest and the first full professor of American history (at Cornell) in the United States. He invited him to take the North Church pulpit for a Sunday.[57] As a young clergyman, Theodore T. Munger, later the most literary advocate of the "New Theology" of the 1880s and 1890s, preached often in Hartford. During an initial visit with Bushnell, Munger found him "very entertaining, more so than anyone I ever conversed with." In addition to spoken counsel, Bushnell wrote him, frankly questioning whether for all the merit of his pulpit work, he was not "too nearly a literary gentleman in your habit—not enough an apostle?" The relationship flourished during the rest of the Doctor's life, and Munger ultimately became his initial nonfamily biographer.[58]

Among these master-journeyman relationships, Bushnell's friendship with Washington Gladden had special depth and color. Gladden was destined to be a great Congregational herald of the social gospel, though he is now best remembered as the author of the still-popular hymn "O Master, Let Me Walk With Thee." Early in his career he had been impressed and theologically liberated by Bushnell's writings. Years later he was to say that he could not have remained in the ministry as an honest man had it not been for this discovery. If he had had any Gospel to preach, he confessed, it was Bushnell who "led me into the light and joy of it."[59]

Hence, when Gladden was called to the Congregational Church in the factory town of North Adams, Massachusetts, in the mid-1860s, he was determined to have the Doctor preach his installation sermon. On receiving Gladden's invitation, the wasting Hartford veteran demurred. Much as he appreciated Gladden's cordiality, he warned him that to ask as controversial figure as himself to take his pulpit on so important an occasion might get him off to a bad start. Gladden, however, insisted that he was prepared to accept the consequences, and the Doctor promptly agreed to come, hopeful that "heresies" would cause "no difficulty."[60]

They spent nearly a week together before the installation. In something of a ministerial idyll, the two rode over the Berkshire Hills and day after day lay in the June shade discussing "things visible and invisible." If his visitor did most of the talking—"Horace Bushnell was one of the great talkers," Gladden observed—his young host took delight in the attention of his illustrious guest, relishing the flow of sturdy, Carlylean rhetoric and the homely speech "lit up with poetic touches."[61]

For all his liberal zeal, the new minister managed to squeeze by his ecclesiastical examination, and his more conservative people found they had nothing to fear from Bushnell's installation sermon on "The Gospel of the Face."[62] Ill health noticeably impaired Bushnell's delivery. But warmth of conviction was unmistakable as he preached the love of God shining in the face of Christ and through him, waiting to shine on the world through ours. Mark Hopkins, legendary president of Williams College whom Bushnell always had found "very friendly,"[63] was in the congregation. Someone asked him after the service, "Is not that the Gospel?" In words that foreshadowed a slowly widening acceptance of Bushnell's views, Hopkins replied without hesitation, "Nothing else is the Gospel."[64]

CHAPTER 20

Rights of African Americans, Rights of Women

THE STREAM OF BOOKS CONTINUED. During the last years of the decade two more came from the Doctor's study. *Moral Uses of Dark Things,* issued in 1867, stands among Bushnell's best.[1] The other, his much-debated *Women's Suffrage; the Reform Against Nature,* published two years later, was among his least successful writings.[2]

Moral Uses brought together an unusual sequence of sermons, subsequently published serially in the magazine *Hours at Home,* a Scribners' periodical which at one time had on its list of contributors the Russian novelist Leo Tolstoy.[3] As noted earlier,[4] the discourses had a common theme: the positive, moral significance of puzzling and painful elements in life, "the night-side of creation," as he called them. In a certain way Bushnell appears here as a prose Milton, seeking to justify the ways of God to man. Why should the supposedly benevolent Deity permit us to be tormented by plagues and poverty, by physical danger and insanity, or even by such marginal threats as winter cold or "things unsightly or disgustful?"

At times he argues that these negative forces are divinely provided to help reduce our human pride and turn us with new appreciation to the better blessings of a fundamentally gracious God. At other times he justifies them as elements in a moral school, obstacles to be dealt with and overcome on the way to mature character. Yet again, these life-threatening, or merely unattractive, elements cause us to look more deeply into life than unmarred happiness and benignity ever would lead us to do, and so also more rigorously into our own moral condition.

As he runs through his catalog of sixteen different enigmas, there are touches of the unusual and the personal. When he faces the problem of noxious insects, it is not hard to see Bushnell the climber and fisherman, knowing firsthand how "a single mosquito will defy and torture a man all night!"[5] Insanity (mental illness) he sensitively calls the "the darkest of all dark things," but along with modern psychology, he considers it largely the imbalance of all of us writ large. We are not all insane. But most of us, in our abuse of nature, our prejudices, our hidden motives, and mismanaged drives, the Doctor contends, are "unsane." A brilliantly endowed Bushnell, who now and then could be irritatingly overconfident, turns modestly tender and open in this essay, hesitant to pass judgment on the so-called madness of others because of the "general distemper" that affects "us all." A moral use of insanity is thus to help show those of us who consider ourselves normal "how far we off we have been from sanity" and, by contrast, what true health of mind and spirit would be.[6]

For the most part, these unusual articles have slipped from memory. One, however, has surfaced in more recent years and stirred heated debate. Along with such "dark things" as storms at sea and decimating pestilences, Bushnell included a chapter entitled "Of Distinctions of Color." Obviously he had in mind primarily, though not exclusively, the black-white question.[7] The very fact that he associated the presence of African Americans with such malignant forces could seem to indicate that he was lapsing again into racism. Some modern critics have said as much.[8] But there is room for a different interpretation.

Bushnell was not dealing here with abstract theory. He was attempting to shed Christian light on an acute public dilemma. The nation had poured out its blood, settled the future of the Union, and put an end to slavery. But with all its agonies and sacrifices, the war had provided no solution to the future of African Americans in American society. What role were millions of newly freed slaves to have, and how were they to be equipped to play it? It was a pressing concern, hotly debated from private homes to the halls of Congress.

During Reconstruction, opinion on the subject went through wide swings, influenced by the tides of politics, sectional differences, and alternating waves of devoted benevolence and brutal violence.[9] At the time Bushnell was writing his essay, egalitarian Radicals, led by Charles Sumner and Thaddeus Stevens, were in the ascendancy. Hopeful African Americans were feeling intensely American and, though hindered by enormous impediments, were mounting brave initiatives in business, education, religion, and political action.

In both the North and South, however, racism continued to be pervasive, and there were powerful negative voices. Early in the Reconstruction experience, future president James A. Garfield, then a prominent Ohio Congressman, winced at the thought of African Americans as his political equals. Privately he admitted, "I would be glad if they could be colonized, sent to heaven, or got rid of in any decent way."[10] Already sitting in the White House, an opinionated Andrew Johnson clung to same hostile position throughout his term of office.[11]

Little wonder that Bushnell had misgivings when he stopped to notice a neatly dressed African American child on the streets of Hartford. Given the persistent degree of prejudice against African Americans, what hope could there possibly be for that young life? The detail of what would come no one could foresee. But the Doctor rightly sensed an ominous future. Despite the promising Thirteenth, Fourteenth, and Fifteenth amendments to the Constitution, Darwinian racists soon would be writing off African Americans as a vanishing race; Northern businessmen would refuse them insurance as unacceptable risks; and Southern negrophobes would be rejecting them as degenerate beasts.[12]

Perplexed and troubled by this monumental prejudice, Bushnell sought to address the problem theologically, hoping to provide greater perspective for whites, and perhaps even to help lighten the burden of African Americans. What good purpose could God have had, he asked himself, in creating a multicolored humanity when it would seem that so many difficulties—such as a terrible Civil War—might have been avoided had we all been made alike?

Unwittingly he exposed himself to sharp twentieth-century attack by referring to African Americans early on as "a quadruman people" (nonhuman primates) and as "physically speaking, animals, and nothing else."[13] These remarks rightly have been seized upon as insufferably racist, acceptable as they would have sounded in the ears of many of his contemporaries.

Yet they are so out of keeping with the supportive tone of the rest of the chapter, that one has to venture the conclusion that Bushnell was describing—and very accurately—a common cultural "supposition" (he uses such a term more than once)[14] as to African Americans, rather than offering his own judgment. Such an explanation seems the more plausible in that he immediately went on to insist that even if African Americans were not descended from Adamic stock—he still clung to Agassiz's theory of multiracial origins—they were as fully human as if they had been. Admittedly most of them lacked cultivation. But African Americans, he claimed, were as far removed from animals as whites, and they were intimately joined to humanity, "where the African race have [*sic*] always been." He had no patience with "low-minded scorners" willing to "insult" Africans "by any most cruel caricature of their physical type" and trying, on some supposedly scientific basis, "to put them outside of humanity"along with "African gorillas and chimpanzees."[15]

As to God's purpose in creating "distinctions of color," it was Bushnell's perception that varieties of color on the outside were intended to make us look more carefully at what it means to be a human being on the inside. They force us to get beneath accidental surface differences of type and color and to honor "the undersoul" of each individual, "the unreducible diamond of moral nature" at the center of every human life. If we all looked the same, he speculated, this immortal, God-given "core" might well be "swamped" under our similarities. Different colors challenge us to probe more deeply after "the everlasting man [human being], the same as to kind, under all colors and aspects and configurations."[16]

Having stated this, he was ready to say without qualification that African Americans carry with them the identical moral dignity as all peoples everywhere. "That is, we are all men, all moral natures," he wrote, "so completely akin to each other that truth to one is truth to another, right principle to one, right principle to another, God, love, and worship, and joy the same to all."[17] It followed that African

Americans, although facing staggering obstacles, were the equal of any person and were entitled to civil as well as moral rights, including the right to vote on the same terms as any other citizen. Anything less, he urged, "is but a name for oppression, whether it be the law of Connecticut, or of South Carolina."[18]

Bushnell also had come to entertain great hopes for African Americans spiritually. For decades the idea had been blowing about among a few American intellectuals that Africans were "natural Christians," temperamentally more gifted for the attainment of true Christianity than their Caucasian despisers. A Scottish-born, Swedenborgian teacher in Cincinnati, Alexander Kinmont, had floated the thought as early as the late 1830s. Unitarians such as Channing, James Freeman Clarke, and James Russell Lowell also had endorsed it, as had Harriet Beecher Stowe in *Uncle Tom's Cabin*. During a rare happy interlude in Tom's experience, Stowe reflects on the potential of his race, predicting that the time will come when African Americans like him "will exhibit the highest form of the peculiarly *Christian life*."[19]

No doubt influenced by Stowe, by the simple piety of his untutored friend "Old Law," and by more gifted African Americans whom he had known personally, Bushnell appropriated this prophetic belief and gave it his own eloquent expression in his *Moral Uses*. African Americans, he declared, "are now the true Nazarenes of the world— they are humble enough, and know how to believe." It had been "the great defect" of Western whites, he confessed, that "they speculate overmuch, and strangle the Gospel." By contrast, he was convinced, "these Africans are constitutionally inspirable." Bushnell gave his reading of their religious future a further biblical underpinning, as Stowe had in her novel, by pointing to God's way of reversing the ways of human history so that the last turn out to be first. Following the pattern ofthese "grand inversions," the Doctor peered ahead, and tried to imagine the day when African Americans, "this very singular people" would prove the finest of God's creation. Could it be, he asked, that it is "God's plan to finish this race last, and set them on the summit, when their day shall come, as the topstone of all righteous peace, and most inspired religion?"[20]

For whatever reason, Bushnell seems not to have been in touch with the many courageous African American advances of the Reconstruction period. This may have left him more pessimistic about the American prospects for this minority than he might otherwise have been. He did not suggest African Americans ought to return to Africa, as Kinmont and Mrs. Stowe did.[21] But with them he doubted that the New Jerusalem, which he believed African Americans might one day build, would be created in this country.[22] It probably could happen in the United States, he thought, "if their friends in the white race could have them [African Americans] to themselves, separated from the plunder and poison of their enemies."[23] But such was not possible. Through "our wrong," and not African American inadequacy, Bushnell confessed, the divinely ordained consummation likely must come not on American but on African soil.[24]

The Doctor's final comprehensive statement on race, this discourse continues to be studied and discussed—and misunderstood—by whites and African Americans from numerous different viewpoints. Beyond question, however, the Bushnell of 1867 had come a long way from his prewar "The Census and Slavery." He remained a man of his time, as every leader inescapably must, using the idiom of his period and affected by the atmosphere of his generation. But whatever the limitations of his thought for a later era, Bushnell's Christian defense of racial equality and his anticipation of the rise of African Americans made him something far broader and deeper than a cultural echo of his prejudiced age.[25]

While African Americans were struggling to gain a new place in postwar society, women were doing the same. For a long time they had chafed, sometimes angrily, in their restricted "women's sphere," sharing their problems with each other privately—if not, out of necessity, secretly—and hiding resentment under thin layers of romance in popular novels.[26] Occasionally an enlightened male would speak a word of encouragement. As early as 1816 Bushnell's future parishioner, John P. Brace, was telling young women students at Miss Pierce's School in Litchfield that he hoped their education would better their prospects in the world. He wanted to see the time when woman would become "the rational companion of men, not the slave of his pleasures or the victim of tyranny."[27]

In many respects abolitionism, and especially the influence of William Lloyd Garrison, provided the women's movement with its initial ideological and political framework.[28] Some of the earliest women leaders won their spurs on abolitionist platforms and in antislavery strategy meetings during the 1830s and 1840s. The fledgling crusade took institutional form at the landmark Seneca Falls Convention in 1848, and with the push for African American suffrage after Appomattox, women hoped that they, too, might share in the coming new day. But it was not to be. In 1867 a promising pilot attempt to amend the Kansas constitution and enfranchise women failed miserably. Women were further humiliated in 1870 when the Fifteenth Amendment to the U.S. Constitution, removing race as a barrier to suffrage, omitted any mention of women.[29]

Bushnell's book on women's suffrage was a response to this turmoil. Its provocative subtitle, "The Reform Against Nature," more than implied that the idea of women in politics went against the very grain of Creation. Except for suffrage, however, Bushnell had moments when he was a surprisingly unapologetic advocate of women's rights. Some of the statements in this little volume might have been written by an Elizabeth Cady Stanton or a Susan B. Anthony. As assertively as they did, Bushnell deplored the long subjugation of women in America and elsewhere, condemning their traditional servitude to men as a condition "no principle of legality permits, and no pretense of reason or necessity justifies." When he considered the history of this injustice, he could well understand the "anger" and the "shame" women had endured. He went so far as to imagine himself as a Victorian woman. When, as best he could, he pondered the feminine lot from the inside—unfair wages for hard work, restricted employments, very possibly a tyrannical husband, the silent suffering over domestic problems, and the ridicule that went with every effort to enter a profession—he was tempted to justify women in staging "a riot against sexhood itself." And he was sure that in a similar situation he would want to be a man.[30]

As to the slowly widening the range of opportunities for women,[31] he had no difficulty seeing them as educators—not only as teachers, but as administrators filling "the highest and most responsible places of management and presiding trust" and entitled to "the rewards that men have in the same." He knew too well the work of such women as Catherine Beecher, Sarah Porter, and his own sister-in-law, Elizabeth Apthorp, to have any reservations in this field.[32] When it was far from generally accepted, he not only strongly favored higher education for women, but was almost passionately supportive of the admission of women to men's colleges. He never forgot his impressions of Oberlin in the 1850s. Furthermore, he and Mrs. Bushnell gave their own daughters the nearest thing to a Yale education they could contrive. He had no use for "the lady style of women, [who] have nothing to do but dress, look pretty, and enjoy themselves."[33] Accordingly, he and his wife saw to it that their children were instructed in ancient and modern languages, science, geography, literature, moral philosophy, and religion. At different times at least two of them served as teachers, and all of them became actively involved in community affairs.[34]

Bushnell was pleased that women were beginning to find their way into medicine, convinced there were situations where they could outdo men as doctors. He wanted to see women as preachers, though not as pastors, and as office lawyers, but not attorneys in court or as judges. He applauded the literary achievements of Margaret Fuller, Mrs. Stowe, and Gail Hamilton (Mary Abigail Dodge), a journalist who once worked as a reporter in Hartford. He was hopeful, too, that women soon would be entering many areas of the business world, anticipating with approval the acceptance of women as "managers of hotels," brokers, insurance actuaries, "private bankers," bank tellers, and "overseers of printing."

As a foundation for all these endeavors, he wanted as much as any liberationist to see both sexes enjoy more nearly equal legal standing. "The law must be for women, as truly as for men," he insisted, and it must offer them such protection as would secure them their full rights "and multiply the chances of industry for women."[35] Not many leading men were willing to go so far. With some hesitation, Emerson in Concord eventually went further;[36] and with steady humanitarian zeal, Thomas W. Higginson and Henry B. Blackwell in Boston espoused the cause.[37]

If only Bushnell could have continued as he began! But when it came to women's suffrage and all it implied, he balked. For women to vote would be "a reform against nature." Yet even here he was not altogether true to his title. Early in the book he admitted that if women could show that giving them the vote and the right to hold political office would be for "the real benefit of their sex, and for the solid and permanent good of society," all controversy on the subject would then and there "be effectually ended." They should have their ballot.[38]

But he could not see any likelihood that this would happen. Always part democrat and part theocrat, he long had questioned the inalienable natural right of suffrage even for men.[39] Now he had grown uncharacteristically pessimistic about the whole future of American political institutions. For thirty years, at least since the coarse campaigns of 1840 and 1844, and his sermons on them, he had been discontented with the working out of the democratic process. Always, though, he had expressed sincere regard for the Founding Fathers and the principles of the Constitution. He had been especially hopeful for a devoutly renewed nation after the war.

Here, however, as though he were writing on a bad day, this basic confidence seemed to go from him. Dejectedly he spoke of "our dreadfully inferior, cheap way of suffrage." It was "a pell-mell operation," "dreadfully loose," and in danger of going down "by the rotting process of its own corruptions." Vaguely he thought the country would do better with some kind of West Point, or even Chinese merit system, in choosing its leaders. Meanwhile, what possible good could it do for women to be pitched into this depressing arena of dissolute politics?[40]

More soberly, Bushnell was convinced that men were by nature the governors of the world. It was "against nature" for women to undertake this role, as it would be for them to be soldiers, builders of railroads, or sea captains. Women had another task. Religiously speaking, men represented the Mosaic Law thundering out of Sinai and "rough-hewing the work of government." Women embodied the

Gospel, as he so often romantically perceived it: full of grace, self-effacing, gentle and lovely, the longed-for fulfillment of the commanding, but incomplete Old Testament Law and prophecy.[41] To Bushnell this meant women had "a divinely superior ministry," one that placed them "above equality with men."[42] Permit this civilizing domestic vocation to be worn away in the hurly-burly of political battle and everyone would lose—men and women, faith and society. To contemplate such an eventuality was to look into an awful abyss where family and public virtue would be wrecked permanently. Let this come to pass, he gloomily predicted, and "our sun is set; is there any other sun to rise?"[43]

Such was his theory. But sequestered women had not been the whole of his experience. His wiry little Bushnell grandmother had helped conquer a Vermont wilderness, yet she remained a woman he highly honored. His worldly wise mother had run a "factory" on a farm without losing qualities that had fundamentally shaped his life. His own wife, who lived to be over 100, was no mere passive parlor angel. When the Hartford Female Seminary acquired a new principal from Virginia in 1845, Mrs. Bushnell served on a committee with Mary Beecher Perkins, Mrs. John Olmsted, and others to advise her on the best ways of improving the school. Quietly conventional as she was in many of her attitudes, she was her husband's strength in depression (as he was hers when she was ill), and to a significant degree she served as his active, working partner. While he was in California she filled in for him in various parish tasks—visitation, entertaining, and forming a new Bible class, for which she already had at hand a lesson guide she had published on the life of Christ.[44] Bushnell's substitute, James Hyde, often was out of town lining up a more permanent pulpit for himself. This left Mary to help bolster morale among the North Church people, who without him or her husband were "as sheep without a shepherd."[45]

Independent as he was, it seems clear that Bushnell frequently talked over sermon questions with Mary. On at least one occasion when she was absent in New Haven he asked her to write, or even telegraph, ideas that might help with his theme for the following Sunday.[46] When his friend Henry Trumbull once inquired why he had omitted part of a discourse when he preached it a second time, he dutifully confessed, "So *you* liked that—did you? So did *I*, but Mrs. Bushnell made me change it."[47]

There are hints, too, that she would have welcomed the chance to play some small part on the Hartford political scene. On election day in 1856, "when everyone was full of excitement" over the race between John C. Frémont, standard-bearer of the newborn Republican Party, and the Democratic Southern sympathizer from Pennsylvania, James Buchanan, she occupied herself writing a letter. She was in no mood to sit at home. "But as I cannot either vote or work," she hoped such routine domesticity would not "dishonor my patriotism."[48] There was all this in the Doctor's own family. Yet his staunch opinion that suffrage would threaten the unique role of women remained fixed.

Such, of course, was also the ingrown opinion of the age. Bushnell's phrase "the reform against nature" fed the predispositions of many readers, and he was pleased by the initial reception of his latest volume. Full of confidence, he mailed off copies to his Boston friends Cyrus Bartol and Edwin P. Whipple, an established lyceum lecturer,[49] and derived "the greatest satisfaction" from Henry Bellows's approval in New York.[50] He chafed unnecessarily over a few points in a generally friendly review in Edwin L. Godkin's *Nation*, but the article occasioned a cordial exchange of correspondence with the independent Irish-born editor.[51] Reassured by these responses, he wrote his publishers that the book seemed to be "well spoken of" and optimistically predicted a second edition might soon be needed.[52]

As in the days of Christian nurture, however, he kept his guard up. "The day of fury, I suppose, is yet to come," he suspected.[53] And with good reason. Prosuffrage women soon were pouncing on him without mercy. Because she was on personal good terms with the Bushnell family, Mrs. Stowe did not feel free to speak her mind publicly. She did, however, let out her feelings to Sarah Willis Parton, the spirited New York novelist "Fanny Fern," telling her she was "immensely tickled" that another woman had put Bushnell on "a nice, lady like 'toasting fork,'" and roasted him in *Hearth and Home*.[54]

Undaunted by the reception he must have known it would receive, he presented an inscribed copy of the book to the redoubtable Isabella Beecher Hooker at Nook Farm. She repaid him by peppering the margins with critical notes. Where he cautioned women not to leap into the abyss of emancipation before they had seen the bottom of it, she counseled him, "Try it, dear friend, you will never touch bottom till you leap." Other passages were "shameful" or "utterly false." Sometimes she added her initials for emphasis. But if "Belle," as her intimates called her, lectured him, he hesitated not at all to lecture her in return. "Be quite easy, my dear friend," he wrote her the same year, declining to withhold an article he had written of which she disapproved, "you are not going to be hurt. Even salvation sometimes takes on a shape that is unwelcome."[55]

Suffragists who were infuriated by much of what Bushnell had to say could find comfort in John Stuart Mill's *Subjection of Women*, which also appeared in 1869. Influenced by his talented wife, Harriet Taylor, the English economist and philosopher had pondered women's rights as long as Bushnell had and had reached opposite conclusions. To Mill, keeping women from the polls had "not a shadow of justification." It was part of a general domination of one sex by the other that was a "relic of an old world of thought and practice exploded in everything else."

Like Bushnell, Mill believed all his life that a married woman's first responsibility was to husband, home, and children, and he saw no benefit in her attempting to contribute to the family income. In this regard, Bushnell at times may have been the more liberal of the two. Unlike his Hartford contemporary, however, Mill found no necessary conflict between a woman's right to vote and her fulfillment of domestic duty. Giving her a voice concerning the leaders and laws under which she must live readily fit his ideal of marriage and the family, an ideal Bushnell in most respects shared: "a school of sympathy in equality, of living together in love, without power on the one side or obedience on the other."[56]

Inevitably the two books invited comparison. Mary Cheney felt Mill had much the better of the argument. In her biography of her father, she gave *Woman's Suffrage* faint praise and in retrospect could say bluntly, "I did not like it then, and do not now." Nor did she think Mrs. Bushnell was comfortable with it, even though the Doctor, without her prior knowledge, had ventured to dedicate the book to her.[57] In a double review of both volumes in *The North American Review,* future Harvard philosopher William James, unmarried and not yet thirty, sympathized with Bushnell's ideal of woman as a dependent homebody. A man needed "one tranquil spot," he thought, where he was accepted and secure. In this, he was certain, "the universal sense of mankind hitherto, and its almost universal sense now, will uphold him [Bushnell]." Still, he thought Mill's book much the better and could not see why Bushnell was so worried that an occasional visit to the polls would sweep away a woman's fundamentally domestic calling.[58]

From a sickbed, Bushnell himself gave Mill a cursory reading. He thought he might "reconstruct" the last chapter of his book to comment on him, but was unimpressed—perhaps, as he put it, "because I am too unimpressible."[59] Possibly he was more affected than he realized. After some reflection he began to feel "mortification" over some of his own pages. If there were to be another printing, he informed the Scribners in New York, he wanted to make alterations. He was especially unhappy with his last two chapters on the harrowing consequences that could be expected if women's suffrage were adopted. "I am sick of some things in the later part of the 7th chapter," he lamented. These sections of the book, he explained, were written "as I was going down, and represent my pains and discomposures more than my thoughts."[60]

This candid admission suggests that the Doctor penned many passages in his controversial book when he was too ill to think or write clearly on anything. He told Bellows he had drafted the final chapter while lying flat on his back.[61] It needs to be said, too, that along with the advantages of change he was willing to recognize, he foresaw only too accurately the new problems expanded activities for women would pose in the next century: less committed marriages, a higher rate of divorce, and added difficulties for children.

These allowances made, however, it remains that he never was fully comfortable with the ultimate aims of the feminist movement: freedom of opportunity for women as women on an equal basis with men as men in both private and public spheres. There were moments, suffrage aside, when he caught a glimpse—or more than a glimpse—of that liberation vision and spoke well for it. But his mindset left him ill-equipped to dream the entire dream. Moved by his faith and his positive experience of marriage and a distaff family, he skirted the Promised Land. Yet he was unable to ally himself with the small advance forces struggling bravely as the decades wore on to cross the Jordan.

CHAPTER 21

"No Give-Up With Him"

BY 1870 HARTFORD WAS AGAIN BECOMING a different city. The population had jumped to a booming 38,000, a total that would more than double by the end of the century.[1] With this influx, the intimacy of downtown was breaking up. Old families, such as the Watkinsons (of the Watkinson Library) and the Wadsworths (of the trailblazing Wadsworth Atheneum) were gone, and a new entrepreneur elite had arisen. Its leading symbol, Samuel Colt, who had acquired enormous means through his prosperous arms factory, had died suddenly at age forty-eight in 1862. His widow, however, continued on for a generation as the *grande dame* of Hartford society.[2]

Leading Hartford families were abandoning the core city and building lavish estates on the fringes of town. Harriet Beecher Stowe, who had settled permanently in Hartford in 1863, noted that while other cities developed "dirty suburbs," Hartford could boast "elegantly kept country places, near enough to the city to enjoy all its pleasures, and yet far enough in the country to have all its quietude and repose."[3] Establishments like these reflected expanding riches. The fact was that situated halfway between commercial New York and genteel Boston, Hartford, with its river shipping, insurance, munitions plants, printing and publishing establishments, factories, and banks, may well have enjoyed the highest per capita wealth of any American city.[4]

An older Hartford had been small enough for Bushnell to exert individual influence in nearly every area of its multifaceted life. Now it was growing beyond him. Nonetheless, he was still a familiar figure, and the aura of age made him even more conspicuously the community's first citizen. As he shuffled about the streets with his cane and his stove-pipe hat, people inquired after his well-being. "How is your health?" people would ask him. A stock reply, not meant unkindly, was, "You know I haven't any."[5] Yet on wheels he seemed as vigorous and daring as ever. He still drove like a biblical Jehu on Farmington Avenue, passing everybody. If a passenger in his gig asked him, "Why so fast, Doctor?" he would call back airily, "My boy, I don't like dust!"[6] Such driving was typical of the way he kept pressing on despite deepening inroads of illness. If his physique was failing, his mind remained clear and his services in demand.

In 1866 and 1868 he gave two important discourses on preaching, one at Andover and one at the Chicago Theological Seminary.[7] It was a time when churches were placing a high priority on impressive preaching, causing many a young minister to dream of being another Henry Ward Beecher—or Horace Bushnell. There is a certain racy quotability to the Doctor's advice to such would-be pulpit stars. The heart of it was that from the eminence of their platforms and their ambitions they not lose living contact with their everyday people. "Of what use is it to know the German, when we do not know the human?" he pointedly asked, not wanting to demean scholarship but questioning an overemphasis on German biblical exegesis then increasingly popular. "A great many preachers die of style," he warned his young listeners, "that is, of trying to soar; when if they would only consent to go afoot as their ideas do, they might succeed and live." The best preaching, he argued, is not imposing thought, but "the bursting out of light" from hard-won, hidden stores of learning and the experience of God and human life. He added a characteristically earthy note. Ministers should not get so lost in lofty homiletics that they neglected the more mundane task of detailed parish administration. "The success and power of the preacher," he told his Andover audience, ". . . will not seldom depend even more on a great administrative capacity, than it will on his preaching."[8]

In the early 1870s Bushnell followed up these addresses with one of his more enduring contributions, a series of nine articles on prayer, published in the weekly Congregational paper, *Advance*. His concern here was not with the exacting duty of saying prayers, but with the open "permission" of speaking or wrestling with God in actual prayer.[9] Though not always clearly audible, he preached often in Hartford pulpits; took several Sundays at the Church of the Pilgrims in Brooklyn, New York, for the celebrated Richard Salter Storrs, in a sense a Brooklyn counterpart of Bushnell; spoke at Williams College; and frequently addressed students and faculty at Yale.[10]

Not only was he sought after professionally, his outside interests continued to be lively and diverse. Edwin Pond Parker thought he worked as hard on projecting the best route for a ship canal across the Isthmus of Panama as though he were personally responsible for its construction.[11] When Congress was considering changes in the tariff, he tried his hand again at economics and produced an article for *Scribner's Monthly* on "Free Trade and Protection."[12] Ever since his "Gihon" sermon in 1847, and his ideas on the building of the city's new reservoir on Asylum Hill in 1855, he had been actively interested in Hartford's water system. In the early 1870s he rode out to West Hartford to give advice to the president of the water board on how the flow of water there might be increased.[13] Railroads, too, both in Connecticut and nationwide, continued to be a prime fascination. Before the war he had pored over ten massive volumes of Congressional reports on plans for a transcontinental line, particularly the maps produced by the cultivated Indian fighter and government surveyor Edward Fitzgerald Beale, "pioneer in the path of empire," as Bushnell's friend Bayard Taylor once called him.[14] At the time the Doctor rather hoped the project would not be attempted. He was convinced that the "forlorn" Buchanan Administration was so weak and so beholden to Southern interests, that if it were to run a railroad from the East "to Puget Sound, they certainly would lay it through Texas."[15] But when at last the ambitious undertaking was completed in 1869, Bushnell noted with some pride that the Central Pacific had chosen for its approach to San Francisco essentially the route he had favored when he was in California.[16]

For the Doctor, roads and railroads were not simply evidences of technological progress. As part of his bursting Victorian optimism, he thought of them as instruments of organic society, opening channels of culture, commerce, law, and religion. He was impressed that so many nations were simultaneously spinning out highways and "roads of iron," and he believed they would make a unique contribution to a unified, peaceful world, resulting at last in a global Christian community.[17]

In the winter of 1871–72 Bushnell undertook his last round of civic campaigning. From time immemorial, Connecticut had been the only state in the Union to have two capitals—one in New Haven, one in Hartford, the legislature meeting alternately in the two cities. By the 1860s, however, the needs of government had so increased that this double arrangement was no longer workable. After much political wrangling, and not a little shady sectional maneuvering, an amendment to Connecticut's constitution was approved in 1873 designating Hartford as the sole capital of the state.[18]

Before this settlement was reached, and as part of the competitive bidding for exclusive title to capital honors, Hartford bestirred itself to offer a more adequate facility than the old eighteenth-century Bullfinch Statehouse. The question then arose, "Where in Hartford should the new building be placed?" A heavy majority opinion favored the western section of Bushnell's City Park. It was land the city already owned, and it would provide a spectacular setting. As 1872 opened, a state commission appointed to carry out the project assumed the decision on that site had been made.[19] But again, Hartford was reckoning without the Doctor. Unwilling to sit by and let the park be savaged, even for this good purpose, Bushnell set out to defend it. A statehouse site that faced the park would be ideal, but carving acres out of the hard-won park itself was quite another matter.

He was in no condition for a struggle. Almost seventy, he had grown deaf, was losing his voice, and had no reserves of energy. Moreover, the prospects of success seemed nil. The impatient commissioners already had dismissed his alternate proposal of land immediately to the west, and the press was solid in support of the commission. "If I had only a few grains of strength left," he told Edwin Pond Parker when they met one day on the street, "I would grapple with this business and overthrow it." But a sympathetic Parker advised him against any such effort. "Do not distress yourself, Doctor; though you had an archangel's strength, you could not accomplish such a miracle." The remark saddened Bushnell, and Parker long remembered the sight of the old man "as he turned wearily away, and walked on under his burden."[20]

Few thought anything further would happen, but despite the odds against him, Bushnell successfully made arrangements to be heard at a public meeting. On a January 1872 evening a good crowd gathered in Central Hall, including influential leaders of the city, many of whom he had known a long time as neighbors and friends. It was his swan song on Hartford's civic platform, and there were those who marveled that he could speak at all. Yet he made of it a scintillating performance. Direct, cogent, witty, and persuasive, as the *Courant* described his style, he was interrupted repeatedly by good-natured laughter and applause. As a kind of secular text, he read from a letter he may well have solicited from Frederick Law Olmsted supporting his position. An aroused Olmsted stated emphatically that "the Park is of more consequence than the state House." It was a shrewd move on the Doctor's part. As a landscape architect the reputation of this native son had become so unassailable that his word to Hartford citizens was little short of command.

With this as an opener, Bushnell made his own strong arguments. He rebutted what seemed to him false fears as to the cost of another location and questioned the proposed plans for orientation and grading. To those who claimed the new capitol would be an ornament to the park, he painted a grim picture of the new building confronting the truncated spectacle of its "murdered mother." He played on the social conscience of his audience. Cut the park nearly in half, he pointed out, and the humbler people of the city would be further deprived of a much-needed recreational space, one of the main reasons for creating the park in the first place. Indulging the privilege of age and respect, he pleaded more personally on their behalf. "It grieves me," lamented, "that you will take away what I tried to give them." He closed with a personal adieu to the public scene. "I have done my last work for Hartford," he said, and sat down to loud applause.[21]

Despite this warm reception, the response of the meeting was not unanimous. It did, however, pass a nonbinding resolution leaving the Common Council free to offer the commission either the park or

Bushnell's alternative site, but indicating a clear preference for the latter.[22] Bushnell felt he had achieved a victory and went home to his fireside. Out of the corner of her wifely eye, Mrs. Bushnell watched him as he slumped contentedly into his chair. Half anxious and half marveling, she thought to herself, "There is no give-up with him."[23]

In the end neither location was chosen. Alfred E. Burr, nationally regarded editor of the *Hartford Times,* resolved the issue by proposing that the city buy the campus of Trinity College adjacent to the park and place the capitol building on that land. Since Trinity soon would need more room for expansion in any case, it was a happy solution. Bushnell was comfortable with it, and Richard M. Upjohn's "gothic chateau" capitol still graces the old college hill.[24] The Doctor's alternative suggestion may not have been altogether wise. Yet his plucky interference kept matters open until the right solution appeared, one that saved the integrity of the historic park. As evidence of the part he played, his head-and-shoulders effigy still looks out on the passing scene from a medallion on the east wall of the gold-domed pile, in company with Jonathan Edwards, Noah Webster, and the celebrated Connecticut literary "Wit" Joel Barlow, among others.[25]

His family doubted he would stand by his promise not to take on further public causes.[26] But he did. From then on he stayed in his study and wrote—when he could, for even writing took every ounce of strength he had. Of his third volume of discourses, *Sermons on Living Subjects,* he told Scribners that he could only put it together gradually, "getting along slowly as my little stock of health permits."[27] The book appeared in 1872, and a receptive *New Englander* greeted it as "an event in literature." The reviewer, James M. Hoppin, art and religion teacher at Yale, had some problems with Bushnell's less-than-human Jesus and with a certain cerebral quality in the Doctor's style, a failing he felt marked too much American preaching. But if the discourses were somewhat lacking in emotional appeal, he felt Bushnell caused them to "breathe and burn with intellectual life." Fully aware of the Doctor's condition, Hoppin still claimed that "there are few men who can hold an audience like him."[28]

The last of his books to come out in his lifetime was theologically more significant, *Forgiveness and Law*.[29] Only months before he died, Bushnell observed to a friend that always he had tried to "mend" his work in constant efforts to come closer to the truth.[30] It was so with his views of the Atonement. Hardly was *The Vicarious Sacrifice* off the press than he wanted to "mend" it. A "new view" had caught him "unexpectedly, when not looking for it." In "duty to the truth," he wanted now to place more emphasis on the Cross as objectively reconciling God to humankind, thus balancing his previous subjective stress on it as reconciling the world to the Divine.[31]

Before writing out his new thought, he commented with a touch of wistfulness that he might be "coming out so orthodox as to make some people think better of me."[32] Yet when he put pen to paper he stoutly denied he was in any way retreating to the traditional legalism he had so long rejected. "I still assert the 'moral view' of the atonement as before," he insisted, "and even more completely than before."[33]

The Doctor's "fresh light" came while he was working over a sermon on forgiveness.[34] It struck him that genuine Christian pardon involves more than merely saying "I will forgive, and forget if I can," or simply letting the offense go by. Full forgiveness, he began to see, comes when the person injured identifies closely with the offender, "going through into good, if possible, with the wrong-doer, and meeting him [or her] there, both reconciled." This can only be done at considerable cost of material sacrifice, shared pain, and donated time by the one injured. In the process, not only may an adversary be moved to repent of his or her deed and embark on a new life, but the person offended also is set into a new peace, free from resentment and any smoldering desires for revenge.[35]

To Bushnell this change was an important part of atonement, namely, a new gaining of self, or, as he stated it more technically, a "propitiation" of ourselves. The consequence was a new relationship between both parties freed of every hindrance to genuine Christian love. Even if the offender should reject such offers, the self-propitiation would remain. The person injured, having done everything possible, simply would share the lot of Christ, "who came unto his own, and his own received him not."[36]

As already noted, the Doctor thought of the moral nature of human beings as corresponding closely to that of God. Hence if this was experience of forgiveness at the human level, why should it not hold true also of the Divine? He was ready now to say that while on Calvary's cruel hill God was "reconciling the world to himself," the Deity, too, was undergoing self-propitiation, being thus reconciled to the world. Not, to be sure, by obtaining any legal satisfaction or by requiring the punishment of an innocent Jesus to pay the debt of our sin; rather, God accomplished it by stooping down in Christ and indentifying self-sacrificially with our sinful condition, just as one human being must do fully to forgive another. Faith looks at Christ Jesus on the Cross, the Doctor claimed, and sees there a "sublime act of cost, in which God has bent himself downward, in loss and sorrow, over the hard face of sin, to say, and saying to make good, 'thy sins are forgiven thee.'"[37]

Theoretically and practically it was a difficult concept, though Bushnell thought he knew from his own experience, not from something beyond human capacity. He knew what it was to be unjustly tied to "the moral whipping post," he wrote in another connection, adding that when it came to forgiveness he had experienced the truth of Paul's testimonial to grace: "I can do all things through him who strengthens me."[38] Although the harm was to society and not to him personally, one wonders to what extent his active concern for the condemned Starkweather may have been motivated by this view of pardon.

To his more complete understanding of the Atonement he joined more "fresh light," this time on the relationship between the law of Moses and the commandments of Jesus in the God's redemptive scheme. With the excitement of sudden discovery, Bushnell in his old age was amazed to realize for the first time the naturalness and finality with which the Great Teacher of Galilee delivered his commandments to his followers. "Neither Socrates, nor Plato, nor Bacon, nor Kant," he suggested to his readers, "ever thought of putting his commandment[s] on the world in such a way." Yet they came freely, and with no trace of hesitation or apology from Jesus, "this peasant going as a foot passenger through the world, this wise man who is not a philosopher." [39]

Bushnell felt both the Mosaic Law, with its penal sanctions, and the grace-filled commandments of Jesus, were necessary to restore a wandering humanity to the love and liberty of the Eternal.[40] But he was captivated by the contrast between the two. Where the law was largely negative, the commandments were richly positive. Where the law was coldly impersonal, the commandments were warmly personal. The law of Sinai was addressed to the natural self. The commandments were addressed to the transformed self, offering not penalty but "promise, always promise, working thus by comforts, inspirations [and] openings upwards into God."[41]

Many of the Doctor's books had elicited hostility. This one produced a wealth of confusion. Did his thought on the propitiation of God and the uniqueness of Christ's commandments contain really new insights, or did the author merely think so? Bushnell felt the volume was "the newest thing I have written." Wishing to check his thought before venturing too far, he had inquired early on of George Park Fisher, church historian at Yale, whether he was breaking fresh ground. Fisher had assured him that for the most part he was.[42] Faithful Amos Chesebrough was supportive when the book appeared, as was a writer in Henry Ward Beecher's widely read *Christian Union*.[43]

Other readers reacted differently. Despite his disclaimer, it seemed to them that the Doctor was falling back on the traditional New England theology, as though at last coming to his orthodox senses. When he tried out the manuscript on the intimate circle of his Hartford ministerial associates, conservative Calvin Stowe commented good-naturedly, "The Doctor's gaining. If he revises a few more times, he'll be pretty near the truth." Others present doubted he should publish the work. It would not satisfy Bushnell's enemies, they feared, and would only be a confusion to his friends.[44]

New teaching or not, Bushnell was not solicitous of theological novelty. He was trying to cope further with what seemed to him both a pastoral and a missionary crisis. At home he saw "a time of jeopardy," when preachers were being more and more challenged by scientific minds, and well-informed pewholders were no longer conditioned to accept without question what they heard from the pulpit. Unitarianism, "an egg trying to get on without a shell," as he genially remarked to Bartol, was no more satisfactory on the Atonement than it always had been, but for lack of a clear alternative people were turning to it.[45] Many signs indicated a new statement was needed, such as he had hoped to supply.

Nor were all the danger signals at home. Foreign missions were expanding rapidly. The Doctor, who had a broad view of the mission field and an open approach to indigenous, non-Christian faiths, worried that the message overseas was still being handicapped by legalistic preachments on the Cross. He knew that in many cases other religions were held by highly cultured people who had "much valuable truth." Such intelligent potential converts, he suspected, were no more ready than educated American churchgoers to accept uncritically whatever a missionary might tell them. In such situations he hoped his reinterpretation of Calvary might be of some service.[46]

Busy as health permitted with his books and his community concerns, Bushnell also continued to enjoy social contacts. Always gregarious, he knew nearly as many people in New Haven as he did in Hartford; and when he visited the Sampsons in New York, he participated freely in their sociable lives. Henry Ward Beecher was a conspicuous part of the New York scene, and Bushnell was "dreadfully overwhelmed" when news of Beecher's alleged affair with Mrs. Tilton broke in 1874. "Well, here is a gulf into which I might have fallen," he wrote Finney in a rare moment of sexual self-revelation, adding that safety had been more God's doing than his own.[47]

He still attended Yale commencements and class reunions, but with less regularity. In April 1871 he wrote Theodore Woolsey that he was not up to preaching in the chapel, and might not be again.[48] Though absent from the graduation exercises that year while vacationing in Ripton, Vermont, the university gave him an honorary degree as Doctor of Laws. He thanked "the dear mother" for the parchment, while denying with evident weariness that he was worthy of the status of "honorable."[49] A month later he wrote his old friend

Noah Porter, Jr., to congratulate him on his elevation to the Yale presidency.[50]

Summer vacations remained an important resource for him, whether on the shores of Lake Waramaug near his native New Preston; in Keene Valley, New York; in Ripton, Vermont; or, finally, in Norfolk, Connecticut. Repeatedly he hoped these breaks would restore a certain "fund" of energy for the winter.[51] But if he rested at times, he also drove himself as though he were a well man, fishing, climbing, and bushwhacking in the wilderness. On the lake, young Charley Clark often was his companion. Clark remembered Bushnell vividly, sitting in the boat half lost in discussing some big subject. Suddenly he would jump as though hit by a charge of electricity, and cry, "My kingdom!" and haul in a fish. Little ones he always let go with kindly warnings to be more careful in the future. Big ones he kept and displayed with boyish pride.[52]

In Keene Valley, he tramped with various guides and friends, as often as possible with leathery old Orson Phelps, a local woodsman of whom the Doctor grew fond.[53] On one strenuous expedition in the Adirondacks with Joseph Twichell, the Doctor lost so much blood Twichell thought he was going to die on the spot. But after resting two nights and a day in the open, in the course of which rain added to his troubles, he insisted on going forward, trudging on for three more days to complete the trip.[54] In August of 1872 he could report from Ripton that he had "walked about twelve miles in the woods, including two miles of the most awful tussle with logs, briers, and all the horrid fencing of tree-falls." Four days later he "took about eight miles of brook fishing again in the woods, to show I am as good as ever."[55]

Even on holiday, however, this cheerful front was not the whole story. In the summer of 1873 his doctor told him he was down to one lung. Bushnell claimed he had suspected as much for some time and was not much shaken by the news. Other factors, however, led him into renewed depressions. Mrs. Bushnell, busy tending her aged mother in New Haven, did all she could by mail to bolster his morale. She diverted his thoughts with accounts of books she had read

and, in inspirational vein, reminded him of heroes such as John the
Baptist or Napoleon who had been subject to more severe limitations
than his and yet persevered. Her one great fear was that with his
high-strung temperament he might suffer a stroke. "I beg you to let
your brain rest," she urged him, hoping he could avoid a calamity
"worse than death of the body."[56]

Fortunately the "calamity" never occurred. Back in Hartford he
continued to meet with the Hartford Central Association to within a
year of his death. His manner in these meetings was all his own. Energetic and usually taut, he would at times speak out in a way his associates could only describe as "magnificent." Yet he was just as
likely to slip into slangy "it ain't" or "it don't"—a liberty he seldom,
if ever allowed himself in print—or use some quaint expression that
clarified his point and stuck in the minds of his audience.[57]

One day as he was about to read a discourse, he announced to his
colleagues in a shaky voice, "Brethren, I am going to read to you
what is probably the last sermon I shall write." There followed a
homily on "Our Relations to Christ in the Future Life." When he had
finished and asked for criticisms, no one spoke. Nathaniel Burton finally attempted to speak for the little circle on his mentor's valedic-
tory, but his emotions were too much for him. He barely managed to
finish his sentence.[58]

Even in his declining years, his pastoral concern stayed alive,
whether for people near at hand or at a distance. When Hartford
headlines brought word of the Chicago fire of 1871, he used the Congregational press to send a letter of sympathy and encouragement to
his friends there.[59] Nor did his dry sense of humor desert him. In June
of 1874, a bronze statue of the Revolutionary War hero Gen. Israel
Putnam was dedicated in the city park. Bushnell went, got soaked by
a passing shower, and suffered a setback as a result.[60] Not long afterward someone told him Hartford citizens were sure to want a statue
of him as well. Where would he like it to be? He looked all around
and then, pointing with his cane, quipped, "Down under the bridge
yonder!"[61]

Although lacking time to focus on the arts, he always was, and
continued to be, sensitive to them. During his last stay at the Bread

Loaf Inn in Ripton, he listened to recitals by the talented Hartford organist Henry Wilson and other musicians. He was so refreshed by the experience that he speculated whether in heaven pure music might not be the chief mode of expressing thought, superior to the best human dialects.[62]

In the 1871 Christmas season he read Henry W. Longfellow's new poem "The Divine Tragedy," an attempt to put the scriptural narrative of Christ into dramatic form. Bushnell wrote him to express the pleasure he had found in it. He was glad that in seeking to portray the figure of Jesus, Longfellow had remained a poet, not succumbing to the temptation to become a preacher![63] Critics, however, gave it a cool reception, and there were objections from theological conservatives. In the face of disappointing reviews, Longfellow found the Doctor's letter "highly complimentary" and was cheered by it.[64]

In his last years Bushnell also came to know Mark Twain. Samuel Clemens, his young wife (née Olivia Langdon), and their short-lived infant son, Langdon, arrived in Hartford from Elmira, New York, in 1871, renting the Nook Farm house of John and Isabella Beecher Hooker before building their own outrageously fascinating house on Farmington Avenue three years later. Already Twain had tasted bitter personal tragedy, but for the first time he also was enjoying the sweet savor of international fame and fortune following the success of his *Jumping Frog* and *Innocents Abroad,* which had been published in Hartford.[65]

In all likelihood Twain had heard of Bushnell before they met. Prior to moving to town, he had been a bachelor guest in the Hooker household and doubtless heard his hosts inveigh against the Doctor's impossible social views. More favorably, he must have picked up at least a few impressions from Thomas Beecher and Joseph Twichell, both of whom officiated at Mark and Livy's Elmira wedding in 1870.[66]

Though a dark doubter himself, Twain always was drawn to ministers he could respect, and Bushnell was no exception. A mutual esteem developed between the younger man and older man. When Twain's rollicking account of his experiences in the West appeared in *Roughing It* in 1872, Bushnell was impatient to read it. He had "roughed it" in California years before Twain and teased the author for not sending him a complimentary copy. Embarrassed at having overlooked so obvious a recipient, Mark was more remorseful than the Doctor felt was necessary. "You blame yourself over much," he wrote him, while accepting a copy through Twichell's good offices. He went on to say that if "another storm in my eyes" did not trouble him, he and Mary would call on Livy Twain's widowed mother, Mrs. Jervis Langdon, "the valued friend of my valued friend T. K. Beecher," who was visiting Mark and Livy in Hartford.[67]

Before long Twain joined the Monday Evening Club.[68] Pretentiously modeled after the London coteries founded by Sir Walter Raleigh, and later Samuel Johnson, this select Hartford group of approximately twenty members had been started by Bushnell, Gen. Joseph R. Hawley, Calvin Stowe, William J. Hamersley, and others in 1868–69, the Doctor framing its Articles of Association in his own hand. Destined to last for over a century, the club met biweekly in private homes, feasted royally on elaborate dinners, and listened to presentations on all manner of topics by the members. Bushnell was strong enough to speak only twice, but this unusual company was a significant forum for Twain for twenty years.[69]

Apparently the two celebrities seldom saw each other, but Bushnell supportively lent his signature to an 1872 copyright petition of Twain's, only stipulating that his name appear "a long way down," to "let the literary gentlemen have their head."[70] The Doctor also was enough of a lingering presence in the Twain household that as late as 1890, when their unusually thoughtful daughter Susy was puzzling out spiritual issues before entering Bryn Mawr College, one of his discourses from *Sermons for the New Life* figured in her teenage gropings.[71]

As he looked out from his vermilion-and-black-trimmed mansion, Twain readily could have seen Bushnell speeding by on the avenue, outracing the choking clouds of dust. In any case he deferentially referred to him as "that noble old Roman," and in his *Autobiography* he spoke of Bushnell with evident awe as a "theological giant."[72]

What Twain was hardly in a position to appreciate was that his friend also was part of the backdrop of his own success as a writer.

The Doctor had been among those who had looked for the coming of an indigenous American literature, to which the future author of *Tom Sawyer* and *Huckleberry Finn* already was contributing. Before Yale alumni in 1837 Bushnell had envisioned a native literary flowering. At Yale's Civil War commemoration he had seen its growth more clearly. "Henceforth," he announced, "we are not going to write English but American...think our own thoughts, rhyme our own measures." No one fulfilled that prophecy more fully than the rising humorist from Nook Farm.[73]

CHAPTER 22

Not the Same City

ON FRIDAY, 22 JANUARY 1875, Bushnell struggled into his study, shut the door, and sat down to start yet another book. He doubted he could ever finish it. "But," as he wrote with his usual fortitude, "I can begin it."[1] Reaching feebly for a sheet of paper, he penned as ambitious a title as he ever had composed, "Inspiration: Its Modes and Uses, Whether as Related to Character, Revelation, or Action."[2] His subject was to be the Holy Spirit. It was a doctrine, as he acknowledged, "far removed from the mere natural intelligence of men," but one of utmost Christian importance. From his many-sided desk, he looked beyond himself for light: "Help me, O Eternal Spirit, whose ways I am engaged to interpret," he prayed, "to be in the sense at all times of Thy pure teaching, and to speak of what thou givest me to presently know!"[3]

The Doctor had come to believe that "the summit of our human nature," what most set human beings apart from the rest of creation, was the capacity to respond to the power of invisible spirit, and above all to the spirit of God. "Inspirableness, or the faculty of inspiration, is the supreme faculty of man," he wrote in his first sentence. A window pane, he pointed out, receives light but cannot retain it, and so continues unchanged. "The sun has been shooting its beams for many thousands of years through the illimitable spaces of the sky, and has not raised their heat even by a degree," he contended, "because it has not encountered anything there that has receptivity for heat." By analogy, however, when some power of spirit, whether religious or not, encounters a human being, it meets a life that can respond. Supremely, the Spirit of God can strike a human heart and not only illumine it, but warm it and change it to conform to itself in its moral and believing nature. Job in the Old Testament had said it well: "There is a spirit in man; and the inspiration of the Almighty giveth them understanding."[4] In a more specifically Christian context, this was to be his great theme.

To Bushnell, a Trinitarian, the Spirit was the saving power communicated to us from God through Christ, having a more potent and pervasive effect than Christ could have had under the human limitations of his earthly ministry. It was directly personal, as it must be to reach us as human personalities, and not merely a vaguely formative influence. With his usual facility for homely analogies, the Doctor remarked that "a carpenter makes a tight joint by making it, and not by an influence on the timber." At the same time the Spirit was not so literally an individual as to be separate in any way from the other persons of the Godhead, as the social Trinitarians maintained. It was universal, much in the manner of Emerson's "oversoul," a comparison Bushnell found it "pleasant" to make.

But Spirit was not irresistible. It might or might not find "true lodgment" in a human heart, depending on the disposition of the recipient, "a grace resisted, or a grace accepted in true welcome." Harking back to the 1830s when he was questioning sudden, lightning-stroke conversions, he saw the Spirit here operating on us to awaken us to our need of redemption and to sensitize us to the things of Christ. But there it "stops short,...laying no hand of force" on any person, but leaving us free to respond according to our own gifts and to move, as one modern critic has put it in describing Bushnell's doctrine, "from searching to finding, from inspirableness to inspiration, from promise to fulfillment."[5]

Every word cost him almost more energy than he had. When he was too weak to write he thought of dictating his thoughts to someone else and letting that person put them into finished form.[6] As it was, he kept on himself and got as far as what now takes up some thirty pages. Then one day he laid down his pen, evidently in the middle of a sentence, and never took it up again.[7]

By mid-March he had become critically ill. In the heat of high fever his mind wandered, and family and friends could not doubt he was at death's door. Yet in lucid moments he was considerate and could even manage a sally of wit. Once a friend remarked that he must have a great deal of patience to lie there in bed so long. "Well," he replied, "I have a great deal of weakness to support it."[8] He still could give as well as receive encouragement. When his Hartford protégé and mountain-climbing companion, Joseph Twichell, looked in on him for "not many seconds," Bushnell reached out his hand and exclaimed, "Joe!" in such a cheerful, half-humorous, and affectionate tone that Twichell went away "vastly refreshed."[9]

During a late-winter trip to New York, Edwin P. Parker hastily drafted an advance obituary for the *Hartford Courant,* certain that word of the Doctor's death would come at any moment.[10] But the news never came. Contrary to every expectation Bushnell got better and began to take renewed interest in his surroundings. He found new delight in the beauty of flowers. "Why, father, you never used to be so fond of flowers," one of his daughters commented. "My child, I hadn't time," he replied. One day he was told a man—perhaps "Old Law"—had called to inquire for him. He was pleased. At another time he learned a poor woman he once had befriended was praying for him, along with some of her friends. "I don't know," he responded gratefully, "but I am kept alive by the prayers of these people."[11]

He reached the point where he was able to take drives and even to sit in the park, watching the progress of the new capitol building. By autumn he was back in church, using a special chair placed up front so he could hear. "I do love to go to church!" he remarked one Sunday to Dr. Burton.[12] On New Year's Day of 1876, he managed a trip to Manchester to frolic as best he could with his grandchildren.[13]

His approaching end held no terrors for him. During the years of his active pastorate he had talked easily and naturally with his parishioners of death and dying. Now that he faced the Great Adventure himself, he was just as unruffled. Calmly he wrote letters of farewell to old friends, not sure how much longer he would live, but confident they all would enjoy unlimited visits on the Other Side. "My boat swings drowsily," he wrote Bartol on the last day of 1875, "and I am in no way disturbed or put to strain by what is before me."[14]

Those close to him thought they could see the glow of the beyond already shining through him. But one more touch of earth was still to come. Hearing his life was ebbing away, Hartford's mayor, Joseph H. Sprague, pressed the city council to put through a vote officially naming the city park "Bushnell Park." Unanimous consent was speedily obtained. On 15 February, his next-to-last day of anything like consciousness, a council messenger hurried to the door of 10 Winthrop Street to deliver the news in person. Bushnell concentrated as best he could while the flattering "Whereases" were read to him, leading up to the main point: *Resolved,* that the public park, now commonly called "The Park," be and hereby is named, "Bushnell Park." He was also told that the Irishman who brought the dispatch had explained that "this is the way we all wanted it to be." At that, Bushnell's face brightened. "Your park, Doctor," his attending physician repeated, wanting to be sure his failing patient understood. "My park," Bushnell whispered faintly.[15]

Not much was said during the hours that followed. Then there came the time when he struggled to say goodbye. With long pauses for breath he got the words out: "Well, now, we are all going home together; and I say, the Lord be with you—and in grace—and peace—and love—and that is the way I have come along home." Very early in the morning of 17 February, while the winter stars were bright and most of Connecticut still slept, Home he went.

Later that day, at Plymouth Church in Brooklyn, New York, with most of the country following the sensational details, the ecclesiastical trial of Henry Ward Beecher was in full swing. Twichell and Parker were among those present, Parker sitting as one of the judges. Suddenly a telegram arrived announcing Bushnell's death. Just as suddenly the proceedings broke off. Many members of the blue-ribbon tribunal owed much to the Doctor and had great fondness for him. When the first stir of reaction had subsided, Leonard Bacon stood to give a brief, impromptu eulogy. Beecher himself was asked to offer a prayer for his long-time, if never close, friend. "Such a prayer was seldom heard on earth," Twichell wrote in his Journal.[16]

In Hartford, at the head of four columns of obituary, the *Courant* announced, "The dear old Doctor!—is gone." In a letter to Mark Twain's literary collaborator, Charles Dudley Warner, then abroad on a trip to the Nile and the Levant, a local resident predicted, "You will not find Hartford the same city on your return." Usually staid Sarah Porter went even further. From her fashionable Farmington finishing school, she let herself go in a note to Mary Cheney. "For me," she wrote sadly, "his death empties the world."[17]

With its heavenly minded piety, late-nineteenth-century America made much of important funerals. At the service for its "foremost citizen," Hartford mourners packed every Gothic niche in the sizable Park Church sanctuary. The *Courant* reporter spotted nearly thirty Connecticut and Massachusetts ministers, and was certain there were more. Like a riderless horse at a state cortege, Bushnell's special chair stood empty near the pulpit, draped in the inevitable crepe of the period.[18]

As the Park Church pastor, it fell to Nathaniel Burton to deliver the principal eulogy. Discriminating lawyer John Hooker used to say he never knew anyone who could use the English langage with such elegance and power as did Burton.[19] This gifted Gospel voice of the Gilded Age rose impressively to the occasion. He reviewed the Doctor's career as a preacher and writer, recalling that his mind was "one of the rarest." He was "independent" and "courageous," at times "too little considerate of the wisdom of the past, but truth-loving (intensely so), debative, soldierly, massive, mobile..." He evoked memories of a pastor and public servant who had displayed personal magnetism and an irrepressible spirit of youth, even while he battled gallantly against disease. In Burton's imposing periods, the man they all had known stood out again as one who kept a "sharp outlook upon the moving, great world" but also sustained a "perfectly undaunted outlook into eternity."

In his peroration, Burton, too, peered over the edge of time. He presented Bushnell as caught up in the Resurrection Life and looked forward with "immense expectation" to meeting his friend and teacher again in that new dimension of being. Meantime, for himself, and for all present, he bade Horace Bushnell Godspeed: "Farewell, O master in Israel, O man beloved! God give thee light on thy dark questions now! God give thee rest from thy tired body! God bring us to thee when eternal morning breaks!"[20]

Epilog

HORACE BUSHNELL NO LONGER WALKED THE STREETS or pushed his unwearied pen. But memory would not let him go. Not yet forty, and busy with eight (eventually twelve) children, intelligently devoted Mary Cheney began her full-length biography of her father, to be followed by the publication of one, and ultimately two, posthumous collections of his writings. Able now to see his life whole, those who had known him best began issuing a steady flow of recollections and appraisals of his character and achievements. Pro and con, this output by contemporaries continued for over twenty-five years.

The 1902 centennial of his birth stimulated renewed interest. At its annual meeting that year, the General Association of Connecticut Congregational clergy spent two days recalling different aspects of his unusual career.[1] Yale, which already had claimed him as a "genius" on a par with Edwards at its bicentennial the year before,[2] went on to publicize "The Centenary of a Great Alumnus."[3] In 1897 the state officially designated a mountain by the shores of Lake Waramaug as "Mount Bushnell" and later set apart just north of it the Mount Bushnell State Park.[4] In time there was an endowed chair at the Yale Divinity School in his memory,[5] and those who recalled his love of the Adirondack woods saw to it that a picturesque waterfall along the Old North Trail up Mount Marcy was named Bushnell Falls.[6]

He was more, however, than a memory. During a critical period in American religious development,[7] Bushnell lived on as a considerable influence. The nature and scope of his legacy is debated still—whether, for example, he was a seminal thinker or chiefly a mediator, a bridge between the old New England orthodoxy and a theology for a different day. Some see him as having helped set the tone for a new social liberalism, but for more critical scholars he was an obstacle to liberation of African Americans and women and, unwittingly, perhaps, played into the hands of a sometimes superficial conservativism.[8]

Some continuing contributions, however, are beyond dispute. Undeniably his thought was a turning point in American Protestantism. He was a background force in the emergence of the so-called New Theology, or Progressive Orthodoxy, a further modification of the aging Calvinism he had challenged.[9] In certain respects this movement went beyond what he could have endorsed, but it served the churches well in its generation and could hardly have developed without his earlier pioneering. Bushnell's teachings on the organic nature of society, not to mention his own civic involvements and his confidence in the Christianization of the world, became factors in the thinking of Gladden, Walter Rauschenbusch, and Josiah Strong. Even if his own formulations did not fully mature in this area, they helped pave the way for the Social Gospel, a landmark feature of American Protestant thought and action well into the twentieth century.[10] He was not himself comfortable with the higher biblical criticism, and he certainly was not a close biblical scholar. By some he has been faulted for this. Nevertheless, his theories of language and comprehensiveness, incomplete though they may have been, served a significant purpose. They helped create an openminded setting where at last it was possible to study the Bible with the same rigorous scrutiny as one would examine any other book, and to do so without loss of faith.[11] In expanding youth work his *Christian Nurture* provided Francis E. Clark with important motivation for founding the Young People's Society of Christian Endeavor, a worldwide youth movement, dating from 1881, that enlisted hundreds of thousands of new young Christians.[12] He was also an inspiration for a generation of preachers and teachers well into the next century, among them

George A. Gordon of Boston, Graham Taylor of Hartford and the Chicago Commons, Newman Smyth and Luther A. Weigle in New Haven, and Warren S. Archibald of Hartford, another of his biographers.[13]

The importance of his writings also continued to be felt in Britain and on the Continent.[14] It was rare, one contemporary observed, to find a British free church minister of any standing who was not familiar with Bushnell's books.[15] The Scottish teacher and evangelist, Henry Drummond, author of the famous sermonic address "The Greatest Thing in the World," felt much indebted to Bushnell, who "started me on lines of entirely new thought." When later he met Henry Trumbull in this country and discovered that he had known the Doctor personally, Drummond eagerly pressed his American friend for every last detail about him.[16] In time Bushnell's legacy in England was considered similar to that of Robertson and to the religious writings of the poet Matthew Arnold.[17]

If this was the nature of Bushnell's impact from the late nineteenth and on into the twentieth century, what of Bushnell's significance as an ultra modern twenty-first century approaches? Admittedly his Victorian literary style, his concern with many theological issues that are no longer central, and the romantic optimism of much of his thinking hardly speak our language today. Yet in other respects he remains strikingly relevant.

In an age of religious pluralism, with wide spiritual swings between a rigid right and an often shapeless left within most high religions, Bushnell lives on as a model of commitment combined with an open catholicity. It is no longer possible to doubt his essential Christian integrity or to question his concern for religious knowledge and serious theological reflection. Those who think of him as a bland, loosely tolerant liberal (a term he much distrusted)[18] have forgotten the quasi-Puritan struggle out of which much of his thought was born. To a degree, too, a seasoned Bushnell also became a sobered, less-optimistic Bushnell, a tragic optimist.[19] In words that seem made for "a [modern] world trembling in darkness," as a current historian has described our condition,[20] he could say that "Christianity is a mighty salvation, because it is a tragic salvation, . . . in an essentially tragic universe . . . with a fall and an overspreading curse at the beginning, and a cross in the middle, and a glory . . . at the end. . . ."[21]

But while he stood firmly by his Gospel insights as long as he believed them true, he held the windows of his mind open. For him there was no place in human experience for the idea of finality.[22] New truth always was a possibility, and if sometimes he failed to recognize it, as with evolution, race, or suffrage for women, his habitual stance was expectant and receptive. This creative tension between tradition and fresh winds from the Spirit is not always realized in the Christian community, yet it is clearly enjoined by the New Testament, celebrating as it does the householder "who brings out of his treasure what is new and what is old."[23] The Doctor's lifelong effort to fulfill this difficult calling still speaks today.

Then, too, in a period that heatedly debates the issue of church and state, Bushnell has a relevant word to say about religion as the root of public, as well as private, morality. Where faith and politics are concerned he is not always a dependable guide. Nonetheless, there is a cutting edge to his repeated contention that a free democracy needs a reverence higher than a humanistic social compact. With considerable plausibility, as we have seen, he argued that the absence of such a national allegiance contributed to the outbreak of the Civil War. The problem now is not sectional breakdown. It need hardly be said that our modern difficulty is a weakening of moral nerve in places of power. The intimate complexity of our common existence, linked with unprecedented global responsibilities, make increased attention to national integrity urgent at every level. Thoughtful voices again are questioning whether we can hope to regain fundamental moral health without taking intelligent religion with new seriousness. Here the Doctor's prophetic confidence in the God of nations, as well as his more personal Gospel, still can be instructive.

Likewise, in a century when children and family life are under heavy pressure, Bushnell's thought on these subjects is perennially pertinent. Of all his writings, *Christian Nurture* remains the most easily read and closest to our day. In a 1979 poll of Christian educators as to which writings they considered indispensable in their field, *Christian Nurture* led all other choices.[24] Qualified historians still speak of it as "one of the most influential books ever to be published in America."[25]

Finally, among the lasting influences is the one that impressed his contemporaries the most: simply the person of Bushnell himself[26]— this complex, sometimes contentious, yet positive and affectionate man whom nobody outside his family ever thought of addressing as "Horace;"[27] this born leader who charmed secular or religious opponents against their will and whom Yale alumni would call out to hear even when he was not scheduled to speak;[28] this pastoral theologian beset by crippling disease for nearly half his years and assailed as a heretic, yet a leader respected and widely beloved. Regardless of the era in which they appear, it is rewarding to encounter human beings of such ability, courage, and hope.

With the Doctor there was this further enduring trait: he had about him an authentic atmosphere of God. Bushnell's Eternal had come closer to the human condition than consistent Calvinists could allow, and he was more gentle, thus opening a new theological day. Yet for him, the Divine never lost majesty or moral command. His faith was highly intellectual. But it was much more than that. It was a continuing personal encounter, equally real to him whether he was sailing the Pacific or laboring intensely in his Hartford study. Religious certainty could leave him; he knew what it was to encounter a "private Gethsemane,"[29] as his periods of suicidal depression made plain. But the storms passed, and the Presence would return to reassure him, beckoning him further into the "new life" of the Gospel.

Speaking to the faculty and students of the Chicago Seminary in the late 1860s, Bushnell reminded them that the city might have built its main water intake close to the Lake Michigan shore. It would have been easier that way, and ostensibly more economical. Yet the Chicago fathers deliberately built a costly line far out into the deeps of the lake in order to obtain for the citizenry the purest possible supply. Bushnell suggested that religious leaders need to reach out beyond the easy shore, where thought is shallow and popular faith grows thin, and draw on the central deep, where God's truth in Christ is tremendous and available.[30]

From long waiting, searching, and suffering, the Doctor knew something of that. Since most human beings at some time hunger for at least an intimation of that final Reality, Horace Bushnell remains among the great Christian believers who are a resource for every age.

Bushnell Falls, Old North Trail, Mount Marcy, Adirondacks, New York. Courtesy of Eileen R. Learned and the late Horace Bushnell Learned, West Hartford, Connecticut

Notes

INTRODUCTION
"Did You Know Horace Bushnell?"

1. Lester L. Potter, "Memorial Sermon on Nathaniel J. Burton," in *The Prow of the Ship: Preachers and Preaching Over 150 Years,* ed. Robert L. Edwards (Hartford: Bond Press, 1979), 129.

2. Reuen Thomas, "My Week with Horace Bushnell," *Congregationalist and Christian World* 87, 23 (7 June 1902): 813.

3. Henry C. Trumbull, *Litchfield County, Connecticut, or One Rural County's Contributions to the Nation's Power and Fame* (Philadelphia: Sunday School Times, 1902).

4. United States Patent Office, Horace Bushnell of Hartford, Connecticut, "Mode of Changing the Draft of Stoves by Means of an Elliptical Valve," Letters Patent No. 1177 (21 June 1839); and "Air Heating Furnace," Letters Patent No. 6238 (27 Mar. 1849). Horace Bushnell Collection, Yale University Divinity School Library.

5. John Dyer, "Dr. Horace Bushnell," *Penn Monthly* 7, 4 (Apr. 1876): 295. The reference omits two of Bushnell's books published posthumously subsequent to this article.

6. Ann Douglas, *The Feminization of American Culture* (1977; New York: Avon Books, 1978).

7. Barbara M. Cross, *Horace Bushnell: Minister to a Changing America* (Chicago: Univ. of Chicago Press, 1958).

8. Jack Mendelsohn, *Channing the Reluctant Radical: A Biography,* (Westport, Conn.: Greenwood Press, 1971), Author's Note.

CHAPTER 1
A Birth in Bantam

1. William C. Langdon, *Everyday Things in American Life, 1776–1876* (New York: Scribner's, 1941), 308.

2. Samuel E. Bushnell to Mary Bushnell Cheney, 6 Nov. 1888, Bushnell Collection, Manuscripts and Archives, Yale University Library.

3. Lee Soltow, "Watches and Clocks in Connecticut, 1800: A Symbol of Socioeconomic Status," *Connecticut Historical Society Bulletin* 45, 4 (Oct. 1980): 119.

4. Partially from a source I have been unable to trace.

5. Albert E. Van Dusen, *Connecticut: A Fully Illustrated History of the State* (New York: Random House, 1961), 213.

6. Sydney E. Ahlstrom, *A Religious History of the American People* (New Haven: Yale Univ. Press, 1972), 365ff.

7. Rom. 8:3, NRSV.

8. Vital Records, Town of Washington, Connecticut, 1:26, Barbour Index to Connecticut Vital Records, Connecticut State Library, Hartford.

9. William D. Love, *The Colonial History of Hartford* (Hartford: Case, Lockwood and Brainard, 1914), 2.

10. George E. Bushnell, *Bushnell Family Genealogy: Ancestry and Posterity of Francis Bushnell (1580–1646) of Horsham, England, and Guilford, Connecticut* (Nashville, 1945), 25, 34. Early Bushnell family ancestry is still a matter of great uncertainty, despite endless amounts of time and ink spent trying to trace it.

11. Bernard C. Steiner, *A History of the Plantation of Menunkatuck, and of the Original Town of Guilford, Connecticut* (Baltimore: Privately published, 1897), 25.

12. Leonard A. Bradley, *Descendants of Isaac Bradley of Branford and East Haven, Connecticut, 1650–1898* (New York: Privately published, 1917), 38.

13. Frederick W. Chapman, *The Chapman Family* (Hartford: Case, Tiffany, 1854), 26–30; Saybrook Vital Records, 1:6, Connecticut State Library, Hartford; Mary W. Ferris, *Dawes-Gates Ancestral Lines* (Privately published, 1943) 2:165–66; Saybrook Tercentenary Committee, *In the Land of the Patentees: Saybrook in Connecticut* (Saybrook, Conn.: Acton Library, 1935), 13.

14. Divorce Records, Superior Court Litchfield County, 1752–1922, Aug., 1793 Term, Connecticut State Library, Hartford. Lucretia divorced

him, married a neighboring widower, Daniel Stoddard, and raised a second family; Vital Records, 2:66, Town of Litchfield, Connecticut.

15. HB, MSS Record Book, 1833–1872, Cheney Collection, Connecticut Historical Society, Hartford.

16. HB memorandum, 1874, in Mary Bushnell Cheney, *Life and Letters of Horace Bushnell* (New York: Harpers, 1880), 24ff.

17. Martha E. E. Nelson, *Record of the Descendants of James Ensign and His Wife Sarah Elson, 1634–1939–1960* (Privately published, 1960), 52.

18. Cheney, *Bushnell,* 25–26; and "Elijah Hedding," in *Dictionary of American Biography,* edited by Allen Johnson and Dumas Malone (New York: Scribner's, 1928–36), 8:497–98.

19. Mary E. Bushnell to Horace Bushnell, 7 June 1823, Horace Bushnell Collection, Manuscripts and Archives, Yale University Library.

20. Cheney, *Bushnell,* 26.

CHAPTER 2
By the Splash of Waterwheels

1. Alain C. White, *The History of the Town of Litchfield, Connecticut, 1720–1920* (Litchfield: Enquirer Press, 1920), 128–29.

2. White, *Litchfield,* 199.

3. Land Records, Town of Litchfield, Deeds, 19 (1798–1826), pp. 366, 398, Town Hall.

4. Cheney, *Bushnell,* 28.

5. Ensign Bushnell, grantee, from Stephen and Nathaniel Cogswell, grantors, 19 June 1804, Land Records, Town of Washington, Index to Deeds, 6 (1779–1849), pp. 206–7, Connecticut State Library, Hartford.

6. Kenneth T. Howell and Einar W. Carlson, *Empire Over the Dam: The Story of Waterpowered Industry, Long Since Passed from the Scene* (Chester, Conn.: Pequot Press, 1974), 3–30, 126ff.

7. Cheney, *Bushnell,* 5–7. Ensign Bushnell served as justice of the peace from 1821 to 1835; *Connecticut Register and U.S. Calendar . . . 1821* (New London, Conn.: Samuel Green, 1821), 36. Ensign Bushnell appears in the *Register* each year through 1835. He engaged in a steady stream of land transactions from 1804 to 1836; see Land Records, Town of Washington, Index to Deeds, 6 (1779–1849), Connecticut State Library, Hartford. On his investment in Marble Dale quarries, see Howell and Carlson, *Empire,* 165.

8. HB, "Age of Homespun," *Work and Play; or Literary Varieties* (New

York: Scribner, 1864), 396; Cheney, *Bushnell*, 7.

9. 1874 sketch by HB in Cheney, *Bushnell*, 26–30.

10. HB, "Age of Homespun," *Work and Play*, 395.

11. Cheney, *Bushnell*, 30, 9.

12. Ibid., 29.

13. Ibid., 15–17, 29, 32.

14. Ibid., 30, 456.

15. Ibid., 18.

16. Ibid., 8.

17. Milton Rugoff, *The Beechers: An American Family in the Nineteenth Century* (New York: Harper, 1981), 44–45.

18. Cheney, *Bushnell*, 15; Jonathan Edwards, "Personal Narrative," in Clarence H. Faust and Thomas H. Johnson, *Jonathan Edwards: Representative Selections* . . . (New York: American Book, 1935), 60.

19. Cheney, *Bushnell*, 28.

20. HB, "Age of Homespun," *Work and Play*, 388–89.

21. Cheney, *Bushnell*, 21.

22. The only known mention of such a possibility is in Noah Porter's eulogy of Bushnell in 1876, "Horace Bushnell, A Memorial Sermon," *The New Englander* 36, 1 (Jan. 1877), 153–54.

23. Cheney, *Bushnell*, 15.

24. Ibid., 21.

25. Ibid., 21, 32; Hannah Josephson, *The Golden Threads: New England's Mill Girls and Magnates* (New York: Duell, Sloan and Pearce, 1949), 33–40.

26. Cheney, *Bushnell*, 36. The tutor was Lyman Coleman, Yale 1817. He taught on a number of well-known college faculties, outlived Bushnell, and for a time was the oldest active college professor in the United States. "Lyman Coleman," *DAB* 4:294.

CHAPTER 3
The Great World of Yale

1. Charles E. Cuningham, *Timothy Dwight, 1752–1817: A Biography* (New York: Macmillan, 1942), 166.

2. Cuningham, *Dwight*, 164–90. A more favorable view of the legacy of Ezra Stiles, Dwight's predecessor, is in Brooks M. Kelley, *Yale: A History* (New Haven: Yale Univ. Press, 1974), 11–12.

3. *New Haven Register,* 16 Sept. 1826, cited in *Hartford Courant,* 18 Sept. 1826.

4. Cuningham, *Dwight,* 247; faculty names from *Catalogue, Yale College,* 1823, 4, Manuscripts and Archives, Yale University Library.

5. The makeup of the class varied during undergraduate years. *Obituary Record of Graduates of Yale College . . .* (New Haven: Tuttle, Morehouse and Taylor, 1870 and following years); Ralph D. Smith, "History of the Class of 1827," Manuscripts and Archives, Yale University Library.

6. Out of a freshman class of eighty-seven, more than sixty were younger than Bushnell, including two who were only fourteen. Thirteen members were older than he. Ralph D. Smith, Manuscripts and Archives, Yale University Library. Cheney, *Bushnell,* 38.

7. Catalogue of Faculty and Students in Yale College, Nov. 1823, p. 23, Manuscripts and Archives, Yale University Library; Cheney, *Bushnell,* 41.

8. Experiences of David Trumbull, class of 1842, Irven Paul, *A Yankee Reformer in Chile: The Life and Works of David Trumbull* (South Pasadena, Calif.: William Carey Library, 1973), 126; Kelley, *Yale,* 209ff.

9. Brothers in Unity Records, 4 (1816–28), Manuscripts and Archives, Yale University Library; Cheney, *Bushnell,* 40–41.

10. Church of Christ Records, 1817–77, p. 25, Manuscripts and Archives, Yale University Library; Cheney, *Bushnell,* 41–42; Kelley, *Yale,* 227–28.

11. Henry Durant, Horace Bushnell, et al., to President [Jeremiah] Day, n.d., Student Petitions and Riots Records, Manuscripts and Archives, Yale University Library. Horace Bushnell, Cortlandt Van Rensselaer, et al., to the Faculty of Yale College, n.d., Day Family Collection, ibid.

12. John M. Clagett, et al., Committee of the Class of 1827, to Elijah Clark, Point Coupee, Louisana, n.d., Conic Rebellion of 1825, Student Petitions and Riots Records, ibid.

13. Yale College Faculty Records, Minutes, Meetings, Committees, 1817–51, 15 July 1825, ibid. Unsigned, undated letter in Day's hand, Conic Rebellion of 1825, Student Petitions and Riots Records, ibid.

14. Yale College Faculty Records, 15–27 July 1825, ibid. For parental pain, see David L. Perry to Jeremiah Day, 1 Aug. 1825, saying he was "among perhaps an hundred parents, whose hearts now bleed," ibid.

15. Cheney, *Bushnell,* 40.

16. Ibid., 37–38.

17. Yale Commencement Exercises, 12 Sept. 1827, Manuscripts and Ar-

chives, Yale University Library; [Lyman Bagg], *Four Years at Yale* (New York: Henry Holt, 1871), 303–5, 665ff.

18. Deemed "ablest" judging by the number of the class appearing in the *Dictionary of American Biography*—eight members, or 10 percent, Bushnell being one. From 1817, when Dwight died, to 1827, no other Yale class came close to this figure.

CHAPTER 4
Feeling after a Profession

1. Cheney, *Bushnell*, 32.

2. Frances M. Caulkins, *History of Norwich, Connecticut* (1866; Chester, Conn.: Pequot Press, 1976), 545–46.

3. HB to Henry N. Day, 20 Oct. 1827, Day Family Collection, Manuscripts and Archives, Yale University Library.

4. Cheney, *Bushnell*, 50–51; "William Maxwell" in Franklin B. Dexter, *Biographical Sketches of the Graduates of Yale College with Annals of the College History* (New York: Henry Holt, 1911) 5 (June 1792–Sept. 1805):520–22.

5. Gideon Welles, Mss Diary, pp. 53, 57–58, Gideon Welles Collection, Connecticut Historical Society, Hartford.

6. Frank L. Mott, *American Journalism: A History of Newspapers in the United States Through 250 Years, 1690–1940* (New York: Macmillan, 1941), 181, 182.

7. Jack Shepherd, *The Adams Chronicles: Four Generations of Greatness* (Boston: Little, Brown, 1975), 306.

8. Cheney, *Bushnell*, 52.

9. Twenty-eight members eventually entered the ministry, and an equal number chose law; business claimed nine and medicine seven.

10. Frederick C. Hicks, *Yale Law School: The Founders and the Founders' Collection*, (New Haven: Yale Law Library, 1935); Roger W. Tuttle, ed., *Biographies of Graduates of the Yale Law School, 1824–1899* (New Haven: Tuttle, Morehouse and Taylor, 1911), 29–31.

11. Cheney, *Bushnell*, 32–33, 52–53.

12. Ibid., 32–33.

13. Kelley, *Yale*, 159; Cheney, *Bushnell*, 57.

14. Fitch to the Rev. Seth Bliss, 21 Mar. 1831, in John T. Wayland, *The Theological Department in Yale College, 1822–1858* (1933; New York: Garland, 1987), 370.

15. Lyman H. Atwater, "Horace Bushnell," *Presbyterian Review* 2 (Jan. 1881): 116. Atwater was a member of the Yale class of 1831.

16. HB, *Sermons on Living Subjects* (New York: Scribner, Armstrong, 1872), 175–76.

17. Porter, "Horace Bushnell" (1877), 155.

18. The account rests on the recollections many years later of Bushnell's classmate and fellow-tutor, Robert McEwen; Cheney, *Bushnell*, 55–56.

19. HB, "Dissolving of Doubts," *Living Subjects*, 176–77.

20. Untitled, Horace Bushnell Collection, Manuscripts and Archives, Yale University Library.

21. Sidney E. Mead, *Nathaniel William Taylor, 1786–1858: A Connecticut Liberal* (Chicago: Univ. of Chicago Press, 1942), 8ff. This is the standard biography. Unless otherwise indicated, Taylor material is taken from this source.

22. Roland H. Bainton, *Yale and the Ministry* (New York: Harper, 1957), 82, citing Theodore T. Munger.

23. Nathaniel W. Taylor, "*Concio ad Clerum,* " in Ahlstrom, *Theology in America,* 213–49.

24. Phil. 2:12–13, RSV.

25. Curtis M. Geer, *The Hartford Theological Seminary, 1834–1934* (Hartford: Case, Lockwood and Brainard, 1934), chaps. 1–4.

26. Theodore T. Munger, *Horace Bushnell: Preacher and Theologian* (Boston: Houghton Mifflin, 1899), 28; Mead, *Taylor,* 161.

27. Mead, *Taylor,* 163.

28. 1 Cor. 2:10, KJV.

29. Cheney, *Bushnell,* 62.

30. [James F. Clarke], "Bushnell on Vicarious Sacrifice," *Christian Examiner* 81, N.S. 1 (May 1866): 277.

31. Jerry W. Brown, *The Rise of Biblical Criticism in America, 1800–1870: The New England Scholars* (Middletown, Conn.: Wesleyan Univ. Press, 1969), chap. 11. Bushnell's regard for Gibbs appears in his *God in Christ, Three Discourses . . .* (Hartford: Brown and Parsons, 1849), 28–29, 31–32.

32. Samuel Taylor Coleridge, *Aids to Reflection, In the Formation of a Manly Character . . .* (Burlington, Vt.: Chauncey Goodrich, 1829), 106–7, 123; lix, 131–35; 116.

33. Ibid., lviii.

34. Cheney, *Bushnell,* 207–9. Just when Bushnell first read Coleridge is debatable. See David L. Smith, *Symbolism and Growth: The Religious*

Thought of Horace Bushnell (Chico, Calif.: Scholars Press, 1981), 34.

35. MSS, July, 1832, Horace Bushnell Papers, MSS Group No. 39, Special Collections, Yale Divinity School Library.

36. Ibid.

37. Records, New Haven West Association, Vols. 3–4 (1787–1832): 173, Archives, Connecticut Conference, United Church of Christ (U.C.C.), Hartford.

38. Cheney, *Bushnell*, 66.

39. HB, "Twentieth Anniversary: A Commemorative Discourse" (Hartford: Elihu Geer, 1853), 7.

40. HB to Judge Thomas Day, 4 May 1833, Day Family Collection, Manuscripts and Archives, Yale University Library.

41. HB, "Twentieth Anniversary," 8.

CHAPTER 5
New Minister in a Port City

1. *Hartford Courant,* 17 Mar. 1991.

2. J. Hammond Trumbull, ed., *The Memorial History of Hartford County, Connecticut, 1633–1884* (Boston: Edward L. Osgood, 1886) 1:653–66. Melancthon W. Jacobus, *The Connecticut River Steamboat Story* (Hartford: Connecticut Historical Society, 1956), 13ff.

3. J. Bard McNulty, *Older Than the Nation: The Story of the Hartford Courant* (Stonington, Conn.: Pequot Press, 1964), 49.

4. State of Connecticut, *Register and Manual for 1869* (Hartford, 1869), 580.

5. Edwards, *Prow of the Ship,* 1–2, 19–20, 25–26, 35–37.

6. H. Shelton Smith, ed., *Horace Bushnell* (New York: Oxford Univ. Press, 1965), 3–4; Sydney E. Ahlstrom, "Theology in America: A Historical Survey" in James W. Smith and A. Leland Jamison, eds., *The Shaping of American Religion* (Princeton: Princeton Univ. Press, 1961), 279ff.

7. Samuel Pease, MSS Diary, 1–3 Mar. 1833, Connecticut Historical Society; HB, "Twentieth Anniversary," 7.

8. Pease Diary, 3 Mar. 1833, Connecticut Historical Society; Heb. 2:3, KJV; Cheney, *Bushnell*, 67.

9. Edward A. Lawrence, *The Life of Reverend Joel Hawes, D. D.* (Hartford: William J. Hammersley, 1871), 55.

10. Robert L. Edwards, "Portrait of a People: Horace Bushnell"s Hart-

ford Congregation," in *Studies of the Church in History: Essays Honoring Robert S. Paul,* edited by Horton Davies (Allison Park, Pa: Pickwick Press, 1983), 152; HB, "Twentieth Anniversary," 8.

11. North Congregational Church Records, 1:54–55, Connecticut State Library, Hartford; HB, "Twentieth Anniversary," 22; Cheney, *Bushnell,* 70–71. The comment on Skinner is in Genealogical Notes, Mary B. Cheney Collection, Connecticut Historical Society.

12. 13 Sept. 1833, Vital Records, New Haven, 6:20, Lucius B. Barbour Collection, Connecticut State Library.

13. Antoinette Cheney Crocker, *The Great Oaks* (Concord, Mass.: Privately published, 1977), 163–64.

14. Mary B. Cheney, MSS note, in the private collection of the late Horace Bushnell Learned, a great-grandson of Horace Bushnell, and Mrs. Learned, of West Hartford Connecticut, hereafter designated as the Learned Collection.

15. Cheney, *Bushnell,* 72.

16. Ibid., 79–80.

17. HB, "Twentieth Anniversary," 13, 14.

18. HB, "Christian Comprehensiveness," *New Englander* 6 (Jan. 1848): 81–111; republished in *Building Eras in Religion* (New York: Scribners, 1881); H. Shelton Smith, ed., *Horace Bushnell,* 106ff.

19. H. Shelton Smith, *Bushnell,* 27–28, 106–8.

20. HB, *Sermons for the New Life* (New York: Scribner, 1858), 364–81. Bushnell's sermons are not always datable. Mrs. Cheney says this one came from his first year of ministry; *Bushnell,* 77.

21. Cheney, *Bushnell,* 73.

22. North Congregational Church Records, 1:61–77, Connecticut State Library; Edwards, "Portrait," 156.

23. HB, "Living to God In Small Things," *Sermons for the New Life,* 300. Cheney dates this sermon 1837; *Bushnell,* 77.

24. Catalogs, North Congregational Church Records, 1832, 1836, 1839, Connecticut State Library; HB, "Twentieth Anniversary," 10–12.

25. HB, *Views of Christian Nurture and of Subjects Adjacent Thereto* (1847; Rpt ed. Philip B. Eppard. Delmar, NY: Scholars' Facsimiles and Reprints, 1975), 247.

26. Geer, *Hartford Seminary,* 279; Catalogs, North Congregational Church Records 1832, 1836, Connecticut State Library.

27. HB, *Views of Christian Nurture,* 246–47.

28. Samuel H. Riddel of Glastonbury was an early secretary, or "Scribe," of the Institute. HB to Riddel, 16 Apr. [?] 1842, Horace Scudder Collection, Washington University Libraries, St. Louis, Missouri; Geer, *Hartford Seminary,* 32.

29. HB, *Views of Christian Nurture,* 120.

30. HB, "A Discourse on the Slavery Question, Delivered in the North Church, Hartford, Thursday Evening, 10 Jan. 1839" (Hartford: Case, Tiffany, 1839), 25; Cheney, *Bushnell,* 40.

31. Nancy Jackson vs. J. S. Bulloch, dissenting opinion, quoted in Bernard C. Steiner, *History of Slavery in Connecticut* (1893; New York: Johnson, 1973), 55.

32. U.S. Department of Commerce, *Historical Statistics of the United States, Colonial Times to 1970* (New York: Basic Books, 1976), 25; Steiner, *Slavery,* 84.

33. Smith's obituary, *Hartford Courant,* May 23, 1860.

34. Edwards, "Portrait," 151; Bushnell, MSS Record Book of Marriages, Horace Bushnell Collection, Connecticut Historical Society.

35. Edmund Fuller, *Prudence Crandall: An Incident of Racism in Nineteenth Century Connecticut* (Middletown, Conn.: Wesleyan Univ. Press, 1971).

36. David E. Swift, *Black Prophets of Justice: Activist Clergy Before the Civil War* (Baton Rouge: Louisiana State Univ. Press, 1989), 57–59, 181, and chs. 8, 9.

37. HB, "Crisis of the Church" (Hartford: Daniel Burgess, 1835), 15, 18–20.

38. HB, "Discourse on the Slavery Question"; Russell G. Talcott to John Seymour, 15 Jan. 1839, Seymour Collection, Stowe-Day Foundation, Hartford.

39. HB, "Discourse on the Slavery Question," esp. 32.

40. Robert C. Senior, "New England Congregationalists and the Anti-Slavery Movement, 1830–1860" (Ph. D. diss., Yale Univ., 1954), 210ff.

41. HB, "Discourse on the Slavery Question," 29–32.

42. Ibid.

43. *Hartford Courant,* 12 Jan. 1839.

44. Francis Gillette, *A Review of Rev. Horace Bushnell's "Discourse on the Slavery Question"* (Hartford: S. S. Cowles, 1839), esp. 39 and 41.

45. Russell Talcott to John Seymour, 15 Jan. 1839, Seymour Collection, Stowe-Day Foundation; HB, "Twentieth Anniversary," 19.

46. HB to Leonard Bacon, 24 June 1840, Bacon Family Collection, Manuscripts and Archives, Yale University Library.

47. Minutes, Consociation of the Eastern District of Fairfield County, Connecticut, 13 Oct. 1840, p. 36, Archives, Connecticut Conference, U.C.C. Bushnell likewise consulted Noah Porter, Jr., then pastor in New Milford, Connecticut, who in turn encouraged Bacon to go along. Noah Porter, Jr., to Leonard Bacon, 27 June 1840, Bacon Family Collection, Manuscripts and Archives, Yale University Library.

48. HB, "Discourse on the Slavery Question," 12; opinions as to African American inferiority, Swift, *Black Prophets,* 140–41, 237.

49. Howard A. Barnes, "Horace Bushnell: An American Gentleman" (Ph. D. diss., State Univ. of Iowa, 1970); in addition to what he had said in 1835, he spoke in 1854 of the possibility of "civil war" and warned that "matters are now verging toward an array of section against section in our country." HB, "The Northern Iron..." (Hartford: Edwin Hunt, 1854), 27. Even in Bushnell's extraordinarily myopic "Census and Slavery," he could not dismiss "the always boding [foreboding], and tempestuous evil" that slavery was. HB, "The Census and Slavery..." (Hartford: L.E. Hunt, 1860), 24.

50. Cheney, *Bushnell,* 465–67; HB, *Nature and the Supernatural, as Together Constituting the One System of God* (1858; AMS Press, 1973), 486–90.

51. Swift, *Black Prophets,* 216; HB to Jeremiah Day, 7 June 1838, Jeremiah Day Collection, Yale Collection of American Literature, Beinecke Rare Book and Manuscript Library, Yale University. Charles Ray (at Wesleyan), and Pennington (at Dartmouth) were rebuffed when they attempted to enter white colleges. Swift, *Black Prophets,* 79–81, 236–37.

52. Howard A. Barnes, "The Idea that Caused a War: Horace Bushnell *versus* Thomas Jefferson," *Journal of Church and State* 16, 1 (Winter 1974): 79; George M. Frederickson, *The Black Image in the White Mind: The Debate on Afro-American Character and Destiny, 1817–1914* (New York: Harper and Row, 1971), ch. 5.

53. Although he is in no way responsible for my formulation, I am indebted to Professor Swift for helping me shape these conclusions.

54. Cheney, *Bushnell,* 85–87. On Ensign Bushnell's move, Monroe County, New York, Index of Deeds, 37:189; 2:123, and 286, Rochester.

55. Cheney, *Bushnell,* 87.

56. Ibid.; Charles H. Clark, "Bushnell the Citizen," in *Bushnell Centenary: 193rd Annual Meeting of the General Association of Connecticut,*

Hartford, June 17, 18, 1902 (Hartford: Case, Lockwood and Brainard, 1902), 62.

57. Cheney, *Bushnell*, 239.

58. Ibid., 75–76, 86.

CHAPTER 6
First Steps toward Center Stage

1. Minutes, Trustees of Wesleyan University, 2 Aug. 1842, 70, Archives, Olin Library, Wesleyan University.

2. HB to Jeremiah Day, 16 Feb. 1836, Jeremiah Day Collection, Yale Collection of American Literature, Beinecke Rare Book and Manuscript Library.

3. David M. Stameshkin, "The Town's College: Middlebury College, 1800–1915" (Ph. D. diss., Univ. of Michigan, 1978), chs. 1–5. Oddly, the minutes of the Middlebury Trustees for 1840 make no reference to HB.

4. Undated memorandum, Mary A. Bushnell to Mary B. Cheney, Learned Collection; Frank R. Shipman, "Some Letters from Horace Bushnell to Leonard Bacon," *Hartford Times*, 31 Aug. 1931.

5. Mary A. Bushnell to George Bushnell, 22 Mar. 1841, Blake Family Collection, Manuscripts and Archives, Yale University Library.

6. HB to Andrews, Mar. 1840, Samuel J. Andrews, *William Watson Andrews, A Religious Biography*... (New York: G. P. Putnam's Sons, 1900), 37–38.

7. Minutes, Porter Rhetorical Society, Andover Seminary, 20, 21 Dec. [1838]; Cheney, *Bushnell*, 88–89.

8. Ps. 19:1–2, RSV.

9. It seems clear that Bushnell had read Emerson's *Nature* (1836), and drew on some of its ideas. Donald A. Crosby, "Horace Bushnell's Theory of Language: An Historical and Philosophical Study" (Ph. D. diss., Columbia Univ., 1932), 189–93.

10. HB "Revelation," MSS in Bushnell Collection, Yale Divinity School Library. Transcript in David S. Steward, "Horace Bushnell and Contemorary Christian Education" (Ph.D. diss., Yale Univ., 1966), 305–35.

11. Quoted in James D. Bloom's review of Herman Melville's *Journals*, edited by Howard C. Horsford and Lynn Horth (Evanston, Ill.: Northwestern Univ. Press and Newberry Library, 1989), *New York Times*, 12 Nov. 1989, 58.

12. Introduction to *Nature,* Norman Foerster and Robert M. Lovett, eds., *American Poetry and Prose* (Boston: Houghton Mifflin, 1934), 515.

13. On HB and Parker: Cheney, *Bushnell,* 108; HB to Noah Porter, Jr., 23 Oct. 1844, and Parker to Noah Porter, Jr., 18 May 1848, Graves Collection, Archives, Unitarian Society, Hartford, courtesy of The Rev. Nathaniel P. Lauriat. On HB and Ripley, Cheney, *Bushnell,* 108. On HB and Emerson: Emerson to George P. Bradford, 28 Aug. 1854, Ralph L. Rusk, ed., *The Letters of Ralph Waldo Emerson* (New York: Columbia Univ. Press, 1939), 4:460.

14. HB, "Principles of National Greatness" (New Haven: Herrick and Noyes, 1837), 24–25; republished as "The True Wealth or Weal of Nations," *Work and Play,* 43–77.

15. HB, "A Discourse on the Moral Tendencies and Results of Human History" (New Haven: A. H. Maltby, 1843); republished in *Work and Play* as "The Growth of Law."

16. Catholicus [pseud.], *A Letter to Dr. Bushnell, of Hartford, on the Rationalistic, Socinian, and Infidel Tendency of Certain Passages in His Address before the Alumni of Yale College* (Hartford: H. S. Parsons, 1843), esp. 19.

17. "Henry Noble Day," *DAB* 5:158–59.

18. Cheney, *Bushnell,* 102–4; *Ohio Observer,* 18 Aug. 1842. His addresses were probably much the same as "Of the Mutabilities of Life," in *Moral Uses of Dark Things* (New York: Scribner, 1868), 319–43, and "Life, or the Lives," *Work and Play,* 262–307. Duke, *Bushnell,* 96.

19. Cheney, *Bushnell,* 105.

20. HB, "National Greatness," 22. An important dimension of Bushnell's work, his statement on the significance of public education still makes relevant reading; "Common Schools in Cities...," *Connecticut Common School Journal* 4, 1 (1 Dec. 1841): 7–13. See also Floyd L. Roberts, "Horace Bushnell and the Common Schools of Connecticut" (MA thesis, Yale Univ., 1927); and Carl F. Kaestle, *Pillars of the Republic: Common Schools and American Society, 1780–1860* (New York: Hill and Wang, 1983), 129, 169–70.

21. Samuel Hart, "Henry Barnard, LL. D.," *New England Historical and Genealogical Register* 56 (1902): 176; on HB's esteem for Barnard, see his "Speech for Connecticut..." (Hartford: Boswell and Faxon, 1851), 40–41 (republished in *Work and Play,* 167–226); and Edith N. MacMullen, *In the Cause of True Education: Henry Barnard and Nineteenth Century School*

Reform (New Haven: Yale Univ. Press, 1991), 100. Connecticut General Association, *Minutes of Annual Meetings,* 1834–1845.

22. Hartford Central Association, Minutes, 6–7 June 1843, Archives, Connecticut Conference, U.C.C., Hartford; Edwin P. Parker, "The Hartford Central Association and the Bushnell Controversy" (Hartford: Case, Lockwood and Brainard, 1896), 5–7. Frank L. Mott, *A History of American Magazines, 1850–1905* (Cambridge: Harvard Univ. Press, 1957), 2:312–14, 4:293, 451.

23. 13 Oct. 1844, Thomas Robbins, *Diary of Thomas Robbins, D.D. 1796–1854,* edited by Increase Tarbox (Boston: Thomas Todd, 1886), 2:754.

24. HB, "Politics Under the Law of God..." (Hartford: Edwin Hunt, 1844).

25. HB, "American Politics," *American National Preacher* 14, 12 (Dec. 1840): 189–204.

26. HB "Politics Under the Law of God," 8, 9–10, 13, 18.

27. *Hartford Times,* 23 Apr. 1844.

28. HB, "Review of [Thomas C. Brownell's] the Errors of the Times," *New Englander* 2 (Jan. 1844): 143–75.

29. Nathaniel H. Egleston, "Bushnell on Henry Clay," *Supplement to the Connecticut Courant* 45, 20 (7 Oct. 1880): 157. Many of the details of the Clay episode are taken from this source.

30. Even so pro-Bushnell a writer as Sydney Ahlstrom makes such a claim; Ahlstrom, "Horace Bushnell," in *A Handbook of Christian Theologians,* edited by Martin E. Marty and Dean C. Peerman (Nashville: Abingdon, 1965), 47.

31. Donald G. Mitchell, *American Lands and Letters: Leather-Stocking to Poe's "Raven"* (New York: Scribner's, 1899), 2:87.

32. *The Christian Freeman* (Hartford), 28 Nov. 1844; Glyndon G. Van Deusen, *The Life of Henry Clay* (Boston: Little, Brown, 1937), 377.

33. Charles H. Clark, "Bushnell the Citizen" in *Bushnell Centenary,* 64; Cheney, *Bushnell,* 110.

34. John B. Moses, M. D., Scarsdale, N.Y., to the author, June 1981.

35. Cheney, *Bushnell,* 75, 87–90; HB, "Politics Under the Law of God," Preface.

36. 26 Jan. 1845, Robbins, *Diary* 2:768; Cheney, *Bushnell,* 113.

37. HB to Leonard Bacon, 11 June 1845, Bacon Family Collection, Manuscripts and Archives, Yale University Library.

38. HB to Henry White, 9 June [1845], ibid.; HB, "The Evangelical Alliance," *New Englander* 5, 1 (Jan. 1847): 102–25.

39. *Hartford Courant,* 19 June 1845; 24 June 1845, Robbins, *Diary* 2:785; William A. Fairburn, *Merchant Sail* (Center Lovell, Maine: Fairburn Educational Foundation, 1945–55), 1175; Cheney, *Bushnell,* 114.

CHAPTER 7
Europe

1. Cheney, *Bushnell,* 115.

2. HB, "A Discourse on the Moral Uses of the Sea" (New York: Dodd, 1845); revised in HB, *Moral Uses of Dark Things* (New York: Scribner's 1867), 344–60.

3. Cheney, *Bushnell,* 115, 116.

4. For identifying this squadron, I am indebted to Mr. J. D. Brown, Naval Historical Branch, Ministry of Defense, London. Details are from the logs of the ships involved, Public Record Office, Kew, Richmond, England. See also William R. O'Byrne, *A Naval Biographical Dictionary* (London: Murray, 1849), 857–58; Sidney Lee, ed., *Dictionary of National Biography, Index and Epitome* (London: Smith Elder, 1906), 1001; HB, MSS, European Journal, 19 July 1845, Yale Divinity School Library; Cheney, *Bushnell,* 116–17.

5. HB, European Journal, 22 July 1845, Yale Divinity School Library; Cheney, *Bushnell,* 117–18.

6. HB, European Journal, 27 July, 3 Aug. 1845, Yale Divinity School Library.

7. Cheney, *Bushnell,* 168; HB, European Journal, 25, 28 July 1845, Yale Divinity School Library.

8. Ibid., 30–31 July, 20 Aug. 1845.

9. Ibid., 20–21 Aug. 1845.

10. Ibid., 28, 29 Aug., 1, 7, 16 Sept. 1845.

11. Ibid., 8 Sept., 7, 10, 15, 20 Nov. 1845.

12. Ibid., 21 Jan. 1846; Corporation Records, 9 (1847–56), p. 214, Harvard Univ. Archives, Pusey Library.

13. HB, European Journal, 3 Nov. 1845, Yale Divinity School Library.

14. Ibid., 12, 13, 17, 18 Sept. 1845.

15. Ibid., 24 July, 23–24 Aug., 26 Sept. 1845; Cheney, *Bushnell,* 124, 135.

16. HB, European Journal, 10 Sept., 8 Dec. 1845, Yale Divinity School

Library; Cheney, *Bushnell,* 152.

17. HB to Leonard Bacon, 18 Apr. 1843, Bacon Family Collection, Yale University Library. Bushnell devoted major energy and time to this project from 1843 to 1847, both at home and overseas. Cheney, *Bushnell,* 107, 138, 172, 175. HB to Noah Porter, Jr., 23 Oct. 1844, Graves Collection, Archives, Unitarian Society; HB to Bacon, 2 Mar., 2, 15 Apr. 1846, Bacon Collection, Yale University Library; and HB, "Evangelical Alliance. "

18. HB, "Letter to His Holiness, Pope Gregory XVI," *Building Eras In Religion, Literary Varieties III* (1881; New York: Scribner's, 1903), 357–58; Cheney, *Bushnell,* 171–72; Ray A. Billington, *The Protestant Crusade, 1800–1860: A Study of the Origins of American Nativism* (New York: Rinehart, 1952), 282.

19. Unsigned article, "The German Anti-Papal Movement," *New Englander* 5, 2 (Apr. 1847); HB, "Evangelical Alliance."

20. Billington, *Protestant Crusade,* 33ff. HB to Bacon, 18 Apr. 1843, Bacon Collection, Manuscripts and Archives, Yale University Library.

21. HB, "Letter to His Holiness," *Building Eras,* 171–72; Billington, *Protestant Crusade,* 282; Eric John et al., eds., *The Popes: A Concise Biographical History* (New York: Hawthorne Books, 1964), 436ff; HB, European Journal, 14, 25 Dec. 1845, Yale Divinity School Library.

22. HB, "Littera al Romano Pontifice, di Orazio Bushnell, Dottore di Teologia di Hartford, Stati Uniti d'America," in *Sulle Attuali Condizioni della Romagna, di Gino Capponi; La Questione Italiana, di M. Canuti; Littera al Romano Pontifice, di Orazio Bushnell, Dottore di Teologia di Hartford, Stati Uniti d'America,* ed. Gino A. G. G. Capponi (Italy, 1846).

23. *Religious Herald,* 9 May 1846; *Supplement to the Courant,* 11, 10 (16 May 1846); *Religious Herald,* 20 June 1846.

24. HB, European Journal, 19 Feb. 1846, Yale Divinity School Library.

25. Ibid., 3 Feb., 27 Mar., 10, 18 Apr. 1846.

26. *London Universe,* 3 Mar. 1846, reprinted in *Religious Herald,* 4 Apr. 1846 and *Hartford Times,* 6, 7 Apr. 1846.

27. HB, European Journal, 21 Mar., 8 Apr. 1846, Yale Divinity School Library.

28. Ibid., 21, 29 Mar. 1846; D. Tyssil Evans, *The Life and Ministry of the Rev. Caleb Morris...* (London: Alexander and Shepheard, 1902); "Caleb Morris," *Congregational Yearbook, 1866* (London: Jackson, Walford and Hodder, 1866), 269–70.

29. HB, *Sermons for the New Life,* 186–205; published in London,

1846, and in *American National Preacher* 20 (Aug. 1846); HB, European Journal, 29 Mar. 1846, Yale Divinity School Library.

30. Charles L. Brace first heard it in Hartford in 1842 and said later it "affected my whole life." [Emma Brace, ed.], *The Life of Charles Loring Brace* (1894; New York: Arno Press, 1976), 7–8. It was also a major influence on Frederick L. Olmstead. Charles C. McLaughlin and Charles E. Beveridge, eds., *The Papers of Frederick Law Olmsted* (Baltimore: Johns Hopkins Univ. Press, 1977), 1:74.

31. HB, European Journal, 8, 12 Apr. 1846, Yale Divinity School Library.

32. Ibid., 12, 29, 30 Apr. 1846.

33. Marie Hanson-Taylor and Horace E. Scudder, *Life and Letters of Bayard Taylor* (Boston: Houghton Mifflin, 1884), 1:65–66; "Bayard Taylor," *DAB* 18:314–16.

34. HB, European Journal, 9 May 1846 and following, Yale Divinity School Library.

35. On his forty-fourth birthday, he noted "the improvement of my health since the last birthday." Ibid., 14 Apr. 1846.

CHAPTER 8
Champion of Children

1. Cheney, *Bushnell,* 171.

2. Ibid., 175–76.

3. HB, *Moral Uses of Dark Things;* Conrad Cherry, ed., *Horace Bushnell: Sermons* (New York: Paulist Press, 1985), 21. For fuller treatment of *Moral Uses,* see Chapter 20.

4. HB, "Agriculture at the East," *Work and Play,* 227–61.

5. Luther A. Weigle, Introduction, HB, *Christian Nurture* (1860; New Haven: Yale Univ. Press, 1947), xxxi; Daniel W. Howe, "The Social Science of Horace Bushnell," *Journal of American History* 70, 2 (Sept. 1983): 305–22.

6. Philip Greven, *The Protestant Temperament: Patterns of Child-Rearing, Religious Experience, and the Self in Early America* (New York: New American Library, 1979).

7. Jared B. Flagg, Autobiography, typescript, Stowe-Day Foundation Library.

8. Rugoff, *The Beechers,* 205.

9. Cheney, *Bushnell,* 15.

10. HB, "Argument for Discourses on Christian Nurture," *Views,* 82.

11. Ibid.

12. James H. Nichols, *Romanticism in American Theology: Nevin and Schaff at Mercersburg* (Chicago: Univ. of Chicago Press, 1961), 238–39. In 1856 Congregationalists could report only 1. 6 baptisms per 100 members.

13. Charles E. Hambrick-Stowe, "An Engaging Sign: Baptism in the History of American Congregationalism," *Bulletin of the Congregational Library* 41, 1 (Fall 1989): 11–12.

14. HB, "Spiritual Economy of Revivals of Religion," *Building Eras in Religion,* 150–81.

15. HB, "Barbarism the First Danger, A Discourse for Home Missions" (New York: American Home Missionary Society, 1847), 16; reprinted in *Work and Play,* 9–42.

16. HB, "Argument," *Views,* 83.

17. Ibid., 82.

18. HB summarizes his change of mind in "Discourses on Christian Nurture," *Views,* 38–39, and "Argument," *Views,* 82–84.

19. HB, "Discourses," *Views,* 6.

20. Marked in Bushnell's hand, "N[orth] C[hurch] H[artford], Mar. 1835," the manuscript of the second of the two sermons survives; in it, however, Bushnell summarizes the import of the first. Bushnell Collection, Bushnell Memorial Hall, Hartford.

21. Cheney, *Bushnell,* 92–93. Eventually Terry took his membership away from the North Church.

22. HB, "The Kingdom of Heaven As a Grain of Mustard Seed," *New Englander* 2, 4 (Oct. 1844): 600–19.

23. Minutes, Hartford Central Association, 2 June 1846, 18; HB," Argument," *Views,* 49.

24. HB, "Discourses," *Views,* 40; "Argument," *Views,* 82.

25. HB, "Discourses," *Views,* 13; Jonathan Edwards had declared in 1750 that "every Christian family ought to be, as it were, a little church. " "Farewell Sermon," Faust and Johnson, *Jonathan Edwards,* 197.

26. HB, *Discourses on Christian Nurture* approved by the Committee of Publication, Boston Sabbath School Society, 1847. Minutes, Hartford Central Association, 4 Aug. 1846, 20–21. That Noah Porter made the motion to publish is presumed from Bushnell's reference to a "venerable father, whose name is a name of confidence and respect, second to no other in our churches." No one else present fitted that description. HB, "Argument,"

Views, 50. See also Eppard's Introduction to *Views,* and 49–51; and Cheney, *Bushnell,* 178–80.

27. This copy is in the Bushnell Collection, Bushnell Memorial Hall, Hartford.

28. HB, "Argument," *Views,* 50–51, 82.

29. Nichols, *Romanticism,* 240–41.

30. James H. Nichols, ed., *The Mercersburg Theology* (New York: Oxford Univ. Press, 1966), 4, 17ff.

31. HB, *Views,* 84, 95ff. John W. Nevin, "Educational Religion," *Weekly Messenger of the German Reformed Church* N.S. 12 (23, 30 June, 7, 14 July 1847).

32. HB, *Views,* 51.

33. HB, "Argument," *Views,* 52–53; "Discourses, *Views,* 31ff; "Revivals of Religion."

34. Bennett Tyler, *Dr. Tyler's Letter to Dr. Bushnell* (East Windsor Hill: Massachusetts Sabbath School Society, 1847), 22.

35. Bennett Tyler, "An Address to the Alumni of the Theological Institute of Connecticut..." (Hartford: Case, Lockwood, 1857), 5. Shakespeare reference is to *Hamlet,* 1.3.62, the famous advice of Polonius.

36. Tyler to A. C. Thompson, 30 June 1847, A. C. Thompson Collection, Archives, Hartford Seminary; *Religious Herald,* 6 Nov. 1847; Walter H. Bidwell to Leonard Bacon, 25 July, 29 Sept. 1847, Bacon Family Collection, Manuscripts and Archives, Yale University Library. Bidwell, the editor, was another of HB's Yale classmates.

37. Quoted in Shelton Smith, ed., *Horace Bushnell,* 376–77.

38. Atwater to A. C. Thompson, 14 July 1847, A. C. Thompson Collection, Archives, Hartford Seminary; *Religious Herald,* 11 Sept. 1847.

39. HB, "Argument," *Views,* 87. Records, Board of Managers, Massachusetts Sabbath School Society, 70–72 (20 July 1847), Congregational Library, Boston.

40. Nichols, *Romanticism,* 238–39.

41. HB, "Argument," *Views,* 115, 117–21.

42. Records, Board of Managers, Massachusetts Sabbath School Society, 73–74 (27 Sept. 1847), Congregational Library; A. Bullard, [Secretary of the Board of the Society] to HB, 28 Sept. 1847, Horace Bushnell Collection, Manuscripts and Archives, Yale University Library.

43. A. C. Thompson to Lyman Atwater, 27 July 1847, Thompson Collection, Hartford Seminary.

44. Nichols, *Romanticism,* 238–39.

45. Bennett Tyler, *Letters to the Reverend Horace Bushnell, D. D., Containing Strictures on His Book, Entitled "Views of Christian Nurture and Subjects Adjacent Thereto"* (Hartford: Brown and Parsons, 1848).

46. Noah Porter, Jr., "Bushnell on Christian Nurture," *New Englander* 5, 4 (Oct. 1847), and 6, 1 (Jan. 1848): 142.

47. William A. Johnson, *Nature and the Supernatural in the Theology of Horace Bushnell* (Lund, Sweden: CWK Gleerup, 1963), 27.

48. HB, *Christian Nurture.*

49. *Congregationalist*, 8 Feb. 1861.

50. Randolph C. Miller, *The Theory of Christian Education Practice: How Theology Affects Christian Education* (Birmingham: Religious Education Press, 1980), 154.

51. HB, "Discourses," *Views*, 41; "Revivals of Religion," *Building Eras*, 172.

52. HB to an unidentified Hartford woman, 19 Feb. 1849, Correspondence, Bushnell Collection, Bushnell Memorial Hall; HB to Elijah H. Owen, 19 Oct. 1859, Learned Collection; HB, *The Spirit in Man: Sermons and Selections* (New York: Scribner's, 1903), 70–89.

53. HB, "Thoughts Fit Bread," *Spirit in Man*, 87–88.

54. Mary B. Cheney, undated typescript, Cheney Genealogical Collection, Connecticut Historical Society. Almost certainly written long after the event, it still has a ring of accuracy.

CHAPTER 9
Pivotal 1848

1. J. S. Holliday, *The World Rushed In: The California Gold Rush Experience* (New York: Simon and Schuster, 1981), 42, 451.

2. Robbins, *Diary* 2:892–95; Cheney, *Bushnell*, 191–93.

3. Albert Schweitzer, *Out of My Life and Thought: An Autobiography*, trans. C. T. Campion (New York: Holt, 1949), 156.

4. HB, *God in Christ*, 185.

5. Cheney, *Bushnell*, 193, 192.

6. On Mme. Guyon, he used Thomas C. Upham, *Life, Religious Opinions and Experience of Madame de la Mothe Guyon . . .* (1843; London: Sampson, Low, 1856). Upham was a Bowdoin College professor.

7. *New England Puritan*, 13 July 1848.

8. Cheney, *Bushnell*, 191–92.

9. HB, "Christ the Form of the Soul," *The Spirit in Man,* 39–51; Gal. 4:19–20, NRSV.

10. Upham, *Mme Guyon,* 170.

11. HB, "Christ the Form of the Soul," *Spirit in Man,* 41, 47, 49, 50; Cherry, *Bushnell Sermons,* 17.

12. David L. Smith, ed., *Horace Bushnell: Selected Writings on Language, Religion, and American Culture* (Chico, Calif.: Scholars Press, 1984), 15.

13. Samuel E. Morison, *Three Centuries of Harvard, 1636–1936* (1936; Cambridge: Harvard Univ. Press, 1965), 275, 268.

14. Morison, *Harvard,* 258–59.

15. Ahlstrom, *Religious History,* 395.

16. President Quincy's 1845 statement above reflects accurately Calvinist hostility to the college at this period.

17. *New York Evangelist,* 19 Aug. 1847.

18. HB to [James Freeman Clarke], 30 Aug. 1847, James Freeman Clarke Collection, Houghton Library, Harvard Univ.

19. HB, *God in Christ,* 97.

20. Theodore Parker to Noah Porter, Jr., 18 May 1848, Graves Collection, Unitarian Society Archives; Cheney, *Bushnell,* 108. HB to Sears, 16 Jan. 1863, Edmund Hamilton Sears Collection, Andover-Harvard Theological Library, Cambridge.

21. Joseph Allen to Edward Everett, 12 Sept. 1848, Harvard College Papers, 2d ser., 16 (1848–49):148–50, Pusey Library; *Religious Herald,* 23 Dec. 1848.

22. Tyler, *Letters* (1848), 4:43.

23. *Christian Register,* 15 July 1848.

24. This stanza is now frequently omitted from the hymn. *Boston Recorder,* 21 July 1848.

25. William E. Channing, *A Selection from the Works of William E. Channing, D.D.* (Boston: American Unitarian Association, 1855), 54, 202–5; George E. Ellis, *A Half-Century of the Unitarian Controversy* (Boston: Crosby, Nichols, 1857), 184, 189–92.

26. HB, *God in Christ,* 186–67, 218.

27. Ibid., 196.

28. 2 Cor. 5:19, RSV. It seems strange that Bushnell did not fill out the quotation, "not counting their trespasses against them...," which would appear to have strengthened his case still further.

29. HB, *God in Christ*, 189.

30. Ibid., 247, 245, 190.

31. Ibid., 258–61, 245.

32. Ibid., 203–5.

33. Ibid., 268–70.

34. *New England Puritan*, 20 July 1848; H. Shelton Smith, *Bushnell*, 276–77; *Christian Register*, 15 July 1848.

35. HB to Cyrus A. Bartol, n.d., Cheney, *Bushnell*, 200.

36. *Religious Herald*, 12 Aug. 1848.

37. Col. 1:19, NRSV.

38. See Gen. 2:23, NRSV. Here "bone of *my* bones, and flesh of *my* flesh" (emphasis added).

39. For Bushnell's description of this, see *God in Christ*, 155, 163; fifth-century Nestorianism, for example, took a similar position.

40. HB, *God in Christ*, 158.

41. Ibid., 127, 155–58.

42. Ibid., 130–31.

43. Ibid., 134.

44. Friedrich E. D. Schleiermacher, "On the Discrepancy Between the Sabellian and Athanasian Method of Representing the Doctrine of the Trinity," trans. by Moses Stuart, *The Biblical Repository and Quarterly Observer* 5 (Apr. 1835): 265–353; and 6 (July 1835): 1–116; HB, *God in Christ*, 175, 111–12; H. Shelton Smith, *Bushnell*, 6–8.

45. Ahlstrom, "Horace Bushnell," *Handbook*, 36.

46. HB, *God in Christ*, 174; see also his later "The Christian Trinity, A Practical Truth," *Building Eras*, 106–49.

47. HB, *God in Christ*, 180.

48. *New England Puritan*, 24 Aug. 1848; quoted in the *Boston Recorder*, 25 Aug. 1848; Munger, *Bushnell*, 116.

49. HB, "Work and Play," *Work and Play*, 9–42.

50. Ibid., 38.

51. Samuel Longfellow, ed., *Life of Henry Wadsworth Longfellow, with Extracts from His Journals and Correspondence* (Boston: Ticknor and Co., 1886), 1:122.

52. *Boston Recorder*, 1 Sept. 1848; *Religious Herald*, 2 Sept. 1848.

53. Cherry, ed., *Bushnell Sermons*, 17–19; *Religious Herald*, 2 Sept. 1848.

54. HB, *God in Christ*, 277–356.

55. Ibid., 352.

56. Ibid., 292, 354–56.

57. "A masterly production in all respects," the *Boston Recorder* told its readers, 15 Sept. 1848. *Religious Herald,* 16 Sept. 1848.

58. Douglas, *Feminization of American Culture,* 17–50.

59. Ahlstrom, *Religious History,* 405.

60. *Christian Observatory,* June 1849, 241.

CHAPTER 10
A Book New England Was Waiting For

1. HB to Cyrus A. Bartol, 11 Oct. 1848 and 8 Jan. 1849, Cheney, *Bushnell,* 211–13; HB to Leonard Bacon, 14 Feb. 1849, Bacon Collection, Manuscripts and Archives, Yale University Library; Frank B. Carpenter, "Studio Talks with Dr. Horace Bushnell," *The Independent,* 11 Jan. 1900. The book proved financially profitable for Bushnell.

2. HB, *God in Christ,* 9–117.

3. *Boston Recorder,* cited in *Religious Herald,* 7 Apr. 1849.

4. HB, *God in Christ,* 11–12. To Mary Cheney, language was "*the key to Horace Bushnell*" (*Bushnell,* 203). Over a century later, a Bushnell scholar was still saying of Bushnell's thought, "Mankind, nature, and God . . . are woven together in one web, and the term that relates them all is language." David L. Smith, *Selected Writings,* 9.

5. Crosby, "Bushnell's Theory of Language," 72; Thomas M. Clark to Mary B. Cheney, 26 Apr. 1878, Cheney, *Bushnell,* 294–95. With their originality of mind, both men used books to stimulate their own thinking more than to master the author's ideas.

6. HB, *God in Christ,* esp. 16, 26, 34, 43.

7. Conrad Cherry, *Nature and the Religious Imagination, from Edwards to Bushnell* (Philadelphia: Fortress Press, 1980), 99–100; Dumas Malone, *Jefferson and the Rights of Man* (Boston: Little, Brown, 1951), 215.

8. Nathaniel W. Taylor, *Essays, Lectures, etc., Upon Select Topics in Revealed Theology* (1859; New York: Garland, 1987), 16.

9. HB, *God in Christ,* 57, 159, 43–48.

10. Ibid., 88.

11. Crosby, "Bushnell's Theory of Language," 22.

12. HB, *God in Christ,* 93.

13. Ibid., 87.

14. Quoted in Halford E. Luccock, "The Gospel According to Mark," *The Interpreter's Bible* (New York: Abingdon-Cokesbury, 1951) 7:656.

15. HB, *God in Christ,* 45–46.

16. Nathan Mitchell, quoted in Avery Dulles, *Models of Revelation* (Garden City, N.Y.: Doubleday, 1983), 136.

17. HB, *God in Christ,* 48–49, 174.

18. Crosby, "Bushnell's Theory of Language," 224–25, calls Bushnell's language theory "a stroke of genius. " See also, David L. Smith, *Selections,* 8–9.

19. HB to Henry M. Goodwin, 12 Apr. 1849, Cheney, *Bushnell,* 221. Goodwin's article was entitled "Thoughts, Words, and Things," *Bibliotheca Sacra* 6, 22 (May 1849): 271–300, Duke, *Bushnell,* 106. See also Crosby, "Bushnell's Theory of Language," 74–75.

20. Enoch Pond, *Review of Dr. Bushnell's "God in Christ"* (Bangor, Maine: Duren, 1849), 5, 13.

21. Omicron [Chauncey A. Goodrich], *What Does Dr. Bushnell Mean?* from the *New York Evangelist* (Hartford: Case, Tiffany, 1849), 8.

22. Pond, "Review," esp. 114–16.

23. Omicron [Goodrich], *What Does Dr. Bushnell Mean?*

24. Julian M. Sturtevant to Theron Baldwin, 18 Sept. 1848, Sturtevant-Baldwin Correspondence, 1830–70, Archives, Schewe Library, Illinois College, Jacksonville.

25. *Congregationalist,* 25 May 1849.

26. *Christian Observatory,* June 1849, 245, 287.

27. [Charles Hodge], "Bushnell's Discourses: Review of *God in Christ...*" *Biblical Repertory and Princeton Review* 21, 2 (Apr. 1849): 260–64, 296.

28. [J. H. Morison], "Bushnell's Discourses," *Christian Examiner and Religious Miscellany* 46, 11 (Sept. 1849): 453–84.

29. Orestes A. Brownson, "Bushnell's Discourses," *Brownson's Quarterly Review,* 1849–51, in *The Works of Orestes A. Brownson,* edited by Henry F. Brownson (New York: AMS Press, 1966), 7:21–22, 61.

30. HB to Mary A. Bushnell, 30 May 1849, Cheney, *Bushnell,* 222.

31. HB to Bacon, 30 Mar. 1849, Bacon Family Collection, Manuscripts and Archives, Yale University Library.

32. HB to Bartol, 31 July 1849, Cheney, *Bushnell,* 223.

33. [Leonard Bacon], "[Review of] *God in Christ...* by Horace Bushnell; *Review of Dr. Bushnell's Theories of Incarnation and Atonement...,* by

Robert Turnbull; 'What Does Dr. Bushnell Mean?'—from the *New York Evangelist*," *New Englander* 7, 2 (May 1849): 324–26.

34. *Methodist Quarterly Review*, 4th ser., 1 (Apr. 1849): 329–30.

35. Robert Turnbull, *Review of Dr. Bushnell's Theories of the Incarnation and Atonement (A Supplement to "Theophany")* (Hartford: Brockett and Fuller, 1849).

36. [Amos S. Chesebrough], *Contributions of CC, Now Declared in Full as Criticus Criticorum* (Hartford: Brown and Parsons, 1849).

37. Amos S. Chesebrough, "Reminiscences of Controversy," *Bushnell Centenary*, 51, 53.

38. HB to Chesebrough, Nov. 5, 1849, Cheney, *Bushnell*, 228, 224.

39. Henry C. Trumbull, *My Four Religious Teachers* (Philadelphia: Sunday School Times, 1903), 119–22; Stopford A. Brooke, ed., *Life, Letters, Lectures and Addresses of Fredk. W. Robertson, M. A., Incumbent of Trinity Chapel, Brighton, 1847–1853* (New York: E. P. Dutton, 1883), 220.

40. Frederick L. Olmsted, *Walks and Talks of an American Farmer in England in the Years 1850–51* (New York: Putnam, 1852), 2:48.

41. Everett to Rev. Henry Bromfield Pearson, 30 Oct. 1848, Edward Everett Collection, Massachusetts Historical Society, Boston.

42. Everett to Milman, 4 Dec. 1849, ibid.

43. Joseph H. Twichell, "Personal Reminiscences," *Bushnell Centenary*, 82.

44. HB, "Twentieth Anniversary," 23.

CHAPTER 11
The Bushnell Battle Royal

1. Williston Walker, *The Creeds and Platforms of Congregationalism* (1893; Boston: Pilgrim Press, 1960), 506.

2. Ibid., 506n. 3; Parker, *Bushnell Controversy*, 20, discusses the second option in Bushnells' case.

3. Leonard Bacon, "Historical Discourse," in *Contributions to the Ecclesiastical History of Connecticut . . .* (1861; Hartford: Connecticut Conference, U.C.C., 1973), 2–72.

4. Records, Hartford Central Association, 1843–1901, 5 June 1849. In a 6 June 1849 letter to Bacon, Bushnell refers to "the overture," but gives no clue as to its source. Bacon Family Collection, Manuscripts and Archives,

Yale University Library. Records of other Connecticut Associations are equally silent on the matter.

5. HB to Bacon, 6 June 1849, Bacon Family Collection, Manuscripts and Archives, Yale University Library.

6. HB to George Bushnell, 20 Apr. 1857, Blake Family Collection, Manuscripts and Archives, Yale University Library.

7. HB to Bacon, 6 June 1849, ibid.

8. HB to Bartol, 24 Oct. 1849, Cheney, *Bushnell,* 227–28.

9. HB to Chesebrough, 29 Aug. 1849, ibid., 225.

10. Records, Hartford Central Association, 18 Sept. 1849, esp. 36, 42, and 55.

11. Cheney, *Bushnell,* 464–65.

12. Records, Hartford Central Association, 22, 23 Oct. 1849; Robbins, *Diary* (22, 23 Oct. 1849), 2:954; Parker, *Bushnell Controversy,* 11. There is doubt about Robbins's vote. Parker has noted that after the result was known, one of the minority offered "to exchange pulpit services with Dr. Bushnell. " Robbins had no regular pulpit to offer. Possibly the third vote was that of William W. Patton, pastor of the Fourth Church where the vote was taken. See also Cheney, *Bushnell,* 252–53.

13. Cheney, *Bushnell,* 226.

14. Ellsworth to Leonard Bacon, 9 May 1849, Bacon Family Collection, Manuscripts and Archives, Yale University Library.

15. Newspaper comments are from a roundup in the *Religious Herald,* 17 Nov. 1949.

16. Walker, *Creeds and Platforms,* 509–11.

17. "Lyman Hotchkiss Atwater," *DAB* 1:416–17. Parsonage comment, *Religious Herald,* 21 July 1849.

18. Dexter, *Biographical Sketches of the Graduates of Yale College* 6:202–6. Regarding involvement against Tyler, see Parker, *Bushnell Controversy,* 14.

19. Records, Fairfield West Association, 29–30 May 1849, Archives, U.C.C. Conference Center, Hartford.

20. *Minutes of the General Association of Connecticut, at their Meeting in Salisbury, June, 1849* (New Haven: J. H. Benham, 1849), esp. Appendix E, 15.

21. Records, Hartford Central Association, 5 Mar. 1850.

22. *Remonstrance and Complaint of the Association of Fairfield West to the Hartford Central Association* (New York: S. W. Benedict, 1850); Re-

cords, Fairfield West Association, 19 Mar. 1850.

23. Records, Fairfield West Association, 19 Mar. 1850.

24. Records of the several associations, Connecticut Conference, Archives, U.C.C.; Noah Porter to Bushnell, 16 Nov. 1850, Cheney, *Bushnell,* 241–43.

25. Records, New Haven West Association, 24–25 Apr. 1850, Archives, Connecticut Conference Center.

26. Records, Tolland Association, 7 May, 4 June 1850, ibid.

27. *Congregationalist,* 14 June 1850.

28. Bellows to Cyrus A. Bartol, 4 Feb. 1850, Henry W. Bellows Collection, Massachusetts Historical Society.

29. Details gleaned from various sets of General Association minutes.

30. The *Religious Herald,* 29 June 1850, carried full details of the entire meeting, as the official minutes did not. Except where otherwise indicated, this is the source for the Litchfield meeting.

31. Cheney, *Bushnell,* 235.

32. Ibid., 236.

33. Ibid., 237–38; Bellows to Bartol, 1 July 1850, Bellows Collection, Massachusetts Historical Society.

34. Parker, *Bushnell Controversy,* 16.

35. Cheney, *Bushnell,* 241; Porter to Bushnell, 16 Nov. 1850, ibid., 241–42.

36. Records, Fairfield West Association, 30–31 Oct. 1850.

37. Atwater, "Bushnell," 129.

38. Edwards A. Park, "Theology of the Intellect and That of the Feelings," *Bibliotheca Sacra* 7 (July 1850): 553–69; Douglas, *Feminization,* 177–79; Ahlstrom, "Theology in America," 284–85.

39. HB, *Christ in Theology; Being the Answer of the Author, Before the Hartford Central Association of Ministers, October, 1849, for the Doctrines of the Book Entitled "God in Christ"* (1851; New York: Garland, 1987); "Review of *Christ in Theology* by Horace Bushnell," *New Englander* 9, 2 (May 1851): 310–11.

40. HB to Leonard Bacon, 11 June 1849, Bacon Family Collection, Manuscripts and Archives, Yale University Library. He took up Calvin at Bacon's suggestion.

41. HB to Bartol, 10 Mar. 1851, Cheney, *Bushnell,* 247; Leonard Bacon, "Concerning a Recent Chapter of Ecclesiastical History," *New Englander* 38 (1879): 701–12; Cheney, *Bushnell,* 245.

42. HB, "Twentieth Anniversary," 24.

43. HB, *Christ in Theology,* 335, 340; "Commemorative Discourse," 24–25.

44. North Congregational Church, Records, 4:5 (28 June 1852), Connecticut State Library.

45. HB to Leonard Bacon, 3 Jan. 1853, Bacon Family Collection, Manuscripts and Archives, Yale University Library. Nearly seven months after the decision, Bushnell was still bothered, and he pressed his friend for historical precedents to ease his mind. HB, "Twentieth Anniversary," 23–26; *Hartford Courant,* 9 Oct. 1852

46. Records, Hartford Fourth Association, 1852, 3, 7; Records, Hartford Central Association, 15 June 1853, ibid. Cheney, *Bushnell,* 306–7.

47. *Religious Herald,* 26 June 1852.

48. Records, Fairfield West Association, 31 May 1853; Parker, *Bushnell Controversy,* 21–22.

49. Cheney, *Bushnell,* 206.

50. *A Protest of the Pastoral Union to the Pastors and Churches of Connecticut* (Wethersfield, Conn. [?], 1854 [?]).

51. *Puritan Recorder,* 30 June 1853.

CHAPTER 12
Meanwhile, a Christian Pastor

1. Munger, *Bushnell,* 95.

2. HB, *Christ in Theology,* 175; HB to Amos S. Chesebrough, 23 Jan. 1854, Cheney, *Bushnell,* 324.

3. Not altogether hyperbolically, Chesebrough saw Bushnell's situation in just such medieval terms, thinking his "martyrdom" might be at hand. As he thought about it, however, Bushnell could not see "how the fire is going to be kindled. " HB to Chesebrough, 6 July 1852, ibid., 261.

4. HB to Henry M. Goodwin, 26 May 1851, ibid., 248.

5. Unless otherwise indicated, data on Bushnell's congregation is from Edwards, "Portrait of a People," Davies, 149–63.

6. David F. Ransom, "Biographical Dictionary of Hartford Architects," *Connecticut Historical Society Bulletin* 54 (Winter/Spring 1989): 61–62.

7. Charles H. Clark, "Bushnell the Citizen," *Bushnell Centenary,* 59.

8. Austin Phelps, "A Vacation with Dr. Bushnell," *Christian Union,* 1876, in Cheney, *Bushnell,* 534.

9. Mrs. Horace Holley, ibid., 289.

10. Ibid., 473.

11. Duke, *Bushnell,* 79.

12. "Horace Bushnell," *DAB* 3:351.

13. Nathaniel J. Burton, funeral sermon for Bushnell, Cheney, *Bushnell,* 564–65.

14. "Horace Bushnell," *DAB* 3:352. The other two were British Canon James B. Mozley's "Reversal of Human Judgments" and Phillips Brooks's "Gold and the Calf."

15. Charles R. Brown, *They Were Giants* (New York: Macmillan, 1934), 39; as illustration of his sermons still being republished, see Cherry, *Bushnell Sermons,* 1984.

16. Titles taken at random from: *Sermons for the New Life; Christ and His Salvation: In Sermons Variously Related Thereto* (New York: Scribner, 1864); *Sermons on Living Subjects* (New York: Scribner, Armstrong, 1872); and *The Spirit in Man.* For sermons on the future, see Richard E. Burton, ed., *Yale Lectures on Preaching, And Other Writings, by Nathaniel J. Burton* (New York: Charles L. Webster, 1888), 423; and HB, *The Spirit in Man,* 52–69. The sermon was delivered in September 1854.

17. Cheney, *Bushnell,* 289–90.

18. John 20:8, KJV.

19. HB, "Unconscious Influence," *Sermons for the New Life,* 186–205. For hints of Freud in Bushnell's thought, see Howe, "Social Science of Horace Bushnell," 312, 321.

20. 2 Chron. 32:30, KJV.

21. HB, "Prosperity Our Duty: A Discourse Delivered at the North Church, Hartford, Sabbath Evening, Jan. 31, 1847" (Hartford: Case, Tiffany and Burnham, 1847); republished in HB, *The Spirit of Man,* 135–58.

22. Duke, *Bushnell.* 77.

23. HB, *Christ and His Salvation,* 28–50.

24. HB, "The Spirit in Man," *Sermons for the New Life,* 35.

25. Ralph Waldo Emerson, "Self-Reliance," *The Complete Works of Ralph Waldo Emerson* (Boston: Houghton, Mifflin, 1903), 2:90; Gay Wilson Allen, *Waldo Emerson, a Biography* (New York: Viking, 1981), 438.

26. HB, "Salvation by Man," *Christ and His Salvation,* 272–74.

27. HB, "Regeneration," *Sermons for the New Life,* 121–22; Cherry, *Nature and the Religious Imagination,* 56.

28. HB, "How To Be a Christian in Trade," *Living Subjects,* 243–67.

29. HB, "Dignity of Human Nature Shown from Its Ruins," *Sermons for the New Life,* 69–70, and "The Hunger of the Soul," 85.

30. HB, "Respectable Sin," ibid., 330–31.

31. Cheney, *Bushnell,* 478.

32. Sketch by Mrs. Horace Holley, n.d., ibid., 289.

33. Charles L. Brace to John P. Brace, 11 Dec. 1842, [Brace, ed.], *Brace,* 10; Timothy Dwight, *Memories of Yale Life and Men, 1845–1899* (New York: Dodd, Mead, 1903), 85–86.

34. McLaughlin and Beveridge, *Olmsted Papers,* 1:72–74.

35. Clark, "Bushnell the Citizen," *Bushnell Centenary,* 58–69; Howe, "Social Science of Horace Bushnell," 319–20; Trumbull, *Religious Teachers,* 8ff; and "Henry Clay Trumbull," *DAB* 19:8–9.

36. Rugoff, *Beechers,* 290, 436; Thomas K. Beecher to Harriet Beecher Stowe, 3 Sept. 1848, Beecher-Stowe Collection, Arthur and Elizabeth Schlesinger Library, Cambridge, Mass.

37. Matt. 12:30, KJV.

38. Joseph H. Twichell, "Personal Reminiscences," *Bushnell Centenary,* 73.

39. Trumbull, *Four Religious Teachers,* 122–24.

40. Rugoff, *Beechers,* xv.

41. Lyman Beecher to Mrs. Lyman Beecher, 28 Aug. 1848, White Collection, Stowe-Day Foundation Library. On the clandestine visit, in 1849, Mary B. Perkins warned her sister Isabella it was "a *profound secret,* so you must not mention a word about it to anyone. " Mary B. Perkins to Isabella B. Hooker, [27 Aug. 1849], Joseph K. Hooker Collection, Stowe-Day Foundation Library.

42. Kathryn K. Sklar, *Catherine Beecher, A Study in American Domesticity* (New York: Norton, 1976), 153–54, 246, 266–67; Catherine and Lyman Beecher to John Hooker, 27 Nov. 1839, Joseph K. Hooker Collection, Stowe-Day Foundation Library. Bushnell served as a trustee of the Hartford Female Seminary from at least 1839 until the 1850s. Catalogs of the Hartford Female Seminary, 1839–53, Stowe-Day Foundation Library.

43. *Congregationalist,* 25 May 1849.

44. Harriet Beecher Stowe to Isabella Hooker [Nov. 1850], Beecher Family Papers, Schlesinger Library; same to Sarah W. Parton, 25 July 1869, Sarah Payson Willis Parton Papers, Sophia Smith Collection, Smith College, Northampton, Mass. For these references I am indebted to Professor Joan D. Hedrick, Trinity College, Hartford. On HB and *Uncle Tom's Cabin,* see HB's "The Northern Iron," 23.

45. Mary B. Perkins to Isabella Hooker, [27 Aug. 1849], Joseph K. Hooker Collection, Stowe-Day Foundation Library.

46. Marie Caskey, *Chariot of Fire: Religion and the Beecher Family* (New Haven: Yale Univ. Press, 1978), 234, 274; Mabel C. Donnelly, "Comments," *The Harriet Beecher Stowe House and Library* [*Bulletin*], Sept. 1987, 3; Isabella's marginal comments on her copy of HB, *Women's Suffrage; the Reform Against Nature,* Stowe-Day Foundation Library.

47. Thomas K. Beecher to Harriet Beecher Stowe, 3 Sept. 1848, Beecher-Stowe Collection, Schlesinger Library; Rugoff, *Beechers,* 436; Thomas K. Beecher to Lyman Beecher, 18 June 1851, White Collection, Stowe-Day Foundation Library.

48. Clifford E. Clark, Jr., *Henry Ward Beecher: Spokesman for a Middle-Class America* (Urbana: Univ. of Illinois Press, 1978), 81–83; Caskey, *Chariot of Fire,* 271.

49. *Boston Recorder,* 18 Nov. 1847; Paxton Hibben, *Henry Ward Beecher: An American Portrait* (New York: George H. Doran, 1927), 129–30.

50. Clark, *Beecher,* 277; "Henry Ward Beecher," *DAB* 2:133; Caskey, *Chariot of Fire,* 268ff.

51. Caskey, *Chariot of Fire,* 233–34.

52. HB, "The Capacity of Religion Extirpated by Disuse," *Sermons for the New Life,* 177.

53. Clark, *Beecher,* 82.

54. HB to Mrs. Bushnell, 11 May 1858, Cheney, *Bushnell,* 413–14.

55. Henry Ward Beecher, *Sermons* (New York: Harper, 1868) 1:31.

56. HB to Mrs. E———, 22 Mar. 1860, Cheney, *Bushnell,* 436–67.

57. HB to George Bushnell, 25 Sept. 1851, Blake Family Collection, Manuscripts and Archives, Yale University Library.

58. Holley, "Sketch," Cheney, *Bushnell,* 288.

59. Cheney, *Bushnell,* 290.

60. Bishop Thomas M. Clark, to Mrs. Bushnell, 26 Apr. 1878, ibid., 294–95.

61. Ibid., 291.

62. Ibid., 292–93.

63. HB to a Mrs. Enis [?], 23 Oct. 1862, Learned Collection.

64. HB to an unidentified "Friend," 19 Feb. 1849, Bushnell Memorial Hall Collection, Hartford.

65. HB to Mrs. Thomas Day, 23 Apr. 1855, Day Family Collection, Manuscripts and Archives, Yale University Library.

66. Unsigned letter to Mary Bushnell Cheney, Buckland, Connecticut, 1 May 1891, Learned Collection.

67. HB, "Twentieth Anniversary."

68. Ibid., 3.

CHAPTER 13
Burning Issues, Hazardous Journeys

1. Howe, "Social Science of Horace Bushnell," 318.

2. HB, "Barbarism"; reprinted in *Work and Play,* 2d ed. (New York: Scribner's, 1903), 227–67.

3. Nathan O. Hatch, *The Democratization of American Christianity* (New Haven: Yale Univ. Press, 1989), 62–63.

4. *The Catholic Encyclopaedia for School and Home* (New York: McGraw Hill, 1965) 5:383–92; Ahlstrom, *Religious History,* 749.

5. Ahlstrom, *Religious History,* 547.

6. Diary of Johann Georg Joseph Anton Rieger, 19 Feb. 1836–14 June 1844, Archives, Eden Theological Seminary Library, St. Louis, entry for 8 June 1836; Carl E. Schneider, *The German Church on the American Frontier: A Study in the Rise of Religion Among the Germans of the West* (St. Louis: Eden Publishing House, 1939), 84–91, 407.

7. Theron Baldwin to Julian M. Sturtevant, 31 Mar. 1865, Baldwin-Sturtevant Letters, 1830–70, Archives, Schewe Library.

8. Society for the Promotion of Collegiate and Theological Education at the West, [*Annual*] *Reports of the Society, 1844–1858* (New York: J. F. Trow, 1844–58); Theron Baldwin to Leonard Bacon, 26 Jan. 1847, Bacon Family Collection, Manuscripts and Archives, Yale University Library; Theron Baldwin to Julian M. Sturtevant, 6 Aug. 1847, 18 Aug. 1853, and Sturtevant to Baldwin, 18 Sept. 1848 and 30 July 1853, Baldwin-Sturtevant Letters, 1830–70, Archives, Schewe Library; and Sturtevant to Jonathan B. Turner, and the Faculty of Illinois College, 2 Oct. 1844, Archives, Schewe Library. I am indebted to Dr. Travis Hedrick of Middletown, Conn., and to Professor Iver F. Yeager of Illinois College for referring me to this correspondence. For Bushnell's policy ideas, see also his "Barbarism," 27–28. Later he came to play a more positive role on the board. In 1858, for example, he served on a financial committee and successfully helped plead the cause of the College of California.

9. HB, "Barbarism," 5.

10. Ibid., 24, 32.

11. Ibid., 26–28, 32.

12. Hatch, *Democratization of American Christianity*, 62–63.

13. "Cyrus Augustus Bartol," *DAB* 2:17.

14. Bartol to Bellows, 4 June 1850, and Bellows to Bartol, 20 Jan. 1855, Bellows Collection, Massachusetts Historical Society. Bellows-Bartol exchanges in this collection contain frequent references to Bushnell.

15. Payne K. Kilbourne, *Biographical History of the County of Litchfield, Connecticut* (New York: Clark, Austin, 1851), 355.

16. HB, "The Fathers of New England: An Oration Delivered Before the New England Society of New York, Dec. 21, 1849" (New York: George P. Putnam, 1850); reprinted under the "Unconsciousness" title in *Work and Play*, 124–66.

17. HB, "Speech for Connecticut," 43; republished as "Historical Estimate of Connecticut," in *Work and Play*, 167–226; MacMullen, *Henry Barnard*, 171–72.

18. *Litchfield County Centennial Celebration*... (Hartford: E. Hunt, 1851), 23ff.

19. HB, "Age of Homespun," reprinted in *Litchfield County Centennial*, 107–30, and in HB, *Work and Play*, 368–402. Quotations here from *Work and Play*, 374–75.

20. Justin Kaplan, *Walt Whitman: A Life* (New York: Simon and Schuster, 1980), 102–3.

21. Arthur J. Heffernan, "A History of Catholic Education in Connecticut" (Ph.D. diss., Catholic Univ. of America, 1936), 26–33; George Stewart, Jr., *A History of Religious Education in Connecticut to the Middle of the Nineteenth Century* (New Haven: Yale Univ. Press, 1924), 289 and ch. 12; Van Dusen, *Connecticut*, 343.

22. HB. "The Common School: A Discourse on the Modifications Demanded by the Roman Catholics" (Hartford: Case, Tiffany, 1853); Kaestle, *Pillars of the Republic*, 169–70.

23. For all his support of public education, there is no evidence that the Bushnell's sent their own children to public school. This may have been because they had less feeling about such instruction for girls than for boys, or because they had private educational resources in their own family, especially under Mrs. Bushnell's sister, Elizabeth Apthorp. Bushnell did send his nephew, Frederick Belden, from western New York to the Hartford Public High School during the winter of 1850 when he lived in the Bushnell

household. Register, Hartford Public High School, 1847–77, Archives, Connecticut State Library.

24. Cross, *Bushnell*, 80.

25. *Religious Herald*, 29 May 1847.

26. HB to Dixon, 24 Feb. 1847, Correspondence, Bushnell Memorial Hall Collection.

27. HB to Bartol, 6 May 1851, Cheney, *Bushnell*, 247–48.

28. Oscar Sherwin, *Prophet of Liberty: The Life and Times of Wendell Phillips* (New York: Bookman, 1958), 315–16.

29. James M. Burns, *The American Experiment: The Vineyard of Liberty* (New York: Knopf, 1982), 543ff; Sherwin, *Wendell Phillips*, 316.

30. HB, "The Northern Iron."

31. Jer. 15:12, KJV.

32. HB to Bartol, 20 Apr. 1854, Cheney, *Bushnell*, 325.

33. *Hartford Courant*, 20 May 1854.

34. *Congressional Globe*, 33d Cong., 1st sess., vol. 28, pt. 2 (Washington, D.C.: Rives, 1854), 1254.

35. Henry S. Commager, *Theodore Parker* (1936; Gloucester, Mass.: Peter Smith, 1978), 250; Van Dusen, *Connecticut*, 225–27.

36. HB to Bacon, 16 Dec. 1846, Bacon Family Collection, Manuscripts and Archives, Yale University Library.

37. Mary A. Bushnell to Mary B. Cheney, handwritten memo, [Hartford], n.d., Learned Collection.

38. HB to Mary A. Bushnell, Aug. 1852, Cheney, *Bushnell*, 265–66.

39. HB to Mary A. Bushnell, n.d., ibid., 267–68; on coeducation, see HB, *Women's Suffrage*, 13–17.

40. Garth M. Rosell and Richard A. G. Dupuis, eds., *The Memoirs of Charles G. Finney: The Complete Restored Text* (Grand Rapids, Mich.: Zondervan, 1989), 520–23; HB to Mary A. Bushnell, n.d., and 3 Dec. 1852, Cheney, *Bushnell*, 267, 275; HB, Letter of Introduction for Finney in England, 26 Nov. 1858, HB to Finney, 24 July [1874?], Finney Collection, Oberlin College Library, Oberlin, Ohio; Keith J. Hardman, *Charles Grandison Finney, 1792–1875: Revivalist and Reformer* (Syracuse: Syracuse Univ. Press, 1987), esp. 426–27.

41. The only account of this journey is in Cheney, *Bushnell*, 267–78, where Bushnell's letters home comprise a kind of diary.

42. HB to Chesebrough, 15 Dec. 1854, ibid., 345.

43. New York City Census Records, 1850, 15th Ward, New York Public

Library; *New York City Directory*, 1854–55, 618, and 1859–60, 748.

44. Henry Durant, Sidney L. Johnson (Class valedictorian), Robert K. Richards, an attorney, and Forrest Shepherd, a geologist and miner: *Obituary Records of College Graduates of Yale, 1870–90.*

45. Bellows to Bartol, 20 Jan. 1855, Bellows Collection, Massachusetts Historical Society.

46. HB to Mary A. Bushnell, 30 Jan. 1855, Cheney, *Bushnell,* 348.

47. HB to Mary A. Bushnell, 4, 16, 18 Feb. 1855, ibid., 349–51.

48. John S. C. Abbott, *South and North, or Impressions Received During a Trip to Cuba and the South* (New York: Abbey and Abbott, 1860), 49.

49. HB to Mary A. Bushnell, 4 Feb. 1855, Cheney, *Bushnell,* 349–50.

50. HB to Mary A. Bushnell, 18 Feb., 4 Mar. 1855, ibid., 351–53.

51. Mary A. Bushnell to Mary Bushnell, 25 Sept. 1855, Learned Collection.

52. HB to Nathaniel H. Egleston, 26 Dec. 1855, Horace Bushnell Collection, Manuscripts and Archives, Yale University Library.

53. HB to Bartol, 26 Dec. 1855, Cheney, *Bushnell,* 364.

54. HB to Bartol, 29 Feb. 1856, ibid., 365–66.

CHAPTER 14
"An Outdoor Parlor"

1. Laura W. Roper, *FLO, A Biography of Frederick Law Olmsted* (Baltimore: Johns Hopkins Univ. Press, 1973), 124–25.

2. Christine Stansell, *City of Women: Sex and Class in New York, 1789–1860* (New York: Knopf, 1986), 3–10.

3. Trudy K. Jones, "Hartford's Bushnell Park: Antidote to Urban Ills," *The Connecticut Antiquarian* 41, 2 (Fall 1990): 11.

4. Frederick Law Olmsted, Jr., and Theodora Kimball, eds., *Frederick Law Olmsted, Landscape Architect, 1822–1903* (New York: Benjamin Blom, 1970), 2:178.

5. Petition to the Mayor and Common Council of the City of Hartford, 12 Apr. 1827, Park Records, City Clerk's Office, Hartford.

6. Clark, "Bushnell the Citizen," *Bushnell Centenary,* 62–63.

7. HB, European Journal, 30 Aug. 1845, Yale Divinity School Library.

8. HB, "Hartford Park," *Hearth and Home* 1, 6 (6 Feb. 1869): 101–2:

9. Clark to Mary A. Bushnell, 26 Apr. 1878, Cheney, *Bushnell,* 294, 297.

10. Report of the Committee on the New Park to the Hartford Common

Council, 14 Nov. 1853, Park Records, City Clerk's Office, Hartford. Although not explicitly attributed to Bushnell, the wording of this section of the report is unmistakeably his.

11. HB, "Hartford Park," 101–2; Roper, *Olmsted,* 125–26.

12. Elizabeth Stevenson, *Park Maker: A Life of Frederick Law Olmsted* (New York: Macmillan, 1977), 155.

13. HB, "Hartford Park," 101; Sherman Adams, "The Hartford Park System: Bushnell Park," *The Connecticut Quarterly: An Illustrated Magazine* 1 (Jan.–Dec. 1895): 69–71.

14. HB, "Hartford Park," 101.

15. Ibid.; *Public Acts . . . of the State of Connecticut,* May Session, 1853 (Hartford: Alfred E. Burr, 1853), 14; *Hartford Courant,* 15, 16 July 1853.

16. Minutes, Hartford Court of Common Council, 25 July 1853, as reported in the *Hartford Courant,* 26 July 1853. On Nook Farm, George Beach to Mayor and Court of Common Council, 8 Aug. 1853, Park Records, Office of the City Clerk, Hartford.

17. His map is reproduced in John Alexopoulos, *The Nineteenth Century Parks of Hartford: A Legacy to the Nation* (Hartford: Hartford Architecture Conservancy, 1983), 15.

18. HB to the Court of Common Council, 26 Sept. 1853, Park Records; Minutes, Court of Common Council, 5 Oct. 1853, Office of the City Clerk, Hartford.

19. Catalogs of the North Church for 1845 and 1859 (only ones available for this period) include no 1853 Council members.

20. J. Bard McNulty, *Older Than the Nation,* 66–67.

21. Memorandum by Emily Cheney Learned summarizing recollections of her mother, Mary B. Cheney, Learned Collection.

22. HB, "Hartford Park," 102.

23. *Hartford Courant* and *Hartford Times,* 7 Oct. 1853. The minutes of the Common Council furnish no details.

24. Minutes, Common Council, 14 Nov. 1853, Office of the City Clerk; Alexopoulos, *Nineteenth Century Parks,* 14.

25. *Hartford Courant,* 21 Nov. 1853.

26. Ibid., 3–7, 11 Jan. 1854.

27. HB to Bartol, 16 Jan. 1854, Cheney, *Bushnell,* 322–23.

28. Bruce Clouette, "Ante-Bellum Urban Renewal: Hartford's Bushnell Park," *Connecticut History* 18 (Nov. 1976): 9–13. On Noble Jones, see Hartford Land Records, General Index 1839–65, 737, Office of the City Clerk.

29. Minutes, Common Council, 22 Dec. 1853, Office of the City Clerk.

30. Minutes, Common Council, as reported in the *Hartford Courant*, 24 Apr., 3 May 1854.

31. HB to Bartol, 16 Jan. 1854, Cheney, *Bushnell*, 323.

32. Minutes, Common Council, 13 Apr. 1858, Office of the City Clerk.

33. *Hartford Courant*, 14 Apr. 1858.

34. Minutes, Common Council, 24 May, 28 June 1858, Office of the City Clerk; *Hartford Times*, 9 July, 8 Sept. 1858.

35. Minutes, Common Council, 12 July 1858 and following, Office of the City Clerk. Council minutes, however, are sparse. The *Hartford Times*, 8 Sept. 1858, contains a detailed summary of the boisterous proceedings.

36. F. L. Jewett to Marsh, 29 Aug. 1859, Park Records, Office of the City Clerk.

37. "Jacob Weidenmann," *DAB* 19:605–6.

38. HB, "Hartford Park," 102.

39. *Hartford Times*, 3 June 1858.

40. Roper, *Olmsted*, 114.

41. Albert Fein, "Frederick Law Olmsted: His Development As a Theorist and Designer of the American City" (Ph.D. diss., Columbia Univ., 1969), 41, 43.

42. McLaughlin and Beveridge, eds., *The Papers of Frederick Law Olmsted*, 1:328.

43. Olmsted to Charles L. Brace, 9 Sept. 1847, ibid., 296–97.

44. Irving D. Fisher, *Frederick Law Olmsted and the City Planning Movement in the United States* (Ann Arbor: UMI Research Press, 1976), 19–20.

45. McLaughlin and Beveridge, eds., *Olmsted Papers*, 1:72–74, gives the best brief estimate of HB's relationship with Olmsted.

46. Mary A. Bushnell to Mary Bushnell, 15 Aug. [1859], Learned Collection.

47. HB, "Hartford Park," 102.

CHAPTER 15
California in the Wake of the Gold Rush

1. HB to Bartol, 29 Feb. 1856, Cheney, *Bushnell*, 365.

2. HB to [Mary A. Bushnell], 4 July 1856, ibid., 382.

3. David McCullough, *The Path Between the Seas: The Creation of the Panama Canal, 1870–1914* (New York: Simon and Schuster, 1977), 34.

Unless otherwise noted, Panama references are from this source, ch. 1.

4. HB to Elijah H. Owen, 17 May [1856], Learned Collection; *Hartford Courant,* 30 Apr., 12, 16 May 1856.

5. Lulu M. Garrett, "San Francisco in 1851, as Described by Eyewitnesses," *California Historical Society Quarterly* 22, 3 (Sept. 1943): 253.

6. *Daily California Chronicle,* 29 Mar. 1856; Bushnell to Mary A. Bushnell, 31 Mar. 1856, Cheney, *Bushnell,* 366.

7. Robin W. Winks, *Frederick Billings, A Life* (New York: Oxford Univ. Press, 1991), 87, 90. The close relationship is documented in the Horace Bushnell to Frederick Billings, Correspondence, 1856–69, Billings Mansion Archives, Woodstock, Vt.

8. William G. Chrystal, "A Beautiful Aceldama: Horace Bushnell in California, 1856–1857," *New England Quarterly* 57, 3 (Sept. 1984): 388; HB to Mary A. Bushnell, 3 Apr. 1856, Cheney, *Bushnell,* 366–67.

9. On Beard, see M. W. Wood, *History of Alameda County, California* (Oakland, 1883), 845–46; HB to Mary A. Bushnell, 28 Apr., 2 May 1856, Cheney, *Bushnell,* 372–75.

10. Wood, *Alameda County,* 846.

11. Sherman Day to [Jeremiah Day], 30 Nov. 1856, Day Collection, University Archives, Bancroft Library, Univ. of California, Berkeley.

12. HB to [Mary A. Bushnell], 28 Apr. 1856, Cheney, *Bushnell,* 372.

13. Ibid., 372–73.

14. Chrystal, "Beautiful Aceldama," 393–94.

15. HB to [Mary A. Bushnell], 15 Apr., 19 May 1856, Cheney, *Bushnell,* 369–70, 379.

16. HB, "California, Its Characteristics and Prospects," *New Englander* 16, 1 (Feb. 1858): 18–19.

17. Harlan E. Hogue, *The Long Arm of New England Devotion* (San Francisco: Northern California Congregational Conference, 1956).

18. *Daily California Chronicle,* 5 May 1856.

19. HB, "California," 33. For "toughest town," see James M. McPherson, *Battle Cry of Freedom: The Civil War Era* (New York: Oxford Univ. Press, 1988), 163.

20. Chrystal, "Beautiful Aceldama," 396–97; *Daily California Chronicle,* 15, 23 May 1856; HB to Mary A. Bushnell, 18, 19, 20 May 1856, Cheney, *Bushnell,* 375–80.

21. *Daily California Chronicle,* 20 June 1856. Judging by the wording and other internal evidence, the author unquestionably was Bushnell.

Chrystal, "Beautiful Aceldama," 398.

22. *Daily California Chronicle,* 23 June 1856.

23. HB to [Mary A. Bushnell], 4 July 1856, Cheney, *Bushnell,* 383.

24. HB, "Society and Religion: A Sermon for California, Delivered on Sabbath Evening, July 6, 1856, at the Installation of Rev. E. S. Lacy, as Pastor of the First Congregational Church, San Francisco" (Hartford: L. E. Hunt, 1856).

25. Jer. 1:10, KJV.

26. *The Pacific,* 10, 17 July 1856.

27. *Daily California Chronicle,* 8 July 1856.

28. *Hartford Courant,* 16 Aug. 1856.

29. *Religious Herald,* 28 Aug. 1856.

30. Records of the Board of Trustees of the College of California, 8 July 1856, Bancroft Library.

31. Ibid., 27–29; "An Interview with President Durant on the Origin of the University of California," typescript, p. 12, Bancroft Library.

32. Trustees, "Movement for a University of California: A Statement to the Public by the Trustees of the College of California, and An Appeal by Dr. Bushnell" (San Francisco: Pacific Publishing, 1857); reprinted in Samuel H. Willey, *A History of the College of California* (San Francisco: Samuel Carson, 1887), 21–34.

33. HB to Samuel H. Willey, Secretary of the Board of Trustees, 10 July 1856, Cheney, *Bushnell,* 384–85; Records of the Trustees, 8 July 1856, Bancroft Library.

34. HB to [Mary A. Bushnell], 18 July 1856, and to the North Congregational Church and Society, 14 July 1856, Cheney, *Bushnell,* 385–87; HB to Elijah H. Owen, 14 July 1856, Learned Collection.

35. William W. Ferrier, *Henry Durant, First President of the University of California . . .* (Berkeley: Privately published, 1942), 34.

36. In his detailed reports to the trustees, HB mentioned at least three routes that seemed to him feasible. Just which one he thought of as "his" solution, is not clear. Records of Trustees, 13 Nov., 23 Dec. 1856, Bancroft Library.

37. HB's detailed reports are given in the Records of the Trustees, 13 Nov. 1856–2 Jan. 1857, ibid.

38. HB to [Mary A. Bushnell], 19 Aug., 3 Sept. 1856, 3 Jan. 1857, Cheney, *Bushnell,* 387–89, 402.

39. HB to [Mary A. Bushnell], 5 Dec. 1856, ibid., 401.

40. HB, *Nature and the Supernatural,* 475–77.

41. Records of the Board of Trustees, 2 Jan. 1857, 23 Feb. 1858, Bancroft Library; Winks, *Billings,* 92–93.

42. Cheney, *Bushnell,* 404; Washington Gladden, *Recollections* (Boston: Houghton Mifflin, 1909), 166–67; Munger, *Bushnell,* 202; Charles A. Dinsmore, "Horace Bushnell," *DAB* 3:351; Johnson, *Nature and The Supernatural,* 38; Cherry, *Bushnell Sermons* (1985), 6; Jones, "Bushnell Park" (1990), 21.

43. William W. Ferrier, "The Story of the Naming of Berkeley" (Berkeley, 1929), 21; HB to [Mary A. Bushnell], 15 Nov. 1856, Cheney, *Bushnell,* 398–99.

44. Samuel H. Willey to President Benjamin I. Wheeler, 16 Jan. 1901, Records of the President of the University, Bancroft Library.

45. "Movement for a University, and Appeal," Willey, *History,* 27, 28.

46. HB to James T. Hyde, 4 June 1856, Horace Bushnell Collection, Archives, Hartford Seminary.

47. HB to [Mary A. Bushnell], 17 Nov. 1856, Cheney, *Bushnell,* 399–400.

48. HB to Billings, 4 Mar., 18 Nov. 1857, Horace Bushnell to Frederick Billings, Correspondence, 1856–69, Billings Mansion Archives.

49. HB to Alexander T. Stewart, Alexander Autograph Collection, Firestone Library, Princeton Univ.; "Alexander T. Stewart," *DAB* 18:3–5; Mary A. Bushnell to Mary Bushnell, 17 Dec. 1856, Learned Collection.

50. HB to Frederick Billings, 2 Feb. 1858, Bushnell to Billings, Correspondence, 1856–69, Billings Mansion Archives.

51. HB, "California, Its Characteristics and Prospect," 142–82.

52. Theron Baldwin to Julian M. Sturtevant, 18 Dec. 1857, Baldwin-Sturtevant Letters, Schewe Library.

53. Henry Durant to Edward B. Walsworth, 20 Nov. 1857, Edward B. Walsworth Collection, Bancroft Library.

54. Durant, "Origin of University," 18–19; Ferrier, *Durant,* 45–46.

55. Trustees, "Movement for a University and Appeal," 7.

56. Records of the Board of Trustees, 2 Jan. 1857, Bancroft Library.

57. *The Pacific,* 29 Aug. 1858, quoted in Jeremiah Day to Elizabeth (Mrs. Sherman) Day, 18 Sept. 1858, Day Collection, Bancroft Library.

58. HB to George Bushnell, 20 Apr. 1857, Blake Family Collection, Manuscripts and Archives, Yale University Library; Jeremiah Day to Mrs. Sherman Day, 18 Aug. 1856, Day Family Collection, Bancroft Library.

59. HB to the Trustees, 9 July 1861, Records of the College of California, Archives, Bancroft Library; Records of the Board of Trustees, 24 Sept. 1861, ibid.

60. "Henry Durant," *DAB* 5:541.

61. Ferrier, "Naming of Berkeley," 6; Winks, *Billings,* 92–93.

62. *Map of Berkeley, California* (Berkeley: Mason-McDuffie, 1911) and *Map of Oakland, Berkeley, Alameda and Piedmont* (Oakland: Bekins Van and Storage, 1924).

63. HB to Mary Bushnell, 5 Dec. 1856, Records of the College of California, Archives, Bancroft Library.

64. Gladden, *Recollections,* 166–67.

65. Chrystal, "Beautiful Aceldama," 401–2.

66. August Heckscher, *Woodrow Wilson: A Biography* (New York: Charles Scribner's: 1991), 111–12. Bushnell was not entirely negative. He saw in Western character "many powerful and promising qualities." "Barbarism," 21.

CHAPTER 16
"Fresh Married to My People"

1. HB to Frederick Billings, 4 Mar. 1857, Bushnell to Billings, Correspondence, 1856–69, Billings Mansion Archives; Mary A. Bushnell to Mary Bushnell, 26 Feb. [1857], Learned Collection.

2. Jer. 48:11. The sermon was reprinted in HB, *Sermons for the New Life,* 415–33.

3. HB to Bartol, Mar. 1857, Cheney, *Bushnell,* 408.

4. *Hartford Courant,* 28 Feb. 1857.

5. Mary A. Bushnell to Mary Bushnell, 26 Feb. [1857], Learned Collection.

6. HB to Mary A. Bushnell, 5 Aug. 1857, Cheney, *Bushnell,* 409; Smith, "History of Yale Class of 1827. "

7. HB, *Spirit in Man,* 199–213. "The Finite Demands the Infinite" apparently was first preached as "Nothing in God's Attributes to Be Spared." MSS in Bushnell Collection, Yale Divinity School Library, which also has the MSS of "Power from On High." For extracts from "The Eternity of Love," see *Spirit in Man,* 240–45; MSS of "Preparations for Eternity" is in Yale Divinity School Library. "The Power of an Endless Life" appears in HB, *Sermons for the New Life,* 304–25.

8. *Hartford Courant,* 10 Oct. 1857.

9. *Hartford Courant,* 24 Apr. 1858.

10. Kenneth M. Stampp, *America in 1857, A Nation on the Brink* (New York: Oxford Univ. Press, 1990), 179–80.

11. Cheney, *Bushnell,* 411.

12. Frank B. Carpenter, "Studio Talks with Dr. Horace Bushnell," *The Independent,* 11 Jan 1900, 119.

13. Henry F. May, *Protestant Churches and Industrial America* (New York: Harper, 1949), 56.

14. The sermon was printed in the *Courant,* 20 Oct. 1857, and reprinted in the *Courant Supplement,* 31 Oct. 1857. For background comment Cheney, *Bushnell,* 410–11. *Journal of Commerce* comment, in *Courant,* 31 Oct. 1857.

15. Cheney, *Bushnell,* 412–13.

16. Trumbull, ed., *Memorial History* 1:670; *Religious Herald,* 18·Nov. 1858.

17. HB to [Mary Bushnell], 13 Apr. 1857, Cheney, *Bushnell,* 408; Mary A. Bushnell to Mary Bushnell, 27 Mar. 1857, Learned Collection.

18. [Normand Smith, A. M. Collins, and Others] to HB, 17 May 1858; and HB to ibid., 15 June 1858, Cheney, *Bushnell,* 415–17.

19. Henry M. Goodwin, "Dr. Bushnell's *Sermons for the New Life,* " *New Englander* 17, 2 (May 1859): 382. On HB popularity, Cheney, *Bushnell,* 417.

20. *Independent,* 18 June 1858; HB to Mary A. Bushnell, 11 May 1858, and to Bartol, 19 May 1858, Cheney, *Bushnell,* 413–15.

21. Kirk to HB, 8 Sept. 1858, Cheney, *Bushnell,* 417–18.

22. Untitled Dudleian Lecture, 12 May 1852, Dudleian Lectures, 1842–57, Pusey Library, Harvard Univ.

23. HB, *Nature and the Supernatural,* 19–27, 61.

24. Ibid., 30, 19.

25. Ibid., Preface, iii-iv.

26. Ibid., 15–18.

27. Coleridge, *Aids,* 273.

28. HB, *Nature and the Supernatural,* 36–37, 41.

29. Coleridge, *Aids,* 273; Cherry, *Religious Imagination,* 100–105.

30. HB, *Nature and the Supernatural,* 37.

31. Ibid., 20, 38.

32. Ibid., 41, 43–44.

33. Ibid., 43–44.

34. Ibid., 59.

35. Ibid., 78.

36. "John Fiske," *DAB* 6:421.

37. James D. Dana, "Anticipations of Man in Nature: Review of Chapter VII of *Nature and the Supernatural,* by Horace Bushnell," *New Englander* 17, 2 (May 1859): 297.

38. HB, "Science and Religion," *Putnam's Magazine* 1, 3 (Mar. 1868): esp. 267, 271; William R. Hutchinson, *The Modernist Impulse in American Protestantism* (Cambridge: Harvard Univ. Press, 1976), 43–48. Munger thought it "pathetic" that Bushnell stood on the border of evolution, without being able to enter; Munger, *Bushnell,* 344.

39. HB, *Nature and the Supernatural,* 218.

40. Ibid., 96.

41. Ibid., 110ff; Duke, *Bushnell,* 53–55.

42. Jonathan Edwards, "The Doctrine of Original Sin Defended," *The Works of President Edwards* (Worcester, Mass.: Isaiah Thomas, 1809), 6:430.

43. HB, *Nature and the Supernatural,* 107–9.

44. Ibid., 214.

45. Ibid., 174.

46. Ibid., 31–32, 42, 278, and ch 10.

47. Ibid., 277.

48. Claude Welch, *Protestant Thought in the Nineteenth Century,* Vol. 1, *1799–1870* (New Haven: Yale Univ. Press, 1972), 265–68; Duke, *Bushnell,* 62–64.

49. HB, *Nature and the Supernatural,* 318.

50. HB, *The Character of Jesus: Forbidding His Possible Classification with Men* (New York: Scribner, 1860); Duke, *Bushnell,* 62.

51. Noah Porter, Jr., "Nature and the Supernatural," *New Englander* 17, 1 (Feb. 1859): 256–57.

52. HB to Bartol, 3 Dec. 1858, Cheney, *Bushnell,* 419–20; [Cyrus A. Bartol], "Dr. Bushnell and Dr. Furness: A Question of Words and Names," *The Christian Examiner* 66, 5th ser., 4 (Jan.–May, 1859): 112–24.

53. The Andover review by Edwards A. Park (?), appeared in *Bibliotheca Sacra and Biblical Repository* 16, 2 (Apr. 1859): 426–37. Princeton did a relatively short notice in *Biblical Repository and Princeton Review* 31, 1 (Jan. 1859): 153–56. For Mercersburg, see John W. Nevin, "Notice of *Na-*

ture and the Supernatural, by Horace Bushnell," *Mercersburg Review* (Apr. 1859). Extensive extracts reprinted in Theodore Appel, *The Life and Work of John Williamson Nevin* (Philadelphia: Reformed Church Publication House, 1889), 529–50.

54. Appel, *Nevin,* 529.

55. David N. Lord, "Dr. Bushnell's *Nature and the Supernatural,* " *Theological and Literary Journal* 11, 4 (July 1858–Apr. 1859): 529–76.

56. Twichell, "Personal Reminiscences," *Bushnell Centenary,* 70–71.

57. HB to George Bushnell, 24 Dec. [1858], Blake Family Collection, Manuscripts and Archives, Yale University Library.

58. North Congregational Church, Records, 4:44–51, Connecticut State Library.

59. Jer. 22:10, KJV. HB, "Parting Words: A Discourse Delivered in the North Church, Hartford, July 3, 1859" (Hartford: L. E. Hunt, 1859).

60. *Hartford Evening Press,* 7 July 1859; HB to the North Church, 3 Aug. 1859, reprinted in *Hartford Courant,* 9 Aug. 1859.

61. HB to Frederick Billings, 4 Apr. 1859, Bushnell to Billings, Correspondence, 1856–69, Billings Mansion Archives.

CHAPTER 17
Minnesota and the Eve of Conflict

1. HB to the *Hartford Courant,* Aug. 1859; published 12 Aug. 1859.

2. HB to Mary A. Bushnell, 30 Aug. 1859, Cheney, *Bushnell,* 428–29.

3. HB to "Mrs. E.," 22 Mar. 1860, ibid., 437.

4. Frances Louisa Bushnell to Mary A. Bushnell, 29 Oct. 1859, Learned Collection.

5. HB to Frances Louisa Bushnell, 6 Dec. 1859, Cheney, *Bushnell,* 433; Mary A. Bushnell to Mary Bushnell, 31 Jan. 1860, Learned Collection.

6. HB to Henry Barnard, 26 Oct. 1859, Barnard Collection, Connecticut Historical Society; MacMullen, *Henry Barnard,* 227.

7. Mary A. Bushnell to Mary Bushnell, 31 Jan. 1860, Learned Collection.

8. John Barnard Phillips, M. D., undated letter to an undesignated recipient, John Barnard Phillips Collection, Minnesota Historical Society, St. Paul.

9. Mary A. Bushnell to Mary Bushnell, 15 Jan. [1856?], Learned Collection.

10. These thumbnail sketches are based on Bushnell family correspondence, in which everybody in the household participated, as well as members of the extended family on Mrs. Bushnell's side. It covers the years from 1848 to the turn of the century. Learned Collection. For the lines of Louisa's verse, see Frances Louisa Bushnell, *Poems* (DeVinne Press, 1900), 18.

11. Frances Louisa Bushnell to Mrs. George Bushnell, 9 Feb. 1862, Blake Family Collection, Manuscripts and Archives, Yale University.

12. Mary Bushnell to Mary A. Bushnell, 7 Nov. 1859, Learned Collection.

13. Mary A. Bushnell to Mary Bushnell, 23 Nov. 1859, ibid.

14. HB to Bartol, 7 Feb. 1860, Cheney, *Bushnell*, 434.

15. Mary A. Bushnell to Mary Bushnell, 18 May 1860, Learned Collection.

16. Ibid.

17. HB to Mary A. Bushnell, 13 June 1860, Cheney, *Bushnell*, 439.

18. HB, "Census and Slavery."

19. HB, "Northern Iron," 27–28.

20. HB to Bacon, 14 June 1855, Bacon Family Collection, Manuscripts and Archives, Yale University Library; "Edward Everett Hale, *DAB* 8:99–100; Senior, "New England Congregationalists," 384–86.

21. HB to unspecified recipient, 4 July 1856, Cheney, *Bushnell*, 384.

22. Commager, *Theodore Parker*, 201.

23. HB, "Census and Slavery," 7, 16, 23.

24. For illustration, Glenn Tinder, *The Political Meaning of Christianity* (Baton Rouge: Louisiana State Univ. Press, 1989), esp. 159–65.

25. Stephen B. Oates, *With Malice Toward None: The Life of Abraham Lincoln* (New York: New American Library, Mentor Books, 1978), 211–12.

26. Senior, "New England Congregationalists," 410–13.

27. *Hartford Courant*, 12 Apr. 1861.

28. HB, "Census and Slavery," 12.

29. Ibid., 4.

30. Connecticut African Americans provided one illustration of progress during these years. Swift, *Black Prophets,* 270ff.

31. Frederickson, *Black Image,* ch. 5, esp. 134–57. On Whitman, see Kaplan, *Whitman,* 132, 291–92.

32. Frederickson, *Black Image,* 187.

CHAPTER 18
"This Gigantic and Fearfully Bloody War"

1. McPherson, *Battle Cry,* 273, 854.
2. HB, "Our Obligations to the Dead," *Building Eras in Religion,* 320.
3. *Hartford Courant,* 13, 15 Apr. 1861.
4. Glenn Weaver, *Hartford, An Illustrated History of Connecticut's Capital* (Woodland Hills, Calif.: Windsor Publications, 1982), 82.
5. Austin C. Dunham, *Reminiscences* (Hartford: Case, Lockwood and Brainard, n.d.), 78.
6. Frances Louisa Bushnell to Mary Bushnell, 16 Feb. 1861, Horace Bushnell Collection, Manuscripts and Archives, Yale University Library.
7. HB to Mary A. Bushnell, 7 Mar. 1861, Cheney, *Bushnell,* 448.
8. Ibid.
9. Oates, *Lincoln,* 275; Carl Sandburg, *Abraham Lincoln, The War Years* (New York: Harcourt, Brace, 1939), 1:301–2.
10. Sandburg, *War Years,* 1:302–4.
11. For examples of more mixed Southern feelings, see C. Vann Woodward, ed., *Mary Chesnut's Civil War* (New Haven: Yale Univ. Press, 1981) 111, 117–18.
12. *Hartford Times,* 22, 29 July 1861.
13. *Hartford Evening Press,* 23 July 1861.
14. *Hartford Courant,* 2, 5 Aug. 1861.
15. HB, "Reverses Needed, A Discourse Delivered on the Sunday after the Disaster of Bull Run, in the North Church, Hartford (Hartford: L. E. Hunt, 1861), reprinted in *The Spirit in Man,* 159–84.
16. Malone, *Jefferson and His Time,* 105–7, 274ff; Barnes, "Idea that Caused a War," 77.
17. HB, "Reverses Needed," *Spirit in Man,* 166.
18. Barnes, "Idea that Caused a War," 73–83.
19. Ibid., 75–78. HB underestimated Jefferson's linkage of God and government. Quotations in the Jefferson Memorial in Washington are enlightening in this respect.
20. HB, "Reverses Needed," *Spirit in Man,* 177.
21. Ibid., 180.
22. Ibid., 183.
23. Bruce Catton, *The Coming Fury* (Garden City, N.Y.: Doubleday, 1961), 468; McPherson, *Battle Cry,* 348; George W. Smith and Charles

Judah, *Life in the North During the Civil War* (Albuquerque: Univ. of New Mexico Press, 1966), 331–34.

24. Oates, *Lincoln*, 353, 356.

25. HB, "Reverses Needed," 23–24; HB to Frederick Billings, 7 Aug. 1861, Bushnell to Billings, Correspondence, 1856–69, Billings Mansion Archives. Doubtless wishing her father's mistaken judgment of McClellan to be forgotten, Mrs. Cheney edited out this reference in the reprint in *The Spirit in Man*, 180–81.

26. HB to George Bushnell, 17 Feb. 1862, Blake Family Collection, Manuscripts and Archives, Yale University Library.

27. Sandburg, *War Years*, 1:629–30; Oates, *Lincoln*, 355.

28. HB to George Bushnell, 15 Dec. 1862, Blake Family Collection, Manuscripts and Archives, Yale University Library.

29. Cheney, *Bushnell*, 481.

30. HB to Gideon Welles, 8 July 1861, Gideon Welles Collection, Connecticut Historical Society.

31. *Records of Connecticut Men in the War of the Rebellion, 1861–1865* (Hartford: Adjutant General's Office, 1889), 619; HB to Frank W. Cheney, Dec. 7, 1862, Learned Collection.

32. Henry C. Trumbull, *The Knightly Soldier: A Biography of Henry Ward Camp, Tenth Connecticut Volunteers* (Boston: Nichols and Noyes, 1865).

33. "Henry Clay Trumbull," *DAB* 19:8–9.

34. HB, "Reverses Needed," 181–82; "Popular Government by Divine Right," Delivered Thanksgiving Day, 24 Nov. 1864, before the congregations of the South and South Baptist Churches, Hartford (Hartford: L. E. Hunt, 1864), reprinted in *Building Eras*, 286–318, esp. 314.

35. Trumbull, *Religious Teachers*, 82–83.

36. HB, *The Vicarious Sacrifice, Grounded in Principles Interpreted by Human Analogies* (New York: Scribner's, 1907) 1:208–9.

37. HB, "The Doctrine of Loyalty," *Work and Play*, 337–67.

38. HB, "Popular Government by Divine Right," *Building Eras*. Charles Eliot Norton invited Bushnell to submit his viewsto the *North American Review*. Under pressure of work, Bushnell declined. HB to Norton, 10 Nov., 28 Dec. 1864, Charles Eliot Norton Collection, Houghton Library, Harvard Univ.

39. HB, "Popular Government," *Building Eras*, 288, 310; George M. Frederickson, *The Inner Civil War: Northern Intellectuals and the Crisis of*

the Union (New York: Harper Torchbooks, 1968), 137–44.

40. Frederickson, *Inner Civil War,* 141.

41. HB, "Popular Government," *Building Eras,* 307.

42. *Hartford Courant,* 10, 11 Apr. 1865.

43. Ibid., 20 Apr. 1865.

44. McPherson, *Battle Cry,* 853.

45. Paul H. Buck, *The Road to Reunion* (Boston: Little, Brown, 1937), 12.

46. *Hartford Courant,* 28 July 1865; [Franklin B. Dexter, ed.] *The Commemoration Celebration Held at Yale College, Wednesday, July 26, 1865* (New Haven: Morehouse, Tuttle and Taylor, 1866).

47. "William M. Evarts," *DAB* 6:215–18.

48. Frederickson, *Black Image,* 183.

49. *New Haven Evening Register,* 27 July 1865.

50. *Hartford Times,* 26 July 1865.

51. Trumbull, *Religious Teachers,* 83.

52. *Hartford Courant,* 28 July 1865.

53. Quoted in Ahlstrom, *Religious History,* 684–85.

54. William A. Clebsch, "Christian Interpretations of the Civil War," *Church History* 30, 2 (June 1961): 214–15; "Robert Lewis Dabney," *DAB* 5:20–21.

55. Eric Foner, *Reconstruction: America's Unfinished Revolution, 1863–1877* (New York: Harper and Row, 1988), ch. 9; Roger Butterfield, *The American Past: A History of the United States from Concord to the Nuclear Age* (New York: Simon and Schuster, 1947), 213.

56. HB, ""Our Obligations to the Dead," *Building Eras,* 331.

57. Clebsch, "Christian Interpretations of the Civil War," 215ff; Ahlstrom, *Religious History,* 685, and "Comment on the Essay of Professor Clebsch: History, Bushnell and Lincoln," *Church History* 30 (1961): 223–30; Conrad Cherry, ed., *God's New Israel: Religious Interpretations of American Destiny* (Englewood Cliffs, N.J.: Prentice-Hall, 1971), 155–60.

58. HB to Mary A. Bushnell, 14 Apr. 1866, Cheney, *Bushnell,* 487–88.

59. Michael B. Chesson, *Richmond After the War, 1865–1890* (Richmond: Virginia State Library, 1981), 57–97.

60. This was likely the First African Baptist Church, at College and East Broad streets. Virginia Historical Society, memo to the author, 30 June 1988.

CHAPTER 19
The Cross "Wickedly" Perverted

1. Woodward, ed., *Mary Chesnut's Civil War,* Introduction, xl, 346–49, 429–32.

2. Robert M. Myers, ed., *The Children of Pride: A True Story of Georgia and the Civil War* (New Haven: Yale Univ. Press, 1972), 925, 1002–3, 1008–9, 1160, for example.

3. Smith and Judah, *Life in the North,* 201–3, 290, 311.

4. Frances Louisa Bushnell to Mrs. George Bushnell, 9 Feb. 1862, Blake Family Collection, Manuscripts and Archives, Yale University Library.

5. Horace Bushnell Record Book, 3 Nov. 1863, Connecticut Historical Society; Mary Bushnell Cheney to her family, 7 Nov. 1863, Mary A. Bushnell to Mary B. Cheney, 24 May 1864, Learned Collection; Mary B. Cheney to Frances L. Bushnell, 24 May 1864, in Eileen R. Learned, ed., *The Letters of Mary Bushnell Cheney and Frank Woodbridge Cheney* (Hartford: Privately published, 1988), 16–19.

6. HB, *Christ and His Salvation,* 10 June 1864.

7. Cheney, *Bushnell,* 480–81.

8. *Work and Play,* 440–64. Previously published, along with a similar address by Thomas M. Clark of Christ Church Cathedral, Episcopal, Hartford, as "Religious Music: Two Discourses, the First by Rev. Horace Bushnell, the Second by Rev. Thomas M. Clark" (Hartford: F. A. Brown, 1852).

9. Cheney, *Bushnell,* 31.

10. *Boston Recorder,* 16 Dec. 1864.

11. Stanley B. Weld, *The History of Immanuel Church, 1824–1967* (Hartford: Connecticut Printers, 1968), 16–18; HB, "Building Eras in Religion," *Building Eras in Religion,* 9–34.

12. HB to Barnard, 28 June [1867?], Henry Barnard Collection, Fales Library New York University; MacMullen, *Barnard,* 273.

13. HB to Gideon Welles, 15, 17 May 1866, Gideon Welles Collection, Connecticut Historical Society.

14. "David Bushnell," *DAB* 3:348–49.

15. State of Connecticut vs. Albert L. Starkweather, Superior Court, Hartford County, 5 Sept. 1865, Criminal Records, 1848–1874, Connecticut State Library.

16. *Hartford Courant,* 18 Aug. 1866.

17. HB, *Moral Uses of Dark Things,* 107; "Obligations to the Dead,"

Building Eras, 350–52; see also, HB, *Vicarious Sacrifice,* 330.

18. *Hartford Courant,* 21 May 1866.

19. HB to Welles, 17 May 1866.

20. *Hartford Courant,* 18 Aug. 1866; the paper devoted nearly a full page to the macabre event.

21. *Hartford Courant,* 28 Feb. 1866.

22. See Chap. 18, note 34.

23. HB to an unidentified recipient, 1 Jan. 1859, Cheney, *Bushnell,* 422.

24. HB, *Vicarious Sacrifice,* 48.

25. Ibid., 47–48, 56.

26. A pertinent 1866 statement of this viewpoint is in W. W. Andrews, *Remarks on Dr. Bushnell's "Vicarious Sacrifice"* (Hartford: Case, Lockwood, 1866), 9–10.

27. HB, *Vicarious Sacrifice,* 124, 381, 121; Cherry, *Nature and Religious Imagination,* 182–83; Duke, *Bushnell,* 74.

28. Rom. 12:1, NRSV.

29. HB, *Vicarious Sacrifice,* 113, 117.

30. Ibid., 14–19.

31. Ibid., 147–50.

32. Ibid., 241.

33. Ibid., 464, 481.

34. Ibid., 130–31.

35. Ibid., 277–80.

36. [Goodrich], "What Does Dr. Bushnell Mean?" 21.

37. Andrews, *Dr. Bushnell's "Vicarious Sacrifice,* " 26.

38. HB, *Vicarious Sacrifice,* 47, 69, 70, 73, 475.

39. Munger, *Bushnell,* 270.

40. Raymond W. Albright, *Focus on Infinity: A Life of Phillips Brooks* (New York: Macmillan, 1961), 106.

41. Charles H. Fowler, "Bushnell's *Vicarious Sacrifice,*" *Methodist Quarterly Review* 43, 4th ser. (July 1866): 350–70.

42. [Henry James, Sr.], "Dr. Bushnell's Book Once More," MSS draft of letter to *New York Tribune* [1858 or 1859], James Family Collection, Houghton Library.

43. Henry James, Sr., "Review of *Vicarious Sacrifice,*" *North American Review* 102 (Apr. 1866): 556–71.

44. Records of the Hartford Fourth Association of Ministers, Mar. 20,

1866, Archives, U.C.C. Center, Hartford; Andrews, *Bushnell's "Vicarious Sacrifice."*

45. James Freeman Clarke, "Bushnell on Vicarious Sacrifice," *The Christian Examiner* N.S., 1 (May 1866): 377.

46. Noah Porter, Jr., "Review of Dr. Bushnell's *Vicarious Sacrifice,* " *New Englander* 25, 2 (Apr. 1866): 228–82.

47. HB, *Vicarious Sacrifice,* 14.

48. Trumbull, *Four Religious Teachers,* 76–79, 88.

49. Ibid.

50. Ibid.

51. John Updike, "Emersonianism," *New Yorker Magazine* 60, 16 (4 June 1984): 112.

52. Kenneth R. Andrews, *Nook Farm: Mark Twain's Hartford Circle* (Seattle: Univ. of Washington Press, 1950), 29.

53. Cheney, *Bushnell,* 463.

54. Trumbull, *Religious Teachers,* 71–72.

55. Burton, "Horace Bushnell," *Yale Lectures,* 417–29; Parker, "[Bushnell's] Ministry at Large,", Cheney, *Bushnell,* 470ff; Leah A. Strong, *Joseph Hopkins Twichell: Mark Twain's Friend and Pastor* (Athens: Univ. Georgia Press, 1966), 7–9, 47, 55–58; and Twichell, "Personal Reminiscences," *Bushnell Centenary,* 70–85.

56. Albright, *Focus on Infinity,* 106, 203, 424.

57. HB to Tyler, 30 Mar. [1858], Moses Coit Tyler Collection, Cornell University Libraries, Ithaca; "Moses Coit Tyler," *DAB* 19:92–93.

58. Benjamin W. Bacon, *Theodore Thornton Munger, New England Minister* (New Haven: Yale Univ. Press, 1913), 140–41; Hutchison, *Modernist Impulse,* 95.

59. Munger, *Bushnell,* 375.

60. HB to Washington Gladden, 13 Mar., 7 Apr., 23 May 1867, Gladden Collection, Ohio Historical Society, Columbus.

61. Gladden, *Recollections,* 165–67; Jacob H. Dorn, *Washington Gladden: Prophet of the Social Gospel* (Columbus: Ohio State Univ. Press, 1966), 42–44.

62. HB, *Sermons on Living Subjects,* 73–95.

63. HB to Washington Gladden, 23 May 1867, Gladden Collection, Ohio Historical Society.

64. Gladden, *Recollections,* 167–68. The installation occurred on 12

June 1867; *Congregational Quarterly Record,* July 1867, 299, Congregational Library, Boston.

CHAPTER 20
Rights of African Americans, Rights of Women

1. See Chap. 8, note 3.
2. See Chap. 12, note 46.
3. Mott, *American Magazines,* 32–33.
4. Ibid., 105–6.
5. HB, "Of the Animal Infestations," *Moral Uses,* 291.
6. HB, "Of Insanity," ibid., 249, 267, 272–73.
7. HB, *Moral Uses,* 296–318.
8. Charles C. Cole, Jr., "Horace Bushnell and the Slavery Question," *New England Quarterly* 23, 1 (Mar. 1950): 19–30; Cross, *Bushnell,* 41; Frederickson, *Black Image,* 155–56; and in a different vein, Louis Weeks, "Horace Bushnell on Black America," *Religious Education* 63, 1 (Jan.–Feb. 1973): 28–41. A positive interpretation of this chapter appears in Ralph E. Luker, "Bushnell in Black and White: Evidences of the 'Racism' of Horace Bushnell," *The New England Quarterly* 45, 3 (Sept. 1972): 408–16. This view is endorsed by Howe, "Social Science," 318–19.
9. A full acount is given in Foner, *Reconstruction.*
10. Frederickson, *Black Image,* 185.
11. Foner, *Reconstruction,* 179–81.
12. Frederickson, *Black Image,* Chs. 8, 9, esp. 228, 250, 259, 281.
13. HB, "Distinctions," *Moral Uses,* 303.
14. Ibid., 302, 303.
15. Ibid., 302–3.
16. Ibid., 301–2.
17. Ibid., 311–12.
18. Ibid., 312–13.
19. Frederickson, *Black Image,* 102–17; On Kinmont, Thomas F. Gossett, *Uncle Tom's Cabin and American Culture* (Dallas: Southern Methodist Univ. Press, 1985), 83–85; Harriet Beecher Stowe, *Uncle Tom's Cabin, or Life Among the Lowly* (1851–52; New York: New American Library, 1966), 197.
20. HB, "Distinctions," *Moral Uses,* 308, 314–18.
21. Gossett, *Uncle Tom's Cabin and American Culture,* 85.
22. Stowe, *Uncle Tom,* 197.

23. HB, "Distinctions," *Moral Uses*, 297–98.

24. Ibid., 296; Bushnell's looking to Africa has been taken as a sign that deep down he remained a child of his time, wedded to colonization and still longing for an all-white America. Weeks, "Bushnell," 40. The whole tenor of his argument seems clearly to deny this.

25. Luker, "Bushnell," 416; Howe, "Social Science," 318–19.

26. Ellen C. DuBois, *Feminism and Suffrage: The Emergence of An Independent Women's Movement in America, 1848–1869* (Ithaca: Cornell Univ. Press, 1978), 21.

27. Emily N. Vanderpoel, *More Chronicles of a Pioneer School, 1792–1833* (New York: Cadmus Book Shop, 1927), 202.

28. Dubois, *Feminism and Suffrage*, 31, 33ff.

29. Ibid., 66, ch. 6; Foner, *Reconstruction*, 447–48.

30. HB, *Women's Suffrage*, 9–11, 90–91.

31. This painful progress is treated in Mabel C. Donnelly, *The American Victorian Woman: The Myth and the Reality* (New York: Greenwood Press, 1986), ch. 10.

32. Elizabeth D. Apthorp, younger sister of Mrs. Bushnell, was neighbor to the Bushnells on Winthrop Street in Hartford from the mid-1850s to the mid-1860s; she kept a select school for girls in her house. Mary A. Bushnell to Mary Bushnell, 25 Sept. 1855, and Elizabeth D. Apthorp to Mary A. Bushnell, 20 Nov. [1859], Learned Collection.

33. HB to a daughter [Mary?], 27 June 1860, Cheney, *Bushnell*, 440–41.

34. We have only hints on the education of the Bushnell children. They are enough, however, to indicate the scope of it, received through members of the family and tutors in Hartford and New Haven and in local private schools. Family letters are revealing: Frances Louisa Bushnell to HB, 25 Dec. 1847, 20 Jan. 1848; Mary A. Bushnell to Mary Bushnell, 17 Dec. 1856, 26 Feb. 1857, Learned Collection; HB to Frances Louisa Bushnell, 6 Oct. 1845, and to Mary Bushnell, 1 Aug. 1859, Cheney, *Bushnell*, 139–43, 427. See also Hartford Female Seminary Catalogs, 1848–49, 1850–51. Mary's teaching and learning while on the staff of Miss Porter's School in Farmington also gives cluesto her own education: Mary Bushnell to Mary A. Bushnell, 12 Oct. 1859, Learned Collection.

35. HB, *Women's Suffrage*, 13–29.

36. Allen, *Emerson*, 558–61.

37. "Henry Brown Blackwell," *DAB* 2:321, and "Thomas Wentworth Higginson," *DAB* 9:16–18.

38. HB, *Women's Suffrage*, 44.

39. Full treatment of this is in "Popular Government by Divine Right," *Building Eras,* 293–300; and *Women's Suffrage,* ch. 2. Bushnell's position here is also noted in Howe, "Social Science and Horace Bushnell," 319.

40. HB, *Women's Suffrage,* 44–48.

41. Ibid., 64–66.

42. Ibid., 62.

43. Ibid., 31.

44. "Reunion [of the] Hartford Female Seminary, 9 June 1892, Addresses and Papers..." (Hartford: Case, Lockwood and Brainard, 1892), 7, Library, Stowe-Day Foundation; Mary A. Bushnell to Mary Bushnell, 5 Sept., 4 Nov. 1856, Learned Collection. [Mary A. Bushnell], *Lessons for a Year on the Life of Christ, Arranged for the Sabbath School of the North Church* (Hartford: Elihu Geer, 1851), Bushnell Memorial Hall Collection. This leaflet bears a notation in Mary B. Cheney's hand, "Arranged by M. A. B."

45. Mary A. Bushnell to Mary Bushnell, 17 Dec. 1856, Learned Collection.

46. HB to Mary A. Bushnell, [15] Nov. 1846, Cheney, *Bushnell,* 176.

47. Trumbull, *Religious Teachers,* 87–88.

48. Mary A. Bushnell to Mary Bushnell, 4 Nov. 1856, Learned Collection.

49. HB to Whipple, 11 June 1869, Autograph File, Houghton Library.

50. HB to Henry W. Bellows, 15 June 1869, Bellows Collection, Massachusetts Historical Society.

51. [Edwin L. Godkin], "Dr. Bushnell on Women's Rights," *The Nation* 8, 208 (24 June 1869): 496–97; HB to Godkin, 19 July 1869, Godkin Collection, Houghton Library.

52. HB to Scribner and Company, New York, 25 June 1869, Charles Scribner's Sons' Collection, Firestone Library, Princeton University.

53. HB to Scribner and Company, 25 June 1869, ibid.

54. Harriet Beecher Stowe to Sarah [Willis Parton], 25 July [1869], Sophia Smith Collection, Smith College Library. Courtesy of Joan D. Hedrick, Trinity College, Hartford. The critical article was Jerushy Wilkerson, "Wilkerson's Journal," *Hearth and Home* 1, 29 (10 July 1869): 452.

55. Isabella Hooker's annotated copy of *Women's Suffrage,* 29–31, 53, 86, Stowe-Day Foundation Library; Mabel C. Donnelly, "Comments [on Bushnell and Isabella Beecher Hooker]," *Harriet Beecher Stowe House and Library [Bulletin]* (Sept. 1987), 3; HB to Isabella Beecher Hooker, 4 May 1869, Joseph K. Hooker Collection, Stowe-Day Foundation.

56. John Stuart Mill, *The Subjection of Women,* in Alice S. Rossi, ed., *Essays on Sex Equality* [*by*] *John Stuart Mill and Harriet Taylor Mill* (Chicago: Univ. of Chicago Press, 1970), 184, 146, 23, 175.

57. Cheney, *Bushnell,* 503; Mary Bushnell Cheney to "Mr. Merriam," 8 Mar. 1912, Learned Collection.

58. William James, "*Women's Suffrage; the Reform against Nature,* by Horace Bushnell, and *The Subjection of Women,* by John Stuart Mill," *North American Review* 109, 225 (Oct. 1869): 557, 563, 560ff, 558.

59. HB to Scribner and Company, 30 June [1869], Charles Scribner's Sons' Collection, Firestone Library.

60. HB to Scribner and Company, 25 June 1869, ibid.

61. HB to Henry W. Bellows, 15 June 1869, Bellows Collection, Massachusetts Historical Society.

CHAPTER 21
"No Give-Up With Him"

1. *Connecticut State Register and Manual, 1969,* 580–81.

2. Weaver, *Hartford,* 79–80.

3. "Harriet...Here and There," Stowe-Day Foundation, *Harriet Beecher Stowe House and Library [Bulletin]* (Oct. 1988): 2–3.

4. Justin Kaplan, *Mr. Clemens and Mark Twain, A Biography* (New York: Simon and Schuster, 1966), 139–40.

5. Cheney, *Bushnell,* 536.

6. Andrews, *Nook Farm,* 29.

7. HB, "Pulpit Talent" (Andover), and "Training for the Pulpit Manward" (Chicago), *Building Eras,* 182–248.

8. Ibid., 187, 189, 215, 188.

9. HB, [A Series on the Subject of Prayer], *Advance* 4–6: (13 Apr. 1871–3 Oct. 1872): 189–265; reprinted in *Chicago Theological Seminary Register* 80, 1 (Winter 1990): 1–43.

10. Cheney, *Bushnell,* 504–5.

11. Ibid., 508–9.

12. HB, "Free Trade and Protection," *Scribner's Monthly* 2, 3 (July 1871): 266–73.

13. Ezra Clark, [Jr.] to Mary B. Cheney, 20 Jan. 1880, Learned Collection.

14. HB to "Mrs. C.," [Mrs. Ezra Clark, Jr.], 23 Jan. [1859?], ibid.;

"Edward Fitzgerald Beale," *DAB* 2:88–89.

15. HB to "Mrs. C" [Mrs. Ezra Clark, Jr.], Hartford, 23 Jan. [1859], Learned Collection.

16. The route Bushnell had in mind ran from Stockton through Livermore Pass, following Alameda Creek down through the Sierra and approaching San Francisco via a causeway from Oakland. For the most part this was approach the Central Pacific chose. Cheney, *Bushnell*, 404–5; L. Nell, *Topographical Railroad and County Map of the States of California and Nevada* (New York: A. C. Frey, 1868); and U.S. Coast and Geodetic Survey, *San Francisco Entrance, California*, #5581, Aug. 1884.

17. HB, "The Day of Roads," *Work and Play*, 436–39.

18. Van Dusen, *Connecticut*, 244.

19. HB's 6 Jan. 1872 speech in Central Hall, *Hartford Courant*, 8 Jan. 1872, and Cheney, *Bushnell*, 506–7.

20. Cheney, *Bushnell*, 507.

21. *Hartford Courant*, 8 Jan. 1872; *Hartford Times*, 9 Jan. 1872.

22. *Hartford Times*, 9 Jan. 1872.

23. Mary A. Bushnell to Mary B. Cheney, 10 Jan. 1872, Learned Collection.

24. *Hartford Courant*, 8, 9 Jan.; *Hartford Times*, 9–17 Jan. 1872; Melancthon W. Jacobus, "The Connecticut State Capitol," *Connecticut Historical Society Bulletin* 33, 2 (Apr. 1968): 41–50; Cheney, *Bushnell*, 507. On Burr, see Trumbull, *Memorial History* 1:615–19, and *DAB* 3:321.

25. "Connecticut State Capitol," General Reference Unit, Vertical File, Connecticut State Library.

26. Mary A. Bushnell to HB, 20 July 1873, Learned Collection.

27. HB to Scribner and Company, New York, 4 Feb. 1871, Charles Scribner's Sons' Collection, Firestone Library.

28. James M. Hoppin, "Bushnell's *Sermons on Living Subjects*, " *New Englander* 31,1 (Jan. 1873): 95–109.

29. HB, *Forgiveness and Law, Grounded in Principles Interpreted by Human Analogies* (New York: Scribner, Armstrong, 1874).

30. HB to an undesignated "Friend," 2 Nov. 1875, Cheney, *Bushnell*, 553.

31. HB to Charles Scribner, 20 Aug. [no year], Charles Scribner's Sons' Collection, Firestone Library.

32. Ibid.

33. HB, *Forgiveness and Law*, 14.

34. Ibid., 11–12. The sermon on forgiveness may have been that published in *Christ and His Salvation*, 372–92; H. Shelton Smith, *Bushnell*, 311. Since, however, this sermon must have been composed two years or more before the publication of *Vicarious Sacrifice* in 1866, it is curious Bushnell did not include its thought in that work.

35. Ibid., 40–42.

36. Ibid., 51; John 1:11, KJV.

37. HB, *Forgiveness and Law*, 33, 73.

38. HB to "a stranger in a distant place" [Mrs. Cheney's note], n.d., Cheney, *Bushnell*, 518–19. Phil. 4:13, NRSV.

39. HB, *Forgiveness and Law*, 98–99.

40. H. Shelton Smith, *Bushnell*, 310–12.

41. HB, *Forgiveness and Law*, 114.

42. HB to Scribner and Co., 4 Feb. 1871, Charles Scribner's Sons' Collection, Firestone Library.

43. HB to Chesebrough, 21 May 1874, and HB to *The Christian Union*, 2 Aug. 1874, Cheney, *Bushnell*, 538–39, 540–41.

44. Trumbull, *Religious Teachers*, 90–93.

45. HB, *Forgiveness and Law*, 23–24, 28–30; HB to Bartol, Mar. 29, 1872, Cheney, *Bushnell*, 525–26.

46. HB, *Forgiveness and Law*, 24–28.

47. HB to Charles G. Finney, 25 June 1874, Finney Collection, Oberlin College Archives.

48. HB to Woolsey, 6 Apr. 1871, Woolsey Family Collection, Manuscripts and Archives, Yale University Library.

49. "Horace Bushnell," *Obituary Records, Graduates of Yale College, 1870–1880*, 214. HB to Franklin B. Dexter, Aug. 2, 1871, Dexter Secretarial Records, Manuscripts and Archives, Yale University Library.

50. HB to Porter, 21 Sept. 1871, Graves Collection, Archives, Unitarian Society, Hartford.

51. Ibid.

52. Clark, "Bushnell the Citizen," *Bushnell Centenary*, 60; HB to Clark, 3 Sept. 1866, and to Orson Phelps, 28 Sept. 1868, Bushnell Collection, Manuscripts and Archives, Yale University Library.

53. HB to Orson Phelps, 28 Sept. 1868, Bushnell Collection, Manuscripts and Archives, Yale University Library.

54. Cheney, *Bushnell*, 500–501.

55. HB to Mary A. Bushnell, 5 Aug. 1872, Cheney, *Bushnell*, 526.

56. Mary A. Bushnell to HB, 20 Aug. 1872, 18 Aug. 1873, Learned Collection; HB to Mary A. Bushnell, 10, 21 Aug. 1873, Cheney, *Bushnell,* 529–30.

57. Dyer, "Bushnell," 295–96, citing Rev. William Leonard Gage of Hartford.

58. Records, Hartford Central Association, Connecticut Conference, U.C.C., 138–89; Parker, "Bushnell Controversy," 26–27. Bushnell's last recorded appearance at the Association was on 7 Feb. 1875. It is hard to doubt Parker's memory of Burton's emotional response, but the Association records contain no reference to such a meeting or to the Doctor's sermon. A sermon with that title was reprinted in *Living Subjects* in 1872.

59. "The Conflagration—Letter from Dr. Bushnell," *Advance,* 16 Nov. 1871.

60. *Hartford Courant,* 18 June 1874; HB to Mary B. Cheney, 22 June 1874, Manuscripts and Archives, Yale University Library.

61. Cheney, *Bushnell,* 512.

62. Ibid.; Austin Phelps, "A Vacation with Dr. Bushnell," *The Christian Union* 14 (12 July 1876): 24; and 14 (19 July 1876): 47–48.

63. HB to Longfellow, 28 Dec. 1871, Longfellow Collection, Houghton Library.

64. Samuel Longfellow, ed., *Final Memorials of Henry Wadsworth Longfellow* (Boston: Ticknor and Company, 1887), 178–79; Thomas Wentworth Higginson, *Henry Wadsworth Longfellow* (Boston: Houghton Mifflin, 1902), 245–46; "Henry Wadsworth Longfellow," *DAB* 11:386.

65. Kaplan, *Mr. Clemens and Mark Twain,* ch. 6.

66. Ibid., 112–13.

67. HB to Samuel L. Clemens, 20 Dec. 1872, Mark Twain Papers, Bancroft Library.

68. Francis Goodwin, II, *The Monday Evening Club of Hartford, Connecticut, Its Members, and the Titles of Papers Read at Their Meetings, 1869–1970* (Hartford: Privately published, 1970).

69. Goodwin, *Monday Evening Club,* 10, 29; Kaplan, *Mr. Clemens and Mark Twain,* 146, 193, 287, 341.

70. HB to Clemens, 20 Dec. 1872, Mark Twain Papers, Bancroft Library.

71. Edith C. Salsbury, ed., *Susy and Mark Twain, Family Dialogues* (New York: Harper and Row, 1965), 275.

72. For HB as an "old Roman," see Mark Twain, *Europe and Else*

where (New York: Harper, 1923), 143; for HB as a "theological giant," see *Mark Twain's Autobiography*, with an Introduction by Albert Bigelow Paine (New York: Harper, 1924) 2:294.

73. HB, "Principles of National Greatness," 24; "Obligations to the Dead," *Building Eras*, 336.

CHAPTER 22
Not the Same City

1. HB, "Inspiration by the Holy Spirit," *Spirit in Man*, 3–4.

2. Cheney, *Bushnell*, 546.

3. HB, "Inspiration by the Holy Spirit," *The Spirit in Man*, 3–5.

4. Ibid., 7–9; Job 32:8, KJV.

5. HB, "Inspiration by the Holy Spirit," *The Spirit in Man*, 10, 15–16, 23; Cherry, *Sermons*, 25.

6. Joseph H. Twichell, Personal Journal, 1874–1918, 1:110 (26 June 1875), Twichell Collection, Yale Collection of American Literature, Beinecke Rare Book and Manuscript Library, Yale Univ.

7. Cheney, *Bushnell*, 549.

8. Ibid., 550.

9. Twichell, Personal Journal, 1:67–68 (15 Mar. 1875), Twichell Collection, Beinecke Library.

10. Ibid., 1:73 (18 Mar. 1875).

11. Cheney, *Bushnell*, 550–51.

12. Ibid., 551–52.

13. Ibid., 561.

14. HB to Cyrus A. Bartol, 31 Dec. 1875, ibid., 560.

15. Sprague to the Court of Common Council, 14 Feb. 1876, Park Records, Office of the City Clerk, Hartford; Records, Court of Common Council, (Apr. 1870–June 1878), 476 (14 Feb. 1876); Cheney, *Bushnell*, 562–63.

16. Andrews, *Nook Farm*, 41; *Hartford Times*, 17 Feb. 1876; Twichell, Journal, 2:22 (17 Feb. 1876), Twichell Collection, Beinecke Library.

17. *Hartford Courant*, 18 Feb., 11 Apr. 1876; Sarah Porter to Mary B. Cheney, 22 Feb. 1876, Learned Collection.

18. Special Resolution in honor of Bushnell, 28 Feb. 1876, Records, Hartford Court of Common Council; *Hartford Courant*, 21 Feb. 1876.

19. John Hooker, *Some Reminiscences of a Long Life, with a Few Articles on Moral and Social Subjects of Present Interest* (Hartford: Belknap and Warfield), 1899), 92.

20. Cheney, *Bushnell*, 563–65; *Hartford Courant*, 21 Feb. 1876.

EPILOG

1. *Bushnell Centenary*.

2. Daniel C. Gilman, *The Relations of Yale to Letters and Science, An Address Prepared for the Bicentennial Celebration, New Haven, Oct. 22, 1901* (Baltimore: Privately published, 1901), 22–23.

3. Theodore T. Munger, "Horace Bushnell: The Centenary of a Great Alumnus," *Yale Alumni Weekly* 11, 27 (9 Apr. 1902): 309–10.

4. Arthur H. Hughes and Morse S. Allen, *Connecticut Place Names* (Hartford: Connecticut Historical Society, 1976), 622; Cheney, *Bushnell*, 1903 ed., [Appendix] Note II.

5. Bainton, *Yale and the Ministry*, 208.

6. Nathan Farb, *The Adirondacks* (New York: Rizzoli Press, 1985), 38.

7. Arthur M. Schlesinger, Sr., "A Critical Period in American Religion," *Massachusetts Historical Society Proceedings* 64 (1930–32), 523–46.

8. For examples: Frederick Kirschenmann, "Horace Bushnell: Cells or Crustacea?" in Jerald C. Brower, ed., *Reinterpretation in American Church History* (Chicago: Univ. of Chicago Press, 1968), 67–89; Douglas, *Feminization of American Culture*, 38–39, 43, 167–68; A. David Bos, "Horace Bushnell Through His Interpreters: A Transitional and Formative Figure," *Andover Newton Quarterly* 18 (Nov. 1977), 122–32.

9. Hutchinson, *Modernist Impulse*, 81–87; Winthrop S. Hudson, *Religion in America* (1965; New York: Scribner's, 1981), 179; David E. Swift, "The Future Probation Controversy in American Congregationalism, 1886–1893" (Ph.D. diss., Yale Univ., 1947), 81–100.

10. Robert T. Handy, ed., *The Social Gospel in America, 1870–1920: Gladden, Ely, and Rauschenbusch* (New York: Oxford Univ. Press, 1966), 21–22, 255; Paul M. Minus, *Walter Rauschenbusch, American Reformer* (New York: Macmillan, 1988), 43, 187; Josiah Strong, *Our Country: Its Possible Future and Its Present Crisis* (New York: Baker and Taylor, 1885), 175–76, 182; Sidney E. Mead, *The Lively Experiment: The Shaping of Christianity in America* (New York: Harper and Row, 1963), 173; Johnson, *Bushnell*, 236–57; Duke, *Bushnell*, 1, 4.

11. John Dillenberger and Claude Welch, *Protestant Christianity Interpreted Through Its Development* (New York: Scribner's, 1954), 197; Duke, *Bushnell*, 89–93.

12. Francis E. Clark, *Worldwide Endeavor: The Story of the Young People's Society of Christian Endeavor from the Beginning and In All Lands* (Philadelphia: Gillespie, Metzgar and Kelley, 1895), 135–37.

13. George A. Gordon, *My Education and Religion: An Autobiography* (Boston: Houghton Mifflin, 1925), 63, 247, 311–12; Louise C. Wade, *Graham Taylor: Pioneer for Social Justice, 1851–1938* (Chicago: Univ. of Chicago Press, 1964), 23–26, 84; Charles T. Russ, "The Theological Views of Graham Taylor, With Reference to the Social Gospel" (Ph.D. diss., Hartford Seminary Foundation, 1964), 96, 145–47, 224; Ahlstrom, "Theology in America," 285; on Weigle, see Bainton, *Yale and the Ministry,* 246; Warren S. Archibald, *Horace Bushnell* (Hartford: Edwin Valentine Mitchell, 1930).

14. In a recollection of Bushnell in 1902, one writer told of an occasion when "three Romish priests walked into Galignani's bookstore in Paris, desiring to buy three volumes of Bushnell's sermons"; William V. Kelley, "A Preacher's Preacher," *Congregationalist and Christian World* 87, 23 (June 1902): 821.

15. Trumbull, *Religious Teachers,* 117, quoting Reuen Thomas.

16. Ibid., 114–16.

17. Stewart D. F. Salmond, "The Theology of Horace Bushnell," *London Quarterly Review* 95, N.S. 5 (Jan.–Apr. 1901): 140, 144; Robert S. Paul, *The Atonement and the Sacraments* (New York: Abingdon, 1960), 149ff.

18. HB, "Christian Comprehensiveness," *Building Eras,* 398–400.

19. R. W. B. Lewis, *The American Adam: Innocence, Tragedy and Tradition in the Nineteenth Century* (Chicago: Univ. of Chicago Press, 1955), 7–8.

20. Harry S. Stout, *The New England Soul: Preaching and Religious Culture in Colonial New England* (New York: Oxford Univ. Press, 1986), 316.

21. Quoted in Ahlstrom, "Horace Bushnell," *Handbook of Christian Theologians,* 44.

22. Thomas, "My Week with Bushnell," 814.

23. Matt. 13:52, NRSV.

24. Boardman W. Kathan, "Outstanding Books in Christian Education," *Reflection* (Yale Divinity School) 78, 3 (Apr. 1981).

25. Hudson, *Religion in America,* 177.

26. Cf. Frank H. Foster, *A Genetic History of The New England Theology* (1907; New York: Garland, 1987), 404: "Bushnell's first and greatest contribution to the world of thought was himself. " This judgment is repeated in scores of tributes extending over many years.

27. Bishop Thomas M. Clark, Cheney, *Bushnell*, 298.

28. Laura H. Moseley, ed., *Diary of James Hadley, Tutor and Professor of Greek in Yale College, 1845–1872* (New Haven: Yale Univ. Press, 1951), 305.

29. HB, "Pulpit Manward," *Building Eras*, 245.

30. Ibid., *Building Eras*, 247–48.

Bibliography

BIBLIOGRAPHICAL NOTE

Any Bushnell bibliographer must be deeply indebted to the bibliographies of works by and about Horace Bushnell compiled by Henry Barrett Learned in *Horace Bushnell, The Spirit in Man* (New York: Scribner's, 1903), and by James O. Duke in his *Horace Bushnell on the Vitality of Biblical Language* (Chico, Calif.: Scholars Press, 1984). No attempt is made to duplicate these definitive compilations here, though I have borrowed somewhat from their format. In listing manuscript collections, I also have borrowed the pattern used by Robin W. Winks of Yale University in his definitive biography of Bushnell's friend Frederick Billings, *Frederick Billings, A Life* (New York: Oxford Univ. Press, 1991). Bushnell's sermons, addresses, and articles subsequently included in his published works are not listed separately; they are cited in detail in the endnotes.

No substantial collection of Bushnell papers is known to have survived. His will directed that, with few exceptions, his wife was to burn his manuscripts. Aside from the fact that he could think of no other way to dispose of them, he was fearful that "transitional and generally undigested" material might be misinterpreted by those who came after him and "weaken me in things published" (Last Will and Testament, 11 June 1875, Probate Court Records, 94:267–68, Hartford).

Although Theodore Munger unaccountably says otherwise (*Bushnell*, 135), Bushnell was an active, quotable correspondent all his years. Yet here again, no major collection of letters remains. As to those he wrote, Mrs. Bushnell and her daughters saw to it that some were saved. This makes Mary Bushnell Cheney's biography of her father, *Life and Letters of Horace Bushnell* (New York: Harper, 1880), not only a biographical narrative, but an indispensable source book. Thanks to the Learneds and with the cooperation of libraries across the country, several hundred unpublished Bushnell letters, and letters written by members of his family, also have sur-faced. These often-intimate communications help make him more acces-sible, shedding light on his private life, on his public activities, and occasion-ally on his thinking.

As to letters he received, we have no way of knowing how many he kept. In the absence of evidence to the contrary, we can only assume that they have been almost entirely lost, a tragedy for the annals of New England church history. In general we are left to surmise what they said from what the Doctor wrote in reply.

One of the quirks in Bushnell's nature was that he had no high regard for institutional libraries (Cheney, *Bushnell,* 533). Nevertheless, his personal li-brary seems to have been quite large and was essentially intact at least until the 1960s (Johnson, *Theology of Horace Bushnell,* 7). Unfortunately it now seems to have been dispersed, depriving us of important detailed knowledge as to how extensive his reading was, not only of such classic theologians as Anselm, Luther, Calvin, Baxter, Edwards, or Schliermacher, but also of his-tory, the new science, current periodicals, the work of contemporary English preachers,and American literature. He makes so few references to it, that it would be interesting to know, for example, whether or not he had a copy of Harriet Beecher Stowe's *Uncle Tom's Cabin* on his shelves, and whether he made any marginal notations in it. We know he at least half-heartedly read John Stuart Mill's *Subjection of Women,* but we are left to wonder whether he ever owned Darwin's *Origin of Species,* or how thor-oughly he was acquainted with it.

Quite clearly his reading was wider than it was deep. Beyond that, lack of access to the volumes he used, or to any systematic record of them, often leaves us in the dark as to the extent of many of his intellectual journeys.

PRIMARY SOURCES

Bushnell's Major Works
(Chronological)

Discourses on Christian Nurture. Boston: Massachusetts Sabbath School Society, 1847.
Views of Christian Nurture and of Subjects Adjacent Thereto. 1847. Rpt.

Bibliography

ed. Philip B. Eppard. Delmar, N.Y.: Scholars' Facsimiles and Reprints, 1975.

God in Christ, Three Discourses, Delivered at New Haven, Cambridge, and Andover, With a Preliminary Dissertation on Language. Hartford: Brown and Parsons, 1849.

Christ in Theology; Being the Answer of the Author, Before the Hartford Central Association of Ministers, Oct., 1849, for the Doctrines of the Book Entitled "God in Christ." 1851. New York: Garland, 1987.

Sermons for the New Life. New York: Scribner, 1858.

Nature and the Supernatural, as Together Constituting One System of God. New York: Scribner, 1858.

The Character of Jesus: Forbidding His Possible Classification with Men. New York: Scribner, 1860. Reprint. New York: AMS Press, 1973.

Christian Nurture. 1860. New Haven: Yale Univ. Press, 1947.

Work and Play; or Literary Varieties. New York: Scribner, 1864. 2nd ed., New York: Scribner's, 1903.

Christ and His Salvation: In Sermons Variously Related Thereto. New York: Scribner, 1864.

The Vicarious Sacrifice, Grounded in Principles of Universal Obligation. New York: Scribner, 1866.

Moral Uses of Dark Things. New York: Scribner, 1868.

Women's Suffrage: The Reform Against Nature. New York: Scribner, 1869.

Sermons on Living Subjects. New York: Scribner, Armstrong, 1872.

Forgiveness and Law, Grounded in Principles Interpreted by Human Analogies. New York: Scribner, Armstrong, 1874. Republished, with Supplementary Notes, as *Vicarious Sacrifice* Vol. 2. New York: Charles Scribner, 1877.

Building Eras in Religion, Literary Varieties III. New York: Scribner's, 1881.

The Spirit in Man: Sermons and Selections. New York: Scribner's, 1903.

Bushnell Sermons, Addresses, and Articles
Not Included in His Books
(Chronological)

"Crisis of the Church." Hartford: Daniel Burgess, 1835.

"Discourse on the Slavery Question, Delivered in the North Church, Hartford, Thursday Evening, 10 January 1839." Hartford: Case, Tiffany, 1839.

"Revelation." Address at Andover Seminary, 1839. Transcript in David S. Steward, "Horace Bushnell and Contemporary Christian Education." Ph.D. diss., Yale Univ., 1966. 308–35.

"American Politics." *American National Preacher* 14, 12 (Dec. 1840): 189–204.

"Common Schools in Cities: City of Hartford, Annual Report of the Board of School Visitors of the First School Society,... Report of the Sub-Committee on the Reorganization of the City Districts, Rev. H[orace] Bushnell, Chairman." *Connecticut Common School Journal* 4, 1 (1 Dec. 1841): 7–13.

"Politics Under the Law of God, A Discourse Delivered in the North Congregational Church, Hartford." Hartford: Edwin Hunt, 1844.

"Review of [Thomas C Bownell's] *The Errors of the Times,*" *New Englander* 2 (Jan. 1844): 143–75.

"Reply to Dr. Taylor." (Signed "Constans.") *Christian Freeman*, Dec. 12, 1844.

Letter on the Oregon Question, Addressed to the Editor of the *London Universe,* Mar. 3, 1846, signed "An American." Reprinted in *Religious Herald,* 4 Apr. 1846.

"Littera al Romano Pontifice, di Orazio Bushnell, Dottore di Teologia di Hartford, Stati Uniti d'America." In *Sulle Attuali Condizioni della Romagna, di Gino Capponi; La Questione Italiana, di M. Canuti; Littera al Romano Pontifice, di Orazio Bushnell, Dottore di Teologia di Hartford, Stati Uniti d'America,* ed. Gino A. G. G. Capponi. Italy, 1846.

"The Evangelical Alliance." *New Englander* 5, 1 (Jan. 1847): 102–25.

"Twentieth Anniversary: A Commemorative Discourse... May 22, 1853." Hartford: Elihu Geer, 1853.

Report of the Committee Concerning the Proposed Public Park, to the Honorable, the Court of Common Council of the City of Hartford, 14 Nov. 1853.

"The Northern Iron, A Discourse Delivered in the North Church of Hartford, on the Annual State Fast, Apr. 14, 1854." Hartford: Edwin Hunt, 1854.

"Society and Religion, A Sermon for California, Delivered on Sabbath Evening, July 6, 1856, at the Installation of Rev. E. S. Lacy as Pastor of the First Congregational Church, San Francisco." Hartford: L. E. Hunt, 1856.

Bibliography

"Movement for a University in California: A Statement to the Public by the Trustees of the College of California, and an Appeal by Dr. Bushnell." San Francisco: Pacific Publishing Co., 1857.

"Thanksgiving for Kansas." Sermon delivered in the North Church, Hartford, 26 Nov. 1857. *Hartford Evening Press,* 30 Nov 1857.

"California, Its Characteristics and Prospects." *New Englander* 16, 1 (Feb. 1858): 142–82.

"Parting Words: A Discourse Delivered in the North Church, Hartford, July 3, 1859." Hartford: L. E. Hunt, 1859.

"The Census and Slavery: A Thanksgiving Discourse Delivered in the Chapel at Clifton Springs, New York, Nov. 29, 1860." Hartford: L. E. Hunt, 1860.

"Science and Religion." *Putnam's Magazine* 1, 3 (Mar. 1868): 265–75.

"Hartford Park." *Hearth and Home* 1, 6 (6 Feb. 1869): 101–2.

"A Series on the Subject of Prayer." *Advance* 4 (1871–72). Reprinted as "Bushnell on Prayer." *Chicago Theological Seminary Register* 80, 1 (Winter 1990): 1–58.

"Free Trade and Protection." *Scribner's Monthly* 2, 3 (July 1871): 266–73.

"The Conflagration—Letter from Dr. Bushnell." *Advance* 5 (16 Nov. 1871): 219.

"The Capitol Site." *Hartford Courant,* 8 Jan. 1872.

Manuscript Sources

Permission to make use of these manuscript materials has been granted by the respective libraries and other owners of collections.

California
University Archives, Bancroft Library, University of California, Berkeley
   Day Family Collection
   Edward B. Walsworth Collection
   Records of the President of the University
   Records of the Trustees, College of California, 1855–1861
   Samuel Clemens (Mark Twain) Papers
Connecticut
Bushnell Memorial Hall, Hartford
   Bushnell Correspondence
   Bushnell Family Materials

Bibliography

Bushnell Manuscript Sermons
Connecticut Conference, Archives, United Church of Christ Conference Center, Hartford
    Association Records, Congregational Churches
    Minutes, Consociation of Eastern District, Fairfield County
    Minutes, Annual Meetings, General Association of Connecticut, 1834–1856.
Connecticut Historical Society, Hartford
    Diary of Samuel Pease
    Gideon Welles Collection
    Henry Barnard Collection
    Horace Bushnell Collection
    Mary B. Cheney Collection of Family Records
    Spencer Family Collection
Connecticut State Library, Hartford
    Lucius B. Barbour Collection of Connecticut Vital Records
    Horace Bushnell–Walter Burnham Correspondence
    "Connecticut State Capitol," General Reference Unit, Vertical File
    Criminal Records, Superior Court, Hartford County, State of Connecticut v. Albert L. Starkweather, 5 Sept. 1865
    Divorce Records, Superior Court, Litchfield County, 1752–1922
    Land Records, Towns of Litchfield and Washington
    Records, North Congregational Church, Hartford
    Register, Hartford Public High School
    Scrapbooks, Pearl Street, Park, and Immanuel Congregational Churches, Hartford
Office of the City Clerk, Hartford
    Hartford Land Records
    Hartford Tax Records
    Minutes of the Court of Common Council
    Records of the City Park and Bushnell Park
Office of the Probate Court, City of Hartford
    Last Will and Testament of Horace Bushnell
Hartford Seminary Library, Hartford
    Horace Bushnell Collection
    Augustus C. Thompson Collection
Horace Bushnell Learned and Eileen R. Learned Collection, West Hartford
    Horace Bushnell Correspondence
    Bushnell Documents

Bushnell Family Correspondence
Mary Bushnell Cheney Correspondence
Town of Litchfield, Vital Records, Town Hall
Stowe-Day Foundation Library, Hartford
    Annotated Isabella Beecher Hooker copy of HB, *Women's Suffrage*
    Jared B. Flagg, Autobiogaphy
    Joseph K. Hooker Collection
    Seymour Collection
    White Collection
Wesleyan University Archives, Olin Library, Middletown
    Minutes, Cuvierian Society
    Minutes, Trustees, Wesleyan University
Trinity College Library, Hartford
    Trinity College Archives
Unitarian Society of Hartford
    Charles Graves Collection
Beinecke Rare Book and Manuscript Library, Yale Collection of American
    Literature, Yale University
    Jeremiah Day Collection
    Donald G. Mitchell Collection
    Joseph H. Twichell Personal Journal, 1874–1918, Twichell Collection
Yale Divinity School Library, Yale Univ., Horace Bushnell Papers, Special
    Collections
    Bushnell's United States Patents
    European Journal
    Manuscript Sermons and Discourses
Sterling Memorial Library, Yale University
    Map Collections
Manuscripts and Archives, Sterling Memorial Library, Yale University
    Bacon Family Collection
    Blake Family Collection
    George J. Brush Collection
    Enoch F. Burr Collecction
    Horace Bushnell Collection
    Day Family Collection
    Josiah W. Gibbs Collection
    Chauncey A. Goodrich Collection
    William L. Kingsley Collection
    Theodore T. Munger Collection

Theodore D. Woolsey Collection

Records, Brothers in Unity, Yale College
Records, Church of Christ at Yale College
Franklin B. Dexter Secretarial Records
Faculty Records, Yale College
Records, Student Petitions and Riots, Yale College
Ralph D. Smith, History of Yale Class of 1827
Catalogs, Yale College, 1823–1827
Yale College Commencement Excersises, 1827
Illinois
Schewe Library, Illinois College, Jacksonville
    Archives, Illinois College
    Julian M. Sturtevant–Theron Baldwin Correspondence
Massachusetts
Andover-Harvard Theological Library, Cambridge
    Edmund Hamilton Sears Collection
Andover Newton Theological School, Franklin Trask Library, Newton
    Center
    Minutes, Porter Rhetorical Society
Congregational Library, Boston
    Records, Massachusetts Sabbath School Society
Forbes Library, Northampton
    Letters and Papers of the Northampton Young Men's Institute
Houghton Library, Harvard University
    Autograph File
    James Freeman Clarke Collection
    Edwin L. Godkin Collection
    James Family Collection
    Henry W. Longfellow Collection
    Charles E. Norton Collection
Harvard University Archives, Nathan Pusey Library
    Horace Bushnell Dudleian Lecture, 1852
    Harvard College Papers
    Harvard Corporation Records
Massachusetts Historical Society, Boston
    Henry W. Bellows Collection
    Edward Everett Collection
    Washburn Autograph Collection

Arthur and Elizabeth Schlesinger Library on the History of Women in
   America, Cambridge
   Beecher Family Collection
   Beecher-Stowe Collection
Smith College Library, Northampton
   Sara Payson Willis Parton Papers, Sophia Smith Collection
Minnesota
Minnesota Historical Society, St. Paul
   John Barnard Phillips Collection
   Alexander Ramsey Collection
Missouri
Washington University Libraries, St. Louis
   Horace Scudder Collection
Eden Theological Seminary Archives and Library, St. Louis
   Diary of Johann Georg Joseph Anton Rieger
New Jersey
Firestone Library, Princeton University
   Alexander Autograph Collection
   Charles Hodge Collection
   Charles Scribners' Sons Collection
New York
Cornell University Library, Division of Rare and Manuscript Collections,
   Ithaca
   Bayard Taylor Collection
   Moses Coit Tyler Collection
Fales Library, New York University
   Henry Barnard Collection
Monroe County Records, Rochester
   Index of Deeds, Office of County Clerk
   Probate Records, Surrogate's Office
New York Public Library
   New York City Census Records (1850), 15th Ward, Manahattan
Ohio
Oberlin College Library, Oberlin
   Henry Cowles Collection
   Charles G. Finney Collection
Ohio Historical Society, Columbus
   Washington Gladden Collection

Bibliography

Vermont
Billings Mansion Archives, Woodstock
   Horace Bushnell to Frederick Billings, Correspondence
Washington, D.C.
Library of Congress, Manuscripts Division
   Journal of John Olmsted
National Archives
   Military Archives, Service Branch
England
Public Record Office, Kew, Richmond
   Logs of British Naval Vessels, 1845

Diaries and Letters

Learned, Eileen R., ed. *The Letters of Mary Bushnell Cheney and Frank Woodbridge Cheney*. Hartford: Privately published, 1988.

Longfellow, Samuel, ed. *Life of Henry Wadsworth Longfellow, with Extracts from His Journals and Correspondence*. 2 vols. Boston: Ticknor, 1886.

Moseley, Laura H., ed. *Diary (1843–1852) of James Hadley, Tutor and Professor of Greek in Yale College, 1845–1872*. New Haven: Yale Univ. Press, 1951.

Myers, Robert M., ed. *Children of Pride: A True Story of Georgia and the Civil War*. New Haven: Yale Univ. Press, 1972.

Olmsted, Frederick L. *Walks and Talks of an American Farmer in England in the Years 1850–51*. 2 vols. New York: Putnam, 1852.

Rosell, Garth M., and Richard A. G. Dupuis, eds. *The Memoirs of Charles G. Finney: The Complete Restored Text*. Grand Rapids, Mich. : Zondervan, 1989.

Tarbox, Increase N., ed. *Diary of Thomas Robbins, D. D., 1796–1854*. 2 vols. Boston: Beacon Press, 1886.

Woodward, C. Vann, ed. *Mary Chesnut's Civil War*. New Haven: Yale Univ. Press, 1981.

Newspapers

Advance (Congregational, Chicago)
The Calendar (Episcopal, Hartford)
The Christian Freeman (Hartford)

Bibliography

The Christian Register (Unitarian, Boston)
The Christian Secretary (Baptist, Hartford)
The Christian Union (New York)
The Congregationalist (Boston)
Daily California Chronicle (San Francisco)
Hartford Courant
Hartford Evening Press
Hartford Times
The Independent (New York)
New England Puritan (Boston)
New England Religious Herald (Hartford)
New Haven Evening Register
New York Evangelist (Congregational)
New York Journal of Commerce
Ohio Observer
The Pacific (Congregational, San Francisco)
Puritan Recorder (Congregational, Boston)
The Recorder (Congregational, Boston)
Supplement to the Connecticut [Hartford] Courant
Weekly Messenger of the German Reformed Church (Mercersburg, Pa.)
Newspapers of the day often reprinted full excerpts from other papers across the country. This adds to the press coverage given by the above publications.

Public Documents

Congressional Globe, 33d Cong., 1st sess., vol. 28, pt. 2. Washington, D.C.: Rives, 1854.
Connecticut Register and U.S. Calendar . . . 1821 to 1836. New London, Conn.: Samuel Green, 1821–36.
Map of Berkeley, California. Berkeley: Mason-McDuffie, 1911.
Map of Oakland, Berkeley, Alameda and Piedmont. Oakland: Bekins Van and Storage, 1924.
Nell, L. *Topographical Railroad and County Map of the States of California and Nevada.* New York: A. C. Frey, 1868.
Public Acts of the State of Connecticut, May session, 1953. Hartford: Alfred E. Burr, 1853.
Records of Connecticut Men in the War of the Rebellion of 1861–1865.

Hartford: Adjutant General's Office, 1889.

State of Connecticut. *Register and Manual, 1869.* Hartford: 1969.

United States Coast and Geodetic Survey. *San Francisco Entrance, California.* #5581. Aug. 1884.

Works by Bushnell's Contemporaries

1828

Taylor, Nathaniel W. "*Concio ad Clerum.*" In *Theology in America,* by Sydney E. Ahlstrom. Indianapolis: Bobbs-Merrill, 1867.

1829

Coleridge, Samuel Taylor. *Aids to Reflection, In the Formation of a Manly Character . . . Preliminary Essay, and Additional Notes by James Marsh.* Burlington, Vt.: Chauncey Goodrich, 1829.

1835

Beecher, Lyman. "Plea for the West." Cincinnati: Truman and Smith, 1835.

Schleiermacher, Friedrich E. D. "On the Discrepancy Between the Sabellian and Athanasian Method of Representing the Doctrine of the Trinity." Trans. with notes by Moses Stuart. *Biblical Repository and Quarterly Observer* 5 (Apr. 1835): 265–353; and 6 (July 1835): 1–116.

1838

"[Review of] An Oration by Mr. Horace Bushnell, Pronounced Before the Society of Phi Beta Kappa at New Haven, Aug. 15, 1837." *North American Review* 46, 98 (Jan. 1838): 301–2.

1839

Gillette, Francis. *A Review of Rev. Horace Bushnell's "Discourse on The Slavery Question," Delivered in the North Church, Hartford, Jan. 10, 1839.* Hartford: S. S. Cowles, 1839.

Bibliography

1843

Catholicus [pseud.]. *A Letter to Dr. Bushnell, of Hartford, on the Rationalistic, Socinian, and Infidel Tendency of Certain Passages in His Address before the Alumni of Yale College.* Hartford: H. S. Parsons, 1843.

1847

[Hodge, Charles.] "Bushnell on Christian Nurture." *Biblical Repertory and Princeton Review* N.S. 19 Oct. 1847, 502–39.

Nevin, John W. "Educational Religion." *Weekly Messenger of the German Reformed Church* N.S. 12 (23, 30 June, 7, 14 July, 11, 25 Aug., and 1 Sept. 1847).

Porter, Noah, Jr. "The New Theological Controversy" and "Bushnell on Christian Nurture." *New Englander* 5, 4 (Oct. 1847): 613–14.

Tyler, Bennet. *Dr. Tyler's Letter to Dr. Bushnell.* East Windsor Hill: Massachusetts Sabbath School Society, 1847.

1848

Porter, Noah, Jr. "Bushnell on Christian Nurture." *New Englander* 6, 1 (Jan. 1848): 121–47.

Tyler, Bennet. *Letters to the Rev. Dr. Horace Bushnell, D.D., Containing Strictures on His Book, Entitled "Views of Christian Nurture, and Subjects Adjacent Thereto."* Hartford: Brown and Parsons, 1848.

1849

[Leonard Bacon.] "[Review of] *God in Christ* . . . , by Horace Bushnell; Review of *Dr. Bushnell's Theories of Incarnation and Atonement* . . . , by Robert Turnbull; 'What Does Dr. Bushnell Mean?'—from the *New York Evangelist.*" *New Englander* 7, N.S. 2 (May 1849): 324–26.

Brownson, Orestes A. "Bushnell's Discourses." *Brownson's Quarterly Review* 1849–51. In *The Works of Orestes A. Brownson* . . . , edited by Henry F. Brownson. New York: AMS Press, 1966.

[Chesebrough, Amos S.] *Contributions of CC: Now Declared in Full as Criticus Criticorum.* Hartford: Brown and Parsons, 1849.

Bibliography

Goodwin, Henry M. "Thoughts, Words and Things." *Bibliotheca Sacra* 6, 22 (May 1849): 271–300.

[Hodge, Charles.] "Bushnell's Discourses: Review of *God in Christ*, by Horace Bushnell." *Biblical Repertory and Princeton Review* 21, 2 (Apr. 1849): 259–98.

Minutes of the General Association of Connecticut, at their Meeting in Salisbury, June, 1849. New Haven: J. H. Benham, 1849. *Minutes* for 1849–54 is a basic source for Bushnell's years of controversy.

[Morison, J. H.] "Bushnell's Discourses." *Christian Examiner and Religious Miscellany* 46, 11 (Sept. 1849): 453–84; and 47, 12 (Dec. 1849): 238–47.

Omicron [Chauncey A. Goodrich]. *What Does Dr. Bushnell Mean? New York Evangelist*. Hartford: Case, Tiffany, 1849.

Pond, Enoch. *Review of Dr. Bushnell's "God in Christ."* Bangor, Maine: E. F. Duren, 1849.

Records, Hartford Central and Fairfield West Associations, 1849, Archives, Connecticut Conference, United Church of Christ, Hartford. (Records for these Associations, Tolland, New Haven East and West, Middlesex, etc., also basic sources for Bushnell's years of controversy.)

"Review of *God in Christ*." *Christian Observatory* 3, 6 (June 1849): 240–300.

"Review of *God in Christ*, by Horace Bushnell." *Methodist Quarterly Review* 1, 12 (Apr. 1849): 329–30.

Turnbull, Robert. *Review of Dr. Bushnell's Theories of the Incarnation and Atonement (A Supplement to "Theophany")*. Hartford: Brockett, Fuller, 1849.

1850

Park, Edwards A. "Theology of the Intellect and That of the Feelings." *Bibliotheca Sacra and Theological Review* 7 (July 1850): 553–69.

Remonstrance and Complaint of the Association of Fairfield West to the Hartford Central Association, Together with the Reply of the Hartford Central Association. New York: Benedict, 1850.

1851

Kilbourne, Payne K. *A Biographical History of Litchfield County, Connecticut*. New York: Clark, Austin, 1851.

"Review of *Christ in Theology* by Horace Bushnell." *New Englander* 9, 2 (May 1851): 310–11.

Stowe, Harriet Beecher. *Uncle Tom's Cabin, or Life Among the Lowly.* 1851–52. New York: New American Library, 1966.

1852

Appeal of the Association of Fairfield West, to the Associated Ministers Connected with the General Association of Connecticut. New York, 1852.

1854

A Protest of the Pastoral Union to the Pastors and Churches of Connecticut. Wethersfield, Conn. [?], 1854 [?].

1857

S[amuel] G. Goodrich. *Recollections of a Lifetime, or Men and Things I have seen...* New York: Miller, Orton and Mulligan, 1857.

Tyler, Bennet. "An Address to the Alumni of the Theological Institute of Connecticut, Delivered July 15, 1857." Hartford: Case, Lockwood, 1857.

1859

[Bartol, Cyrus A.] "Dr. Bushnell and Dr. Furness: A Question of Words and Names." *Christian Examiner* 66, 4 (Jan.–May 1859): 112–24.

Dana, James D. "Anticipations of Man in Nature: Review of Chapter VII of *Nature and the Supernatural,* by Horace Bushnell." *New Englander* 17, 2 (May 1859), 293–334.

Goodwin, Henry M. "Dr. Bushnell's *Sermons for the New Life.*" *New Englander* 17, 2 (May 1859): 382–99.

Lord, David N. "Dr. Bushnell's *Nature and the Supernatural.*" *Theological and Literary Journal* 11, 4 (Jan. 1859): 529–76.

Nevin, John W. "Notice of *Nature and the Supernatural,* by Horace Bushnell." *Mercersburg Review* (Apr. 1859).

[Park, Edwards A.] "Review of *Nature and the Supernatural.*" *Bibliotheca Sacra and Biblical Repository* 16, 2 (Apr. 1859): 426–37.

Bibliography

Porter, Noah, Jr. "*Nature and the Supernatural.*" *New Englander* 17, 1 (Feb. 1859): 256–57.

"Review of *Nature and the Supernatural,* by Horace Bushnell." *Biblical Repository and Princeton Review* 31, 1 (Jan. 1859): 153–56.

Taylor, Nathaniel W. *Essays, Lectures, Etc. Upon Select Topics in Revealed Theology.* 1859. New York: Garland, 1987.

1861

Goodwin, Henry M. "Dr. Bushnell's *Christian Nurture.*" *New Englander* 19, 2 (Apr. 1861): 519.

1863

Chase, Irah. *Infant Baptism, Bushnell's Arguments Reviewed.* Philadelphia: American Baptist Publication Society, 1863.

1866

Andrews, W[illiam] W. *Remarks on Dr. Bushnell's "Vicarious Sacrifice."* Hartford: Case, Lockwood, 1866.

[Clarke, James F.] "Bushnell on Vicarious Sacrifice." *Christian Examiner* N.S. 80 (May 1866): 360–77.

Fowler, Charles H. "Bushnell's *Vicarious Sacrifice.*" *Methodist Quarterly Review* 43, 18 (July 1866): 350–70.

James, Henry, Sr. "Review of *Vicarious Sacrifice.*" *North American Review* 102 (Apr. 1866): 556–71.

Porter, Noah, Jr. "Review of Dr. Bushnell's *The Vicarious Sacrifice.*" *New Englander* 25, 2 (Apr. 1866): 228–82.

1869

James, William. "1. *Women's Suffrage; the Reform Against Nature.* By Horace Bushnell. 2. *The Subjection of Women,* by John Stuart Mill." *North American Review* 109 (Oct. 1869): 556–65.

Bibliography

1873

Hoppin, James M. "Bushnell's *Sermons on Living Subjects, New Englander*
31, 1 (Jan. 1873): 95–109.

1876

Phelps, Austin. "A Vacation with Dr. Bushnell." *Christian Union* 14 (9 July
1876): 24; and 14 (19 July 1876): 47–48.

1877

Porter, Noah, Jr. "Horace Bushnell, A Memorial Sermon." *New Englander*
36, 1 (Jan. 1877): 153–54

SECONDARY SOURCES

Background Works

Abbott, John S. C. *South and North, or Impressions Recieved During a Trip
to Cuba and the South.* New York: Abbey and Abbott, 1860.
Ahlstrom, Sydney E. *Theology in America.* Indianapolis: Bobbs-Merrill,
1967.
Alexopoulos, John. *The Nineteenth Century Parks of Hartford: A Legacy
to the Nation.* Hartford: Hartford Architecture Conservancy, 1983.
Beecher, Henry Ward. *Sermons.* New York: Harper, 1868.
Brown, Jerry W. *The Rise of Biblical Criticism in America, 1800–1870:
The New England Scholars.* Middletown, Conn.: Wesleyan Univ. Press,
1969.
Burr, Nelson R. *A Critical Bibliography of Religion in America.* Religion in
American Life. Ed. James W. Smith and A. Leland Jamison. Princeton:
Princeton Univ. Press, 1961.
Burton, Richard E., ed. *Yale Lectures on Preaching, and Other Writings, by
Nathaniel J. Burton.* New York: Charles L. Webster, 1888.
Butterfield, Roger. *The American Past: A History of the United States from
Concord to the Nuclear Age.* New York: Simon and Schuster, 1947.
Caskey, Marie. *Chariot of Fire: Religion and the Beecher Family.* New
Haven: Yale Univ. Press, 1978.

Bibliography

Catholic Encyclopaedia for School and Home. New York: McGraw Hill, 1965.

Channing, William E. *A Selection from the Works of William E. Channing, D. D.* Boston: American Unitarian Association, 1855.

Dictionary of American Biography. 20 vols. Ed. Allen Johnson and Dumas Malone. New York: Scribner's, 1928–36.

Donnelly, Mabel C. *The American Victorian Woman: The Myth and the Reality.* New York: Greenwood Press, 1986.

Douglas, Ann. *The Feminization of American Culture.* 1977. New York: Avon Books, 1978.

Dulles, Avery. *Models of Revelation.* Garden City, N.Y: Doubleday, 1983.

Edwards, Jonathan. *The Works of President Edwards* 8 vols. Worcester, Mass.: Isaiah Thomas, 1809.

Emerson, Ralph Waldo. *The Complete Works of Ralph Waldo Emerson.* 12 vols. Boston: Houghton, Mifflin, 1903.

Fairburn, William A. *Merchant Sail.* 6 vols. Center Lovell, Maine: Fairburn Educational Foundation, 1945–1955.

Ferm, Vergilius, ed. *Classics of Protestantism.* New York: Philosophical Library, 1959.

Foerster, Norman, and Robert M. Lovett, eds. *American Poetry and Prose.* Boston: Houghton Mifflin, 1934.

Forell, George W., ed. *Christian Social Teachings: A Reader in Christian Social Ethics from the Bible to the Present.* 1966. Minneapolis: Augsburg, 1971.

Greven, Philip. *The Protestant Temperament: Patterns of Child-Rearing, Religious Experience, and the Self in Early America.* New York: New American Library, 1979.

Hughes, Arthur H., and Morse S. Allen. *Connecticut Place Names.* Hartford: Connecticut Historical Society, 1976.

Hutchinson, William R. *The Modernist Impulse in American Protestantism.* Cambridge: Harvard Univ. Press, 1976.

Langdon, William C. *Everyday Things in American Life, 1776– 1876.* New York: Scribner's, 1941.

Luccock, Halford E. "The Gospel According to Mark." In *The Interpreter's Bible.* New York: Abingdon-Cokesbury, 1951.

May, Henry F. *Protestant Churches and Industrial America.* New York: Harper, 1949.

Miller, Randolph C. *The Theory of Christian Education Practice: How*

Bibliography

Theology Affects Christian Education. Birmingham: Religious Education Press, 1980.

Nichols, James H. *Romanticism in American Theology: Nevin and Schaff at Mercersburg.* Chicago: Univ. of Chicago Press, 1961.

——, ed. *The Mercersburg Theology.* New York: Oxford, 1966.

Rossi, Alice S., ed. *Essays on Sex Equality [by] John Stuart Mill and Harriet Taylor Mill.* Chicago: Univ. of Chicago Press, 1970.

Russ, Charles T. "The Theological Views of Graham Taylor, With Reference to the Social Gospel." Ph.D. diss., Hartford Seminary Foundation, 1964.

Stansell, Christine. *City of Women: Sex and Class in New York, 1789–1860.* New York: Knopf, 1986.

Stout, Harry S. *The New England Soul: Preaching and Religious Culture in Colonial New England.* New York: Oxford Univ. Press, 1986.

Strong, Josiah. *Our Country: Its Possible Future and Its Present Crisis.* New York: Baker and Taylor, 1885.

Tinder, Glenn. *The Political Meaning of Christianity.* Baton Rouge: Louisiana State Univ. Press, 1989.

Walker, Williston. *Creeds and Platforms of Congregationalism.* 1893. Boston: Pilgrim Press, 1960.

Welch, Claude. *Protestant Thought in the Nineteenth Century.* Vol. 1. 1799–1870. New Haven: Yale Univ. Press, 1972.

Genealogies

Bradley, Leonard A. *Descendants of Isaac Bradley of Branford and East Haven, Connecticut, 1650–1898.* New York: Privately published, 1917.

Bushnell, George E. *Bushnell Family Genealogy: Ancestry and Posterity of Francis Bushnell (1588–1646) of Horsham, England, and Guilford, Connecticut.* Nashville: Privately published, 1945.

Chapman, Frederick W. *The Chapman Family.* Hartford: Case, Tiffany, 1854.

Cheney, Mary Bushnell. *Life and Letters of Horace Bushnell, With Portraits and Illustrations.* New York: Harpers, 1880; Scribner's, 1903.

Cone, William W., and George A. Root. *Record of the Descendants of John Bishop, One of the Founders of Guilford, Connecticut in 1639.* Nyack, N.Y.: Privately published, 1951.

Crocker, Antoinette C. *Great Oaks: Memoirs of the Cheney Family.* Concord, Mass.: Privately published, 1977.

Ferris, Mary W. *Dawes-Gates Ancestral Lines.* 2 vols. Privately published, 1943.

Nelson, Martha E. E. *Record of the Descendants of James Ensign and His Wife Sarah Elson, 1643–1939–1960.* Privately published, 1960.

Books on Bushnell's Theology

Cherry, Conrad, ed. *God's New Israel: Religious Interpretations of American Destiny.* Englewood Cliffs, N.J.: Prentice-Hall, 1971.

——. *Horace Bushnell: Sermons.* Sources of American Spirituality. New York: Paulist Press, 1985.

——. *Nature and the Religious Imagination, from Edwards to Bushnell.* Philadelphia: Fortress Press, 1980.

Crosby, Donald A. "Horace Bushnell's Theory of Language: An Historical and Philosophical Study." Ph.D. diss., Columbia Univ., 1962.

Duke, James O. *Horace Bushnell on the Vitality of Biblical Language.* Chico, Calif.: Scholars Press, 1984.

Foster, Frank H. *A Genetic History of New England Theology.* 1907. New York: Garland, 1987.

Johnson, William A. *Nature and the Supernatural in the Theology of Horace Bushnell.* Lund, Sweden: CWK Gleerup, 1963.

Lewis, R. W. B. *The American Adam: Innocence, Tragedy, and Tradition in the Nineteenth Century.* Chicago: Univ. of Chicago Press, 1955.

Paul, Robert S. *The Atonement and the Sacraments.* New York: Abingdon, 1960.

Smith, David L. *Symbolism and Growth: The Religious Thought of Horace Bushnell.* Chico, Calif.: Scholars Press, 1981.

——, ed. *Horace Bushnell: Selected Writings on Language, Religion, and American Culture.* Chico, Calif.: Scholars Press, 1984.

Smith, H. Shelton, ed. *Horace Bushnell.* New York: Oxford Univ. Press, 1965.

Steward, David S. "Horace Bushnell and Contemporary Christian Education: A Study of Revelation and Nuture." Ph.D. diss., Yale Univ., 1966.

Bushnell Biographies

Adamson, William R. *Bushnell Rediscovered.* Philadelphia: United Church Press, 1966.

Bibliography

Archibald, Warren. *Horace Bushnell*. Hartford: Edwin Valentine Mitchell, 1930.

Cheney, Mary Bushnell. *Life and Letters of Horace Bushnell*. New York: Harpers, 1880; Scribner's, 1903.

Cross, Barbara M. *Horace Bushnell: Minister to a Changing America*. Chicago: Univ. of Chicago Press, 1958.

Munger, Theodore T. *Horace Bushnell: Preacher and Theologian*. Boston: Houghton Mifflin, 1899.

General Biographies and Autobiographies

Albright, Raymond W. *Focus on Infinity: A Life of Phillips Brooks*. New York: Macmillan, 1961.

Allen, Gay Wilson. *Waldo Emerson, A Biography*. New York: Viking, 1981.

Andrews, Samuel J. *William Watson Andrews, a Religious Biography, With Extracts from His Letters and Other Writings*. New York: G. P. Putnam's Sons, 1900.

Appel, Theodore. *The Life and Work of John Williamson Nevin*. Philadelphia: Reformed Church Publication House, 1889.

Bacon, Benjamin W. *Theodore Thornton Munger, New England Minister*. New Haven: Yale Univ. Press, 1913.

Bacon, Theodore D. *Leonard Bacon: A Statesman in the Church*. Ed. Benjamin W. Bacon. New Haven: Yale Univ. Press, 1931.

Barnes, Howard A. "Horace Bushnell: An American Gentleman." Ph.D. diss., State Univ. of Iowa, 1970.

[Brace, Emma, ed.] *The Life of Charles Loring Brace*. 1894. New York: Arno Press, 1976.

Brooke, Stopford A., ed. *Life, Letters, Lectures and Addresses of Fredk. W. Robertson, M. A., Incumbent of Trinity Chapel, Brighton, 1847–53*. New York: E. P. Dutton, 1883.

Bushnell Centenary: 193rd Annual Meeting of the General Association of Connecticut, Hartford, June 17, 18, 1902. Hartford: Case, Lockwood and Brainard, 1902.

Bushnell, Frances L. *Poems*. DeVinne Press, 1900.

Clark, Clifford E., Jr. *Henry Ward Beecher: Spokesman for a Middle-Class America*. Urbana: Univ. of Illinois Press, 1978.

Commager, Henry S. *Theodore Parker*. 1936. Gloucester, Mass.: Peter Smith, 1978.

Bibliography

Congregational Yearbook, 1866. London: Jackson, Walford and Hodder, 1866.

Cuningham, Charles E. *Timothy Dwight, 1752–1817: A Biography.* New York: Macmillan, 1942.

Dexter, Franklin B. *Biographical Sketches of the Graduates of Yale College with Annals of the College History.* 6 vols. New York: Henry Holt, 1911.

Dorn, Jacob H. *Washington Gladden: Prophet of the Social Gospel.* Columbus: Ohio State Univ. Press, 1966.

Dunham, Austin. *Reminiscences.* Hartford: Case, Lockwood and Brainard, n.d.

Dwight, Timothy. *Memories of Yale Life and Men, 1845–1899.* New York: Dodd, Mead, 1903.

Edwards, Robert L., ed. *The Prow of the Ship: Preachers and Preaching Over 150 Years...in Hartford, Connecticut.* Hartford: Bond Press, 1979.

Evans, D. Tyssil. *The Life and Ministry of the Rev. Caleb Morris.* London: Alexander and Shepheard, 1902.

Faust, Clarence H., and Thomas H. Johnson. *Jonathan Edwards: Representative Selections.* New York: American Book, 1935.

Fein, Albert. "Frederick Law Olmsted: His Development As a Theorist and Designer of the American City." Ph.D. diss., Columbia Univ., 1969.

Ferrier, William W. *Henry Durant, First President of the University of California, the New Englander Who Came to California With College on the Brain.* Berkeley: Privately published, 1942.

Fisher, Irving D. *Frederick Law Olmsted and the City Planning Movement in the United States.* Ann Arbor: UMI Research Press, 1976.

Fuller, Edmund. *Prudence Crandall: An Incident of Racism in Nineteenth Century Connecticut.* Middletown, Conn.: Wesleyan Univ. Press, 1971.

Gallaudet, Edward Miner. *Life of Thomas Hopkins Gallaudet, Founder of Deaf-Mute Instruction in America.* New York: Henry Holt, 1888.

Gladden, Washington. *Recollections.* Boston: Houghton Mifflin, 1909.

Gordon, George A. *My Education and Religion: An Autobiography.* Boston: Houghton Mifflin, 1925.

Hanson-Taylor, Marie, and Horace E. Scudder. *Life and Letters of Bayard Taylor.* 2 vols. Boston: Houghton Mifflin, 1884.

Hardman, Keith J. *Charles Grandison Finney, 1792–1875, Revivalist and Reformer.* Syracuse: Syracuse Univ. Press, 1987.

Heckscher, August. *Woodrow Wilson: A Biography*. New York: Charles Scribner's, 1991.

Hibben, Paxton. *Henry Ward Beecher: An American Portrait*. New York: George H. Doran, 1927.

Higginson, Thomas W. *Henry Wadsworth Longfellow*. Boston: Houghton Mifflin, 1902.

Hooker, John. *Some Reminiscences of a Long Life, With a Few Articles on Moral and Social Subjkects of Present Interest*. Hartford: Belknap and Warfield, 1899.

Johns, Eric, et al., eds. *The Popes: A Concise Biographical History*. New York: Hawthorne Books, 1964.

Kaplan, Justin. *Mr. Clemens and Mark Twain, A Biography*. New York: Simon and Schuster, 1966.

———. *Walt Whitman: A Life*. New York: Simon and Schuster, 1980.

Kilbourne, Payne K. *Biographical History of the County of Litchfield, Connecticut*. New York: Clark, Austin, 1851.

Kring, Walter D. *Henry Whitney Bellows*. Boston: Skinner House, 1979.

Lawrence, Edward A. *The Life of Reverend Joel Hawes, D. D.* Hartford: William J. Hammersley, 1871.

McLaughlin, Charles C., and Charles E. Beveridge, eds. *The Papers of Frederick Law Olmsted*. Vol. 1. *The Formative Years, 1822–1852*; Vol. 2. *Slavery and the South, 1852–1857*; Vol. 3. *Creating Central Park, 1857–1861*. Baltimore: Johns Hopkins Univ. Press, 1977, 1981, 1983.

MacMullen, Edith N. *In the Cause of True Education: Henry Barnard and Nineteenth Century School Reform*. New Haven: Yale Univ. Press, 1991.

Malone, Dumas. *Jefferson and The Rights of Man*. Boston: Little, Brown, 1951.

Mead, Sidney E. *Nathaniel William Taylor, 1786–1858: A Connecticut Liberal*. Chicago: Univ. of Chicago Press, 1942.

Mendelsohn, Jack. *Channing the Reluctant Radical: A Biography*. Westport, Conn.: Greenwood Press, 1971.

Minus, Paul M. *Walter Rauschenbusch, American Reformer*. New York: Collier Macmillan, 1988.

Mitchell, Donald G. *American Lands and Letters: Leather-Stocking to Poe's "Raven."* 2 vols. New York: Scribner's, 1899.

Oates, Stephen B. *With Malice Toward None: The Life of Abraham Lincoln*. 1977. New York: American Library, Mentor Books, 1978.

Obituary Records of Graduates of Yale College, . . . Presented at the An-

nual Meetings of the Alumni. New Haven: Tuttle, Morehouse and Taylor, 1870 and following years.

Olmsted, Frederick Law, Jr., and Theodora Kimball, eds. *Frederick Law Olmsted, Landscape Architect, 1822–1903*. 2 vols. New York: Benjamin Blom, 1970.

Paul, Irven. *A Yankee Reformer in Chile: The Life and Works of David Trumbull*. South Pasadena, Calif.: William Carey Library, 1973.

Roper, Laura W. *FLO, A Biography of Frederick Law Olmsted*. Baltimore: Johns Hopkins Univ. Press, 1973.

Rugoff, Milton. *The Beechers: An American Family in the Nineteenth Century*. New York: Harper, 1981.

Rusk, Ralph L., ed. *The Letters of Ralph W. Emerson*. 6 vols. New York: Columbia Univ. Press, 1939.

Salsbury, Edith C., ed. *Susy and Mark Twain, Family Dialogues*. New York: Harper and Row, 1965.

Sandburg, Carl. *Abraham Lincoln, The War Years*. 4 vols. New York: Harcourt, Brace, 1939.

Schweitzer, Albert. *Out of My Life and Thought: An Autobiography*. Trans. C. T. Campion. New York: Holt, 1949.

Shepherd, Jack. *The Adams Chronicles: Four Generations of Greatness*. Boston: Little, Brown, 1975.

Sherwin, Oscar. *Prophet of Liberty: The Life and Times of Wendell Phillips*. New York: Bookman, 1958.

Sklar, Kathryn K. *Catherine Beecher, A Study in American Domesticity*. New York: Norton, 1976.

Stevenson, Elizabeth. *Park Maker: A Life of Frederick Law Olmsted*. New York: Macmillan, 1977.

Strong, Leah A. *Joseph Hopkins Twichell: Mark Twain's Friend and Pastor*. Athens: Univ. of Georgia Press, 1966.

Trumbull, Henry C. *Knightly Soldier: A Biography of Ward Camp, Tenth Connecticut Volunteers*. Boston: Nichols and Noyes, 1865.

——. *My Four Religious Teachers*. Philadelphia: Sunday School Times, 1903.

Tuttle, Roger W., ed. *Biographies of Graduates of the Yale Law School, 1824–1899*. New Haven: Tuttle, Morehouse and Taylor, 1911.

Twain, Mark. *Mark Twain's Autobiography*. Intro. by Albert Bigelow Paine. 2 vols. New York: Harper, 1924.

Upham, Thomas C. *Life , Religious Opinions and Experience of Madame*

Bibliography

de la Mothe Guyon. 1843. London: Sampson, Low, 1856.

Van Deusen, Glyndon G. *The Life of Henry Clay.* Boston: Little, Brown, 1937.

Wade, Louise C. *Graham Taylor: Pioneer for Social Justice, 1851–1938.* Chicago: Univ. of Chicago Press, 1964.

Weiss, John. *Life and Correspondence of Theodore Parker, Minister of the Twenty-eighth Congregational Society, Boston.* 2 vols. New York: Appleton, 1864.

Winks, Robin W. *Frederick Billings: A Life.* New York: Oxford Univ. Press, 1991.

Histories

Ahlstrom, Sydney E. *A Religious History of the American People.* New Haven: Yale Univ. Press, 1972.

Andrews, Kenneth R. *Nook Farm: Mark Twain's Hartford Circle.* 1950. Seattle: Univ. of Washington Press, 1969.

[Bagg, Lyman.] *Four Years at Yale.* New York: Henry Holt, 1871.

Bainton, Roland H. *Yale and the Ministry.* New York: Harper, 1957.

Billington, Ray A. *The Protestant Crusade, 1800–1860: A Study of the Origins of American Nativism.* 1938. New York: Rinehart, 1952.

Brown, Charles R. *They Were Giants.* New York: Macmillan, 1934.

Buck, Paul H. *The Road to Reunion.* Boston: Little, Brown, 1937.

Burns, James M. *The American Experiment: The Vineyard of Liberty.* New York: Knopf, 1982.

Catton, Bruce. *The Coming Fury.* Garden City, N.Y.: Doubleday, 1961.

Caulkins, Frances M. *History of Norwich, Connecticut: from Its Possession by the Indians, to the Year 1866.* 1866. Chester, Conn.: Pequot Press, 1976.

Chesson, Michael B. *Richmond After the War, 1865–1890.* Richmond: Virginia State Library, 1981.

Clark, Francis E. *Worldwide Endeavor: The Story of the Young People's Society of Christian Endeavor from the Beginning and In All Lands.* Philadelphia: Gillespie, Metzgar and Kelley, 1895.

Contributions to the Ecclesiastical History of Connecticut; Prepared under the Directions of the General Association to Commemorate the Completion of One Hundred and Fifty Years Since Its First Annual Assembly. 1861. Hartford: Connecticut Conference United Church of Christ, 1973.

Bibliography

Curti, Merle. *Human Nature in American Thought, A History*. Madison: Univ. of Wisconsin Press, 1980.

[Dexter, Franklin B., ed.] *The Commemorative Celebration Held at Yale College, Wednesday, July 26, 1865*. New Haven: Morehouse, Tuttle and Taylor, 1866.

Dillenberger, John, and Claude Welch. *Protestant Christianity Interpreted Through Its Development*. New York: Scribners, 1954.

DuBois, Ellen C. *Feminism and Suffrage: The Emergence of an Independent Women's Movement in America, 1848–1869*. Ithaca: Cornell Univ. Press, 1978.

Durant, Henry. "An Interview with President Durant on the Origins of the University of California." Typescript. Bancroft Library, Univ. of California, Berkeley.

Ellis, George E. *A Half-Century of the Unitarian Controversy*. Boston: Crosby, Nichols, 1857.

Farb, Nathan. *The Adirondacks*. New York: Rizzoli Press, 1985.

Ferrier, William W. "The Story of the Naming of Berkeley." Berkeley, 1929.

Foner, Eric. *Reconstruction: America's Unfinished Revolution, 1863–1877*. New York: Harper and Row, 1988.

Frederickson, George M. *The Black Image in the White Mind: The Debate on Afro-American Character and Destiny, 1817–1914*. New York: Harper and Row, 1971.

——. *The Inner Civil War: Northern Intellectuals and the Crisis of the Union*. New York: Harper Torchbooks, 1968.

Geer, Curtis M. *The Hartford Theological Seminary, 1834–1934*. Hartford: Case, Lockwood and Brainard, 1934.

Gilman, Daniel C. *The Relations of Yale to Letters and Science, An Address Prepared for the Bicentennial Celebration, New Haven, October 22, 1901*. Baltimore: Privately published, 1901.

Goodwin, Francis, II. *The Monday Evening Club of Hartford, Connecticut, Its Members, and the Titles of Papers Read at Their Meetings, 1869–1970*. Hartford: Privately published, 1970.

Gossett, Thomas F. *"Uncle Tom's Cabin" and American Culture*. Dallas: Southern Methodist Univ. Press, 1985.

Handy, Robert T. *A History of the Churches in the United States and Canada*. New York: Oxford Univ. Press, 1977.

——. *The Social Gospel in America, 1870–1920: Gladden, Ely, and Raus-*

chenbusch. Library of Protestant Thought. New York: Oxford Univ. Press, 1966.

Hatch, Nathan O. *The Democratization of American Christianity*. New Haven: Yale Univ. Press, 1989.

Heffernan, Arthur J. "A History of Catholic Education in Connecticut." Ph.D. diss., Catholic Univ. of America, 1936.

Hicks, Frederick C. *Yale Law School: The Founders and the Founders' Collection*. New Haven: Yale Law Library, 1935.

Hogue, Harlan E. *The Long Arm of New England Devotion*. San Francisco: Northern California Congregational Conference, 1956.

Holliday, J. S. *The World Rushed In: The California Gold Rush Experience*. New York: Simon and Schuster, 1981.

Howell, Kenneth T., and Einar W. Carlson. *Empire Over the Dam: The Story of Waterpowered Industry, Long Since Passed from the Scene*. Chester, Conn.: Pequoit Press, 1974.

Hudson, Winthrop S. *Religion in America*. 1965. New York: Scribners, 1981.

Jacobus, Melancthon W. *The Connecticut River Steamboat Story*. Hartford: Connecticut Historical Society, 1956.

Josephson, Hannah. *The Golden Threads: New England's Mill Girls and Magnates*. New York: Duell, Sloan and Pearce, 1949.

Kaestle, Carl F. *Pillars of the Republic: Common Schools and American Society, 1780–1960*. New York: Hill and Wang, 1983.

Kelley, Brooks M. *Yale: A History*. New Haven: Yale Univ. Press, 1974.

Lee, Sidney, ed. *Dictionary of National Biography, Index and Epitome*. London: Smith Elder, 1906.

Litchfield County Centennial Celebration . . . Hartford: E. Hunt, 1851.

Love, William D. *The Colonial History of Hartford*. Hartford: Case, Lockwood and Brainard, 1914.

McCullough, David. *The Path Between the Seas: The Creation of the Panama Canal, 1870–1914*. New York: Simon and Schuster, 1977.

McNulty, J. Bard. *Older Than the Nation: The Story of the* Hartford Courant. Stonington, Conn.: Pequot Press, 1964.

McPherson, James M. *Battle Cry of Freedom: The Civil War Era*. New York: Oxford Univ. Press, 1988.

Mead, Sidney E. *The Lively Experiment: The Shaping of Christianity in America*. New York: Harper and Row, 1963.

Bibliography

Morison, Samuel E. *Three Centuries of Harvard, 1636–1936*. Cambridge: Harvard Univ. Press, 1965.

Mott, Frank L. *American Journalism: A History of Newspapers in the United States Through 250 Years, 1690–1940*. New York: Macmillan, 1941.

——. *A History of American Magazines, 1850–1905*. Cambridge: Harvard Univ. Press, 1957.

O'Byrne, William R. *A Naval Biographical Dictionary*. London: Murray, 1849.

Parker, Edwin P. *The Hartford Central Association and the Bushnell Controversy*. Hartford: Case, Lockwood and Brainard, 1896.

Roberts, Floyd L. "Horace Bushnell and the Common Schools of Connecticut." M.A. Thesis, Yale Univ., 1927.

Saybrook Tercentenary Committee. *In the Land of the Patentees: Saybrook in Connecticut*. Saybrook: Acton Library, 1935.

Schneider, Carl E. *The German Church on the American Frontier: A Study in the Rise of Religion Among the Germans of the West*. St. Louis: Eden Publishing House, 1939.

Senior, Robert C. "New England Congregationalists and the Anti-Slavery Movement, 1830–1860." Ph.D. diss., Yale Univ., 1954.

Smith, George W., and Charles Judah. *Life in the North During the Civil War*. Albuquerque: Univ. of New Mexico Press, 1966.

Society for the Promotion of Collegiate and Theological Education at the West. *[Annual] Reports of the Society, 1844–1858*. New York: J. F. Trow, 1844 and following years.

Stameshkin, David M. "The Town's College: Middlebury College, 1800–1915." 2 vols. Ph.D. diss., Univ. of Michigan, 1978.

Stampp, Kenneth M. *America in 1857, A Nation on the Brink*. New York: Oxford Univ. Press, 1990.

Steiner, Bernard C. *A History of the Plantation of Menunkatuck, and of the Original Town of Guilford, Connecticut*. Baltimore: Privately published, 1897.

——. *History of Slavery in Connecticut*. 1893. New York: Johnson, 1973.

Stewart, George. *A History of Religious Education in Connecticut to the Middle of the Nineteenth Century*. New Haven: Yale Univ. Press, 1924.

Swift, David E. *Black Prophets of Justice: Activist Clergy Before the Civil War*. Baton Rouge: Louisiana State Univ. Press, 1989.

——. "The Future Probation Controversy in American Congregationalism, 1886–1893." Ph.D. diss., Yale Univ., 1947.

Trumbull, Henry C. *Litchfield County, Connecticut, or One Rural County's Contributions to the Nation's Power and Fame.* Philadelphia: Sunday School Times, 1902.

Trumbull, J. Hammond, ed. *The Memorial History of Hartford County, Connecticut, 1633–1884.* 2 vols. Boston: Edward L. Osgood, 1886.

Trustees, College of California. "Movement for a University of California: A Statement to the Public . . . and An Appeal by Dr. Bushnell." San Francisco: Pacific Publishing, 1857.

United States Department of Commerce. *Historical Statistics of the United States, Colonial Times to 1970.* New York: Basic Books, 1976.

Van Dusen, Albert E. *Connecticut: A Fully Illustrated History of the State.* New York: Random House, 1961.

Vanderpoel, Emily N. *More Chronicles of a Pioneer School, 1792–1833.* New York: Cadmus Book Shop, 1927.

Wayland, John T. *The Theological Department in Yale College, 1822–1858.* 1933. New York: Garland, 1987.

Weaver, Glenn. *Hartford, An Illustrated History of Connecticut's Capital.* Woodland Hills, Calif.: Windsor Publications, 1982.

Weld, Stanley B. *The History of Immanuel Church, 1824–1967.* Hartford: Connecticut Printers, 1968.

Willey, Samuel H. *A History of the College of California.* San Francisco: Samuel Carson, 1887.

White, Alain C. *The History of the Town of Litchfield, Connecticut, 1720–1920.* Litchfield: Enquirer Press, 1920.

Wood, M. W. *History of Alameda County, California.* Oakland, 1883.

Wright, Conrad. *The Beginnings of Unitarianism in America.* 1955. Hamden, Conn.: Archon Books, 1976.

Yale Alumni Weekly, 20 Oct. 1901 . . . *The Bicentennial . . . Issue of Commemoration.* New Haven, 1902.

Chapters in Books

Ahlstrom, Sydney E. "Horace Bushnell." In *A Handbook of Christian Theologians,* edited by Martin E. Marty and Dean C. Peerman. Nashville: Abingdon, 1965.

——. "Theology of America: A Historical Survey." In *The Shaping of American Religion,* edited by James W. Smith and A. Leland Jamison.

Bibliography

Princeton: Princeton Univ. Press, 1961.

Edwards, Robert L. "Portrait of a People: Horace Bushnell's Hartford Congregation." In *Studies of the Church in History: Essays Honoring Robert S. Paul....*, edited by Horton Davies. Allison Park, Pa: Pickwick Press, 1983.

Kirschenmann, Frederick. "Horace Bushnell: Cells or Crustacea?" In *Essays in Divinity*. Vol. 5 *Reinterpretation in American Church History*, edited by Jerald C. Brauer. Chicago: Univ. of Chicago Press, 1968.

Stephens, Bruce M. "The Trinity as the Language of God: Horace Bushnell." *God's Last Metaphor: The Doctrine of the Trinity in New England Theology*. Chico, Calif.: Scholars Press, 1981.

Weigle, Luther A. Introduction to Bushnell. *Christian Nurture*. New Haven: Yale Univ. Press, 1947.

Willey, Samuel H. "Search for a Permanent Site." *A History of the College of California*. San Francisco: Samuel Carson, 1887.

Articles

Adams, Sherman. "The Hartford Park System: Bushnell Park." *The Connecticut Quarterly: An Illustrated Magazine* 1 (Jan.–Dec. 1895): 69–71.

Abbott, Lyman. "The Life of Horace Bushnell." *Outlook* 63, 7 (Oct. 14, 1899): 413–15.

Ahlstrom, Sydney E. "Comment on the Essay of Professor Clebsch: History, Bushnell and Lincoln." *Church History* 30 (1961): 223–30.

Atwater, Lyman H. "Horace Bushnell." *Presbyterian Review* 2 (Jan. 1881): 114–44.

Bacon, Leonard. "Concerning a Recent Chapter of Ecclesiastical History." *New Englander* 38 (Sept. 1879): 701–12.

Barnes, Howard A. "The Idea that Caused a War: Horace Bushnell *versus* Thomas Jefferson." *Journal of Church and State* 16, 1 (Winter 1874): 73–83.

Bos, A. David. "Horace Bushnell Through His Interpreters: A Transitional and Formative Figure." *Andover Newton Quarterly* 18 (Nov. 1977): 122–32.

Carpenter, Frank B. "Studio Talks with Dr. Horace Bushnell." *The Independent*, 11 Jan. 1900, 116–20.

Chrystal, William G. "A Beautiful Aceldama: Horace Bushnell in California, 1856–1857." *New England Quarterly* 57, 3 (Sept. 1984): 384–402.

Bibliography

[Clarke, James F.] "Bushnell on Vicarious Sacrifice." *Christian Examiner* 81, N.S. 1 (May 1866).

Clebsch, William A. "Christian Interpretations of the Civil War." *Church History* 30, 2 (June 1961): 212–21.

Clouette, Bruce. "Ante-Bellum Urban Renewal: Hartford's Bushnell Park." *Connecticut History* 18 (Nov. 1976): 9–13.

Cole, Charles C., Jr. "Horace Bushnell and the Slavery Question." *New England Quarterly* 23, 1 (Mar. 1950): 19–30.

Donnelly, Mabel C. "Comments [on Horace Bushnell and Isabella Beecher Hooker]." *The Harriet Beecher Stowe House and Library [Bulletin]*, Sept. 1987, 3.

Dyer, John. "Dr. Horace Bushnell." *Penn Monthly* 7, 4 (Apr. 1876): 287–97.

Edwards, Robert L. "First Forays into a New Life Bushnell." *Bulletin of the Congregational Library* 33, 3 (Spring/Summer 1982): 4–13.

Egleston, Nathaniel H. "Bushnell on Henry Clay." *Supplement to the Connecticut Courant* 45, 20 (7 Oct. 1880): 157.

Garrett, Lulu M. "San Francisco in 1851, as Described by Eyewitnesses." *California Historical Society Quarterly* 22, 3 (Sept. 1943): 253.

Gladden, Washington. "Are Dr. Bushnell's Views Heretical?" *Independent*, 17 Oct. 1867.

Godkin, Edwin L. "Dr. Bushnell on Women's Rights." *The Nation* 8, 208 (24 June 1869): 496–97.

Hambrick-Stowe, Charles E. "An Engaging Sign: Baptism in the History of American Congregationalism." *Bulletin of the Congregational Library* 41, 1 (Fall 1989): 4–15.

Hart, Samuel. "Henry Barnard, LL.D." *New England Historical and Genealogical Register* 56 (1902): 173ff.

Howe, Daniel W. "The Social Science of Horace Bushnell." *Journal of American History* 70, 2 (Sept. 1983): 305–22.

Jacobus, Melancthon W. "The Connecticut State Capitol." *Connecticut Historical Society Bulletin* 33, 2 (Apr. 1968): 41–50.

James, William. "*Women's Suffrage; the Reform Against Nature,* by Horace Bushnell, and *The Subjection of Women,* by John Stuart Mill." *North American Review* 109, 225 (Oct. 1869): 556–65.

Jones, Trudy K. "Hartford's Bushnell Park: Antidote to Urban Ills." *The Connecticut Antiquarian* 41, 2 (Fall 1990): 11–21.

Kathan, Boardman W. "Outstanding Books in Christian Education." *Re-*

flection (Yale Divinity School) 78, 3 (Apr. 1981).

Kelley, William V. "A Preacher's Preacher." *Congregationalist and Christian World* 87, 23 (7 June 1902): 821.

Luker, Ralph E. "Bushnell in Black and White: Evidences of the 'Racism' of Horace Bushnell." *New England Quarterly* 45, 3 (Sept. 1972): 408–16.

Munger, Theodore T. "Horace Bushnell: the Centenary of a Great Alumnus." *Yale Alumni Weekly* 11, 27 (9 Apr. 1902): 309–10.

Parker, Edwin P. "Dr. Bushnell's Marks in Hartford." *Congregationalist and Christian World* 87, 23 (7 June 1902): 818.

Ransom, David F. "Biographical Dictionary of Hartford Architects." *Connecticut Historical Society Bulletin* 54 (Winter/Spring 1989): 61–62.

Salmond, Stewart D. F. "The Theology of Horace Bushnell." *London Quarterly Review* 95, N.S. 5 (Jan.–Apr. 1901): 133–58.

Schlesinger, Arthur M., Sr. "A Critical Period in American Religion." *Massachusetts Historical Society Proceedings* 64 (1930–32): 523–46.

Shipman, Frank R. "Some Letters from Horace Bushnell to Leonard Bacon." *Hartford Times*, 31 Aug. 1931.

Soltow, Lee. "Watches and Clocks in Connecticut, 1800: A Symbol of Socioeconomic Status." *Connecticut Historical Society Bulletin* 45, 4 (Oct. 1980): 115–22.

Thomas, Reuen. "My Week with Horace Bushnell." *Congregationalist and Christian World* 87, 23 (7 June 1902): 813–14.

Updike, John. "Emersonianism." *New Yorker Magazine* 60, 16 (4 June 1984): 112–32.

Weeks, Louis. "Horace Bushnell on Black America." *Religious Education* 63, 1 (Jan.–Feb. 1973): 28–41.

INDEX

Index

Index